Journal of Consciousness Studies
controversies in science & the humanities

Vol. 18, No. 1, January 2011

Describing Inner Experience : A Symposium
Debating Descriptive Experience Sampling (DES)
edited by Josh Weisberg

3   About Authors

Editorial Introduction

7   Introduction — Josh Weisberg

Invited Commentaries

21   How to Study Introspection — Christopher S. Hill

44   Describing the Experience of Describing? — Claire Petitmengin

63   Socratic Introspection and the Abundance of Experience — Charles Siewert

92   Response Organization of Mental Imagery, Evaluation of DES and Alternatives — Eric Klinger

102   Scientific Methods Must Be Public, and DES Qualifies — Gualtiero Piccinini

118   Time, Experience, and DES — John Sutton

130   DES: What Is It Good For? — Mark Engelbert & Peter Carruthers

150   Describing, Debating, and Discovering Inner Experience — Michael J. Kane

165   Using First-Person Data about Consciousness — Maja Spener

180   Introspection and the Phenomenology of Free Will: Problems and Prospects — Terry Horgan and Mark Timmons

Replies from R.T. Hurlburt & E. Schwitzgebel

206   Presuppositions and Background Assumptions — RTH & ES

234   Little or No Experience Outside of Attention — RTH & ES

253   Methodological Pluralism, Armchair Introspection, and DES as the Epistemic Tribunal — RTH & ES

274   Nine Clarifications of DES — RTH

288   The Philosophical and Psychological Context of DES — ES

295   A Case Study in Bracketing Presuppositions: Agency — RTH & Neda Raymond

Journal of Consciousness Studies

Editor
Valerie Gray Hardcastle, Dean of McMicken College of Arts and Sciences, University of Cincinnati. *valerie.hardcastle@uc.edu*

Managing Editors (address for submissions)
Anthony Freeman, Imprint Academic, PO Box 200, Exeter EX5 5YX, UK. Tel: +44 1392 851550. *Anthony.jcs@gmail.com*
Graham Horswell (Assistant): *Graham.jcs@gmail.com*

Book Reviews Editor (address for books for review)
Julian Kiverstein, Department of Philosophy, University of Edinburgh, George Sqare, Edinburgh, EH8 9JX, UK. *J.Kiverstein@ed.ac.uk*

Associate Editors
Jean Burns: *jeanbur@earthlink.net*; **Ivo Mosley** (Poetry):*ivomosley@aol.com*
Chris Nunn: *cmhnunn@btinternet.com*

Founding Editors
Joseph A. Goguen (1941–2006), **Robert K.C. Forman**: *Forman@TheForge.org*
Jonathan Shear:*jcs@infionline.net*, **Keith Sutherland**, Publisher: *keith@imprint.co.uk*

Editorial Advisory Board
Bernard J. Baars, Neurosciences Institute; **David Chalmers**, Australian National University; **Ewert Cousins**, Fordham University; **Daniel Dennett**, Tufts University; **Margaret Donaldson**, Edinburgh University; **Peter Fenwick**, Maudsley Hospital; **Stuart Hameroff**, University of Arizona; **Erich Harth**, Syracuse University; **Basil Hiley**, Birkbeck College; **Nicholas Humphrey**, London School of Economics; **Piet Hut**, Institute for Advanced Studies; **Robert Kentridge**, University of Durham; **Christof Koch**, CalTech; **George Lakoff**, UC, Berkeley; **Philip Merikle**, University of Waterloo; **Mary Midgley**, University of Newcastle; **Raimon Panikkar**, UC, Santa Barbara; **Roger Penrose**, Oxford University; **Geraint Rees**, Institute of Cognitive Neuroscience, **Eleanor Rosch**, UC, Berkeley; **David Rosenthal**, CUNY, **John Searle**, UC, Berkeley; **Huston Smith**, Syracuse University; **Susan Leigh Star**, Santa Clara University; **Roger Walsh**, UC, Irvine; **Arthur Zajonc**, Amherst College.

Manuscript Submissions
For style guide and other directions for authors go to the journal's website, imprint-academic.com/jcs

---

Subscription and Ordering Information
Annual Subscription Rates for 2011 (12 monthly issues):

Individuals: $154/£77   **Institutions**: $560/£280

Prices for print journal and include accelerated delivery (UK/USA), surface mail rest of world, and free access to the journal online at Ingenta.com

Orders to : Imprint Academic, PO Box 200, Exeter EX5 5YX, UK.
Tel: +44 1392 851550; Fax: 851178; *Email: sandra@imprint.co.uk*

Cheques (£ or $US 'Imprint Academic'); VISA/AMEX/MASTERCARD

ia imprint-academic.com

ABOUT AUTHORS

Peter Carruthers is Professor of Philosophy at the University of Maryland. His most recent book is *The Opacity of Mind: An Integrative Theory of Self-Knowledge* (Oxford University Press, 2011).

Mark Engelbert is a graduate student in philosophy at the University of Maryland.

Christopher S. Hill is a professor of philosophy at Brown University. He is author of *Sensations: A Defense of Type Materialism* (1991), *Thought and World: An Austere Portrayal of Truth, Reference, and Semantic Correspondence* (2002), and *Consciousness* (2009), all published by Cambridge University Press.

Terry Horgan and ***Mark Timmons*** are colleagues in philosophy at the University of Arizona, and previously were colleagues in philosophy at the University of Memphis. They have collaborated extensively, mainly in metaethics (including work on moral phenomenology) and occasionally on other philosophical topics.Their recent papers include: 'Untying a Knot from the Inside Out: Reflections on the "Paradox" of Supererogation', *Social Philosophy & Policy* (2010), 'Mandelbaum on Moral Phenomenology and Moral Realism,' in *Maurice Mandelbaum and American Critical Realism*, ed. I. Verstegen (2010).

Russell T. Hurlburt is Professor of Psychology at the University of Nevada, Las Vegas. He has been an investigator of innr experience consistently since the early 1970s. He was one of the founders and principal investigators of thought sampling and is the originator of the Descriptive Experience Sampling (DES) method and the author of a

---

Published in the UK and USA by Imprint Academic, PO Box 200, Exeter EX5 5YX, UK

World Copyright © Imprint Academic, 2011. No part of any contribution may be reproduced in any form without permission, except for the quotation of brief passages in criticism and discussion. The opinions expressed in the articles and book reviews are not necessarily those of the editors or the publishers.

JCS is indexed and abstracted in: *Social Sciences Citation Index®, ISI Alerting Services* (includes *Research Alert®*), *Current Contents®: Social and Behavioral Sciences, Arts and Humanities Citation Index®, Current Contents®: Arts & Humanities Citation Index®, Social Scisearch®, PsycINFO®* and *The Philosopher's Index*.

ISSN 1355 8250

number of books about it, including *Describing Inner Experience: Proponent Meets Skeptic* (MIT Press, 2007) with Eric Schwitzgebel.

Michael J. Kane is a Professor of Psychology at the University of North Carolina at Greensboro, an Associate Editor for *Cognitive Psychology*, and a Fellow of the Association for Psychological Science. He earned his BA in Psychology from Haverford College and his PhD in Cognitive Psychology from Duke University. His first published article presented an introspective case study about the phenomenology of Tourette Syndrome, and his current research combines experimental, psychometric, and experience-sampling methods to investigate individual differences in working memory, cognitive control, and cognitive failures (including action slips and mind wandering).

Eric Klinger is Professor of Psychology Emeritus at the University of Minnesota, Morris and (adjunct) Minneapolis. His research activities focus on motivational processes, especially as these influence mental content, including daydreaming and dreaming. He has contributed to basic theory of motivation, its assessment, and its extension to cognition, substance use, motivational counseling, and depression. A Fellow of the American Association for the Advancement of Science and of the American Psychological Association, and a Charter Fellow of the Association for Psychological Science, Klinger is the author of more than 100 publications.

Claire Petitmengin is a Senior Lecturer at Institut Télécom (Télécom Ecole de Management) and Member of the Centre de Recherche en Épistémologie Appliquée (École Polytechnique/CNRS) in Paris. Since her doctoral thesis of 1998 (under the direction of Franciso Varela), her research has focused on pre-reflective lived experience, the methods enabling us to become aware of it and describe it, and the methods enabling the detection of experiential generic structures. Her research evaluates the reliability of these methods, and their educational and therapeutic applications. She is also interested in the process of mutual guidance and refinement of first person and third person analyses in the context of 'neuro-phenomenological' projects.

Gualtiero Piccinini is associate professor of philosophy in the Departments of Philosophy and Psychology and the Center for Neurodynamics at the University of Missouri, St. Louis. Recent publications include *First-Person Data, Publicity, and Self-Measurement* (Philosophers' Imprint, 2009); 'The Mind as Neural Software?

Understanding Functionalism, Computationalism, and Computational Functionalism' (*Philosophy and Phenomenological Research*, 2010); and 'Information Processing, Computation, and Cognition' (with Andrea Scarantino, in *Journal of Biological Physics*).

Eric Schwitzgebel is Professor of Philosophy at the University of California, Riverside. His research explores connections between empirical psychology and philosophy of mind, especially the nature of belief, the inaccuracy of our judgments about our stream of conscious experience, and the tenuous relationship between philosophical ethics and actual moral behaviour. He is co-author, with psychologist Russell T. Hurlburt, of the book *Describing Inner Experience: Proponent Meets Skeptic* (MIT Press, 2007). He maintains a secondary interest in classical Chinese philosophy.

Charles Siewert is the Robert Alan and Kathryn Dunlevie Hayes Professor of Philosophy at Rice University. He is the author of *The Significance of Consciousness*, and a number of articles on consciousness, introspective self-knowledge, and phenomenology.

Maja Spener is a Lecturer in the Faculty of Philosophy at the University of Oxford and a Junior Research Fellow at St Catherine's College, Oxford. Her research focuses on issues at the intersection of philosophy of mind & psychology and epistemology.

John Sutton is Professor of Cognitive Science at Macquarie University, where he was previously Head of the Department of Philosophy. He is author of *Philosophy and Memory Traces: Descartes to Connectionism*, and coeditor of *Descartes' Natural Philosophy*, and of the journal *Memory Studies*. He has published recent papers on perspective in personal memory, dreaming, and the extended mind, and his current research addresses collaborative recall, skilled movement, and cognitive history. URL: http://www.phil.mq.edu.au/staff/jsutton/.

Josh Weisberg is an assistant professor of philosophy at the University of Houston, and he received his PhD at the City University of New York, Graduate Center, under the supervision of David Rosenthal. His research focuses on the epistemic status of intuitions about consciousness, the reliability of introspection and first-person access, and the prospects for reductive theories of consciousness, in particular the higher-order thought theory. He is at work on an introductory text on consciousness for Polity Press.

HARVARD REFERENCING SYSTEM IN *JCS*

Please note that, effective immediately and in line with UK educational institutions, the *Journal of Consciousness Studies* requires references in the bibliography section to follow the Harvard referencing system.

Examples are given here for ease of reference:

References to books

Jantsch, E. (1980) *The Self-Organizing Universe*, Oxford: Pergamon.

References to articles

Black, A. (1993) The juristic origins of social contract theory, *History of Political Thought*, **16** (4), pp. 157–176.

References to other sources

Book with an editor

Noë, A. & Thompson, E. (eds.) (2002) *Vision and Mind*, Cambridge, MA: MIT Press.

Chapter in a book

Grice, H.P. (2002) Some remarks about the senses, in Noe, A. & Thompson, E. (eds.) *Vision and Mind*, Cambridge, MA: MIT Press.

Conference papers

Jenkins, H. (2008) A catch-22: Psi and explanation, *The Parapsychological Association 51st Annual Convention – Conference Proceedings*, Winchester, pp. 97–110.

Newspaper articles

Cumming, F. (1999) Tax-free savings push, *Daily Mail*, 4 April, pp. 1–2.

Internet resource

Young, C. (2001) *English Heritage Position Statement on the Valletta Convention*, [Online], http://www.archaeol.freeuk.com/EHPositionStatement.htm [24 Aug 2001].

(where the final date is the date the webpage was accessed).

Josh Weisberg

Introduction

Describing Inner Experience? Proponent Meets Skeptic is a unique contribution to consciousness studies. The book presents a detailed and far-ranging debate between psychologist Russell T. Hurlburt, developer and defender of the Descriptive Experience Sampling (DES) method of introspective reporting, and philosopher Eric Schwitzgebel, whose sceptical work challenges the accuracy of any introspective method. It is the format of the work that is especially distinctive: the authors examine the reliability of DES by actually engaging in the method, interviewing a single introspecting subject, given the pseudonym Melanie, over the course six sampling days. This hands-on approach effectively brings out the real-time challenges facing introspective methods, while providing a fruitful entry-point into a number of key empirical and philosophical questions in consciousness studies. But just as importantly, the energetic interplay between Hurlburt and Schwitzgebel, even when they disagree, helps clarify what is at stake in this complex debate, very much in the style of Socratic dialogue. The work is among the best examples of interdisciplinary research in consciousness studies.

This special issue of the *Journal of Consciousness Studies* extends both the spirit and scope of *Describing Inner Experience*. Ten invited commentaries from leading researchers in philosophy and psychology challenge both Hurlburt's impassioned defence of DES and Schwitzgebel's persistent sceptical worries about introspection. The debate moves in new and interesting directions, and problems initially brought out in the book receive extended treatment. Further, the forum allows both Hurlburt and Schwitzgebel to clarify, refine, and, occasionally, reformulate their positions on the complex issues raised in *Describing Inner Experience*. Their replies here form a seamless

Correspondence:
Josh Weisberg, University of Houston, Philosophy
Email: *jweisber@central.uh.edu*

continuation of both the style and substance of the original work. In this brief introduction, I will present a sketch of the DES method and touch on some of the central themes raised in the book and in Hurlburt and Schwitzgebel's replies. I conclude by presenting a short summary of the commentaries.

1. DES and the Challenge of Introspection

Consciousness studies faces a unique and seemingly ineliminable methodological challenge. Our access to the data a theory of consciousness must explain is introspective, but introspection is widely seen as a suspect and unreliable source of data. The history of psychology is famously marked by the failure of introspective methods, and recent psychological research, by Richard Nisbett, Timothy Wilson, Daniel Wegner,[1] and others, has only confirmed introspection's shortcomings as a reliable guide to the workings of the mind. But how can we study consciousness if we can't rely on the introspective reports of conscious subjects? The ordinary behavioural methods of psychology are silent about the phenomenology accompanying many of our mental activities. But it is this phenomenology that constitutes the explanatory target for a theory of consciousness. Without some reliable access to introspective data, there is nothing to study in consciousness studies.

But unreflective reliance on introspective data — or a blissful ignoring of the problems plaguing introspection — is the main source of one of the major frustrations in this field of research. Far too often, theorists arrive at incompatible (and seemingly incommensurable) conclusions because of differences in their initial characterization of the data to be explained. Because they are talking about different phenomena, they pass like ships in the night. One researcher's obvious phenomenological truth, grounding an entire research programme, is another's theory-laden confabulation. And once this is grasped, all the sound and fury of the debate loses its interest: the debaters are talking about different things. Consciousness studies thus cries out for a reasonably accurate introspective method.

A pioneer in the search for such a method is psychologist Russell Hurlburt. Over the course of more than 30 years he's developed and defended Descriptive Experience Sampling (DES).[2] According to Hurlburt, DES avoids the major pitfalls that undermined previous

---

[1] Nisbett and Wilson (1977), Wilson (2002), Wegner (2002), e.g.

[2] For more on DES, see Hurlburt (1979; 1990; 1993; 1997; 2009; in preparation), Hurlburt and Akhter (2006), Hurlburt and Heavey (2006).

introspective methods, and though it certainly has its limitations, DES provides a reliable way to accurately describe inner experience and thus provide the neutral data necessary to put consciousness studies on firm scientific footing.

DES is designed to provide a reliable characterization of the experiences of an individual subject at a series of randomly-chosen times. A key element of the method is the use of a beeper, which at random moments cues the subject to attend to her experience. The subject then makes a brief written note of her conscious experience. Later, the subject is interviewed by a trained DES investigator, whose role is to aid the subject in arriving at as accurate and unbiased description of her experience as possible. As Hurlburt describes the method,

> DES uses a random beeper in the subject's natural environment to signal the subject to pay attention to the experience that was ongoing at the moment of the beep. The subject then jots down notes about that now-immediately-past experience. The subject collects a half-dozen such beeped experiences and then meets with the investigator within 24 hours for an expositional interview, the aim of which is to describe the experiences that were ongoing at each of the six beeped moments. (H&S, p. 20)[3]

The trained DES-practitioner acts as a 'co-investigator' with the subject during the later debriefing. According to Hurlburt,

> The aim of the expositional interview is simple: help the subject stay focused on the experience that was ongoing at the moment of the beeps and no other, to describe the features of that particular ongoing experience and not experience in general, and to describe the ongoing phenomena as they actually present themselves, not according to some a priori understanding or expectation. (Hurlburt and Akhter, 2006, p. 280)

It is clear that the investigator is not a passive recorder. Rather, the investigator is actively involved in developing the final record of the introspective report.

One might worry that the active role of the investigator could bias the results (indeed, this is one of Schwitzgebel's central concerns). But Hurlburt is confident that a properly trained investigator can avoid skewing the books. To achieve this neutrality, both subject and investigator must 'bracket their presuppositions' throughout the procedure, in Hurlburt's terms. This means one should as far as possible refrain from categorizing the described experiences into pre-established categories or according to *a priori* presuppositions. Further,

---

[3] 'H&S' references are to *Describing Inner Experience*.

one should simply describe the particular experience in question, rather than theorize about experience generally. Though Hurlburt acknowledges that complete bracketing is not possible, he offers it as a goal to guide the process of description. As best we can, we should 'apprehend the phenomena as close as possible to the way they actually present themselves' (Hurlburt and Akhter, 2006, p. 283). Hurlburt stresses repeatedly that his own experience with the method reassures him that a practitioner of the method can be neutral. Subjects, he tells us, do not typically feel coerced into making claims. They are encouraged to say 'I don't know' when they are unsure. What's more, both subject and investigator are often surprised by the final results of the method, indicating that the process is not being forced into one predetermined interpretation or another.

The process of beeping, recording, and interviewing is repeated over several days, a process Hurlburt calls 'iterative' (Hurlburt, 2009). This iteration acts to improve the subject's facility with the method and aids in identifying particular features of conscious experience recurring in this subject. By the end of the series of sessions, a purportedly high-fidelity record of the subject's inner experience at a series of random times is generated. What's more, investigations of different subjects can be compared and contrasted to find more general patterns and recurring features. Hurlburt contends that DES avoids the troubles of other introspective methods by targeting brief, naturally-occurring experiences. This serves to minimize the memorial and interpretive demands on the subject, and it helps emphasize the particular features of lived experience, thus avoiding hasty 'faux' generalizations. Further, the presence of a skilled investigator aids in reducing the influence of prior theorizing and presuppositions. DES maintains, according to Hurlburt, a healthy scepticism about introspective reports without undermining the very possibility of success. DES provides a careful, controlled way of investigating the inner experiences of conscious subjects. It appears to supply just the source of neutral data needed to study human consciousness.

2. Schwitzgebel's Scepticism

But does DES deliver on its promises? Philosopher Eric Schwitzgebel, in a range of articles,[4] challenges the reliability of introspection, both in its empirical and everyday uses. In *Describing Inner Experience*, he takes sceptical aim at DES, even as he engages in the examination of

---

[4] Schwitzgebel (2002; 2003; 2005; 2007; 2008; in press a; in press b).

Melanie's experiences under Hurlburt's guidance. Schwitzgebel identifies five main reasons to doubt the reliability of introspection in general and DES in particular. First, conscious states are fleeting and changeable. Close attention makes it apparent that there is rarely a stable, easily observed 'content' of consciousness. Second, we're not often in the habit of introspecting and certainly not with the level of detail demanded by psychologists and philosophers. We just don't spend that much time trying to pin down the details of our conscious experience. Third, because our interest is generally focused outward, we lack good descriptive concepts of conscious experience. Our concepts are generally borrowed from those employed in outward perceptual experience. This creates a confusing double use of many terms, like 'red' or 'sweet'. Is it the apple or the apple experience that is red? Or is it both? And is it the candy or the experience of eating candy that is sweet? With care, these subtleties can be kept clear, but this creates a distinct worry of confusion and equivocation. Fourth, introspection requires focused attention on conscious experience. But this arguably alters the very experience attended to. Further, introspection may generally occur after the conscious 'facts' have passed; it might be better to see it as retrospection, a later reflection on past conscious experience. This potentially alters the data we wish to ascertain, making a clear, unadulterated picture of consciousness difficult if not impossible. Further, it creates a problem of memory, one that grows as the demands of detail and complexity grow. Can we be so sure we are accurately recalling just what occurred in our past experience? Finally, the fifth difficulty directly challenges the notion of 'bracketing' introduced by Hurlburt. Schwitzgebel contends that interpretation and (often implicit) theorizing is ever-present in introspection. This is not a minor issue; according to Schwitzgebel, the influence of theory on introspection can be acute. And even if it is more minimally invasive, it is extremely difficult to tell just where theorizing leaves off and 'uncorrupted' introspection begins. Even the most basic introspective claims are thus threatened with bias and distortion. Schwitzgebel and Hurlburt seem most at odds over the extent of this problem.

Despite (or perhaps because of) these worries, Schwitzgebel eagerly engages in the DES method with Hurlburt and Melanie. Throughout, Schwitzgebel allows Hurlburt to take the lead as the trained DES investigator, but he chimes in whenever his sceptical 'detectors' fire. Here is a sample of the process, from *Describing Inner Experience*. The following is a snippet from the expositional interview wherein Melanie recounts what she was thinking at a particular beep, under the questioning of Hurlburt and Schwitzgebel:

> Melanie: During this little time period I was brushing my teeth in the bathroom. I kind of was letting my mind wander, because it's such a banal thing I do every day. I was aware of being slightly bent over the sink and aware of the kind of rhythmic motion of my hand, you know, brushing up and down and side to side. I was aware of the kind of cold and gooiness of the toothpaste.
>
> Russ:[5] And is that it, in your awareness?
>
> Melanie: Yeah.
>
> Russ: And when you say you're aware of being bent over, so you're sort of...
>
> Melanie: Like hunched over a little bit. I mainly could feel it in my spine, because it's not a super comfortable position to be in.
>
> Russ: So this is like a bodily awareness or a kinesthetic awareness, something like that?
>
> Melanie: Yes.
>
> Russ: And does that seem like a sort of separate awareness? You've got the bent-over awareness and you've got...
>
> Melanie: Yeah, they seemed very localized. Like the feeling in my back feels *in my back*, and the up and down motion I can feel in my mouth and with my hand and my arm, because I'm holding the toothbrush and moving it.
>
> Russ: And the cold and gooiness?
>
> Melanie: Another feeling that is very located, just in my mouth and everything.
>
> Russ: And nothing else is going on at this particular moment.
>
> Melanie: Nope.
>
> (H&S, pp. 123–124)

Schwitzgebel then follows with any questions he has about the specific experience in question.

> Eric: You started by saying your mind was wandering.

---

[5] Editor's note: In *Describing Inner Experience*, as well as in Hurlburt and Schwitzgebel's replies in this issue, and in a number of the commentaries, the authors are at times referred to by first name only. This is in keeping with the friendly, informal tone of the book, and we have left the first names when they were employed. This does not indicate any lack of seriousness about the subject matter; rather, it continues the open, Socratic spirit of the original work.

Melanie: Yeah, well, I mean, that was the best way to say my mind was kind of empty [laughs].

Eric: Oh, okay, so that was… you were just…

Melanie: Pretty much absorbed in what I was doing.

Eric: …pretty much absorbed in that. Because you could think 'your mind was wandering' could mean…

Melanie: Yeah, jumping to different subjects.

Eric: …thinking about, you know, what you are going to do today or something like that, but that's not…

Melanie: No.

(H&S, pp. 124–125)

A bit later, Schwitzgebel presses one of his worries, and Hurlburt and Melanie try to respond. It is not uncommon in the transcripts to find Hurlburt leaping in to clarify what he takes Melanie to have said, and to defend the cogency of her answers to Schwitzgebel's questions.

Eric: It seems to me that we should also bear in mind the possibility (I'm not saying it's the case) that when the beep goes off you think 'Okay, what was my experience? Was I having an experience of the bathroom? Oh, the bathroom floor is cold. I guess I was experiencing that at the time' — letting your knowledge of your environment feed back into your impression of what your experience was at the time of the beep.

Melanie: Right. I'm not defending myself by any means. But I tried specifically to really focus on the moment of the beep and not what came afterwards, because of the discussion last time about how the beep would usually catch me towards the end of a thought. And I wanted to work on trying to hone that, and so I was trying to do that as best I could.

Eric: Right. I guess the concern I have is not so much directly temporal. You could be trying to reconstruct what's going on at the moment of the beep, or immediately prior to the beep, and not confusing it in any way with what's going on now, but noticing what's going on now and then deliberately thinking 'Okay, was this going on a moment before?' And then because it's going on now and because you know certain things about your environment, you might infer that it was going on the moment before as well.

Russ: Well, I don't think Melanie can confidently say she doesn't do *any* of that. I think she just *did* confidently say she *tried* not to do that.

Eric: Right. And again, you know, I'm not saying that I have any specific reason to worry about this particular case. How do we partial out how much is due to a kind of reconstruction?

(H&S, p. 128)

This gives a good feel both for how DES works and how *Describing Inner Experience* is structured. Despite Hurlburt's impassioned defence, however, Schwitzgebel concludes that there are distinct limits to what DES can accomplish. He allows that it is accurate, barring counter-evidence, for reports of gross features of experience — that one is having a pain, or is imagining a red apple, say. But as the level of detail in the reports increases, so, too, do Schwitzgebel's sceptical worries. He concludes (and Hurlburt in fact agrees) that the method is not able to deliver reliable data at the level desired by many researchers in consciousness studies.

Schwitzgebel supports this conclusion by bringing up the question of the 'richness' of conscious experience. Some hold that conscious experience, at any one time, contains a variety of multimodal features. We may not directly attend to all these features, but they are nonetheless present in consciousness. This can be termed the 'rich' view of experience. The 'thin' view, by contrast, holds that only features which are directly attended enter consciousness. Hurlburt, based on his experience with DES, advocates a tentative acceptance of the thin view. Schwitzgebel finds the rich view intuitive, though he is sceptical of any introspective means of settling the debate. Throughout *Describing Inner Experience*, Schwitzgebel stresses the ambiguity of Melanie's responses *vis-à-vis* the rich/thin question. Hurlburt concedes the difficulty, but does not think it undermines the importance of DES in general. Schwitzgebel concludes that DES cannot answer questions at this level of detail, and, unfortunately, many of the questions of interest in consciousness studies may demand data pitched at this level.

Among the key points of disagreement between Hurlburt and Schwitzgebel throughout *Describing Inner Experience* are the question of bracketing presuppositions, the purported success of DES over all-comers (as opposed to a 'pluralistic' approach to introspective methods), and the issue of attention and its role in conscious experience. These three topics are treated once again in the first three of Hurlburt and Schwitzgebel's replies in this issue. Each of these replies again takes on the dialogue form of *Describing Inner Experience* (though Melanie is sadly absent!) Thereafter, Hurlburt and Schwitzgebel then each present an essay summarizing their view of the state of the debate and stressing those elements in the commentaries they find most intriguing. Finally, Hurlburt offers a brief sample of material taken from a training session of a prospective DES investigator. Hurlburt presents this material in order to buttress his case that the relevant presuppositions really can be bracketed in DES. It provides yet another window on the method at work. Taken together, the replies address the key points raised in the commentaries, while continuing the fruitful dialogue of *Describing Inner Experience*. Proponent and sceptic still disagree, which isn't such a surprise, perhaps, but their disagreement helps illuminate the fault-lines in this crucial debate in consciousness studies.

3. Summary of the Commentaries

Philosophers Mark Engelbert and Peter Carruthers concur with Schwitzgebel that DES is reliable when it comes to gross features of conscious experience and that the method loses efficacy when it comes to fine-grained features of experience. However, they agree with Hurlburt (*contra* Schwitzgebel) that there may be considerable individual differences in conscious experience and thus we should take seriously Hurlburt's DES-based claim that some subjects may on occasion have very thin conscious experience. Finally, they propose several possible extensions of DES designed to explore our introspective access to occurent propositional attitudes. *Inter alia*, they defend Carruthers' (2009) model of introspection in light of Hurlburt's claims about 'unsymbolized thinking'.

Philosopher Christopher Hill's extensive commentary introduces seven 'theses' about introspection, and uses these ideas to pose a number of probing questions for DES. The theses are inspired by Hill's reading of *Describing Inner Experience* but are rooted in his previous work of consciousness and introspection (Hill, 1991; 2009). The first thesis holds that introspection is a diverse process and we should not assume that the same mechanisms are involved in all the things we group under that term. This suggests that sweeping claims about the reliability of introspection in general are difficult to make. The second thesis notes the presence of a competence/performance distinction in introspection and stresses the complexities this might create for assessing the reliability of particular introspective judgments. The third thesis highlights the strong influence that attention can have on introspective awareness. Among other things, this raises difficulties for DES when it comes to judging the richness of inner experience. The fourth thesis argues against the possibility of a 'presuppositionless' method of studying introspection. This poses a direct challenge to Hurlburt's goal of 'bracketing presuppositions'. Hill in contrast recommends actively employing scientific presuppositions to guide subjects in introspection and argues that Schwitzgebel underestimates the efficacy of such an approach. Thesis five sketches a theory of introspective judgment predicting accurate introspective judgments for a range of cases. The theory has its origins in considerations of the epistemology of perceptual judgments. Hill contends that such theories need to be taken into account when making judgments about the reliability of introspection. Thesis six points out that folk psychology holds many sorts of very ordinary introspective judgments to be reliable. Hill contends that the authors, especially Schwitzgebel, seem to downplay this sort of introspection. Finally, thesis seven highlights the deep connection between some forms of introspection and non-introspective mental processes. To the extent that introspection relies on these non-introspective processes, and these processes are reliable, we should expect introspection to be reliable as well. In any event, teasing apart these components will influence how we evaluate the reliability of introspection.

Philosophers Terry Horgan and Mark Timmons frame their questions about DES by focusing on a particular (and controversial) type of inner experience: the phenomenology of agency. Introspective claims about the 'feeling' of agency play a crucial role in philosophical theories of free will. Horgan and Timmons present some of the details of this debate and then consider how DES might be used or modified to address questions at this level of phenomenological detail. In particular, they note the difficulties posed by probing subjects with specific requests about inner experience, as this violates Hurlburt's prescription not to influence subjects with presupposition-laden theories of experience. Further, asking about very specific types of experience seems to require targeting probes to specific behaviour, as opposed to randomly beeping subjects. This potentially undermines the naturalness of the probes in DES and may further bias subjects' responses. Horgan and Timmons worry about the difficulties facing any introspective method attempting to answer such precise philosophically-focused questions about inner experience, but they are optimistic that introspection can provide some indirect, abductive support to philosophical and psychological theories.

Psychologist Michael Kane's interesting commentary recounts his participation as a DES subject, with Hurlburt's assistance as the interviewer. Kane has previous experience with introspective methodology in his work investigating individual differences in attention, memory, and mind-wandering. In addition, he suffers from Tourette's Syndrome and has engaged in research on the syndrome, some of it relying on introspective phenomenological claims. He thus is well-placed to evaluate DES, indeed, uniquely so with respect to issues concerning Tourette's. Kane is particularly surprised to find that when sampled, his experience is much more sensory and much less cognitive than he would have expected. This serves to allay the worry that we simply confirm our own prior beliefs about experience in introspection. Kane remains optimistic about the method after his participation, and he sees its potential for generating useful generalizations across subjects to perhaps be better than even Hurlburt is willing to venture at this point in time.

Psychologist Eric Klinger, like Hurlburt, was an early developer of a beeper-driven introspective sampling method (1978). His commentary addresses the debate over mental imagery and the possibility of imageless (or 'unsymbolized', in Hurlburt's terms) thought. He offers a model which explains imageless thought as unconscious, 'overlearned' symbolic thought failing to fully reach the threshold of consciousness. He then expresses his worries about the influence of the interviews on the reports of subjects in DES and his concerns about the time-delay between the beeping of subjects and the debriefing interview. He closes by contrasting DES to two potential rival approaches: a beeper-sampling technique developed by Klinger using questionnaires instead of the intensive DES interviews, and a beeper-sampling technique supplemented by fMRI investigation.

Claire Petitmengin is a psychologist trained in an introspective method differing from DES, the 'explicitation method' (e.g. 1999). She also has some experience with DES, participating in a workshop on the method under Hurlburt's guidance. Her commentary addresses the importance of understanding the *process* by which subjects in introspective interview paradigms actually come to access their experiences. Petitmengin's research suggests a number of crucial elements that allow a subject to access their experiences. One is 'evocation', an involuntary type of recall that can be evoked by replaying the appropriate sensory triggers. The process of evocation can be taught to interviewees, and one role of the interviewer is to guide the subject into the right trigger state. This is just one of the features of the process of accessing one's inner experience noted by Petitmengin. Her main charge throughout her commentary is that these elements of the process of introspective access are not deliberately evoked in DES; indeed, they are not considered at all. This, according to Petitmengin, both weakens the method and makes its assessment for accuracy more difficult.

Philosopher Gualtiero Piccinini argues for the central importance of *public* methods in science, and then investigates whether DES counts as a public method. A method is public, according to Piccinini, 'just in case different investigators can apply the method to answer the same questions and, when they do, they obtain the same data'

(Piccinini, this issue). Piccinini defends the importance of publicity for science, particularly for assuring the accuracy of experimental methods, and offers a number of clarifications and counterarguments in response to worries about the publicity thesis. He then argues that even though inner experience itself may be private, that does not entail that DES is a private *method*. He concludes that DES meets the publicity requirement; however, its reliability in particular cases is still very much an open question.

Philosopher Charles Siewert critiques the DES method by jumping into a key debate in *Describing Inner Experience*, over whether inner experience is ordinarily 'rich' or 'thin'. As noted above, Hurlburt contends that it is a novel result of DES to find that experience is ordinarily much thinner than some would expect. Schwitzgebel, on the other hand, finds the rich view intuitive, but more importantly is sceptical that DES (or any other introspective method) could settle this debate. Siewert argues in favour of a rich conception of experience, and in doing so he raises a number of concerns about DES, particularly the difficulty in interpreting just what subjects *mean* in their reports and interviews. In the face of such ambiguity, Siewert contends that DES is not in a position to overcome our ordinary beliefs about the richness of experience. Further, he contends that other methods of introspection, including self-directed introspection, if practised with care, are not undermined by Hurlburt's defence of DES. What's more, he argues that DES assumes some prior degree of introspective competence, and thus entails that other methods of introspection must be accurate at least some of the time. He concludes, however, by claiming he is a proponent, rather than a sceptic, of DES and introspective methods that are sufficiently careful and 'Socratic'. In this way, he is closer to Hurlburt than to Schwitzgebel, despite his criticisms of DES.

Philosopher Maja Spener takes careful aim at the question of what exactly is at issue between Hurlburt and Schwitzgebel in *Describing Inner Experience*. She notes that there is a difficulty is assessing the debate because Hurlburt and Schwitzgebel are often concerned with quite different phenomena. Spener distinguishes between using data from an introspective method to support claims about the underlying cognitive architecture of the mind *versus* using such data to support 'philosophical theories' about the nature of experience. In the latter context, she argues that introspective methods can provide some support for philosophical claims, but only when there is a loose fit between data and theory. However, if the connection between data and theory is tightened, so that a theory must be 'phenomenally adequate',

Spener concludes that Schwitzgebel's scepticism about introspective methods is warranted. So, to the extent that DES is effective as an introspective method, it will not answer the sorts of questions raised by philosophers about the nature of inner experience.

Philosopher John Sutton addresses the 'snap-shot' nature of DES and considers the possibility of extending the temporal resolution of the method. A range of important experiential phenomena spread over more than just a single moment in time. Further, the very identity of a single 'slice' of experience often depends on the flow of experience in which it's embedded. Sutton takes Hurlburt to contend that the isolation of a punctate moment of experience by DES is one of the key elements allowing it to avoid the problems of theory-laden reconstruction that doomed past introspective methods. Sutton argues that missing such temporally-extended experiential phenomena is a serious shortcoming of DES. But he is generally optimistic about the possibility of expanding DES to include temporally-extended experience, and offers a number of suggestions of how to move forward.

4. In Sum

Though they are inspired by the rich interplay of *Describing Inner Experience*, the commentaries are informative stand-alone articles in their own right. And they in turn spark Hurlburt and Schwitzgebel's spirited replies, making this special issue of the *Journal of Consciousness Studies* a fitting companion to the original work, extending the book's conversation in exciting and productive directions. The issues at the heart of *Describing Inner Experience*, and of this symposium, are the issues at the heart of consciousness studies. Anyone interested in the prospects for a scientific approach to consciousness will find this special issue rewarding — proponents and sceptics of introspection alike.

References

Carruthers, P. (2009) How we know our own minds: The relationship between mindreading and metacognition, *Behavioral and Brain Sciences*, **32**, pp. 121–138.

Hill, C. (1991) *Sensations: A Defense of Type-Materialism*, Cambridge: Cambridge University Press.

Hill, C. (2009) *Consciousness*, Cambridge: Cambridge University Press.

Hurlburt, R.T. (1979) Random sampling of cognitions and behavior, *Journal of Research in Personality*, **13**, pp. 103–111.

Hurlburt, R.T. (1990) *Sampling Normal and Schizophrenic Inner Experience*, New York: Plenum.

Hurlburt, R.T. (1993) *Sampling Inner Experience in Disturbed Affect*, New York: Plenum.

Hurlburt, R.T. (1997) Randomly sampling thinking in the natural environment, *Journal of Consulting and Clinical Psychology*, **65**, pp. 941–949.

Hurlburt, R.T. (2009) Iteratively apprehending pristine experience, *Journal of Consciousness Studies*, **16** (10–12), pp. 156–188.

Hurlburt, R.T. (in preparation) *Investigating Pristine Inner Experience: Moments of Truth*.

Hurlburt, R.T. & Akhter, S.A. (2006) The Descriptive Experience Sampling method, *Phenomenology and the Cognitive Sciences*, **5**, pp. 271–301.

Hurlburt, R.T. & Heavey, C.L. (2006) *Exploring Inner Experience: The Descriptive Experience Sampling Method*, Amsterdam: John Benjamins.

Klinger, E. (1978) Dimensions of thought and imagery in normal waking states, *Journal of Altered States of Consciousness*, **4**, pp. 97–113.

Nisbett, R. & Wilson, T.D. (1977) Telling more than we can know: Verbal reports on mental processes, *Psychological Review*, **LXXXIV** (3, May), pp. 231–259.

Petitmengin, C.P. (1999) The intuitive experience, *Journal of Consciousness Studies*, **6** (2–3), pp. 43–77.

Schwitzgebel, E. (2002) How well do we know our own conscious experience? The case of visual imagery, *Journal of Consciousness Studies*, **9** (5–6), pp. 35–53.

Schwitzgebel, E. (2003) How trustworthy are imagery reports?, *Journal of Mental Imagery*, **27**, pp. 238–241.

Schwitzgebel, E. (2005) Difference tone training, *Psyche*, **11** (6).

Schwitzgebel, E. (2007) Do you have constant tactile experience of your feet in your shoes? Or is experience limited to what's in attention?, *Journal of Consciousness Studies*, **14** (3), pp. 5–35.

Schwitzgebel, E. (2008) The unreliability of naïve reflection, *The Philosophical Review*, **117**, pp. 245–273.

Schwitzgebel, E. (in press a) Introspection, what?, in Smithies, D. & Stoljar, D. (eds.) *Introspection and Consciousness*, Oxford: Oxford University Press.

Schwitzgebel, E. (in press b) *Perplexities of Consciousness*, Cambridge, MA: MIT Press.

Wegner, D.M. (2002) *The Illusion of Conscious Will*, Cambridge, MA: MIT Press.

Wilson, T.D. (2002) *Strangers to Ourselves: Discovering the Adaptive Unconscious*, Cambridge, MA: Belknap Press.

Christopher S. Hill

How to Study Introspection

Abstract: In this paper I celebrate the virtues of Hurlburt and Schwitzgebel's path-breaking book on introspection, but I also express dissatisfaction with a few of its recurring themes. The main body of the paper consists of seven theses about the way in which the study of introspection should be conducted. Thus, to a large extent, the paper is a methodological proposal, though it also makes a number of concrete claims about the nature of introspection, and about the epistemological status of its deliverances. The methodology I endorse is quite different than the one that Hurlburt advocates, but even so, it is compatible with assigning a large role to Descriptive Experience Sampling. Equally, while I am no fan of Schwitzgebel's radical scepticism about introspection, he and I are of like mind on a number of specific epistemological issues, and we share the sense that it would be useful to draw on other areas of cognitive science in extending Descriptive Experience Sampling and refining it.

Introduction

Describing Inner Experience is a splendid book, one that makes important contributions to both science and philosophy.[1] There are four contributions that I find particularly noteworthy.

First, it provides an especially lucid and comprehensive account of Descriptive Experience Sampling, a method of collecting introspective data that was devised by one of the authors, Russell Hurlburt, in the late 1970s. Hurlburt has described DES in a number of earlier writings; but in my view, anyway, the present volume makes the

Correspondence:
Christopher S. Hill, Department of Philosophy, Brown University, Providence, RI 02915   *Email: Christopher_Hill@brown.edu*

---

[1] Russell T. Hurlburt and Eric Schwitzgebel, *Describing Inner Experience? Proponent Meets Skeptic* (2007). Unless otherwise indicated, citations in the text refer to this volume.

advantages of DES more vivid than Hurlburt's prior contributions, in part because long stretches of the book are devoted to dialogues between Hurlburt and the other author, Eric Schwitzgebel. These exchanges keep fundamental questions about the motivation for DES constantly in view, as well as questions about its proper deployment and epistemological validity.

In a DES trial a subject is equipped with a device that emits beeps at random intervals. Immediately after a beep has sounded, the subject focuses attention on the conscious experiences that were occurring at the moment of the beep, and takes notes on them in a diary. Eventually, after several such episodes have occurred, the subject is interviewed by an investigator. The investigator asks questions that are designed to elicit elaborations of the notes, and also qualifications and corrections. Clearly, when introspective data are obtained in this random way, they are less likely to be influenced by any theoretical commitments that subjects might have concerning introspection itself or the nature of experiences. Moreover, DES improves upon several traditional scientific methods for investigating introspection in that it minimizes dependence on memory. The subject's introspections are not precisely concurrent with the experiences that serve as their objects, but since they occur immediately afterwards, the relevant memories should be quite fresh. A third advantage of the method is that it does not involve extended training or supervision by an authority, with the result that data are less likely to be shaped by the instructions of investigators. And a fourth advantage is that it is spontaneous and unconstrained. The classic advocates of introspective psychology, such as Wundt and Titchener, relied on repeated trials involving rigorously controlled stimuli. One of the problems with approaches of this sort is that later trials are heavily influenced by priming and expectation effects, and another is that subjects have little opportunity to report novel experiences, or experiences that are hard to classify. DES avoids these problems.

A second virtue is that the book makes available a wealth of information about conscious experience. It focuses on the testimony of a volunteer the authors call 'Melanie'. Melanie wore a beeper for six days, responded to many beeps, and was interviewed on several occasions by both Hurlburt and Schwitzgebel. Assuming we take Melanie's testimony more or less at face value, at least after it has been refined and qualified during the interviews, it shows that conscious experience is much more variegated, and correspondingly more difficult to taxonomize and explain, than one might otherwise have thought. Moreover, Hurlburt draws on his many years of experience with other subjects in interpreting and evaluating Melanie's observations, thereby providing the reader with a sense of where Melanie's experiences are located within a fairly broad-based probability distribution. We learn, for example, that Melanie is not atypical in finding that some of her thoughts involve a kind of auditory imagery, as if a person were speaking inside her mind. In short, the book is a cornucopia of data. Vision scientists will find passages that interest them, as will psychologists who work on thinking. Scientists of other stripes will find interesting material on attention, imagery, emotion, and episodic memory.

Third, the book addresses structural and phenomenological questions that are of crucial importance to a variety of philosophical programmes. Does the realm of perceptual experience extend beyond the realm of perceptual attention, or can we say that to be perceptually conscious of an item comes to the same thing as attending to it? Does thought have a proprietary phenomenology? Is the phenomenological dimension of emotional experience exhausted by bodily sensations? A highly gifted philosopher, Schwitzgebel is sensitive to the various dimensions of questions of this sort, and is also well aware of the many ways in which introspective data might bear upon them. The queries and observations he directs to Melanie, along with the ones he directs to Hurlburt, are designed to determine whether DES has anything of value to teach us about these larger metaphysical issues. His tentative answer is that DES will not be of much help. More generally, he is sceptical about the role of introspection in metaphysical enquiries. He makes a strong case for these negative views.

Fourth, both Hurlburt and Schwitzgebel make a number of illuminating observations about epistemological issues. Among other things, Hurlburt gives ten general reasons for thinking that the judgments obtained during DES trials are on the whole trustworthy (pp. 28–31), and also argues briefly that it is sometimes possible to derive testable predictions from such judgments (pp. 32–37). These remarks are aimed mainly at establishing that DES is an especially fruitful way to gather introspective data, but they also have some bearing on more general questions about the reliability of introspection. In my view, they leave plenty of room for scepticism, both about DES and about introspection itself; but at the same time, I think that they lay a foundation for future work. Future defenders of DES will find Hurlburt's arguments useful. Schwitzgebel's take on the relevant epistemological issues is quite different, as the following passage makes clear:

> We should tentatively accept the most basic claims Melanie makes about her experiences, pending further evidence. However, we should view the details she provides, even plausible details confidently asserted, with a high degree of skepticism. (p. 222)

He supports this scepticism in a variety of ways — by pointing out that the introspective testimony of most subjects tends to conflict, at many points, with the testimony of others, by calling attention to factors that make introspection more problematic than perception and other modes of awareness, by citing research that calls into question the reliability of eyewitness reports, by raising questions about the inner world that introspection seems unable to answer, and so on. Almost all of his arguments have merit, and many of them are quite persuasive.

Although I admire the book very much, for the reasons I have been reviewing and for others as well, it is also true that I have some views about the nature of introspection and the proper methods of studying it that seem to diverge from the views of one or both of the authors. I will devote the rest of this discussion to stating and explaining these views. In several cases they seem to be flatly inconsistent with claims that are made in the book, but in others the divergence is more a matter of difference in emphasis. There are seven in all. I will refer to them as 'theses'.

I

Thesis 1: Introspective awareness of conscious experiences is highly polymorphous in character, reflecting in the diversity of its forms the highly diverse nature of the mental phenomena that fall within its ken.[2] Accordingly, it is very risky to put forward generalizations about the reliability or unreliability of introspection. It is much safer, and therefore much more desirable, to advance claims of the form 'Introspective judgments about mental states of type T tend to be reliable', or 'The judgments produced by introspective faculty f tend to be reliable'. Also, it is very risky to draw inductive inferences concerning the reliability of one introspective faculty from data about the reliability of another faculty. Before such inferences can be deemed acceptable, it is necessary to show that the two faculties are structurally and functionally similar.

Conscious experiences include pains, images, perceptual experiences, emotions, episodic memories, thoughts of various kinds (suppositions, judgments, etc.), volitions, and inferences. On the face of it, anyway, a mechanism that takes pains as inputs and yields introspective judgments as outputs would have to be quite different in internal

---

[2] I argue for this claim at some length in Hill (2009, Chapter 8).

organization than a mechanism that transforms mental images into introspective judgments, and agencies of these two kinds would have to be quite different from a third agency that has the job of producing introspective judgments about passing wishes. By the same token, one would expect these different faculties to have quite different reliability ratings. Pains can be very complex, but images can be even more so, with the result that it can be more difficult to characterize them accurately. Further, images are more elusive than pains, for they tend to have characteristics like vagueness and 'faintness'. Or so it is said. Still further, there is likely to be interference between images and concurrent visual experience of the external world, with the result that inputs to the faculty charged with the responsibility of keeping track of images are frequently degraded and fragmentary. These differences are quite substantial. Still, assuming that pains and images are alike in that they have little or no conceptual content, the faculties responsible for registering their comings and goings are likely to resemble one another more than either resembles the faculty that is charged with keeping track of passing wishes. When one wishes for something one entertains a proposition — that is, one entertains a representation with a logical structure that is built out of concepts. Hence, an introspective judgment about a wish must contain a representation of a proposition. The job of representing a proposition is inevitably quite different than the job of representing a pain or an image. Accordingly, it would be quite surprising if the wish-registering faculty had the same reliability rating as the pain-registering faculty or the image-registering faculty.

Both Hurlburt and Schwitzgebel have a tendency to speak in general terms about the reliability of introspective judgments, and also a tendency to draw fairly strong inferences about reliability from data that are concerned with relatively small samples. In the case of Hurlburt, we see these tendencies at work when we consider his many positive claims, scattered through the book, concerning the reliability of judgments obtained by DES sampling; and in the case of Schwitzgebel, we see them at work in many of the passages in which he is arguing for *negative* claims about introspective reliability. (Consider, for example, the foregoing quotation from Schwitzgebel: it asserts that introspective judgments about the details of experience are *generally* untrustworthy.) But more: in another publication Schwitzgebel in effect *denies* that there is any ground for thinking that introspection is polymorphous. Thus, toward the end of 'The Unreliability of Naïve Introspection', we find the following claim: 'Neither I, nor [subjects in DES experiments], nor Titchener, nor Hurlburt, nor anyone else I'm aware of, sees any obvious difference in mechanism'

(Schwitzgebel, 2008, p. 267). Perhaps this is true. But I think investigators in this area *should* see differences in mechanism. Indeed, for reasons like the ones given above, I would not be surprised if there was a different introspective mechanism for each kind of conscious experience.

It might be replied, I suppose, that while conscious experiences are highly diverse in point of intrinsic properties and causal powers, they are all alike in being *conscious*, and that this one commonality provides a reason to think that they are all in the domain of a single, multi-purpose introspective mechanism. I disagree with this argument — I think it presupposes a highly questionable principle of individuation for mental faculties. I will not challenge it here, however, for it does not matter too much for present purposes whether there is one introspective mechanism or many. Even if there is only one, it will still be true that this one mechanism is obliged to operate in different ways in dealing with its highly diverse inputs, and it will therefore still be true that introspective judgments about different types of experience are trustworthy to different degrees.

II

Thesis 2: The operations of an introspective agency are governed by a competence/performance distinction. Thus, even if the actual track record of an introspective agency is quite modest, it could still be true that the agency would be highly reliable if it was allowed to operate in ideal circumstances. The factors that degrade performance are legion; they include time constraints, noisy inputs, priming, inebriation, pathology, multi-tasking, inexperience, inattention, and the limits of various memory stores. Often it is possible to design experiments in which the influence of factors of this sort is reduced, perhaps significantly, and when this happens, we can get a sense of the true competence of an introspective agency. In this we see a second reason for eschewing broad generalizations about reliability. Indeed, we see that it is not sufficient to relativize reliability claims to introspective faculties. They must also be relativized to performance-affecting circumstances. Assessments should take the form 'Faculty f is reliable to degree d in circumstances c'.

I will illustrate this thesis by borrowing an example from Schwitzgebel (2008, pp. 254–256). Many subjects are strongly inclined to think that their visual experience enjoys a high degree of resolution across a broad area. Thus, for example, as I sit here in my chair, with a computer on my lap, it seems to me that I have highly detailed experience of a fairly large region of the computer screen, a region that encompasses much more than the words that I am typing at the present moment, and also that I have a fairly detailed grasp of the rest of the computer. It is known, however, that the fovea is the only portion of the eye that takes in highly detailed information, and that 'the visual angle covered by the fovea is only about 2 degrees, the size of your thumbnail held at arm's length' (Palmer, 1999, p. 31). Accordingly, the area of maximum acuity is quite limited in scope; at any one time it includes only a tiny segment of the visual field. Because of this, the judgment that one has a highly detailed grasp of a fairly large portion of the visual environment cannot be correct. Why then are we inclined to make that judgment? The answer is evidently that at any one time, T, we have access not only to the information that the fovea is providing at T, but also, via a visual memory system, to some of the foveal information that was collected in the course of several immediately preceding saccades (several saccades can occur within a single second). Unless we suppress that information by attending resolutely to what is immediately present before the eyes, we have trouble distinguishing it from the information that is currently arriving. Interestingly, however, as Schwitzgebel notes, if a subject becomes aware of the relevant facts about visual acuity, and proceeds to apply this knowledge in some informal experiments, it soon becomes clear *on the basis of introspection itself* that the area of maximal acuity is quite circumscribed.[3]

In view of these considerations, what should we say about our introspective judgments concerning visual acuity? That they are highly unreliable? No. To be sure, they are unreliable when they are produced by casual observation — that is, when no effort is made to reduce the influence of information that derives from immediately preceding saccades. But they are quite reliable when introspection is guided by knowledge and shaped by effort. That is to say, we are *capable* of getting at the truth about visual acuity, though in everyday contexts our assessments of acuity are influenced by extraneous factors.

Our authors are both aware that introspective competence is often poorly reflected in performance, but I feel that they do not take this fact sufficiently to heart. Hurlburt shows that he is sensitive to it when he remarks that he tends to throw out most of the testimony that is concerned with the earliest stages of trials. Subjects are not sufficiently

---

[3] To conduct such an experiment, focus on one of your thumbnails, held at arm's length, and make an effort to keep your eyes stationary. If you do this, you will find that you have very little detailed information about objects in the rest of the visual field.

discerning, he maintains, until they have practised a bit, and have interacted at least once with the investigator. Nor are they sufficiently clear as to what exactly they are expected to do. He is unwilling, however, to allow considerations having to do with expertise to play any greater role in the methodology of DES, as is shown by his strictures against Wundt and Titchener, both of whom assigned great importance to training, supervision, and attention. As I understand him, Hurlburt's vision of DES excludes testimony obtained in experiments like the ones concerning acuity that I described a moment ago. Above all, he wants DES to be innocent of posits and assumptions — to be presuppositionless, much as the pursuit of Husserlian phenomenology is presuppositionless after the epoché has been performed (pp. 262–264). But an enquiry is hardly presuppositionless if it is initiated by beliefs about the size of the fovea and what steps must be taken to suppress saccades. In my view, we need not and in fact should not embrace DES to the exclusion of methods that assign larger roles to assumptions and expertise. As for Schwitzgebel, it is clear that he is more of a pluralist than Hurlburt with regard to methods of investigation, and as I read him, anyway, he is much more sympathetic to methods that assign importance to training and supervision. But I feel that he does not attach sufficient importance to the competence/performance distinction. Thus, for example, he consistently presents the data about awareness of visual acuity as evidence for the unreliability of introspection. As we have seen, that is not the best way to understand the situation. *Some* of the data attest to unreliability, but *other data* show that we are at least *capable* of arriving at accurate assessments of acuity.

III

Thesis 3: Introspective awareness is influenced profoundly by attention, and in more than one way. Attention plays a role in determining the depth to which information about objects of awareness is processed, enhancing figure/ground contrast, and also increasing resolution, thereby providing access to details (see Yeshuran and Carrasco, 1999; Carrasco, Penpecci-Talgar and Eckstein, 2000). Thus, in some cases anyway, experiences are changed by attention. Also, because of the limited capacity of attention, there is a strict limit on the number of items that can be explicitly grasped at any one time.[4] This has important

---

[4] It is known, for example, that people can follow the careers of at most four objects in Multiple Object Tracking experiments: see, e.g. Scholl (forthcoming). For a different sort of experiment, also aimed at establishing the limits of attentional capacity, see also Van Rullen and Koch (2003).

implications for the empirical study of introspection. Thus, when a subject denies that an experience of a certain sort occurred on a particular occasion, it may be that, as a result of the limits of attention, the subject has simply overlooked an experience that was present but not prominent. As a result, *negative* introspective reports should be accorded much less weight than positive reports. Fortunately, today we know a fair amount about the nature and *modus operandi* of attention, and so are able to design procedures for studying introspection that allow for and manipulate its influence. It is crucial to use methods that have this virtue.

I have discussed the way in which attention transforms experience in earlier writings (Hill, 1991), so I will focus here on the limited capacity of attention. One of the jobs of attention is to serve as a kind of gate-keeper for working memory. Roughly speaking, the rule is this: if we attend to an item, it is registered in working memory; and otherwise it is not registered. Now the capacity of attention is quite limited. According to most accounts, it is limited to roughly four items at a time. Because of this, only a small number of concurrent items can be registered in working memory. But it takes time to take explicit notice of an item and to record its presence in a diary, with the result that only those experiences that are registered in working memory will be reported by DES subjects. Because of all this, it seems possible that the diaries of DES subjects are quite incomplete. They record only those parts of an experience, or aspects of the experience, that are sufficiently salient, or sufficiently relevant to present concerns, to attract attention. How important is this point? It may be very important. Thus, for example, Hurlburt tells us that his subjects often fail to report perceptual experiences in their descriptions of introspective episodes, and that they respond to his queries about the episodes by *denying* that any perceptual material was present. It seems possible that on many such occasions, perhaps all, the subjects' experiences actually included a certain amount of perceptual material, but that, due to other concerns, the subjects failed to attend to the perceptual components of their experiences, thereby allowing them to perish without trace.

In my view, Hurlburt does not allow sufficiently for the transformative role of attention in his accounts of DES. Also, as far as I can tell, he sees negative introspective reports as on a par, epistemologically, with positive reports. As we have just seen, this may be a mistake. Schwitzgebel's attitude toward attention is quite different than Hurlburt's, for he lays considerable stress on the ways in which attention can shape experience in explaining his sceptical views about introspection (pp. 51–52). Moreover, in discussing subjects' claims to have had experiences without a perceptual dimension, he recommends a deflationary explanation like the one I just proposed, urging that these claims may be due to a failure to have attended to perceptual material (p. 74).

Incidentally, we see Hurlburt's willingness to accord significant weight to negative testimony at work in his discussion of a famous series of studies by John Flavell and his associates (1995). Flavell put 5-year-old children in circumstances that were calculated to cause them to have thoughts about a certain topic, and then asked them whether such thoughts had indeed occurred. He found that, more often than not, his young subjects denied having had thoughts of the relevant sort, and that many of them denied having had thoughts of any kind (during the targeted temporal window). In effect, Hurlburt takes the children's testimony at face value, accepting it as evidence that 5-year-olds are much less likely to engage in conscious thought than adults. But one might say instead that we will not be in a position to evaluate Flavell's results until more is known about the attention/ working memory system of 5-year-olds. It may be that children in that age group have as many thoughts as adults, but that they are much less adept in attending to them.

I should stress that I mean to claim only that it is *possible* that the capacity limitations of attention cause subjects to neglect significant aspects of their experience. At present this is the strongest claim that can be made, for it is an open question whether the realm of conscious experience extends beyond the realm of attention. To be sure, it is intuitively plausible that we have experiences that are not shaped in any way by attention. Thus, for example, when a subject devotes all of her attention to a tree in the foreground, it no doubt seems to her that she has a broad panoramic awareness of the larger environment, including items that are far to her left and far to her right. As is well known, however, various lines of contemporary research suggest that this may be an illusion of some kind, and that our experience of objects is actually restricted to the few items to which we are actively attending (see, e.g. Rensink, O'Regan and Clark, 1997; Mack and Rock, 1998). In view of this research, it must be acknowledged as a possibility that there are no experiences beyond the ones that are either enhanced by attention, in the sense that they present objects to which we are attending, or are themselves items of which we are attentively aware. By the same token, it must be acknowledged that Hurlburt's practice of taking subjects' negative testimony at face value may turn out to be defensible. My point is just that that we do not at present have an epistemic right to adopt this practice. Or rather, this is my only substantive point. There is also an attendant methodological point — namely, that DES should not be seen as a fixed method, but rather should be allowed to evolve as evidence about attention and experience accumulates.

IV

Thesis 4: It is futile to seek a *presuppositionless* method of studying introspection, for we inevitably use concepts that are associated with a theory when we attempt to characterize the objects of introspective awareness, and also when we attempt to characterize introspection itself. This may be obscured by the fact that we normally use the conceptual vocabulary of common sense psychology in expressing introspective judgments, for use of that vocabulary comes to us as second nature, much as walking and speaking a language do. Because of this, the theoretical nature of common sense psychological concepts is not immediately apparent. Reflection shows, however, that those concepts are shaped by powerful assumptions about mental states and their causal powers, and that when we use them, we are incurring theoretical commitments that are quite robust. There is in fact no alternative to using concepts that are shaped by some theory or other. Hence, we should make a virtue of necessity by drawing on the best available theories in designing methods of investigation, and we should encourage the subjects in experiments to use concepts that belong to such theories in describing their experience. In general, the more use we make of solid scientific results, and well motivated scientific concepts, the better.

The desirability of drawing on science in designing methods of enquiry can be illustrated by invoking Thesis 1, which points out that assessments of reliability should be relativized to particular introspective faculties (or to different types of deployment of a single faculty — I will hereafter suppress reference to this possibility). Now it is one of the flaws of common sense psychology that it fails to recognize a range of introspective faculties: it tells us that there is such a thing as introspection, and pretty much leaves it at that. *A fortiori*, it provides no taxonomy of introspective faculties, and no principled basis for individuating them. Accordingly, if we are to act on the advice of Thesis 1, we must turn to science for an appropriate set of distinctions, and also for a taxonomy and a principle of individuation. Otherwise we will not know how to design experiments so as to obtain information about particular faculties, and our discussions of reliability will be hopelessly confused.

The desirability of encouraging subjects to draw on scientifically motivated concepts in describing their experience can be illustrated by calling attention to some now familiar facts about pain. It has become clear in recent years that the common sense concept of pain is used to keep track of three quite different phenomena — a type of peripheral bodily disturbance, which is generally associated with actual or potential damage, a somatosensory representation of that type of disturbance, and a complex pattern of activity in the anterior cingulate cortex and certain other parts of the limbic system.[5] I will call these phenomena 'peripheral pain', 'somatosensory pain', and 'pain affect'. Now there is generally no need to distinguish between these items in everyday life, for they are highly correlated under normal conditions. We now appreciate, however, that they are fully dissociable. Thus, there are cases in which people sustain serious injuries on the athletic field or in combat, but in which it seems to them that they are not in pain. These are cases in which there is peripheral pain but no somatosensory pain or pain affect. Phantom limb pain illustrates the fact that it is possible for there to be somatosensory pain and pain affect but no accompanying peripheral pain. And the disorder known as 'pain asymbolia' illustrates the fact that it is possible for there to be cases in which peripheral pain and somatosensory pain are present but pain affect is absent.[6] (These are cases in which the body is damaged and subjects claim to be aware of the sensation of pain, but say that the sensation does not bother them.) Further dissociations are possible. Thus, for example, it sometimes happens (though apparently only very rarely) that pain affect occurs without being accompanied either by peripheral pain or by somatosensory pain (see Grahek, 2001, pp. 100–103). Since these claims about dissociations are now pretty well established, there is reason to think that subjects in introspective experiments should use three concepts rather than one in describing the experience of pain, and that investigators should use three concepts in reporting the circumstances under which subjects are inclined or disinclined to make claims about pain. Here one might say: 'Yes, of course, but there is no reason to deploy three concepts in experimental trials in which circumstances are normal — only when there is independent reason to think that dissociations are occurring.' I appreciate the force of this reply, but I think it overlooks a very important possibility. As I see it, the dissociations suggest that, even in normal cases,

---

[5] See the accounts in Price (1999, Chapter 5), and in Basbaum and Jessell (2000). For discussion see Hill (2009).

[6] See Basbaum and Jessell (2000, p. 482). For a more detailed discussion see Grahek (2001).

the three forms of pain may vary independently of one another to some extent. They suggest, for example, that somatosensory pain can remain constant while pain affect waxes and wanes. Clearly, if a subject is to be sensitive to fluctuations of this sort when they occur, and well equipped to describe them in a diary, she must have a system of concepts that fully honours the relevant distinctions.

Hurlburt and Schwitzgebel are of course well aware of the facts I have been reviewing, but I feel that they fail to appreciate fully their methodological implications. As we have observed, Hurlburt stresses the importance of using a 'presuppositionless' method for investigating introspection, and he claims that DES comes close to achieving that status. These views seem quite wrong to me. Every method has substantial presuppositions, and DES presupposes folk psychology. Moreover, in some cases, at least, such as that of pain, concepts belonging to our common sense psychological vocabulary significantly distort the phenomena that they purport to classify. As a result, in so far as introspection makes use of such concepts, it is not in general wise to expect it to reveal either the intrinsic or the functional properties of conscious experiences. Nor is it wise even to take judgments about particular mental states at face value. Efforts to collect introspective data should proceed in tandem with enquiries into the validity of the conceptual vocabulary in which introspective judgments are normally couched, and should evolve as that vocabulary changes. With regard to Schwitzgebel, it is clear that he differs from Hurlburt in being willing to explore methods of enquiry other than DES, and also in being highly concerned about the risks associated with using the conceptual vocabulary of common sense psychology. But if I understand him properly, in his rush to scepticism he fails to do justice to the epistemological benefits that would result from drawing on scientific results in designing methods, and from using scientifically motivated vocabularies.

V

Thesis 5: There are engaging theories of several forms of introspection which imply that those forms are quite reliable. As of now there is not much experimental support for the theories in question – the motivation for them is as yet intuitive and philosophical. But the motivation is nonetheless reasonably strong. Accordingly, while it might be appropriate to be sceptical about the reliability of various specific forms of introspection, and also appropriate to be sceptical as to whether introspection can be used to resolve certain important scientific and philosophical questions about the mind, it would be inappropriate, at the present juncture at least, to adopt a posture of across-the-board scepticism about the epistemic value of introspection. It is arguably a powerful instrument that can be trusted to yield correct judgments about several domains of mental phenomena.

I will illustrate this thesis by sketching an example — a theory that is concerned with introspective awareness of perceptual experiences.

The point of the theory is to explain the truth conditions of certain judgments that describe visual experiences, and to model the processes by which such judgments are produced. The judgments in question are rather heterogeneous in point of logical structure. I will focus here on ones of the form 'It looks to me as if p' and 'I am having a visual experience as of a situation in which it is the case that p', which I will take to be equivalent. Thus, the judgments under consideration are produced by applying operators to propositions — more particularly, to propositions about the visual environment, where a proposition counts as being about the visual environment if it attributes properties and relations that count intuitively as observable to one or more objects that count intuitively as accessible to people with more or less normal visual powers. 'It looks as if there is a red object in front of me' is an example, as is 'I am having a visual experience as of a situation in which it is the case that a black cat is crossing my path'.

To be more specific, the judgments I am interested in use what Roderick Chisholm (1957, Chapter 4) called the *epistemic senses* of 'looks' and 'experience as of', and are therefore to be distinguished from judgments that deploy the *phenomenological senses* of these expressions.[7] To appreciate the distinction, compare 'It looks to me as if the truck in the remote distance is quite large' with 'That (remote) truck looks quite small'. Roughly speaking, the first judgment states that my experience provides grounds for accepting the proposition that the truck in the distance is quite large, while the second one specifies a viewpoint-dependent characteristic of my visual experience — specifically, a characteristic that it shares with experiences that I have when I am viewing genuinely small objects that are close at hand.[8]

---

[7] Chisholm actually used the term 'non-comparative use' to designate what I am calling the 'phenomenological sense' of appearance-words. Chisholm did not explicitly mention the expression 'experience as of' in his discussion. (See also Quinton, 1965.)

[8] In general, judgments that deploy the phenomenological sense of 'looks' are concerned with characteristics that visual experiences have in virtue of such relational factors as the viewer's distance from the object, the way the object is slanted relative to the line of sight, the motion of the object relative to the observer, and the intensity of the light that is reflected from the object to the point in space that the observer occupies.

It seems reasonable to say that the epistemic appearance-statements comprise a large and important class. Moreover, in addition to being important in their own right, they are important because they capture the experiential content of judgments of the form 'I saw that p'. Judgments of the form 'I saw that p' imply judgments of the form 'It looks to me as if p', and it is because they imply the latter judgments that we are inclined to think that they are concerned in part with visual experience. Moreover, it is because they imply the latter judgments that we are inclined to think that introspection plays a role in generating them. I must know what my visual experience is like in order to know how things look to me, and it is introspection (in one of its many forms) that tells me what my visual experience is like. Accordingly, introspection must play a role in the derivation of judgments about seeing.

I can now state the main claims of the theory. One is that judgments of the relevant sorts have truth conditions that can be summarized as follows:

> A judgment of the form 'It looks to me as if p' (or of the form 'I am having a visual experience as of p') is true, for a subject S at a time T, just in case S is having a visual experience at T that entitles S to the perceptual judgment p.

The theory's second main claim is that the cognitive agency charged with producing appearance-judgments of the given forms makes use of the mechanisms that are used to derive perceptual judgments from visual experience. According to the theory, the agency begins its operations by activating the mechanisms in question. Then, after the mechanisms have delivered a perceptual judgment, it prefixes the operator 'It looks to me as if' (or the operator 'I am having a visual experience as of a situation in which it is the case that') to the judgment. To express this in somewhat different terminology, according to the theory, if I wish to know how things look to me at present, I will begin by asking how things stand in my current perceptual environment — what objects are saliently present, and what properties and relations those objects saliently exemplify.[9] Third, the theory claims that it is possible to determine whether the agency that produces appearance-judgments is reliable by considering the outputs of the mechanisms that produce perceptual judgments about the environment. If those outputs tend to be judgments that are genuinely warranted by the visual experiences of subjects, then the outputs of the agency that

---

[9] Perhaps I will arrive at the proposition that a black cat is currently crossing my path. I will then derive the further proposition that *it currently looks to me as if* the first proposition is true.

produces appearance-judgments are reliable. Otherwise not. Fourth, the theory claims that our perceptual judgments about the environment in fact tend to be ones that are warranted by visual experiences. It follows of course that the agency that produces appearance-judgments is reliable. This is the theory's fifth and final claim.[10]

To elaborate: Many philosophers have held that appearance-judgments have the highest possible epistemic status — that we can in effect be certain that they are correct. The present theory does not sustain this assessment, but it does accord appearance-judgments a form of immunity to error that most other contingent judgments do not enjoy. According to the theory, 'It looks to x as if p' is true just in case x is entitled to the perceptual judgment p. Now there are a number of circumstances in which an agent is not entitled to the perceptual judgments that the relevant mechanisms produce. This can happen, for example, when an agent is inebriated, and also in cases in which there is conceptual priming, attention overload, a lapse of memory, or a false belief, either about the way objects of a certain kind look (in the phenomenological sense of 'look'), or about the statistical relationships between phenomenological appearances and various types of object.[11] It would seem, however, that an agent can be entitled to a perceptual judgment in many cases of illusion or hallucination. If so, then the theory implies that appearance-judgments are true in such cases. By the same token, it implies that appearance-judgments can be true in cases in which sceptical scenarios are fulfilled.

I have been moving rather rapidly. Because of this, it might seem that if the present theory is correct, then appearance-judgments are not really *about* experiences, but rather serve *only* to express epistemic facts about perceptual entitlement. Now if appearance-judgments are not about experiences, it is a mistake to think of them as introspective. And of course, if the theory implies that appearance-judgments are not introspective, then it is a mistake to suppose that the theory vindicates introspection by implying that a large group of introspective judgments are trustworthy. Instead of vindicating introspection, the theory in effect implies that the scope of introspection is much more narrow

---

[10] As far as I know, no one has yet proposed a theory of appearance-judgments that has precisely the structure of the theory that I sketch above. But my proposal is similar to, and was in fact inspired by, the account of appearance-judgments that we find in Evans (1982, pp. 226-228).

[11] Thus, you might form the judgment that a raccoon is on the road ahead of you because of a false belief about how raccoons tend to look — in the phenomenological sense — when seen under certain conditions, or because, as a result of your having ignored pertinent defeaters which indicate that you are on a movie set, you hold a false belief about the incidence of real raccoons among all the raccoon-shaped creatures in the local environment.

than might otherwise have been supposed. That is to say, the theory 'vindicates' introspection by diminishing it.

This objection is misguided, for contrary to what it claims, the theory allows that appearance-judgments are concerned with experiences. According to the theory, each such judgment claims that an agent is having a visual experience of a certain sort. To be sure, if the theory is true, then the judgments do not say anything about the intrinsic properties of experiences, nor do they serve to make the representational contents of experiences explicit. But the judgments do provide *implicit* characterizations of representational contents. More specifically, each such judgment tells us that the content of an experience is such as to entitle the relevant agent to a certain specific perceptual judgment. In view of this, it seems fair to say that the theory allows appearance-judgments to count as introspective.[12]

The theory I have been sketching is concerned only with appearance-judgments, but there are theories in the philosophical literature that are concerned with introspective judgments of a number of other kinds.[13] In general, these theories tend to imply that the forms of introspection with which they are concerned are at least moderately reliable. My present point is just that the theories should be taken into account in considering questions about the epistemological status of introspective judgments. As far as I can see, neither Hurlburt nor Schwitzgebel has done this. They proceed as if it is possible to assess the reliability of introspection without considering models of introspective processes.

VI

Thesis 6: As earlier theses point out, there are scientific and philosophical considerations that have illuminating implications concerning the reliability of introspection. But there are also considerations of this sort that are available from the perspective of common sense psychology. The common sense considerations are of course subject to revision, and will no doubt be revised as experimental results accumulate and

---

[12] As noted, the theory does not apply to *phenomenological* appearance-judgments (which are usually expressed by propositions of the form 'x looks F to y'). I believe, however, that there is a related theory that does apply to such judgments. It would take us too far afield to consider that theory here, for it would be necessary to preface an account of it with a lengthy enquiry into the truth conditions of the judgments. Instead of discussing phenomenological appearance-judgments, I will just refer the reader to an investigation of them that I have undertaken elsewhere (Hill, 2009, Chapter 5). With that investigation in view, it is possible to see, I think, how to develop an attractive theory of the processes by which introspection enables us to acquire *knowledge* of phenomenological appearances.

[13] See, e.g. Moran (2001, Chapters 1 and 2), Nichols and Stich (2003, Chapter 4), Goldman (2006, Chapters 9 and 10), and Byrne (2005).

theory rises to new heights. They should, however, be taken into account in contemporary discussions that recommend tentative working hypotheses.

This thesis can be illustrated by invoking introspective awareness of occurrent propositional attitudes — that is, awareness of the judgments, suppositions, wishes, worries, and so on that make brief appearances on the Humean stage of consciousness and then glide away, in most cases remaining just off stage in working memory. Someday we will no doubt know enough about working memory to say how well its contents are preserved, and the extent to which they can be recovered by various 'refreshing' operations. Also, the future will no doubt bring large amounts of relevant data about such things as the eye movements and subvocalizations that accompany occurrent attitudes. In combination with the results of imaging studies, information about these things will no doubt support precise and accurate assessments of reliability. Comparatively speaking, the information that is available today is quite limited. Even so, however, we are able to arrive at tentative assessments of reliability by triangulating from what we know about the causes and effects of occurrent attitudes. We find, for example, that if an agent is in a situation in which it is independently likely that he is thinking about a recipe (because, say, he is cooking dinner), his introspective judgments are likely to be concerned with thoughts about the ingredients that the recipe specifies. Equally, if an agent is attentively watching a soccer match, his introspective judgments are likely to be concerned with thoughts about the events on the field. Generally speaking, we find that introspective reports are concerned with attitudes that agents *should* have, given the concerns that they are known independently to have, and the speech acts that they have recently produced. To be sure, we generally have to ask people to tell us their thoughts. But we are rarely surprised by the answers they give. The thoughts they report are usually ones that it seems appropriate for them to have, given everything else that we know about them.

Everything I have said here is common knowledge, so it would come as no surprise to Hurlburt or Schwitzgebel. In my view, however, they do not attach enough importance to considerations of this sort. This is especially true of Schwitzgebel. If he were to temper his position with common sense observations about reliability, his bottom line would be quite different. Or so it seems to me.

VII

Thesis 7: The faculties and processes that we regard as introspective tend to have components that are principally concerned with non-introspective, first order cognitive endeavours. Thus, for example, a number of introspective processes make use of procedures for searching one or more memory stores. Moreover, in cases of this sort, the part of the faculty or process that is strictly introspective in character can be small, even quite small, in comparison to the part that is charged with first order responsibilties. For this reason, the study of introspection cannot be proprietary to any one branch of science or philosophy. Investigations of it must draw on results from a variety of disciplines. Further, the task of assessing the reliability of introspection will have to focus, in many cases anyway, on the reliability of first order faculties and processes.

I will give three illustrations.

Example 1: I illustrated Thesis 5 by sketching a model of how we acquire introspective knowledge of appearances. According to that model, the strictly introspective component of the process by which we acquire such knowledge consists simply in prefixing operators like 'It looks to me as if' to perceptual judgments. All of the heavy lifting is done by a process that derives warranted perceptual judgments from perceptual experiences. Now of course, it is far from clear at this point whether that model, or anything like it, is correct. But the fact that several people have proposed related models shows that the core ideas have a certain appeal. In view of this, there is at least *some* reason to think that introspective knowledge of appearances derives mainly from the activity of non-introspective faculties.

Example 2: I turn now to the faculty that produces introspective judgments about enduring (i.e. non-occurrent) beliefs. According to an intuitively plausible account of that faculty, it operates by posing a probe question, such as 'How long do I think it would take to paddle a kayak across Narragansett Bay?' The faculty then feeds appropriate key words (e.g. 'kayak' and 'Narragansett Bay') into a Google-like search engine, and directs the engine to look for matches in one or more memory stores. After a best match has been found and 're-freshed', the faculty prefixes 'I believe that' to it, thereby generating an introspective judgment. Now it is clear that all of the hard work here is done by the search engine, and it is also clear that the primary responsibility of this mechanism is to retrieve information about the world, not to serve our introspective concerns. Its role in introspective processing is secondary and is no doubt acquired at a later point in time.

If this model is correct, the only really deep questions about introspective awareness of enduring beliefs are questions about the search engine that the model posits. By the same token, the only deep questions about the reliability of the relevant form of introspective processing are questions about the reliability of the search engine. Does it use a quick and dirty process or a slower and more trustworthy one? Is it usually capable of finding matches between key words and stored propositions when they exist? Does it generally succeed in finding the best match? It is important that these questions can be investigated independently of the reliability of introspective processing. They fall entirely within the purview of scientists and philosophers who investigate memory — specifically, long term memory.

I claimed a moment ago that the model is intuitively plausible. This is shown, I suggest, by the fact that it is closely related to proposals that have come from several different quarters.[14] It would be premature to make a stronger claim about the validity of the model. But plausibility is an important virtue.

Example 3: I will now sketch a theory of introspective awareness of *occurrent* attitudes. The theory consists principally of six claims. First, it asserts that an occurrent attitude has two distinguishable components: (i) a thought or proposition that has a logical form and is built out of concepts, and (ii) a marker of some sort that determines its functional role, and therefore determines whether it counts as a judgment or a supposition or an attitude of some other kind. Second, the theory maintains that we can only come to know occurrent attitudes after they have yielded their place on the Humean stage and are lingering in working memory. For whatever reason, the theory claims, it is difficult for the mind to produce a first order occurrent attitude and a state of second order awareness of that attitude at exactly the same time. It appears that, in normal cases anyway, there is room on the Humean stage for only one actor. As a result, a first order attitude has to precede a second order attitude that refers to it by a brief interval, perhaps consisting of just a few hundred milliseconds in some cases. Knowledge of occurrent attitudes is always retrospective to some degree. Third, the theory claims that introspective processing of the relevant sort generally begins with a probe question such as 'What was I thinking about just now?' or 'What was the major premise of the inference

---

[14] See, for example, Evans (1982, pp. 225–226), Moran (2001, Chapters 1 and 2), and Byrne (2005).

that I just now performed?' Fourth, according to the theory, questions of this sort initiate searches of working memory — searches that are similar to the 'find and refresh' missions that our computers undertake. Fifth, the theory asserts that when a search of the relevant sort arrives at a target attitude <p, M>, where p is the thought-component of the attitude and M is the marker-component, a mechanism for producing introspective judgments is activated. The operations of this mechanism are governed by rules like the following:

(R1) If the input is an occurrent attitude consisting of the proposition p and the marker M_1, then produce a judgment of the form 'I was just now judging that p'.

(R2) If the input is an occurrent attitude consisting of the proposition p and the marker M_2, then produce a judgment of the form 'I was just now supposing that p'.

Sixth, the theory claims that the ability to pose and answer questions of the given sort serves a number of practical interests. We need the ability because we are often interested in assessing the chains of reasoning that have led us to particular conclusions, because we are often interested in recovering and evaluating the rationale that led us to perform a particular action, and because our thought processes are often interrupted by events that grab our attention, with the result that we need to remind ourselves of where the processes were headed.

As with the previous two proposals, the present one has the status of a conjecture. It enjoys a certain intuitive plausibility, I think, but no stronger claim can be made for it. Suppose, however, that the theory is correct, at least in outline. On this assumption, introspective awareness of occurrent attitudes depends to a large degree on working memory, and on procedures for searching it. Now working memory does not exist primarily to serve our introspective interests, but rather to support a range of first order cognitive activities, including planning, decision making, belief fixation, and language processing. Further, it is arguable that procedures for searching working memory are to some extent independent of introspective processing, because they are grounded in the processes by which mental events and perceptual stimuli automatically prime items held in working memory and refresh them. So, like the previous two proposals, the present one suggests that an important form of introspective processing depends heavily on factors that that have independent, more fundamental roles. And by the same token, it suggests that the reliability of this form of processing depends heavily on the reliability of other factors.

It must be acknowledged that the proposal involves a high degree of idealization. Thus, for example, when we enquire into the nature of our recent thoughts, we are more likely to be given paraphrases than exact replicas of the originals. Indeed, more likely than not, we will be given only the bare gist of what was originally a complex discourse. It is clear, however, that the implications of the proposal for our present concern would survive the appropriate qualifications and retrenchments. It would still imply that awareness of occurrent attitudes rides piggyback on more basic mechanisms and processes.

As with the earlier theses, it seems to me that our present reflections point to methods of investigating introspection, and of assessing reliability, that are not sufficiently acknowledged by Hurlburt and Schwitzgebel. In general, while I feel that their discussion of DES is invaluable, I think that there is a larger story that should be kept ever in view, at least in the background.

References

Basbaum, A.J. & Jessell, T.M. (2000) The perception of pain, in Kandel, E., Schwartz, J.H. & Jessell, T.M. (eds.) *Principles of Neural Science*, 4th edition, New York: McGraw Hill.

Byrne, A. (2005) Introspection, *Philosophical Topics*, **33**, pp. 79–104.

Chisholm, R. (1957) *Perceiving*, Ithaca, NY: Cornell University Press.

Carrasco, M., Penpecci-Talgar, C. & Eckstein, M. (2000) Spatial covert attention increases contrast sensitivity across the CSF: Support for signal enhancement, *Vision Research*, **40**, pp. 1203–1215.

Evans, G. (1982) *The Varieties of Reference*, Oxford: Oxford University Press.

Flavell, J.H., Green, F.L. & Flavell, E.R. (1995) Young children's knowledge about thinking, *Monongraphs of the Society for Research in Child Development*, **60** (1), Chicago, IL: Society for Research in Child Development.

Goldman, A.I. (2006) *Simulating Minds*, Oxford: Oxford University Press.

Grahek, N. (2001) *Feeling Pain and Being in Pain*, Oldenburg: Bibliotheks und Informationssystem der Universität Oldenburg.

Hill, C. (1991) *Sensations: A Defense of Type-Materialism*, Cambridge: Cambridge University Press.

Hill, C. (2009) *Consciousness*, Cambridge: Cambridge University Press.

Hurlbert, R.T. & Schwitzgebel, E. (2007) *Describing Inner Experience? Proponent Meets Skeptic*, Cambridge, MA: MIT Press.

Mack, A. & Rock, I. (1998) *Inattentional Blindness*, Cambridge, MA: MIT Press.

Moran, R. (2001) *Authority and Estrangement*, Princeton, NJ: Princeton University Press.

Nichols, S. & Stich, S.P. (2003) *Mindreading*, Oxford: Oxford University Press.

Palmer, S. (1999) *Vision Science: Photons to Phenomenology*, Cambridge, MA: MIT Press.

Price, D.D. (1999) *Psychological Mechanisms of Pain and Analgesia*, Seattle, WA: IASP Press.

Quinton, A. (1965) The problem of perception, in Swartz, R.J. (ed.) *Perceiving, Sensing, and Knowing*, pp. 497–526, Garden City, NY: Doubleday & Company.

Rensink, R.A., O'Regan, J.K. & Clark, J.J. (1997) To see or not to see: The need for attention to perceive changes in scenes, *Psychological Science*, **8**, pp. 368–373.

Scholl, B. (forthcoming) What have we learned about attention from multiple object tracking (and vice versa), in Dedrick, D. & Trick, L. (eds.) *Computation, Cognition, and Pylyshyn*, Cambridge, MA: MIT Press.

Schwitzgebel, E. (2008) The unreliability of naïve introspection, *The Philosophical Review*, **117**, pp. 245–273.

Van Rullen, R. & Koch, C. (2003) Competition and selection during visual processing of natural scenes and objects, *Journal of Vision*, **3**, pp. 75–85.

Yeshuran, Y. & Carrasco, M. (1999) Attention improves performance in spatial resolution tasks, *Vision Research*, **39**, pp. 293–305.

Claire Petitmengin

Describing the Experience of Describing?
The blindspot of introspection

Abstract: *My comments on this pioneering book by Russ Hurlburt and Eric Schwitzgebel do not focus on the descriptions of experiences that it includes, but on the very process of description, which seems to me insufficiently highlighted, described and called into question. First I will rely on a few indications given by Melanie herself, the subject interviewed by the authors, to highlight an essential difficulty which the authors only touch upon: the not immediately recognized character of lived experience. Then I will look for clues about what Melanie does to come into contact with her experience and recognize it. These clues — completed by elements of description of this act collected through explicitation interviews — provide criteria enabling a more precise evaluation of what the authors do to guide Melanie in the realization of this act, and therefore the accuracy of Melanie's descriptions. I will defend the idea that the description of the very process of becoming aware and describing is an essential condition for the understanding, refinement, teaching, and evaluation of introspection methods, as well as for the reproducibility of their results.*

Keywords: Description, explicitation, explicitation interview, Descriptive Experience Sampling, experience, becoming aware, awareness, consciousness, introspection

Correspondence:
Claire Petitmengin, Centre de Recherche en Épistémologie Appliquée (CREA), École Polytechnique/CNRS, Paris
Institut Télécom — TEM, Paris
Email: Claire.Petitmengin@polytechnique.edu

Introduction

My comments on the book by Russ Hurlburt and Eric Schwitzgebel are technical comments, based on fifteen years of practising an interview method aimed to help a subject to describe one moment of lived experience, the explicitation method (Vermersch, 1994/2008; Petitmengin, 2006). I also had the opportunity, in the context of the 'First Person Conference' organized by Jack Petranker in 2007 and 2008, to attend interviews led by Russ, and to experience the Descriptive Experience Sampling (DES) method myself. In other words, like Melanie, the central character of the book, I have worn — but for one day only — a device emitting a 'beep' at random intervals, taken notes on what I had been living just before the beep, and been interviewed by Russ about these experiences. This enabled me to begin to compare the two methods.

The fact that the authors' discussions are anchored in their concrete work of explicitation with Melanie enables them, much more than abstract discussions would have done, to refine the central question of the book significantly: 'To what extent is it possible to obtain accurate descriptions of inner experience?' (p. 14). This is to my mind a pioneering work, and exactly the type of work we need if we want research in the field of consciousness studies to progress. The particular descriptions provided by Melanie enable the authors to raise questions of general interest at two levels, the content of a description and the process of description. The content level is the level of the structure of lived experience: for example, as the authors wonder, is the experience of emotion exhausted by bodily sensations? Does thinking always involve words or images, or does an unsymbolized way of thinking exist? Is experience rich or thin? The process level concerns the difficulties met during this work of description and the devices enabling the interviewer to help the subject to overcome them.

It is to the second level, the level of the description process, that I will devote this commentary, because it seems to me that this process is insufficiently highlighted, described and called into question in the book. *What does Melanie do, what does the subject do* to describe his or her lived experience? In fact, very surprisingly, this act (or set of acts) is seldom explicitly referred to, and even more rarely described in the book, but only glimpsed at, hinted at, from time to time, as if by mistake, by Melanie, Eric or Russ.

First I will rely on a few indications given by Melanie to highlight an essential difficulty which the two authors stress very little: the not immediately recognized character of lived experience. Then I will look for clues about what Melanie does to come into contact with her experience and recognize it. The description of this act — completed by those that the explicitation method allowed me to collect — will enable me to evaluate the way the authors guide Melanie in the realization of this act, and therefore the accuracy of Melanie's descriptions. I will defend the idea that the description of the very process of description is an essential condition for understanding, refining, teaching, and evaluating introspection methods, as well as reproducing the descriptions produced.

Difficulties in accessing lived experience

The authors describe extensively the difficulties in accessing and describing the experience that is actually occurring at the moment of the beep: the fleeting and changeable character of experience, the tendency of the subject to shift from the description of the singular experience toward hasty generalizations, to infiltrate his/her theories, beliefs and presuppositions in the description of the experience, the absorption into exterior objects to the detriment of inner experience, the lack of adequate vocabulary to describe experience, the distorting effect of metaphors. Another difficulty, that seems to underlie all the previous ones, is pointed out repeatedly by Melanie without always being expressly raised by the authors: the not immediately recognized character of experience, the fact that it is not immediately accessible to awareness and therefore to description.

For example, from the first beep of the first day, Melanie notices that 'I couldn't feel myself smiling. I wasn't aware of myself smiling, but after the beep I was, you know, "Oh! I'm smiling right now"' (p. 67). Melanie confirms this lack of awareness in the next part of the interview: 'It wasn't until after the beep that I became much more aware of the fact that, Oh I am sitting with my legs tucked underneath me, and I have this smile on my face, and I am holding this piece of paper. That didn't come until after the beep kind of compelled me to examine what I'm doing' (p. 73).

Here Melanie testifies the surprise ('Oh!') that she feels just after the beep when discovering that she was smiling, without being really aware of it.

Later (beep 5.1, p. 179), Melanie makes a similar observation about a tension in her body:

> Melanie: After the beep I noticed that I was a little bit tense, but not before.

Russ: And so at the beep was there in your awareness any...

Melanie: No.

Russ: So at the very precise moment of the beep is it true to say that really the only portion of the anxiety was the *knowledge of* the anxiety?

Melanie: Um hm.

Russ: So what's happening is that there is something in your body, which is experiencing anxiety, but you're not aware of that.

Melanie: Right.

What Melanie is clearly saying here is that she has a certain knowledge or awareness of being anxious, without being aware of the bodily sensations associated with this anxiety. As Russ reformulates it, the bodily process related to anxiety 'seems to be outside her awareness', or 'isn't in her awareness directly', while the recognition of anxiety 'is in her awareness in a not particularly articulated way'. It is the interruption created by the beep that allows her to become clearly aware of these bodily sensations (pp. 179–180).

Russ calls 'feeling fact of body' these emotional processes that seem to be ongoing in the body (e.g. fists clenching, face flushing, heart pounding) without being immediately noticed (p. 187). However, Melanie's interviews show that this unrecognized character is not limited to the bodily sensations associated with an emotion, and that it can affect other dimensions of experience. Melanie gives us a nice example of this in interview 3.3 (unfortunately unrecorded because of a technical malfunction): 'At the moment of the beep, before the sentence had been completed in her thoughts, she had the general sense of its entire meaning... Since the beep interrupts Melanie mid-speech as it were, we can observe (if the report is accurate) that the conscious thought is already formed before the speech is complete. It runs, half-articulated, somewhat ahead of the speech' (pp. 136–138). What Melanie is discovering here is the existence of a non-verbal meaning, prior to expression. Usually unnoticed, the 'what is about to be said' (Russ, p. 138) is disclosed here thanks to the interruption of the beep. As Russ notes, this interesting observation calls into question the theory according to which thought is of a verbal nature:[1] 'If the thought is complete before the inner speech is complete, inner speech can't be the medium of the thought, can it?' (p. 138).

---

[1] Gendlin has systematically explored this non-verbal dimension and the process enabling us to relate to it in the process of expression (1962, and http://www.focusing.org). I have helped subjects to describe this dimension in numerous interviews (Petitmengin, 2007).

In the three situations described, it seems that it is the absorption of Melanie in the object or objective of her activity which occults the unrecognized part of her experience. For example, at the time of beep 5.1, Melanie is absorbed in the activity of recounting what she has to do the following day, more exactly she is realizing that the time which is available between two appointments may not be sufficient to cross the city. The absorption in this thought masks the sensation of physical tension elicited by this thought. At the time of the beep 3.1, it is the absorption in words and the rapidity of expression that conceal the subtle preverbal meaning that precedes them.

I would like to suggest this interpretation on the basis of hundreds of interviews that I have led, observed, read or lived (including several with Russ as interviewer), and also on the basis of my experience of *vipashyana* meditation: the absorption into the object, and more generally in the 'what' of experience, seems to mask what is closer to us, the experience itself and 'how' it unfolds. This is what Eric expresses in the following sentence, while emphasizing the distinction between the (outer) object of experience and (inner) experience: 'Things nearby and essential may nonetheless be only poorly seen and rarely reflected on — such as one's eyeglasses. I may talk more coherently about, and reach more accurate judgments about, the road I'm driving on than the steering wheel I use to drive on it. (I know that the road curves 90 degrees, but can I say how far I need to rotate the steering wheel to make that turn?)... We normally observe, attend to, think about, and describe *outward* events, not inner ones' (p. 236).

Which generic term should we use to qualify an experience which is lived through without the subject being aware of living it? Is it not a contradiction in terms to speak of 'non conscious experience'? For example, in interview 5.1, Russ says: 'So what's happening is that there is something in your body, which is experiencing anxiety, but you're not aware of that.' But in box 8.4, he rectifies: 'I shouldn't have used the word "experiencing" here, since I'm trying to ask whether the body is undergoing anxiety without that fact being part of her inner experience' (p. 179). On the other hand, using a word imbued with phenomenological history such as 'pre-reflective' — as it is the case in the explicitation method I usually use — gives rise to a risk of misinterpretation or overinterpretation, as Eric signals in box 6.1 (p. 133). For this reason in my commentary I prefer to term these features of experience 'unrecognized'.

In the examples quoted above, it is difficult to contest that the recognition of previously unrecognized features of experience is triggered by the interruption of the beep, which makes Melanie reorient her attention from the object of her experience toward her immediate experience. Russ insists very much on the fact that the beep facilitates the bracketing of presuppositions: by selecting specified moments of experience to be reflected upon and by avoiding retrospection (see for example 'The beep as the first bracketing step', p. 268). But it seems that it is also and mostly the reorientation of attention triggered by the beep which, by enabling the subject to become aware of what is there, stops for an instant her/his usual tendency to substitute theory to experience.

The interruption of the beep brings to mind the gong that in some Zen monasteries calls the monks back to their immediate experience (Hurlburt and Akhter, 2006, p. 296). It also reminds us of some of the protocols designed by the supporters of the method of genetic realization (Aktualgenese), consisting of interrupting or disrupting an activity (for example of visual perception or expression), in order to elicit the awareness and description of phases or characteristics of the activity which are usually concealed by the speed of the process and the absorption into the object (Werner, 1956).

But does the interruption of the beep make it possible to recognize *all* the unrecognized elements? As Eric remarks, it is 'quite possible that Melanie is missing whole modalities of experience that are difficult to discern and report — such as perhaps imageless or "unsymbolised" thinking, if it exists, or unattended visual experience — focusing on and remembering, instead, only those aspects that happen to come to mind first or are easiest to parse' (p. 246). Is not it the function of the interview to lead the subject to become aware of dimensions which are not directly accessible, and that the beep is not sufficient to bring into awareness? And then, how can we help the subject to recognize what is present but unrecognized in his/her experience? How can we elicit the required reorientation of attention?

Coming into contact with one's experience

But how can we help someone to perform an action without knowing what it consists of? To accompany subjects in this act of recognition, it seems to me indispensable to acquire an acquaintance with this act and its variants, and with the different ways to manage or to fail to accomplish it. And therefore to be interested in what subjects *do* to describe their experience. Only a precise knowledge of what they do can allow the investigator to help them, through relevant questions and prompts, to refine, improve, in brief to learn to perform this act accurately.

In their interviews with Melanie as well as in their discussions, I have been struck by the lack of interest of Russ and Eric in what Melanie does to answer their questions. The authors agree on the fact that accurate introspection requires a degree of skill, which in most people is uncultivated. Russ greatly insists on the fact that this skill is acquired progressively, in an iterative way. But what does this know-how precisely consist of? What does the subject iteratively learn? To answer that he learns how to 'bracket presuppositions' seems very insufficient. Very concretely, what does Melanie do at the precise moment where Russ asks her 'what was your experience at the moment of the beep?' What does '*looking back* after the beep' (Russ, p. 166) consist of? What does Melanie do 'when beeped and called to look at [that bodily process which seemed to be outside her awareness]' (Russ, p. 179)? Asked by Russ, a few hours after the beep, to describe the experience which was ongoing just before the beep, Melanie has to recall her experience. On two occasions, Eric leads her to describe how she goes about it. For example, just before beep 2.1, Melanie is reading a novel and forming 'in her head' the image of the scene corresponding to what she is reading. With the objective to ask Melanie to describe the variations of her attentional focus, Eric tries to make her describe what she does to describe the image (p. 100):

> Eric: And were you recreating that image now when you were just reporting it?
>
> Melanie: Yes

We note in passing that Eric's question is very interpretative, a more neutral question would have been: 'What were you doing now when you were just reporting this image?' But the question is interesting because it enables him to collect a first indication about how Melanie goes about describing a past picture: she relies on a present picture.

It is also the case during the experience 1.3 (p. 89):

> Russ: So when you're thinking about this image now, it looks [...] like you're reviewing this image again. Is that true?
>
> Melanie: Yes.

Just before beep 4.1, Melanie is remembering the sensations she feels while scuba diving:

> Eric: And are you generating [this description of a sensation of being 'twisted'], do you think, on the basis of *a sharp memory* [my emphasis] of the emotional experience? Or are you kind of re-creating the emotional experience now and then kind of observing it now as you're reporting? How would you describe that process?

DESCRIBING THE EXPERIENCE OF DESCRIBING? 51

Melanie: Remembering the way it feels like. Because the way I took my notes was to engage my memory to think about the experience…

Eric: Um hm.

Melanie: …and I guess the way I'm trying to do that is to put myself… to remember the exact situation and exactly how it felt.

Although Eric's questions remain interpretative, they allow Melanie to provide interesting details: in order to be able to describe her past bodily sensations, she has to put herself back in the situation where she was feeling them, and to feel again how they felt. But instead of helping Melanie to deepen the description of what she actually does, Eric immediately introduces his own theories about memory. He distinguishes two ways of remembering: 'an abstract remembering' on which he does not give any other details and a 'reconstruction' which consists in 'imaginatively putting yourself back in the situation you were previously in' and 'then kind of provoking some of the old reactions' (p. 150), in other words in 'attempting to re-create the experience, then reporting on the recreated experience, with the expectation that what is true of it will be true of the original experience' (p. 151). Eric notes: 'this may seem perverse, but I think… that her claim here may be more reliable as a reconstruction than as simple recall' (p. 151).

If a 'simple recall' consists in an 'abstract remembering', how could such a memory provide Melanie with the smallest chance of giving any precision about the sensoriality concretely associated with the experience? How could the fact of remembering only in an abstract way having felt a sensation or an emotion, or imagining a scene, allow her to describe this experience in detail? On the other hand, what else is a 'sharp memory' of an experience, than a recall, a refreshment of the past experience, intense enough to allow the whole sensoriality associated with the experience to come back here and now? As Melanie explains very accurately, to describe her experience she has to refresh, to replay or re-enact it.

What does this process, which is indispensible for retrieving past information — even if we were aware of it in the past situation — consist of? To answer this question, the practitioners of the explicitation method have collected hundreds of descriptions of it and closely observed the subjects while in the act of accomplishing it. This process, which in the explicitation method is called 'evocation', does not consist of 'attempting to re-create the experience', as Eric explains, but is in fact involuntary.[2] Not only is the experience memorized

[2]

without any intention of memorization, but the *recalling* of the memory is also involuntary: it does not require any effort, but occurs spontaneously, usually through the intermediary of a sensorial trigger. It allows the recognition of elements of the experience — sensations, emotions, thoughts — which had not been memorized voluntarily, and sometimes even recognized, at the precise moment of the experience. For example, you did not voluntarily memorize the first thought you had when you woke up this morning. But this information is still available. You can turn yourself toward this moment, and make this information reappear. And to do that, it is quite probable that there would be no other way for you than returning in thought to your bed at the moment when you awoke, recalling what you were seeing at that moment, the birds singing or the alarm clock going off, and the position of your body. These sensorial triggers may then allow the emergence into awareness, by itself, of your first thought of the morning.

Precise clues indicate that the subject is in the process of evoking, and thus coming into contact with, his/her experience. For example, verbal indicators such as the use of the word 'I', the present tense, the specific context indicators of place and time, the concrete and detailed character (as opposed to conceptual and general) of the vocabulary used, the slowing down of speech: all these signs indicate that the subject is in touch with a particular situation, and that he is not in the process of reciting theoretical knowledge or reconstructing a false memory. Co-verbal gestures are another sign of evocation. These usually unconscious gestures (McNeill, 1992), which occur even when the interviewer cannot see them (Iverson and Goldin-Meadow, 1998), do not seem to be intended to transmit information to the interviewer. But rather, they occur because the subject is in contact — or attempting to make contact — with his distant past or recent past experience. All these objective clues enable the investigator to recognize an 'embodied utterance position', very different from an 'abstract utterance position' where the subject expresses himself on the basis of a vague memory of an experience, or his representations, beliefs or judgments about his experience. The closer the contact is, the less chance there is that presuppositions will infiltrate the process. In a similar way, the Focusing method has detected precise linguistic and somatic clues making it possible to evaluate precisely the 'experiencing level', that

---

The reader may refer to Vermersch (2004a; 2004b; 2006b; 2009) and Petitmengin (2006). Vermersch throws fresh light on this process based on the model of retention and awakening in Husserl's theory of passive memory (1925/2001), and on the theory of 'involuntary memory' or 'concrete memory' (Gusdorf, 1951).

is the degree of contact of a person with his/her experience (Hendricks, 2009).

Even if the experience to be described has only just occurred, for example at the time just after the beep, a specific act is necessary to evoke it. I have been able to verify by myself while experimenting the DES method that the temporal proximity of the experience doesn't exempt me from accomplishing this act. On several occasions, the interruption created by the beep in the flux of my experience has even in a way 'erased' the immediately previous moment: 'Where was I? What was I doing?' It was only by unwinding again the 'thread' of my experience from a previous instant that had 'come back' to me more easily that I finally succeeded in remembering the instant just before the beep. The accurate accomplishment of the act of evoking is less related to the delay between the initial experience and its description, than to the awareness or 'training' of the subject with regard to entering into contact with his experience. Russ explains this clearly: 'My sense is that the length of the delay is more crucial early in the training of a DES subject, and that the interval can probably be relaxed somewhat with a subject who, because of DES experience, knows what is being asked and what is at stake' (p. 285). In fact, the length of time elapsed plays a very minor role: usually, we are not even in contact with our present experience.

Helping the subject to come into contact with his/her experience

The very specific act which makes it possible to come into contact with one's experience may be achieved in a more or less efficient way. Far from being 'innate', it has to be learnt and practised. In the context of an interview, it is the role of the investigator to help the subject to achieve it accurately. For example, in the explicitation method, it is very important for the interviewer to help the subject to rediscover precisely the spatio-temporal context of the experience (when, where, with whom?), and then with precision the visual, auditory, tactile and kinaesthetic, olfactory and possibly gustatory sensations associated with the experience, until the past situation is 're-enacted', to the point that it is more present than the interview situation. It is only when, thanks to the clues listed above, the interviewer observes that the evocation state is sufficiently intense and stabilized, that he can enable the interviewee, with the help of appropriate questioning, to turn his attention towards his inner experience and describe it. Because of the instability of his attention, and his tendency to move from the singular to the general, it is, however, rare for the interviewee to remain in the evocation state throughout the interview. Sometimes an ill-advised question or reformulation on the interviewer's part, or an external noise, can be sufficient for the interviewee to lose contact with the past experience. When the interviewer observes that the interviewee is leaving the evocation state, one of the processes enabling the interviewer to bring the interviewee back into this state consists of reformulating the description of the sensorial context of the experience, or formulating questions about this context, to which the person cannot reply without referring to the past situation, without 'going back to it'.

However, evoking the experience is not sufficient to become aware of all its dimensions. This awareness requires other reorientations of attention, and other devices for eliciting them.[3] In this commentary I am focusing on the act of evocation which, by allowing us to come into contact with our experience, is the very condition of possibility of this process of recognition.

The elements of description of this act we have collected provide criteria enabling a more precise evaluation of what Russ and Eric do to help Melanie to achieve it, and therefore the accuracy of her descriptions — whereas Eric is reduced to 'radical uncertainty about Melanie's reports. I have no idea where to doubt and where to believe, so I am left only doubting' (p. 249).

Interestingly, Melanie, by herself and apparently without being invited to do it, often starts by describing the context of the experience: my experience as an interviewer leads me to think that it is not only to enable Russ and Eric to understand her experience that she does this, but also to immerse herself in it again. Russ helps her to do this in different ways.

First, the 'contract of communication'[4] that Russ has with Melanie is very important: 'You should know that you may stop sampling at any time, and decline to discuss any experience for any reason.' This is a necessary condition in order for Melanie to feel at ease in accomplishing this unusual task. Russ usually strongly encourages the careful focus on the single experience being described: when Melanie drifts away from a description of this experience to make comments or generalizations, he asks a question that brings her back to the

---

[3] The reader may refer to Petitmengin (2006), Vermersch (1994/2008), Vermersch (2009) and to numerous articles (in French) on www.expliciter.fr. An analysis of the effects of the investigator's prompts (or 'perlocutory effects') is provided in Vermersch (2006a; 2007). Examples are provided in Maurel (2009).

[4] Vermersch (1994/2008, chapter 6) provides a description of this contract and of its function in the context of the explicitation interview.

DESCRIBING THE EXPERIENCE OF DESCRIBING? 55

experience itself. Russ often reformulates Melanie's descriptions, which also has the effect of helping her to stabilize or refocus her attention on the experience being described.

In a very skilful way, by reformulating Melanie's descriptions in the present tense, Russ induces the present tense in Melanie's descriptions, which is a way to help Melanie to come into contact with her experience, here and now. For example (beep 1.3, pp. 81–82):

> Melanie: I said 'Oh, I remember the shed now.' And right I finished speaking the beep came.
>
> Russ: so you're saying 'Oh, I remember the shed now' aloud?
>
> […]
>
> Russ: And in your awareness is…
>
> Melanie: In my awareness is that I can feel my mouth close. And then also I have a mental image of the structure we're talking about, of the shed. […] and I'm just remembering it from the view I saw that day.

But Eric systematically resumes the interview in the past tense, which induces the past tense in Melanie's report and probably makes her lose this contact a little, for example (p. 170):

> Russ: So the apartments that you're talking about are on the street ahead of you?
>
> Melanie: Yeah, they're the ones that are across the street, on the other corner.
>
> Russ: Okay. Sorry, Eric.
>
> Eric: Um hm, that's fine. So you said there were other cars that were in the image?
>
> Melanie: Um, I couldn't tell you that.

In a very relevant way too, Russ draws Melanie's attention to her gestures, for example (beep 5.1, p. 177):

> Russ: And the [feeling of anxiety] seems to be in the back of your mind, you said?
>
> Melanie: Yeah.
>
> Russ: And when you say 'back of your mind' your hands are going…
>
> Melanie: Yeah, it actually felt like it was in the rear of my head.

Melanie's gestures are indications that she is already in touch with her experience, feeling again the sensations she was feeling just before the beep. The description (and maybe the reproduction) by Russ of her gestures enables Melanie to deepen the evocation of this moment, by coming into even closer contact with the felt dimension of her experience. Moreover, as she is not fully aware of these gestures while making them,[5] Russ's prompts have also the effect of helping her to become aware of them, and to draw Melanie's attention to the corresponding — maybe unrecognized — sensations. In another interesting passage of interview 2.2 (p. 115), where Melanie is describing an emotion of sadness and dread she felt while reading a book, Russ's drawing her attention to her gestures helps her to refine the awareness and description of the bodily feeling associated with this emotion:

> Russ: And you've got your hand short on your chest. Is that where the pressing seems to be?
>
> Melanie: Um hm, yeah.
>
> Russ: And is it clearly there? Or does it seem like sort of all over with a center there? Or...
>
> Melanie: I would say that probably all over with a definite center feeling right at that spot.
>
> Russ. Okay. And when you indicate that spot, you have your hands sort of outstretched covering whatever... six or eight inches.
>
> Melanie: Yeah.
>
> Russ: So we're not talking about a small...
>
> Melanie: It's not like a knot, but it's a more diffuse area.

In a passage of interview 4.1, Melanie is describing the sensation of 'twisting' she uses to feel while scuba diving. Once again, Russ draws her attention to her gestures: '...And you sort of twisted with your hands...'; 'And you're aiming forward with your hand...'; 'And you're indicating it from your chest, sort of...' (pp. 140 and 143). The presence of gestures shows that Melanie is retrieving this sensation. Through his questions, Russ keeps her in touch with this sensation, and enables her to refine her awareness and description of it. However, in this example, to answer Russ's questions precisely, Melanie does not seem to evoke the scene preceding the beep — Melanie was at the restaurant with her boyfriend, *evoking* her sensations while scuba diving — but directly her experience of scuba diving, which is in fact quite relevant here. The difficulty is that Melanie, who is not skilled in the act of evoking, does not seem to evoke a particular experience, but her experience of scuba diving 'in general'. To get a precise description of the sensation of 'twisting' that Melanie feels while

---

[5] As we have noticed it in the previous section, co-verbal gestures are usually unconscious (McNeill, 1992).

scuba diving, it would have been useful to ask her to choose a precise experience of scuba diving, situated in space and time. On the other hand, if Russ's goal as an investigator is to make Melanie describe her experience just before the beep, which was to *evoke* her sensations while diving, he would have to ask suitable questions. A better acquaintance with the evocation process would have enabled him to refine his questioning here.

A better knowledge of the process of becoming aware, and especially of evocation, would enable Russ to guide Melanie in an even more relevant way.

For example, the guidance of evocation, at the beginning of the interviews, seems non-existent. The first question is very brusque: 'What was in your awareness at the moment of the beep?' Russ doesn't ask any question — for example about the visual and auditory context of the experience — that would help Melanie to 'put herself back' in the experience preceding the beep. Melanie, who is far from being an expert, is not guided. I also noted, in my own interviews with Russ, that he let me do this work alone, sometimes without even leaving me the necessary time to do it. Indeed evoking a past situation is not immediate, it requires at least a few seconds. Moreover the interviews with Melanie are interspersed with abstract discussions with Eric. After these discussions, Russ as well as Eric resumes his questioning without helping Melanie at all to come into contact again with her experience. This is the main reason why, most of the time, like Eric, I am not convinced of the accuracy of Melanie's descriptions: she is seldom in contact ('in touch', as Russ says it p.120) with her experience, through lack of systematic guidance by Russ in the recalling of experience.

But obviously Russ is not interested in this process. For example, interview 1.3 contains the following exchange (p. 82):

> Russ: Okay. And at the same time you also have an image of the shed.
>
> Melanie: Right, as if you've opened the front door and you're standing just inside. I've only seen this building once, and I'm just remembering it from the view I saw that day.
>
> Russ: And in your image, whether or not it's the same as anything that actually exists on the planet, what do you see in the image?

Melanie is describing a remembered scene. She describes her perceptual position — that is the viewpoint from which she is looking[6] — in the remembered scene: 'as if you've opened the front door and you're

---

[6] See, for example, Andreas and Andreas (2009).

standing just inside', while specifying that it is the same as in the initial situation: 'I'm just remembering it from the view I saw that day.' Through this detail she is giving a precious indication about what she does to recall this scene, to 'put herself back' in it: in imagination, she takes exactly the same position as in the initial situation. Russ brings her back a little abruptly to the description of the content of the scene, missing this structural feature of this experience of Melanie, which is maybe characteristic of what Melanie usually does to recall a scene and maybe characteristic of the evocation act in general. This feature indeed emerges from the numerous descriptions we have collected: one of the essential conditions required to retrieve precisely the experience which has been lived, in other words to evoke a situation, is to adopt in imagination the same perceptual position. It is for this reason that, to guide interviewees toward the evocation of a past situation, we may use prompts such as: 'Take again the position you had', 'Look around you again at what you were seeing'.

On other occasions, his inadequate knowledge of the evocation process leads Russ to ask Melanie to carry out extremely difficult operations. For example, in interview 2.2 (p. 111) he asks her: 'And in what way is this experience the same or different from the experience of the previous beep? In both cases you're reading and watching an image...' What is Melanie supposed to do to answer? Russ asks her to compare two scenes she has evoked at different moments, which involves accomplishing a complex operation of double re-evocation, complemented by an operation of comparison, without helping her at all. In box 5.10, Russ states: 'this "same or different" question is one of the most non-leading questions possible. It focuses Melanie directly on the phenomenon without preferring one explanation to the other' (p. 112). This remark seems to me enlightening about a characteristic of the whole of the interviews: since Russ concentrates on how to *avoid* the infiltration of presuppositions, he is blind to the acts Melanie has to *perform* in order to answer his questions. It is as if his focus on a process of letting go prevented him from recognizing the positive acts — entering into contact with one's experience — which may prepare and elicit this process. And this lack of knowledge weakens his questioning.

Finally, in box 4 (p.76) Russ defends the need to focus on a single moment of the experience being described. My experience of the explicitation interview, as an investigator as well as a subject, has led me to notice on the contrary that the evocation of a single moment often requires retrieving the 'thread' of the preceding moments, and that focusing on a singular moment may even prevent the evocation.

Moreover, when the evocation of a singular moment is intense enough, appropriate guidance may enable the subject to describe the immediately following or previous moments, and instant after instant the whole unfolding of the experience. Such guidance may also enable him to recognize in this single moment an initially unrecognized dynamics. The subject, Russ says, is supposed to try 'to "freeze" and remember whatever experience was ongoing at the last undisturbed moment before the beep began — whatever was "before the footlights of consciousness"' (p. 58). It seems to me that the two metaphors included in this sentence are inadequate. To enter into contact with one's experience, it is necessary to respect its fluid and dynamic character, and therefore not 'to freeze' it. And entering into contact with it on the contrary enables its unfolding. By ignoring the dynamics of experience, the DES method narrows its field of investigation considerably. Moreover, by focusing on what is 'before the footlights of consciousness', it limits itself to a minute part of experience, underestimating the immense part of what is unrecognized.

Describing the process of description

Why does Russ prevent himself from studying the experience of accessing and describing one's experience? It is because he limits himself to the study of the 'pristine experience' which precedes a beep. As he often reiterates, Russ is not interested in the experience which follows the beep. Since the experience of accessing and describing one's experience is triggered by the 'beep' and the questions of the interviewer, it is not a 'pristine experience', and therefore ignored. In a private communication, Russ has invoked two arguments against the reflexive study of the process of description. The first one is the argument of infinite regression: describing the act of description would be 'the start of an infinitely required meta-reflection'. According to the second argument, the only place in this process where contact with lived experience takes place is the initial experience: 'All the other reflections and meta-reflections and meta^n-reflections are delicately balanced on that single point', and no matter how careful they are, that balance, according to Russ, will collapse. I think that both are abstract arguments which do not work in practice. Putting it into practice shows that describing the process of description is both possible and useful. The objective of this meta-description is a pragmatic one: it is to enable investigators to guide and reproduce the process of becoming aware and describing. In both cases, an additional level of meta-description is not required. The infinite regression argument is no more relevant in this case than for the description of any other practice. For example, in scientific publications a researcher is required to describe not only his results, but also the method which enabled him to reach them, in order for them to be reproducible: this reproducibility does not require him to also describe the process which enabled him to design his method. In the same way, the description that a practitioner (for example a weaver) may provide of his know-how in order to facilitate its transfer to other practitioners does not require him to also describe how he went about producing this description. However, the difference is that unlike descriptions of most other skills, the description of the description process is auto-referential. But this does not imply that I leave lived experience for abstract levels, the only point of contact being the initial experience: the experiences of becoming aware of one's experience and describing it are also experiences, which do not belong to a different and more abstract level, but are as concretely and bodily lived as any other experiences. It may even be the case that understanding the process which enables us to become aware of our experience, as well as the process which blinds us to it, makes us enter into closer contact with our experience, and teaches us more about human experience, than the understanding of any other experience. But as it is the case for most skilled practitioners, the concentration on the object of the practice — producing descriptions of lived experience — may conceal the 'how' of this practice, namely the act of description. To deprive oneself of the awareness and of the description of this act is very limiting for several reasons.

First, this description enables the refinement and improvement of this process. In the same way as turning our attention from the content of our reading towards our process of reading would enable us to improve it, turning our attention from the content of our descriptions to the process of description would enable us to understand it better and refine it. For example we would be able to acquire a finer knowledge of the process of co-determination and mutual elicitation of the 'gestures' of bracketing presuppositions and coming into contact with one's experience.

Second, such a description enables us to elicit, guide and teach this process[7] more efficiently. It also makes it possible to evaluate the degree of contact of a subject with his/her experience and thus the accuracy of a description.

---

[7] Even if one could accurately argue that describing a know-how is not enough to teach it, that an implicit part is always left, and that a direct contact with the expert is required in order for a person to appropriate his description, this description is nevertheless extremely useful.

Third, describing the process of becoming aware of one's experience and describing it enables us to compare what different methods do in order to elicit, guide and teach this process. For example, it could enable us to compare the techniques of the DES method and of the explicitation method. We could evaluate to what extent these methods are compatible and complementary, and which one is more adapted to the description of which type or dimension of experience. This would also allow the progressive creation of a more and more refined and shared vocabulary on first-person methods, an essential condition for constituting a research community in this domain.

Finally, the reproducibility of a result is the foundation of any scientific validation. In order to be considered as scientifically valid, a result must be verifiable, at least potentially, by any researcher. And in order to be verifiable, it has to be accompanied by a description of its own process of production. Now if the process of becoming aware and describing a lived experience is not a random event, but has a generic structure, its description makes it possible to reproduce the description of a given type of experience, and therefore to corroborate or invalidate a given description.[8] This opens a path towards a rigorous and disciplined study, a science of lived experience.

References

Andreas, C. & Andreas, T. (2009) Aligning perceptual positions: A new distinction in NLP, *Journal of Consciousness Studies*, **16** (10–12), pp. 217–230.

Gendlin, E. (1962/1997) *Experiencing and the Creation of Meaning*, Evanston, IL: Northwestern University Press.

Gusdorf, G. (1951) *Mémoire et Personne (2)*, Paris: Presses Universitaires de France.

Hendricks, M. (2009) Experiencing level: An instance of developing a variable from a first person process so it can be reliably measured and taught, *Journal of Consciousness Studies*, **16** (10–12), pp. 129–155.

Hurlburt, R. & Akhter, S. (2006) The Descriptive Experience Sampling method, *Phenomenology and the Cognitive Sciences*, **5**, pp. 271–301.

Hurlbert, R. & Schwitzgebel, E. (2007) *Describing Inner Experience? Proponent Meets Skeptic*, Cambridge, MA: MIT Press.

Husserl, E. (1925/2001) *Analyses Concerning Passive and Active Synthesis: Lectures on Transcendantal Logic*, Boston, MA: Kluwer Academic Publisher.

Iverson, J.M. & Goldin-Meadow, S. (1998) Why people gesture when they speak, *Nature*, **396** (6708).

McNeill, D. (1992) *Hand and Mind: What Gesture Reveals About Thought*, Chicago, IL: University of Chicago Press.

Maurel, M. (2009) The explicitation interview: Examples and applications, *Journal of Consciousness Studies*, **16** (10–12), pp. 58–89.

---

[8] This issue is developed in Petitmengin and Bitbol (2009).

Petitmengin, C. (2006) Describing one's subjective experience in the second person: An interview method for a science of consciousness, *Phenomenology and the Cognitive Sciences*, **5**, pp. 229–269.

Petitmengin, C. (2007) Towards the source of thoughts: The gestural and transmodal dimension of lived experience, *Journal of Consciousness Studies*, **14** (3), pp. 54–82.

Petitmengin, C. & Bitbol, M. (2009) The validity of first-person descriptions as authenticity and coherence, *Journal of Consciousness Studies*, **16** (10–12), pp. 363–404.

Vermersch, P. (1994/2008) *L'entretien d'explicitation*, Paris: Éditions ESF.

Vermersch, P. (2004a) Modèle de la mémoire chez Husserl. 1/ Pourquoi Husserl s'intéresse-t-il tant au ressouvenir, *Expliciter*, **53**, pp.1–14.

Vermersch, P. (2004b) Modèle de la mémoire chez Husserl. 2/ La rétention, *Expliciter*, **54**, pp. 22–28.

Vermersch, P. (2006a) Les fonctions des questions, *Expliciter*, **65**, pp.1–6.

Vermersch, P. (2006b) Rétention, passivité, visée à vide, intention éveillante. Phénoménologie et pratique de l'explicitation, *Expliciter*, **65**, pp. 14–28.

Vermersch, P. (2007) Approches des effets perlocutoires 1/ Différentes causalités perlocutoires: demander, convaincre, induire, *Expliciter*, **71**, pp. 1–23.

Vermersch, P. (2009) Describing the practice of introspection, *Journal of Consciousness Studies*, **16** (10–12), pp. 20–57.

Werner, H. (1956) Microgenesis and aphasia, *Journal of Abnormal Social Psychology*, **52**, pp. 347–353.

Charles Siewert

Socratic Introspection and the Abundance of Experience

Abstract: *I examine the prospects of using Hurlburt's DES method to justify his very 'thin' view of experience, on which visual experience is so infrequent as to be typically absent when reading and speaking. Such justification would seem to be based on the claim that, in DES 'beeper' samples, subjects often deny they just had any visual experience. But if the question of 'visual experience' is properly construed, then (judging by the example of Melanie) it is doubtful they* are *denying this. And even if they were, that would not generally warrant overturning belief in the abundance of one's own visual experience.*

I defend use of non-DES introspective judgments in reaching this conclusion. These are no more dubious overall than the near-term retrospective judgments in response to open-ended prompts employed in DES. Moreover, DES itself needs to presuppose subjects enjoy an introspective competence not confined to their beeper reports. The true power of DES to revise introspection thus lies in its interview portion. This view is further supported by considering Hurlburt's and Schwitzgebel's discussion of detail in visual imagery.

Introspectively based conceptions of experience should be improved and corrected, not by means of a supposedly privileged class of reports, but by questioning that clarifies distinctions and makes explicit the implications of what one says in making introspective judgments. My advocacy of this sort of 'Socratic introspection' leads me to broad agreement with many of Schwitzgebel's conclusions. But it also makes me regard myself as a 'proponent' of — not a 'sceptic' about — the use of introspection to study experience.

Keywords: Introspection, Descriptive Experience Sampling, visual experience, visual imager

Correspondence: Charles Siewert, Rice University Philosophy Department MS 14, PO Box 1892, Houston, TX 77251, USA *Email: siewert@rice.edu*

1. Introduction

Describing Inner Experience recounts a conversation among a psychologist (Hurlburt), a philosopher (Schwitzgebel), and a subject of Hurlburt's Descriptive Experiential Sampling (DES) research — the pseudonymous 'Melanie'. In accord with DES methodology, Melanie has supplied a number of reports of her own experience just prior to beeps that occur randomly as she goes about her daily business. Of course, the ultimate interest of this inquiry does not lie simply in what thoughts, feelings or images happened to arise in Melanie's mind right before she was 'beeped'. Her self-reports, along with data from other subjects, provide opportunities to investigate general questions about human experience and the use of introspection. So this is to a large extent an inquiry about methodology — though that dry expression might obscure how enjoyable the book is to read, and how close to home these issues are. For depending on how we sort all this out, we may arrive at vastly different pictures of ourselves, of how we compare to others, and of our capacity to generate and rationally revise our self-conception.

It must be emphasized that Hurlburt does not just tabulate 'beeper reports', and then directly use these to support or refute claims about experience. It is also essential to his method to *elaborate* and *interpret* such (initially meagre and sketchy) reports, in dialogue with the subjects themselves. Hulbert gives a simple illustration of this, when Melanie ventures that, on a certain beeper trial, her thoughts had been 'wandering' (p. 125).[1] Hulburt quite rightly insists that we cannot use such remarks to work up an account of her experience, compare it to others, or generalize from it, *until we are clear about what she means*. For just what she intends to say about herself is not always sufficiently clear from an initial expression of her claim. That may be ambiguous, or may not effectively convey what she intends, or its bearing on some issue at hand may not yet be obvious. Persistent and artful questioning is often needed to expose just what the subjects *mean to say*, hence what *beliefs* they hold about their own experience.

Thus a notable feature of Hurlburt's method is what I want to call its 'Socratic aspect'. For the Socrates of Plato's dialogues assumes, like Hurlburt, that an initial expression of belief may not well reveal our attitudes towards what's important — this may require careful follow-up questioning. Of course we should not minimize differences

---

[1] All page references are to Hurlbert & Schwitzgebel (2007).

between a DES interview and a Socratic examination. But one could say that, in either case, the questioning has the potential to lead us to reconsider what we *thought* we knew about ourselves by prodding us to articulate our attitudes to an uncustomary degree.

Now maybe the participation of a philosopher in the book's DES interviews (together with my own obsessions) make me exaggerate this comparison (and Schwitzgebel does seem — more than Hurlburt — to want to press questions in a challenging Socratic fashion). But I do think Hurlburt's procedures provide an instructive setting in which to consider how philosophical enquiry merges with psychological research. In any case, it seems clear that when thinking about Hurlburt's use of DES, we need to keep well in mind two distinctive phases it involves.

> **Beeper Reports**. 'Surprise' eliciting of first-person judgments about experience in the very recent past, in response to an open-ended query about what 'inner experience' one was having, recorded in brief notes taken at the time.
>
> **Dialogue**. Interpretation and elaboration of those reports in dialogue with a researcher, occurring some time (generally hours) after the initial sampling, in which subjects are posed additional questions about the experience reported, partly in order to clarify what they meant to say by their reports, hence just what they are claiming about their experience.

Now, in my view, part of what makes *Describing Inner Experience* such a valuable study is how it explicitly incorporates and makes prominent what I am calling this 'dialogue phase'. Hurlburt's method brings to the fore how much it matters just how we interpret the terms we deploy in reports of our experience, and what distinctions we recognize. It also strikingly raises the issue of how we might take introspective judgment seriously in studying experience, even as we use it to *overturn* certain introspectively based conceptions of it. For, as we shall see, sometimes Hurlburt seems to envision a pretty extreme overthrow of this kind. My comments will focus on these themes, and on some of the distinctions that seem to me particularly salient in conducting the dialogue phase with Melanie. I will aim to show that a 'Socratic aspect' is indeed crucial to a scrupulous use of introspection. But the resulting picture of experience and method will contrast significantly with Hurlburt's.

2. Visual Experience: What is the Question?

One distinction I want to examine plays a role early on, though it provokes relatively little direct discussion in the book. I focus on it, nevertheless, because I think it can help shed light on the potential of introspection to correct introspection, and the importance of dialogue. This is a distinction Hurlburt assumes between *seeing* something and having *visual experience* of it.

This distinction appears in the discussion of the first sample, in which Melanie recounts an experience connected with having unpacked a chair and found a document with it. Melanie is taken to say that while, just prior to the beep, she *saw* and *looked at* the paper before her, she then had either *no visual experience*, or *very little*. At least that disjunction ('little or none') is used in the summary of the first DES sampling results on p. 305.

But it could be clearer just how Hurlburt wishes to interpret Melanie (and his DES subjects generally) on this issue. When Schwitzgebel takes Hurlburt's interview with Melanie to suggest she's saying she had no visual experience at all just before the beep, Hurlburt denies this interpretation (p. 74). However, in the same breath he says that *many* of his subjects *do* persuasively deny having *any* visual experience in their samples. It's left unclear how what they said distinguished them from Melanie. Further, he earlier objects to Schwitzgebel's description of the experience of reading, and suggests that (contrary to popular belief) typically we have no experience of the text we're looking at when we're reading (p. 50). And he remarks that when DES subjects speak out loud they usually have *no* visual (or any *sensory*) experience at all (p. 138). (In fact, he seems to say they then simply have *no experience* of any sort — neither 'inner' nor 'outer'.) And I think he wants to suggest that this is how things commonly are for us, whether we ordinarily think so or not.

These claims make it hard to see why Hurlburt would want to grant that Melanie has accorded herself at least a little visual experience in her paper viewing episode. In any event, some of the things he says suggest he thinks that it is fairly common for DES subjects to believe correctly they just saw and were looking at something, even while lacking visual experience *entirely*. More astonishingly still, he suggests that they (and we) are ordinarily actually like this for much of our day. For if I usually don't have visual experience while reading and talking, it's unclear to me when I do — but surely it can't be *very often*. Hurlburt's view of visual experience is radically 'thin' (to use Schwitzgebel's terminology).

I myself think my visual experience is abundant in ways that Hurlburt apparently aims to contest. I would say that I enjoy highly variegated visual experience throughout the course of an average day, even while I'm reading or talking. But Hurlburt (if I understand him) would suggest my beliefs about my experience are largely erroneous, because I make a faulty use of introspection, to be corrected by DES. The suggestion is, in effect, that I use the DES introspections to correct my own homegrown ('armchair') introspections. And the revision would be far from minor. The account of typical *visual experience* that emerges on his account is something more like that I might have *expected* for *visual imagery*: infrequent and very sketchy. Meanwhile — although I'm not sure exactly where he comes down on this — he tends to see visual imagery as commonly elaborate and detailed (for some people anyway). This disparity between Hurlburt's picture of mental life and my own seems pretty remarkable.

Because I find myself inclined to dissent more strongly from Hurlburt's views on these basic issues than from Schwitzgebel's, it seems almost inevitable that my initial critical response to the book will dwell on Hurlburt. That, and the fact that these disagreements are too complicated to be treated quickly, mean that here I will refer more to Hurlburt than to Schwitzgebel. However, I will, towards the end, focus on how my assessment of the situation compares with Schwitzgebel's. I might add that I found very thought-provoking much of their discussion on topics I will not be able to address now (e.g. imageless thought and inner speech; (unacknowledged) use of metaphor in the description of experience; the experience of emotion). My neglect of these here is certainly no sign of a lack of interest. I could undoubtedly learn much from what they say about these other issues (and, in the case of imageless thought at least, I could find much more common ground with Hurlburt). But I unfortunately will have to leave these questions to another occasion.

So, I want initially to organize my response to *Describing Inner Experience* around this issue: should I abandon my view of visual experience in favour Hurlburt's apparently much diminished view? My hope is that this will illuminate the general issue of how to use and correct introspection.

To sharpen my focus, it seems we need to try to sort out just what I should count as evidence that subjects *correctly believe they have little or no visual experience*. For evidently their (anti-'abundance') introspections are to be taken as a guide to what human experience is generally like, so as to overrule the allegedly less credible (non-DES) introspections I may have to the contrary. This would seem to be key to correcting my gross exaggeration of experiential abundance. To anchor this discussion, let's go back to what Melanie says, and consider whether we are given reason to think *she* believes that she had 'little or no' visual experience just prior to the beep in the first sample. And let's start with the 'no experience' half of this 'little or no experience' disjunct. Is there reason to think she believes she had *no visual experience whatsoever* at the relevant time? And what would show that she — or any DES subject — did?

Now you might think it should be straightforward what Melanie believes. If she says, with evident sincerity, 'I had no visual experience of what I was looking at just before the beep', then she believes this. If she says the opposite, she believes *that*. But, in *Describing Inner Experience* things do not unfold so simply. Melanie does not start off remarking on how much 'visual experience' she had, or by uttering anything like the sentence I just put in quotation. As far as I can tell from the book, she is never directly asked whether she would assent to such a statement (so I don't actually see why Schwitzgebel says Melanie 'explicitly denies' having visual experience — pp. 231–233). What happens instead: she starts by saying or affirming that (on the occasion in question) she was *looking at* the paper and *saw* it. Hurlburt then asks her whether 'that' (seeing the paper, presumably) seemed to be 'in [her] awareness' (p. 71). To *this* question, she responds negatively. And from this response it seems we are to infer that she thinks she had little or no visual experience of the paper.

However, it's not clear to me just why we should conclude this. And this is the very sort of thing we *need* to understand, if we're to be clear generally about our basis for using DES reports to reach conclusions about the abundance or paucity of experience. So let's try to sort this out. Just what is Hurlburt asking Melanie when he asks her whether 'that' (seeing) was 'in her awareness'? Is he asking her:

(a) Just before the beep, were you attending to, and thereby aware of, the fact that you were seeing the paper? Or:

(b) Just before the beep, by looking at the paper, were you aware of it (i.e. were you visually aware of it)?

One might take Hurlburt's 'was that in your awareness?' question either way. One might, in other words, take him to be asking Melanie either: (a) Was seeing the paper at that moment an *object* of your awareness? Or: (b) Was seeing that paper then a *constituent* of your awareness?

It seems that Melanie herself (who hasn't even been told that her 'visual experience' of the paper is at issue) takes Hurlburt to be asking something more like (a). For she elaborates on her ('not in awareness') answer by immediately adding that (just before the beep) she was not aware of her *bodily orientation or posture* or of *her bodily actions*. She says of the moment in question: 'I'm not aware of how my body is positioned or what I'm holding...' (p. 71). It's hard to see why she would even bring this up, unless she were responding to something more like (a) than (b). Her response seems to bear on her lack of an attentive awareness to her *point of view* on the scene at the time, and her absorption instead in her *thoughts* about the paper ('It's very much just in my head', she says. Hurlburt: 'You're paying more attention to your thought process...'. Melanie: 'Yes, exactly'). Hence plausibly, her remarks about what's 'in her awareness' speak to a lack of attention to the fact of her *seeing*, as her attention is at that moment absorbed in what's going on 'in her head'.

But this sort of ambiguity — (a) *vs.* (b) — is not addressed here. However, it *is* brought out in connection with *another* sample (pp. 79–80), where it becomes fairly clear Melanie is interpreting Hurlburt's 'seeing in awareness?' query in manner (a). Assuming then that Hurlburt's question to Melanie about what was 'in her awareness' *is* something along the lines of (a), we then need to ask: what does that have to do with the issue of whether she believes she had *visual experience* at a given time (and if she had it, how much)? Would it not be enough for Melanie to have had visual experience of the paper she was looking at, simply that she was *aware of it by looking at it*, and that it *looked some way to her*? Shouldn't we just ask her whether *that* was going on, if we simply want to know whether she thinks she had some visual experience of the paper? It's certainly not clear that, merely to have had visual experience at the time, she then had to have been *attending to her own seeing* (by becoming aware of, and attending to, her perspective on what's before her, as determined by her bodily posture). I don't see how the presence or absence of that kind of self-directed attention at the time in question is *relevant* to whether she then had visual experience (or how much she had). If this is what we're interested in, then it seems we should let Melanie know that, and ask her question (b), rather than (a).

My concerns here, though related to one expressed by Schwitzgebel (pp. 232–233), are distinct from his. He worries that Hurlburt encourages Melanie to identify what's 'in awareness' with the focus of attention, thereby tilting reports in favour of a 'thin' view of experience. My concerns are these:

(i) Hurlburt seems to assume that when Melanie first says she saw or looked at a paper she means this in a *non-experiential* sense in which one can see and look at a paper of which one has *absolutely no experience or awareness*. But it's unclear that Melanie recognizes this, or intends to be interpreted in this way, and whether vision without visual experience is even a kind one is normally in a position to report.

(ii) Hurlburt (perhaps unwittingly) encourages Melanie to interpret his 'what's in awareness?' query as asking about whether at the time she was attending to (and had reflective awareness of) *her own seeing*, when it is supposed to be about whether she then had visual awareness (or experience) of *the paper.*

It's possible that the two assumptions work together to hide their effect. If Melanie does not realize the default assumption is that she's employing a *non-experiential* sense of 'look' and 'see' when she talks about herself — a sense that leaves entirely open whether one has any awareness or experience at all of what one is looking at or seeing — then, once she's already said she saw and looked at the paper, it may be harder for her to hear a further question about what's 'in her awareness' as a question about whether she was aware *of the paper* (for hasn't that question *already been covered*?) And so she may naturally be drawn to interpret the awareness question as bearing on something *more* than mere awareness of the paper — an awareness of her (visual) awareness, an awareness of her seeing — where this would involve an unusual attentiveness to perspective and to her bodily situation and activity. But however exactly it happens that the focus shifts to (a) rather than (b), the basic question about her visual experience of the paper is obscured.

3. Evidence of Denial; Evidence of Absence

Let's refocus then on what's supposed to be at issue: when, if ever, would a subject be rightly taken to say that, just before the beep, she was seeing and looking at something, but had no visual experience of what she was seeing? To return to Melanie, I would understand her to be denying she had visual experience at a given time, only if she would say that she was not then *visually aware of anything at all*, and that *nothing* in her surroundings *looked any way to her.* I would want to ask her: 'Right before the beep, did things look to you just the way they look to you when you are in a tightly sealed lightless room — i.e.

not any way at all?' And I would take her to be *denying* visual experience only if she would say: '*Yes, that's exactly how it was in the moment before the beep.*' Now Melanie doesn't actually say this; the question is simply not posed. But *were* it posed, I would be surprised if she did say this. Again, it's not clear to me why Hurlburt turns out not to think she is denying she had any visual experience just before the beep. But that is part of why *I* don't think she's denying visual experience.

I focused on this juncture in the conversation, because I was trying to understand how DES might be used to radically undermine my belief in the abundance of visual experience. And at this point, that only seems more remote. Melanie is not denying visual experience. I am not doing so. Where are the grounds to doubt its abundance then? Perhaps I should now ask how some other DES subjects, including perhaps a *counterfactual* Melanie, *might* provide evidence that they correctly deny having had visual experience. And then I can consider how a case for the general paucity of experience, including my own, could be built up from there.

So suppose now, hypothetically, Melanie *did* respond to my question with a surprising denial of visual experience prior to the beep. And on further questioning, it becomes clear she is not just saying she *doesn't recall* whether she had visual experience, she is emphatically saying she did *not*. Now I want to know: whether I should believe her denial; how to get from this to attributing to her a *general* dearth of visual experience; and how to bring this to bear on my own case. Here is how I would proceed (I will depart from Hurlburt's procedure; later I will consider whether I do so illegitimately). First, I would pose Melanie some targeted questions about her current experience (or lack thereof). For example, in good light, I would ask her: 'And now, as we are talking, when your eyes are open, do things you are looking at look some way to you, or not?' Suppose in such circumstances, she regularly says 'yes, they do'. Then I would wonder, 'Hmm, why does she say she *does* have visual experience when queried directly about her current condition, but sometimes *denies* it when surprised by a beep that asks (in effect) generally what sort of experience she had in the prior moment? Is it that, not just prior to the beep, but commonly as she goes around looking at things, she has no visual experience of them at all, but somehow my direct query about visual experience actually *causes* her to start having some?

To answer that question, once she agrees she's got some visual experience, I could suggest to her that she note what it's like for her visual experience of what's before her to *cease* when she voluntarily shuts her eyes, and then for it to *return* when she opens them. And then I could say, 'When I initially asked you whether things looked somehow to you, did things then *just begin* to look somehow to you, somewhat as when you open your eyes — except in this case, you went from "no visual experience of them" to "some visual experience of them" while you *already had* your eyes open?' Suppose to this she responds: 'No, things didn't *just start* looking somehow to me when I heard your question, somewhat as when I opened my eyes a little while ago.'

Then apparently, while it is rather common for her to believe (correctly) that she has visual experience, sometimes, in the context of retrospective beeper reports, she *denies* having had it during a brief interval. Now the beeper sound presumably cannot bring about antecedent losses of visual experience by backwards causation. It seems there is nothing that could plausibly have briefly extinguished her visual experience just prior to the beep. Under the circumstances then, a reasonable hypothesis would be that sometimes, just before the beep, she is far too absorbed in matters other than her visual awareness for her to retain a memory of it after being interrupted by the 'What did you just experience?' beep; this absorption in other matters keeps her from retaining a memory of her visual experience in that moment, at least memory of a sort that would be readily accessed by such an open-ended question. And in the confident denial of visual experience we are imagining her to make in later follow-up, she mistakes an absence of memory for a memory of absence. And that, plausibly, is why she denies having it, if she does.

Even with this hypothetical case, we still seem to be nowhere near charting a course from DES denials of pre-beep visual experience to more general, far-reaching denials. So far I haven't even got a scenario where we have reason to think that sometimes, even briefly, DES subjects look at things of which they have no visual experience. But let me press on. Again, suppose (counterfactually) Melanie gave us reason to think she did intend some denial of pre-beep visual experience. But now suppose, even more surprisingly, she outright denied having visual awareness of *anything* — even now, *as I am speaking to her.* Suppose she said, 'While I am and have been looking at things in front me, they don't look anyhow to me, and haven't appeared any way to me in the recent past.' *Then* — in this extraordinary turn of events — I would have reason to seriously consider, as one live hypothesis, that perhaps most of the time she has no visual experience. More precisely, in this circumstance Melanie's responses would give me reason to think either:

(a) She has plenty of visual experience, but is making a peculiar extended joke at my expense; or

(b) She may or may not be like me visually, but in any case she doesn't mean what I do by 'looks', 'visual experience', 'aware of', etc. (and I don't understand what she means); or

(c) She has some strange dissociative disorder (like 'hysterical blindness') preventing her from reporting on her visual experience; or finally,

(d) She is *radically different from me visually* (I have lots of visual experience; she has none).

I would see (a–d) as my options because of how I myself would answer some of the questions I have imagined posing to her. That is, in ordinary circumstances, if I ask myself at any given moment whether what I'm looking at looks some way to me, and whether what I was just looking at had been looking some way to me, I would say: *yes indeed, on both counts*. Moreover, I am *never* (so far as I can tell) inclined to say I am (or was) looking at something that doesn't (or didn't) look anyhow to me. In fact, I frankly don't even understand how I am supposed to tell what I'm *looking at*, when this doesn't *look* any way to me. That is, I can certainly imagine that my eyes might be positioned in such a way that something reflected light onto and activated my retinas, even when (because of brain damage) the area before me did not look any way to me. I do not even rule out that I might retain some kind of visual function in this situation (e.g. perhaps I am still able to avoid obstacles in my path better with my eyes open). But were this to happen, it would not constitute 'looking at' the area in question, or 'looking at' anything in it — as I normally understand this. I can frame a notion of some kind of 'vision without visual experience', 'seeing' things that don't look anyhow to me, but that's not the sort of vision I would normally think I had — rather it's the kind of thing I believe is going on in brain damaged 'blindsight' subjects.

Let me take stock. I have been trying to understand what would justifiably lead me to think Melanie correctly claimed to have had little or no visual experience just before the beep, because I'm trying to see how we are supposed to get from DES denials of visual experience to general doubts of its prevalence. The evidence provided in *Describing Inner Experience* does not support the claim that Melanie is *saying* she has no visual experience in the case in question, hence there's no reason to think she then *has* none. And thus far there is no reason to think visual experience is at all *unusual* for her. But beyond this, unless Hurlburt's other subjects would answer the relevant questions in the way needed to make *them* visual experience deniers, I would say the same about them. Without the appropriate questions and responses in the dialogue phase, I would not be convinced that they were correctly denying that they had visual experience. And this makes me doubtful of Hurlburt's claims that many of his subjects 'persuasively deny' they had any visual experience just before the beep. Further, even if we did find some subjects that retrospectively denied pre-beep visual experience, we shouldn't conclude that it is at all *unusual* for them to have it, unless they went on to answer additional questions regarding their *current* experience in negative fashion. And then, even if things got *that* strange, I still would not have reason to conclude *I* rarely had visual experience.

Now I might continue to pursue even more peculiarly counterfactual scenarios and ask what my epistemic situation would be *then* (what if *everyone in the world but me* were a *bona fide* lifelong experience-denier — what then?) I suspect pushing things this far strains intelligibility (how would they even understand what they're denying? How, in this nightmare world, could I have ever learned to talk about my experience?) But we needn't try to pursue these matters now. For the more outlandish these scenarios, the less relevance they have for assessing the prospects of undermining belief in experiential abundance — which is the present concern.

The point remains: I still don't have an acceptable account of how DES introspections should, or even *might* (given a lot of counterfactual assumptions) rightly lead me to conclude I am wrong to think I ordinarily have visual experience quite frequently — most of the time I'm awake, in fact. I haven't argued that I *couldn't* possibly somehow be radically mistaken about my visual experience, only that, so far, DES doesn't show me how I might be justified in arriving at such a conclusion.

4. Only *a Little* Visual Experience?

As I sized up the epistemic situation, I envisaged some reliance on present tense claims in response to targeted questions about visual experience. Now perhaps this will be declared illegitimate. If we really want to know how abundant visual experience is, we should forbid any such reliance. I will return to this idea. But there is something else I need to pursue first.

Recall Melanie was supposed to have believed she had 'little or no' visual experience of what she was looking at prior to the beep. And this led me to consider what would show she had (and thought she then had) *none at all*. But it seems we should get back to the other half of that disjunct, and address the notion that she had (or thinks she had) just 'a little'. This seems relevant, because the background issue here is how DES might flip me from an 'abundance' view of my experience to something more like the extreme 'paucity' view Hurlburt suggests, then I ought to consider the prospect — not of being persuaded that I hardly ever have any visual experience at all — but that even when I do have it, I just never get to have *very much* of it; I only ever have a *little* — anyway I have a *lot less* of it than I think I do. Maybe DES promises to overthrow my introspection in *that* way.

To examine this, we clearly need to consider just what we might mean in this context by saying someone had 'little visual experience' of something. The meaning of such a claim is initially unclear, and needs cautious handling (like that of claims that experience is or is not 'rich'). Now by saying one had only a little visual experience of something, one might mean something like: one had *no more than a glance* at it. That is to say: one had a visual experience of it that was *not very long*. Of course, DES subjects would correctly report having in *that* sense 'only a little' visual experience of something just prior to the beep, because they are being asked about a *brief period of time*: the 'moment' — what happened 'just before' — the beep. But that picks no quarrel with my introspection, and it has no consequences for the abundance of visual experience generally, since it's not true that we rarely get more than a glance at anything we see.

What else then might be meant? By saying one had little visual experience during a certain period of time one might instead mean something like: 'the way things *looked* to me then was relatively *homogeneous or undifferentiated*. An extreme case would be the experience of a uniformly lit, monochromatic expanse: a 'Ganzfeld'. And one could also have, in this sense, relatively little visual experience of something because of *poor lighting*, or because of *visual defects* that severely affect acuity. So, looking at an elaborately patterned Persian rug, or a detailed city map, or the circuit board of a computer, I have little experience of it, *when the lights are quite dim*, relative to what I have *when the lights are turned up*. And, even with good lighting, my legally blind friend Mike has little experience of it, relative to what *I* have. Now it seems Melanie (and other DES subjects) might indeed have *relatively* little visual experience of what they were looking at, just prior to the beep, in this sense as well — little, that is, relative to what she would have had over a longer period of visually examining it. But none of this suggests that, in some sense, *usually* she or we have 'only a little' visual experience of the things that we see. So again, I don't see the prospects for some big overthrow of my pre-DES introspective convictions.

So what *else* might be meant by saying someone has little visual experience? I suppose you might mean something like: during a given time, you do not have visual experience of *many things you can identify in the course of that experience*. A list of items you can visually identify during that time (i.e. classify by how they look to you) would *not be very numerous*. Surely this is true of the pre-beep moments reported by DES subjects. But it also would be upheld by introspection outside DES. Suppose, for example, you look over the rug for awhile (take your time), and are asked to classify the patterns or shapes and areas of colour you see as you do so. Or the rug is removed from view and immediately you are asked to list just what patterns and shapes and colours you then saw. The number of classified objects you provide in your list is likely not to be very large — certainly not relative to the number of distinguishable patterns, shapes, and areas of colour *that are there*. Again there doesn't seem to be much threat to ordinary introspection from DES here.

Anyway, if *this* is what is meant by saying we have 'little visual experience', then it seems true enough. However, I would note this would also be misleading. For recognizing this limitation in our capacity to visually identify what we visually experience over a given stretch of time is compatible with recognizing that the appearance of what is experienced is often much more various than this. The things before me may — and usually do — appear to me much more heterogeneously with respect to colour, shape, and position, than is reflected in the number of distinct classifications of seen objects I will actually report, for that particular duration of experience, if queried.

Now let me sum up. If what I've been saying is correct, the evidence from Melanie we have in the book gives us no reason at all to think she denies that she had visual experience prior to the beep in the first sample. And here at least, it seems I agree with Hurlburt. But my reasons for this make me doubt his other subjects are (any more than Melanie) typically denying they have any visual experience just before the beep. And, if on some such occasions they would deny having had it, it's unclear we should believe them, and even if we should, we'd still have no reason to think they don't *usually* have it — unless they would also deny this, when directly asked about their *current* state. And even if, amazingly, some did deny this as well, then that still wouldn't show that visual experience is for *me* a rare treat. Finally, if we consider the suggestion that whenever subjects have visual experience, they have only a *little*, we always need to ask: *'little' in what respect, and relative to what*? If we mean 'little variegated, relative to other experience we have', or 'of much shorter duration than other experience we have', then clearly there won't be a good prospect of showing we usually have only a little visual experience. For again, we are not limited to getting only a glance at things. And we are not usually limited to Ganzfeld experiences or the experiences of the severely visually impaired, and aren't always stuck with poor lighting. So far then, I see no prospects for using DES to overthrow my introspective judgment that my visual experience is considerably more abundant than Hurlburt seems to claim.

Let me be clear: this is not meant to discredit DES itself. Nor is it supposed to cast doubt on Melanie's beeper reports. Rather it is an attempt to pursue more deeply matters that arise in the dialogue phase of DES, in ways that show why, based on the evidence I've got, I don't think DES supports — or has any prospect of supporting — the radical denials of experience suggested by many of Hurlburt's remarks.

5. Must I Wait for the Beep?

In extending the dialogue as I have, I have at times relied on first-person judgments about experience that are neither themselves beeper reports, nor based on such reports. I have so far put off a certain objection this might arouse. Perhaps Hurlburt would object: 'At crucial points, you would have us give some evidential weight to your "armchair" introspective judgments made outside of, and unconfirmed by, DES beeper reports. And that is illegitimate. We use DES to reveal the paucity of experience by allowing *only* its near-term retrospective reports about experience in response to an open-ended prompt. If it's not to be found in such reports, it's not in experience. Since many beeper reports mention very few types of experience, and whole categories (e.g. visual, aural) are often simply missing, we should conclude those kinds of experience are infrequent, and experience as a whole is much poorer than you think. For *other* reports of experience deserve no credence at all, unless they are backed up by the appropriate beeper reports' (See pp. 50, 109, 185–186, 269–270).

In response to this, I would want first to note that, in this context, I regard it as a little prejudicial to use the term 'armchair' to describe introspective judgments that we make on our own initiative, differing from DES beeper reports by being *present-tense* or responsive to *targeted* questions. There is certainly a pejorative feel about 'armchair'. It suggests that the judgments in question are unwarranted speculations, somehow not respectably 'empirical', as beeper reports are. But this shouldn't be taken for granted. So I propose we set this label aside. The issue is really whether we should suspend reliance on any first-person judgments about experience, except for near-term retrospective judgments in response to an open-ended prompt.

Now even if we did try to privilege these reports as proposed, it's far from clear this would pave the way to undermine other introspective judgments, so as to leave in its wake a barren experiential landscape. It would need to be clear that one's responses to *open-ended questions* about a given time would in fact usually simply be missing whole classes of experiences (e.g. visual, aural) commonly self-attributed in response to *targeted questions regarding one's just-past experience*. But my examination of how the vision/visual experience distinction is handled in Melanie's case leads me to wonder if we appear to get the 'missing experience' result from subjects' beeper reports by imposing dubious (and rather obscure) requirements on what is to count as an attribution of experience. So again, even though subjects report they *saw* or *looked at* something, we don't take them to report *visual experience*, because we implicitly assume they are understanding 'see' and 'look at' in their remarks in a sense in which one can see and look at something of which one has no visual experience or awareness. And we also wind up surreptitiously presupposing that genuine visual experience requires a *concurrent attention to one's own seeing*, or at any rate a kind of *concurrent reflective awareness of one's own seeing*.

But if we understand the relevant terms in *another* way, as I have suggested, then what we have is not evidence for a relative paucity of visual experience, but at most evidence for a relative paucity of *contemporaneous reflective self-consciousness about one's visual experience*. And that is something else entirely. So I would question whether confining our evidence for experience to beeper reports should actually result in such a drastic reduction in our estimate of it. Also, I note that Schwitzgebel's 'beeper' subjects, who were briefed differently than Hurlburt's, and not instructed to look only for 'inner' experience, seemed to have been considerably more generous in their self-attributions of visual experience (pp. 228–231). This too should give us pause.

Next I think we need to ask whether we really have sufficient reason to discard responses to questions about (e.g.) how things look to us as we are looking at them, in favour of responses to surprise generic queries about what we just experienced a moment ago. Suppose subjects don't mention a type of experience in response to an *open-ended* question, which they report in a *targeted* one. Why should we believe the former report, and not the latter? Hurlburt is concerned that targeted questions will presuppose certain types of experience are occurring, where that should be left open — and an open-ended prompt has the desired neutrality (p. 25). But if we risk inducing confabulations because eager-to-please subjects think we're telling them they *should* be having a certain type of experience, we can explicitly tell them from the start that we do not mean to suggest this, much as we might assure them at the outset that it's ok to say they don't remember, to help guard against *denials of past experience* when a disavowal of *memory* would be more prudent. Such precautions are imperfect, undoubtedly. But the dangers of relying on targeted present tense questions appear overall at least no *greater* than the dangers of confabulation and poor memory that, as Hurlburt admits, attend DES (pp. 284–285).

Note also that if we limit ourselves to DES reports, we assume in effect that only the sort of thing that shows up in such reports is to be found in experience. And that seems like a big assumption. One reason to question it is this. Confining ourselves to responses to an open-ended past tense question may actually build in an unwarranted bias in favour of 'thin' experience, precisely because it gives the subject no clue about what is important or what to look for (this 'openness' is not necessarily a strength). For if one is faced with the wide-open question, 'What did you just experience?' with no context to orient attention, and no guidance about what is salient, one may be inclined to notice retrospectively *only what recently so strongly dominated one's attention as to be virtually unignorable in memory* — 'unforgettable'. But why assume this will include everything that is ever 'in experience'?

Furthermore, it may well be that our capacity for detailed articulate memory of experience *we weren't noticing or attending to at the time of occurrence* is very limited. Subjects may record a few aspects of their experience in their notes, and in that time lose access to other aspects, which they might have retained if they had happened to focus on that instead. And, when interviewed about these episodes hours later, and asked simply, 'Was there anything else in your experience/awareness at that moment?', they may be less than vigilant in distinguishing between: 'I don't recall anything else', and 'I recall there was nothing else', and thereby slip into an unwarranted underestimate of experience.

In general I would have to say: I agree with Hurlburt that we should seek to minimize many of the sources of error and distortion in first-person judgments that he decries. But I also agree with Schwitzgebel (pp. 222–225) that this doesn't justify according to beeper reports a place of such high *epistemic privilege* that these should serve as a sort of tribunal, before which *present* tense judgments, and those made in response to more *targeted* questions, can be tried. For there are serious potential drawbacks to treating beeper reports as furnishing complete records of experience, and insufficient reasons have been offered to think other reports are overall inferior to them. Nor is it even clear the court Hurlburt convenes would yield the harsh verdicts he suggests, were it furnished with appropriate rules of evidence.

Finally, there is this basic problem in trying to accord DES beeper judgments such commanding epistemic authority that they might in principle threaten to sweep all other first-person characterizations of experience aside. And that is this. That subjects enjoy a certain competence in reporting on their own experience is *presupposed* when they are deemed fit subjects for DES — or fit interviewers for that matter. But that competence could not have been acquired and exhibited only in *past tense judgments* in response to *open-ended questions*. If I am not entitled to assume that, as things are, I can frequently make accurate judgments in response to targeted questions that I am now *seeing* something, that I am *looking at* something, that something *looks* or *appears* somehow to me, and if I cannot coordinate these uses with my use of terms like 'visually experience', 'visual awareness' and their cognates, then I am not entitled to assume I have enough competence in the use of these expressions to employ them in beeper reports worth taking seriously. If I am no good at answering you now, when you ask me, 'Does A look to you bigger than B?', then I have no business reporting on whether, a moment ago, A look*ed* to me bigger than B. *Nor*, it seems to me, failing such competence, would I understand the crucial terms adequately to make me fit to participate in the dialogue phase of DES.

This is not just about me. *None* of us is equipped to get in the game, unless we bring to the table some such prior competence in the application of these terms to our own case. And that assumes the accuracy of extra-DES introspection.

6. On Introspective Error

I have been arguing, among other things, that there are limits to the manner in which we could expect DES research to debunk introspective judgment, because of how it presupposes a background introspective competence. But I certainly do not deny that introspection can fail significantly in revealing to us the character of experience.

I do not even purport to rule out a discovery that someone's application of certain terms or distinctions suffers from defects so grave as to deprive the first-person reports that employ them of all authority, and rob them of all force in evidence or argument. In the most extreme case, we would find that every use of a type of expression by a particular person to assert something about themselves would be thus disqualified (think, for instance, of blind people who suffer from Anton's syndrome, and of their claims to 'see' and 'look at' things). But the question remains: *should* I in fact regard myself as thus disqualified in my use of 'visual experience', 'looks', and 'aware of'? We should be cautious about such a dire conclusion. And we must distinguish this from subtler, but still significant cases, where a speaker's grasp of a relevant distinction, or their care in handling it in a given instance, should be put in question.

I now want to discuss briefly some examples of this, drawn from Hurlburt's and Schwitzgebel's discussion of visual imagery. This will help me to illustrate and bolster my argument that there are certain built-in limits to how much DES (or any method that relies on introspection) can do to undermine an individual's first-person present tense judgments about experience in response to targeted questions. But at the same time it will also help me show that we can rationally discover — through dialogue — how introspection can go wrong, and what would make it better.

Example #1: 'A discernible difference?'

Consider in this connection Melanie's reports of visual imagery, and the discussion of how much 'detail' was originally 'in the image'. We are in a position to use a subject's report to justify claims that she visualized something just prior to the beep, and just what she visualized, only if we assume, for example, that she can with some accuracy generally report when she is *seeing* something, and when instead she is only '*seeing it in her mind or imagination*'. This is a competence she needs before she signs up for DES. Otherwise she won't be able to provide worthwhile data. For suppose when you ask her something like, 'Do you really see a traffic light before you now, or are you just *imagining* it?', she simply cannot regularly correctly judge *which* is going on. How could we rely on the self-reports of such a subject to reach any warranted conclusions about visual imagery and its level of detail relative to visual experience?

Now I don't at all doubt that Melanie, Hurlburt, Schwitzgebel — and we their readers — share this basic competence. But it is a further matter whether we are always sufficiently attentive in relevant ways to the difference at issue (seeing *vs.* imagining), in the context of certain *unusual, picky* questions about, say, whether this or that detail was 'already in the image'. So, for example, when Melanie reports having 'had a mental image of' being at an intersection, Hurlburt asks her (p. 167) whether 'that' was *'just like* being in the car'. And she answers that it was. Now this response *might* be taken to imply she believes she had visual imagery just as 'detailed' as ordinary visual experience. On the other hand, it might be a mistake to read this into her response. For it might *also* be taken (and perhaps *should* be taken) to have by itself *no immediate bearing at all on this 'detail' question*. For she might be saying simply that *what she imagined* (or had an image of) on this occasion (a.k.a. the 'scene') was a normal situation of being in a car before a red traffic light — and thus a sort of *situation* none other than (in no discernible way different from) that she sometimes *perceives* she's in when she's *actually in the car.* That is to say: she was not imagining being before some *peculiar* traffic light or intersection — just the typical, ordinary sort of scene. But this does not entail that the *experience of imagining* being at the stoplight was for her utterly indistinguishable from the *experience of seeing* that same type of situation, when she is in the car — or even anything close to this. She can, after all, we are assuming, generally tell when she's seeing a traffic light, and when she's just imagining one. And it just may be that part of what makes the experiences distinguishable is that the one in some sense contains a level and type of 'detail' that the other does not. But before we can even consider that issue, we need to distinguish between asking whether *what was imagined* on an occasion was the *very sort of situation one sometimes sees*, and asking whether the *experience* of imagining it is indistinguishable (with respect to type and level of detail) from the *experience* of seeing it.

Part of what I wish to convey here is that, even while we rightly assume a certain introspective competence in reporting episodes of *imagining* as opposed to *seeing* — and in reporting what one sees and what one imagines — this can leave us vulnerable to mistakes about questions like: are my visual experience and my visual imagery *similarly detailed*? For, without explicit care to distinctions of the sort just mentioned, either I myself, or an audience relying on my introspective reports, might wrongly take my response to a question like Hurlburt's to commit me to claiming that the detail of imagining is equivalent or comparable to the detail of seeing. And in this way introspection could lead to error about 'image detail'.

Does Melanie commit such an error? Schwitzgebel worries that Melanie 'overdescribes her imagery' (p. 175) and Hurlburt says she 'describes substantially more image detail' than Schwitzgebel expects (p. 176). But it's not clear to me, in some of these cases, she is even saying she experiences or imagines all that much detail, or just what detail she is claiming that Schwitzgebel doubts was there.

Example #2: Embellishment?

A second illustration of the general point (again crucial to using imagery reports to address 'level of detail' questions), has to do with a difference whose importance Schwitzgebel emphasizes (pp. 97, 102, 239–240). This (as I would put it) is the difference between:

(a) Recalling what one earlier imagined by *re*-imagining it *with some additional embellishments*, and

(b) Simply recalling what was earlier imagined.

In order to distinguish (a) reports from (b) reports, subjects and interviewers both must have the basic prior competence with the seeing/imagining distinction already discussed. But if we want to use their reports to address the *level of detail* question about imagery they need more. They need some introspective competence in distinguishing (a) and (b). Unless they have this, *and* take care to try to heed the distinction in reports and dialogue, we won't be able to draw any worthwhile conclusions about the relative level of detail in the (original) image by using DES. For consider subjects who first assure us in follow up questioning that they imagined a prodigious wealth of detail in some moment before the beep. As we request more and more detail about what was imagined, they happily continue to supply it. But then when we mention the distinction between (a) and (b), and ask them whether they are confident they are not adding in some new details after the fact, they say they aren't clear on the distinction, or seem confused by the question. Or perhaps they say they now get the distinction well enough, but weren't really trying to apply it in giving their earlier reports. Or (more worrisome still, though less likely) they say they grasp the distinction, but don't know at all how to heed it in their responses, because when they imagine something, they can *never* tell whether they are imagining more than they had already imagined. Or maybe they *say* they get the distinction, and are heeding it in their reports, and yet, as it happens — they never or almost never seem to worry that they are embellishing a past image, as opposed to strictly recalling what was 'in' it; they just keep piling on more and more detail, blithely assuring us it was already there in that image briefly formed some hours ago.

All these eventualities could reasonably put into question the reliability of first-person reports in this context. Subjects might have satisfactory competence with the 'seeing/imagining' distinction, but lack it for the 'imagined-already/imagining-new-stuff' distinction. Or they might not have understood the distinction very well. Or they might have understood it, but not have taken care to apply it. Or they might say they're applying it, but do so in a suspiciously lopsided fashion. Which if any of these pitfalls undercuts the usefulness of their testimony needs to be sorted out. And unless we have made reasonable efforts to avoid and remedy these problems, we can't use introspective judgments about imagery (including DES judgments) to tell us anything about how detailed someone's imagery experience is. To some extent at least, such worries can be raised and dealt with in the 'dialogue phase', even while we rely in various ways on a background of introspective competence. But whether this will leave irremediably large indeterminacies in reported detail would then remain to be seen.

It is unclear to me just which of these problems, if any, may be afflicting Melanie's reports in various places. I do not think the question of whether imagery detail is enriched by focusing on or 'looking at' a portion of 'the image' (the question discussed on p. 105) is just the same as whether (and in what respect) the original imagery experience has been embellished in re-imagining. So it is hard to know just what Melanie can be taken to have claimed about the detail she has visualized at a given time, and how trustworthy her claims are.

Example #3: Semantic slippage?

Here is just one more example of how trouble might arise for introspective judgments about imagery even against a background of basic introspective competence. Again, assume a competence in wielding 'see' and 'imagine', as well as the relevant 'embellishment *vs.* simple recall' distinction, on the part of all relevant parties. Still we may go astray when we discuss what was imagined, in a way that abandons explicit 'image' talk for talking simply in terms of what one 'saw', and what was 'in the visual experience' of it (as happens, for instance, on p. 172). We should be alert to a danger that our observations will lose their relevance for the topic of imagery, without our noticing, because we have heedlessly slipped back into thinking of vision, not visualization.

So I may well note that if I saw something that looked to me like a real building (neither, say, a *potential* — i.e. half-finished — building, nor a prop or fake — a trompe l'oeil, a facade) then the real-looking building (and the detail that makes it look 'real' to me) are 'in my visual experience' in some sense. The difference in visual experience, between the way a real building looks, and the way an incomplete or prop building looks, we may say often has to do with the appearance of details in the former not apparent in the latter. But it's not clear what, if anything, this tells us about the level of detail experienced in corresponding *mental imagery*.

For instance, the observations just made about the experience of seeing don't warrant the conclusion that, in *visualizing* a real building, one experiences, or forms, a *more detailed image* of the building, than when one visualizes a merely 'schematic' (incomplete?) building. It seems one might visualize a real, complete building in no more detail overall than one does an *incomplete* building. And this remains so even if, in vision, a building *looks real* (and not e.g. incomplete or fake) partly in virtue of the appearance of more detail in it than is apparent in an incomplete or fake building. But we may lose track of these distinctions, and these points, if we address introspection of imagery in terms drawn straight from the visual context — asking about what was 'in visual experience', how it 'looked', and what one was 'looking at', even when one is ostensibly talking about *visual imagery*. And so again the use of introspection *could* lead us astray, if we are not careful with the distinctions we use in it, and in the interpretation we give of it (as revealed in the inferences we draw). And without attention to these matters, it is hard for us to know what Melanie is claiming or implying about the detail of her imagery in some of her remarks.

I am really trying to make two main points in this section. The first is this. We can employ DES to address the desired questions about the character of experience — by providing usable data in the form of beeper reports — only if we can *already* make rudimentary first-person applications of terms to be used in the beeper reports, fairly accurately, *even prior to hearing our first beep*. And that is to assume some entitlement to such judgments that is not derived from DES. So my argument in the previous section (against denying the abundance of visual experience) does not *illicitly* go outside DES for introspection. For DES itself presupposes the acceptability of extra-DES introspective judgments. We need to assume that people have a reliable (I don't say infallible!) competence in distinguishing (for example) when something looks somehow to them, from when it doesn't, and when it looks somehow to them, from when they are only imagining it, *prior* to joining in DES research, if they are even to be suitable participants. It follows that there are limits to how much that method can rationally throw this competence into doubt.

The second general point I want to make is this. Even against the background of assuming the sort of basic competence I have illustrated, there is still considerable potential for error in what we say based on introspective reports about our experience — error of the sort that can be exposed in dialogue. Previously, I illustrated how (in my view) we could make unwarranted denials of experiential abundance, and just now — how we could make unjustified claims of great detail in visual imagery. And in both cases these are exposed through the dialogue in which we try to clarify what we mean, draw distinctions, and consider the implications of what we say. But the fact that they are exposed through such dialogue also gives us hope they might be prevented and corrected by it.

7. On Introspective Self-Correction

If we are but fallible reporters on the character of our experience, how do we detect and correct our errors? One dispiriting possibility is that introspection, working from its own resources, is (in an unfavourable sense) *incorrigible*. On this view, introspection is merely a (sometimes faulty) gauge of some sort. One can correct its faulty 'readings' only 'from the outside' so to speak. Sometimes introspection spits out judgments that line up with purely 'third-person' evidence, sometimes not — and it's only by appeal to occasions of the latter sort that one can set it aright. It may indeed seem difficult to envisage just how introspection could be self-correcting, as ordinary perceptual experience can be. We can often correct visual illusion by 'getting a better look' at something, or by appeal to other modalities with which it is unified (for example: when I reach where something appears to be, I come up empty-handed). But even if one takes the dead metaphor of 'introspection' seriously, there seems to be no comparable way to employ 'inner sense' to check itself.

One way of responding to such a challenge would be to isolate a certain class of introspective judgments or reports as pre-eminently trustworthy: something about the manner in which they're formed or about their content makes them less liable to error than others. So if we can argue that a conception of experience based on such reports conflicts with what is alleged in the *unfavoured* class of reports, then we can use this to discredit the latter, even if this requires a massive revision, leaving us with a radically different view of ordinary human experience. I see Hurlburt as pursuing a version of this strategy. We grant 'most favoured introspection' status to near-term retrospective reports in response to a random, open-ended prompt (once these are suitably refined and elaborated under questioning). Then we argue that the picture of experience these provide puts the lie to that we get when we admit present tense reports or concurrent judgments, in response to targeted questions. And this is thought to result in a wholesale purge of our experiential lives.

Both the account of introspective self-correction suggested by my criticisms, and the outcome of applying it, are quite different. Not only do I not think DES reports constitute a privileged class of introspective judgments, I am not convinced we can justifiably isolate in a very general way *any* such group of introspective claims, and set them up as a standard before which all others may stand or fall. This is not to deny we can address introspective controversy by trying to reduce our claims, locate and retreat to less controversial ones, and see whether we can reason our way back to conclusions from there. But identification of the relatively 'firmer, safer' ground to which one can withdraw should be done only on a contextual, case-by-case basis, and I don't assume there is some entirely epistemically self-sufficient isle of safety to which we can repair.[2]

On my approach one would instead strengthen and enhance introspection by dogged pursuit of the sort of questioning that Hurlburt initiates in his DES interviews. It seems then that we agree at least on this: we will *not* improve introspection by trust in the 'noble savagery' of raw introspective reports 'unexposed' or unrefined by critical questioning. We must press sensitively worded questions to probe the content and implications of introspective judgments, to see which are worth retaining. But Hurlburt and I apparently differ regarding just what it is crucial to ask, how far to push such questioning, and the dangers of prematurely abandoning it — and it seems, the extent to which the questioners should also similarly examine themselves, while engaging in their own first-person reflection on experience. It seems — and this is my deepest worry about Hurlburt's method — that the very habits of self-reflection I would have us *cultivate*, he would evidently have us *suppress*, since he thinks they only breed error of the sort DES is called in to correct. But on my view we need just such habits of articulate alertness to our own on-going experience, and of

---

[2] This brings up the tricky issue of 'bracketing presuppositions' which I regret I cannot explore here in more detail.

self-examination, if we are to bring the 'personal' into the 'theoretical' as Hurlburt laudably wishes (pp. 257–260). It is just such habitual self-examination that we need to nourish the rational correction of introspectively-based conceptions of experience.

This difference in approach has led me also to a rather different result than Hurlburt's — arguing against his stark conception of visual experience, in favour of my more fulsome view. And it has made me cautious about claims of richly detailed, near instantaneous imagery. But notice, though our views are introspectively grounded, it would not be fair to bring against us both the charge that, because of this, we have been driven into some dead-end of opposed introspections where reason has no recourse. Our disagreement is more diffuse, and seemingly traceable to differences in the standards we assume, the questions we pose, the distinctions we recognize, and our interpretation of these — all of which are indefinitely open to further rational discussion.

Well, that's just the problem, you might think. For now it seems that, on my view, taking introspection seriously ties it closely to the kind of individualistic, idiosyncratic dialectical enquiry that makes philosophy seem so endlessly disputatious. If responsible introspection must have a prominent 'Socratic aspect', that does not bode well for securing widespread agreement, even if, assiduously pursued, it may sometimes afford us improved self-understanding on an individual level. So it may be that psychology's openness to *introspection* will sometimes be an invitation to *philosophize*, and so at least sometimes a threat to establishing the study of consciousness around a solid body of professional consensus. It may be that here again the 'personal' and the 'theoretical' are in uneasy tension. Though I would urge this is not because embracing the personal requires us to abandon the discipline of reason.

This brings me to the matter of where I stand with respect to Schwitzgebel, my colleague in philosophy. Although much of what I have said here (I think!) puts me close to what he says in his exchanges with Hurlburt, I would describe myself as a 'proponent', not (as he does) a *sceptic*, about introspective description of experience. I would apply his label to myself only if (somewhat in the style of the ancient sceptics) I thought we were doomed to directly conflicting reflections supported by equally balanced arguments. But I don't see that as our situation. In this arena I do believe in intellectual *progress*, achieved through the use of reason, even if I am not particularly sanguine about the prospects for *consensus*. Since I see these (progress and consensus) as distinguishable, I anticipate that even when someone makes progress, questions about just *who* has made more progress, and about *what*, are part of what will remain (perhaps interminably) disputed. But this should not make us give up, or succumb to the 'paralysis' Schwitzgebel reasonably warns would ensue if we did not presume some defeasible authority for our own introspective judgments (p. 109). Rather, it should make us strive for humility, and shun complacency, and seek to learn from those whom we think mistaken — until the day we die. This is also part of why I believe I am more reluctant than Schwitzgebel to conclude that introspective disagreements persist even when conditions are 'most favourable' to introspection. For I would say that conditions are *most favourable* only when we have examined the distinctions shaping our judgment, and our understanding of them, and heeded them adequately to declare nothing serious can be had from doing more of this. And I *am* sceptical about determining conclusively that this condition has been fulfilled.

Finally, this leads me to comment briefly on Schwitzgebel's characterization of my own approach to the study of consciousness. Referencing my writings, together with those of William James, Julian Jaynes, Daniel Dennett and John Searle, he says,

> [T]he debate about the richness of experience has thus far been conducted largely impressionistically, or in terms of questionable general theories of consciousness... A version of the beep-and-interview method gives us the opportunity to explore the question in a different and maybe better way... (pp. 233–234)

Though I am certainly grateful for the citation (and the illustrious company!), I admit I am a tiny bit apprehensive that a reader encountering this passage might come away with the idea that Siewert's approach to consciousness consists in making hazy (impressionistic), theoretically loaded remarks about his own experience. However, I should hasten to note that Schwitzgebel also kindly glosses my approach in a way I find easier to endorse (p. 226). But let me just say for the record that, here and elsewhere, I have striven to my utmost to discipline my description of experience with a precise critical discussion of relevant distinctions and reasoned responses to objections. And I strongly believe this kind of rigour *essential* to forming responsible judgments about large questions regarding consciousness — such as worrisomely vague ones about the 'richness' of experience. This is integral to what I mean by 'phenomenology'.

If, despite my efforts to be precise and responsive to opposing ideas, my writings still seem impressionistic and theory-driven, it is not for want of trying to hold myself to higher standards! Anyway, I would not agree, as Schwitzgebel seems to suggest, that some version of the beeper research offers a *substitute* for what I have at least been *attempting* to do, one which will more likely allow us to resolve questions about, say, the richness of experience in a responsible fashion. For the interpretation of data often depends crucially on involved reasoned investigation of the conceptual framework that we impose, or that surfaces in reports and discussions — enquiry that involves critical reflection on one's own experience and on what one means by what one says. I have tried to illustrate and support this point through my discussions here. And — with respect to the particular research that Schwitzgebel initiates regarding the 'richness' question of *just which sensory modalities* are usually experientially active at once — it also seems to me that critical reflection on experience still has a role to play. We need to engage in Socratic introspection (if I can call it that), in order to get needed clarity about difficult notions such as: attention and 'levels' ('degrees', 'amounts') of attention, 'background' experience, 'indeterminacy' in experience, and the distinctness of — and relationship among — the sensory modalities. Without this, beeper methodology will get us only so far.

Now one might find irrelevant the sort of clarification of which I am so enamoured. This seems to be suggested by some of Hurlburt's comments, when he responds to Schwitzgebel's worry that he has been too cavalier with terms like 'awareness' and 'experience' without distinguishing different ways they might be taken. Hurlburt remarks:

> My methods simply don't address such issues... I... explicitly try to use a variety of phrases more-or-less interchangeably, thereby indicating I do not favor any one set of advantages/connotations/implications: 'Is... in your awareness?' 'Do you experience...?' 'Is...in your inner experience?' 'Are you paying attention to...?'... My subjects are almost never confused by these terms and, like me, treat them interchangeably. It is clear enough what the questions are about that the particular label is irrelevant. (p. 181)

However, as I have argued above, we neglect precise, explicit examination of 'such issues' at a cost. For how we handle certain distinctions, and whether we heed them, can affect enormously how we use evidence to support conclusions about the abundance of visual experience, and the detail of visual imagery. For example, in the first case discussed, I argued that because of an unacknowledged ambiguity in the 'was that in your awareness?' question, we actually lose touch with what was ostensibly the topic of discussion: whether the subject had *visual experience* at a given time, and how much. And we are implicitly nudged into conflating *this* question with another — that of whether the subject was *reflectively attending to her own seeing* at the time. Meanwhile, one researcher (Hurlburt) seems to conclude that the subject has only denied having more than a little visual experience at the time in question, whereas another (Schwitzgebel) thinks she has explicitly denied having *any*. And it is unclear (to this reader at least) just why they reach those divergent conclusions, and how they understand what is being asserted or denied.

It's true that people may not feel confused when neglecting examination of the relevant distinctions. And in many ordinary contexts attention to them probably does not matter — and indeed, what we are saying or asking is often 'clear enough' without all this protracted semantic fuss. All the same, such neglect can undermine our efforts, when, in a theoretical context, we want to draw conclusions about decidedly *un*ordinary questions, such as 'how rich is visual experience?' and 'how detailed, or how indeterminate, are visual images?' What is clear enough in most contexts in which terms like 'awareness' and 'experience' appear is not *always* clear enough.

In fact, Schwitzgebel seems to agree with me that care with such distinctions is crucial to the conduct and assessment of DES research, for his concerns about Hurlburt's interviews with Melanie overlap with mine. So I think he should not suppose we can address ourselves rigorously to questions about 'richness' and 'detail' by foregoing entirely my project of critical phenomenology, and replacing it with some version of DES. That is not to say the two efforts must be *antagonistic*. In fact, we can see my approach as continuous with the sort of questioning that Hurlburt rightly recognizes as necessary. And far from supposing I can ignore the sort of research he does or dismiss its relevance, I have done my best to learn from it. While admittedly I have focused here on restraining the use of DES to drastically depopulate consciousness, I hope it is clear that I do not aim to undermine it generally. If my criticisms have been well-reasoned, they may only show Hurlburt's method better suited to help demonstrate that certain contested forms of experience (such as imageless thought) *are* prevalent, than that those commonly claimed (visual experience) are *not*. And I cannot overemphasize how strongly I agree with his belief in the necessity of interview, and his conviction that mere questionnaires cannot expose self-conceptions that deserve our credence, in the absence of direct dialogue.

Reference

Hurlbert, R. & Schwitzgebel, E. (2007) *Describing Inner Experience? Proponent Meets Skeptic*, Cambridge, MA: MIT Press.

Eric Klinger

Response Organization of Mental Imagery, Evaluation of Descriptive Experience Sampling, and Alternatives

A Commentary on Hurlburt's and Schwitzgebel's 'Describing Inner Experience?'

Abstract: This commentary explores a number of issues raised by Hurlburt and Schwitzgebel (2007) in 'Describing Inner Experience'. The commentary argues for expanding the definition of mental imagery, by which it is a virtually universal human attribute; reintroduces a theory of response organization, the meaning complex, *to conceptualize unsymbolized thinking; draws on work with Guided Affective Imagery to comment on the fragility versus robustness of mental imagery; comments on the virtues and probable flaws of Descriptive Experience Sampling (DES), including an evolutionary explanation of the flaws; and describes a pair of alternatives to DES: idiothetic experience sampling in which rating scales immediately follow the narrative reports, in place of delayed interviews, and the growing promise of coupling experience sampling with brain imaging.*

In the early 1970s, three investigators independently hit upon the idea of sampling mental content with beepers: Mihalyi Csikszentmihalyi (e.g. Csikszentmihalyi and Larson, 1987; Csikszentmihalyi, Larson and

Correspondence:
Eric Klinger, Division of Social Sciences, University of Minnesota, Morris; Morris, MN 56267   Email: klinger@morris.umn.edu

Prescott, 1977), Russell Hurlburt (e.g. Hurlburt and Schwitzgebel, 2007; Hurlburt and Sipprelle, 1978), and Eric Klinger (e.g. Klinger, 1978; 1978–79; Klinger, Barta, Mahoney, *et al.*, 1976; Klinger and Cox, 1987–88). Science generally rests on predecessors' shoulders, and this idea had predecessors in dream sampling (e.g. Aserinsky and Kleitman, 1953) and, even earlier, behaviour sampling in industrial settings by so-called efficiency experts (e.g. Tippett, 1935). Csikszentmihalyi, Hurlburt, and Klinger brought sampling to the study of waking inner experience, and all to some extent refined and extended their methods, but perhaps none so intensively as Russ in developing Descriptive Experience Sampling (DES). This commentary explores a number of issues raised in *Describing Inner Experience*, provides a brief evaluation of the DES approach, and describes a pair of alternative methods.

Universality of Mental Imagery

In Box 5.1 (Hurlburt and Schwitzgebel, pp. 96–97), Russ asserts that 'many people simply do not have imagery' (p. 97). However, I have never found one. The generalization depends on how one defines 'imagery'. I have applied the classic window-counting exercise to numerous people, in both group and individual sessions. As most readers know, this simple exercise asks people to count the windows in the houses in which they live. The point of the exercise is not, of course, the answer but instead the process of arriving at the answer. Everyone in my experience uses some variation of imagining walking around the house or, alternatively, walking into each room, and counting the windows. Even those who claim not to have mental images nevertheless turn inward to look at what must be a simulated spatial array to which one can virtually point in counting the windows. I would argue that this is a form of experience that has at least the spatial-array property of visual imagery.

There clearly are large individual differences in the vividness with which people experience their mental imagery. These differences may, among other things, arise from individual differences in the varying thresholds for admitting anything — sensory, cognitive, and emotional properties — into focal consciousness. It is now widely recognized that not entering consciousness is far from not being functional. In the window-counting exercise, for those individuals who claim a lack of mental imagery, conscious operations nevertheless contact the nonconscious operations that enable the counting to proceed. The next section addresses how this might come about.

Unsymbolized Thinking

The reef on which the introspectionist approach allegedly foundered, imageless thought, or 'unsymbolized thinking' in Russ's phrase, would seem resolvable within a theory spun decades ago and never followed up (Klinger, 1971; 1978–79). The theory addresses the problem of how responses of any kind are organized, regardless of whether they are internal, such as mental images or interior monologues, or physical acts. Until the 1960s, response organization was most often conceptualized within classical stimulus-response frameworks, but investigators such as George A. Miller (1960) and Steven Keele (1968), among others, introduced compelling opposing arguments and introduced a paradigm of hierarchical organization. This paradigm has interesting implications for unsymbolized thinking.

In this view, the components of acts, such as the specific words in an utterance or movements in an athletic act, are controlled not sequentially (in which each component depends directly on the preceding component) but rather all together by a central organizing scheme, a momentary brain event, on which each component depends directly. It is hierarchical in the same sense in which all soldiers in a unit depend for their orders on the next-level commanding officer. Miller, a psycholinguist, named the central event a *grammar plan*; Keele, concerned with motor skills, called it a *motor program*. Because I was interested at the time in the structure of fantasy, I sought to generalize the concept beyond specific domains and dubbed the central event for language, motor acts, and mental acts a *meaning complex*. Subsequent research programmes (e.g. Johnson, 1968; Schneider and Schmidt, 1995; Wulf, Schmidt and Deubel, 1993) have borne out the basic concept and extended it.

Theoretically, meaning complexes are overlearned contingency plans whose output depends on stimulus input and that, in any given situation, control the emission of the corresponding response. The meaning complex itself is nonconscious, but, of course, its output generally becomes conscious. It is at this point — the transition from meaning complex to consciousness, or not — that the theory becomes relevant to unsymbolized thinking.

It seems safe to assume that becoming conscious requires exceeding some kind of threshold. This is well established for perceptual processes, and it presumably applies to anything that might become conscious. Thresholds of this kind require gatekeepers. Just as good administrative assistants take care of business and bother the boss only when the boss needs to know, the processes that guard consciousness admit primarily matters that would benefit from conscious attention. There are no doubt a number of factors that determine access to consciousness. One is surely the competition from competing processes. It seems likely that emotional arousal is another prominent factor that weighs on the gatekeeping decision process, such that what arouses strong emotion gains conscious attention. Overlearning is another, in that people focus consciously in learning new tasks, but the details of overlearned responses recede from focal consciousness even while those responses are performed. For example, the student driver taking a car from the curb is focused on coordinating the steering wheel, brake pedal, accelerator, and sensory input through the windshield and mirrors. Here, the relevant meaning complexes are still being learned. In contrast, the experienced driver is focused on the best route to get to the destination, while the mechanics of driving, controlled by overlearned meaning complexes, remain at the periphery of consciousness or even nonconscious.

Cannot this model now be applied to thinking? That is, meaning complexes that subserve thought, including mental imagery, produce outputs that become conscious if the outputs pass the threshold for consciousness because they adequately enlist the various determinants. When thoughts need not be communicated or examined word for word, they can become abbreviated, stunted, perhaps completely unsymbolized. There is a parallel here with communications among people with a long history of interaction, such as a work group. These communications often become shorthand expressions and gestures that nevertheless retain their effectiveness with insiders but may be hard for outsiders to interpret (Kraus and Weinheimer, 1964). Self-communication via one's thoughts becomes similarly vestigial.

Research (e.g. Hassin, Bargh and Zimerman, 2009) has already established that goal pursuits can be primed and behaviour influenced by these primes outside of consciousness. It is not much of a leap to suppose that meaning complexes can become effective — produce functional outputs, such as thoughts — without all of the potential features of that output parading through consciousness. Hence the possible explanation of 'unsymbolized thought'.

There are no doubt wide individual differences in threshold heights and in the verbalization or symbolization of thoughts. This is all an area that needs much more investigation.

Fragility *versus* Robustness of Mental Imagery

It is hard to imagine that the intensive interviewing of participants many hours after their sampling would not influence their responses. For example, it would surely sensitize them to particular properties of their sampled experiences and possibly lead to sometimes finding such properties even if they did not exist. Russ thinks that this happens at a low enough frequency to be tolerable without gross distortion of the results. Perhaps. My experiences with Guided Affective Imagery (GAI; e.g. Leuner, 1978) provide reason for both reassurance and worry.

GAI puts people into relaxed conditions and typically provides a beginning scenario, such as 'Imagine a meadow'. The participant/ client is then instructed to let her/his mind go in whatever direction and is asked to report to the therapist continuously on what the image is like and on the ensuing imagery as it unfolds. The therapist periodically asks questions to clarify the communication of the imagery (for instance: What kind of day is it? Are there any people or animals?) and may make occasional therapeutically crafted suggestions for the direction of the imagery.

Relevant here are a number of observations. First, nearly everyone is capable of performing this exercise, even though people vary dramatically in what they report experiencing. Second, the imagery may become quite intense and emotion-laden. Third, the imagery is remarkably robust, in the sense that clients can usually report on their imagery and answer questions — even discuss them briefly — without losing track of the thread or shattering what often appears to be a semi-trance. This latter observation provides a little reassurance regarding the reportability of beeped experiences and resistance to influence by an interviewer. Fourth, however, the questions sometimes evoke features of the imagery that very likely would have been ignored as absent without the questioning. For example, asking about the weather on the meadow may lead to descriptions of features that may very well have become conscious in response to the question. Responses such as 'Now that you mention it, there is a light drizzle' suggest that there is a certain degree of susceptibility to influence from the questioner. That is less reassuring about the veridicality of DES results.

Conclusions about DES

The method of DES is entirely idiographic. For exploring an individual's reportable mental content, nothing that I know of is superior to this method. That makes it potentially, at least for select cases, a useful clinical tool. It is also an excellent way to explore the range of possibilities for mental content. Russ provides excellent guidelines in Chapter 2 (Hurlburt and Schwitzgebel, 2007, pp. 14–20) for conducting introspective investigations.

As Russ admits, DES is focused on the 'discovery' stage of the science of consciousness — that is, the discovery of phenomena and the creation of hypotheses. That has merit as a starting point for scientific work on inner experience, but for this purpose it is only a starting point. To arrive at nomothetic conclusions — at something generalizable — its subject matter would eventually need to submit to categorization or more elaborate forms of quantification, such as qualitative analysis by raters or quantitative analysis with rating scales used by raters or by the subjects themselves. DES as described here lacks these further formal steps toward generalizable science.

Russ makes a valid point that science is well served by beginning with minute observations of individual cases and gradually building upwards from them into an eventual theoretical structure capable of complexity and generality. One has to ask whether this has not already been partially done with respect to the fields of consciousness and personality, through the many hours spent in clinical examination of individual clients and research participants, as well as armchair observation. The methods and theories now in use did not, after all, arise from purely abstract considerations. It remains unclear to me whether starting over from scratch is a sensible deployment of research resources, but having some investigators try this out does seem to be worthwhile.

DES is a highly labour-intensive procedure. Its scientific cost-effectiveness might be improved by a somewhat more focused approach, in any given investigation, of testing a limited set of hypotheses, or answering a limited set of research questions. Russ will probably object that such an approach destroys the open-ended discovery potential of current DES, but Eric S. seems to have approximated this suggestion and it seems likely that a more focused approach can be reconciled with keeping the discovery option open at least within the realms indicated by the research questions.

Despite Russ's assurances, I am still left with grave doubts about the collection of data from interviews that occur up to 24 hours after the experience samples were recorded. As he himself admits, the reasons for plausibility fall short of clinching the argument. I therefore side with Eric S. in substantially accepting the main thematic content of thought reports and treating the details, especially when reported after a lapse of hours, with great scepticism.

To put this in other words, based on my experience with thought-sampling, dream-sampling, GAI, and the literature on memory, I would generally trust immediately reported thematic content in the form of focal objects, interactions among them, and verbalizations. I would place on average less trust in immediate reports of sensory-like qualities and emotional tone. The degree of my trust for all aspects of reports decreases as an accelerating monotonic function (something like a backward J-curve) of time between beep and report. That is, trust is high while the memory of the experience is still iconic, plummets over the first few minutes after that, but loses less ground per minute thereafter.

All this, by the way, makes good evolutionary sense. Survival depends on interacting adaptively with objects in the environment — attaining one's positive goals and the negative ones of avoiding or escaping threats. That might entail detecting subtle discriminative stimuli that relate to those interactions, but there is little gain for survival in focusing attention on the nuances of inner experience, especially after the iconic stage of memory has faded. This is simply not likely to be one of the skills prominently targeted in natural selection.

Alternatives to DES

There are at least two prominent alternatives to DES. Neither produces the degree of detail that Russ assumes DES produces, but neither is as much subject to erosion of memory that must take place when reports of the details of imagery trail beeps by several hours. One such alternative builds on the kind of 'raw' sampling that Russ himself performed earlier in his programme, and that Csikszentmihalyi and I independently developed at about the same time. The second alternative, which is still largely potential but getting better, is the triangulation of sampling with brain imaging and other measures.

Experience-Sampling Without Subsequent Interviewing

The thought-sampling method we have used is idiothetic (Lamiell, 1981) in that it starts out idiographic but also has built-in quantification. In so far as our subjects faithfully follow instructions, it avoids the time gap between beep and interview that characterizes DES. Originally applied in laboratory settings (Klinger, 1977; 1978), it was subsequently extended to free-living contexts (Klinger, 1978–79; Klinger and Cox, 1987–88; Klinger and Kroll-Mensing, 1995; Kroll-Mensing, 1992). The method equips participants with beepers, response forms to be completed as soon as possible after each beep, and some brief training in reporting.

The reporting consists of briefly narrating the main elements of the experience just preceding each beep and rating it on scales to characterize its duration and its sensory and/or other properties. The rating format generally does not assume the existence of anything, but rather enquires into degrees of presence, with absence being an option. After a little practice, participants zip through the rating scales fairly expeditiously. Our free-living sampling generally spaced beeps at an average of about 45-minute intervals, with wide random variation within participants.

Work with this method has produced and replicated factor structures of self-reported properties of thought flow and related its content to participants' goal pursuits in interaction with controlled preceding stimuli. Continuing in the tradition of dream research, we have also applied it to dream sampling (Hoelscher, Klinger and Barta, 1981; Nikles, Brecht, Klinger and Bursell, 1998), in which it again successfully related dream contents to dreamers' self-reported goal pursuits in interaction with controlled preceding stimuli.

This method is evidently powerful in its use even without subsequent DES-style interviews. It is also highly flexible, in that different training regimens, instructions, and rating scales permit it to explore a wide variety of research questions relating to inner experience. Because there has never been a head-to-head comparison between it and DES, it remains for future research to determine the extent to which the laborious interviewing modelled for us in Russ and Eric S.'s book can make an incremental contribution.

Sampling Combined with Brain Imaging

The application of brain imaging to mental content has recently begun to blossom. In recent years, researchers using fMRI have identified a set of pathways that become active when participants stop working on tasks, their minds presumably at rest. They have dubbed this set of pathways the *default network*. At least two investigations have now shown that activation of this network corresponds to periods of self-reported stimulus-independent thought (SIT) — i.e. mind-wandering (Christoff *et al.*, 2009; Mason *et al.*, 2007). These studies employed thought sampling together with fMRI, cognitive tasks, and questionnaires. Mason *et al.* additionally showed that propensity to report SIT during laboratory sessions correlated well with a questionnaire measure of mindwandering during normal-living periods.

Speer *et al.* (2009) reported that reading stories activates brain areas relevant to the experiences that people are reading about. For example, when the stories reached a point at which a character's goal changed, there was significant activity in prefrontal cortical areas known to be associated with organization of goal-directed behaviours, and some of this activity did not occur significantly with other kinds of changes in the stories. Presumably, the changed brain activity was in some way related to changes in the reader's mental imagery driven by the text. These investigations can be viewed as the entering wedge of refining understanding of the relationships between inner experience and brain activity. So far, they have shown at least that brain activity can signal whether participants are engaged in SIT and the kinds of imaginal changes (from among a limited set) that their reading evoked. This is an impressive breakthrough. Even though these mind-brain relationships are still very crude, one can extrapolate into the future and imagine that the ability to decipher inner experience from brain activity might improve to the point of being able to reflect much more nuanced properties of ongoing mentation. When combined with experience sampling, these methods may provide much more solid information about inner experience than we can now establish through DES interviewing.

References

Aserinsky, E. & Kleitman, N. (1953) Regularly occurring periods of eye motility, and concomitant phenomena, during sleep, *Science*, **118**, pp. 273–274.

Christoff, K., Gordon, A.M., Smallwood, J., Schooler, J.W. & Smith, R. (2009) Experience sampling during fMRI reveals default network and executive system contributions to mind wandering, *Proceedings of the National Academy of Sciences of the United States of America*, **106**, pp. 8719–8724.

Csikszentmihalyi, M. & Larson, R. (1987) Validity and reliability of the experience-sampling method, *Journal of Nervous and Mental Disease. Special Issue: Mental Disorders in their Natural Settings: The Application of Time Allocation and Experience-Sampling Techniques in Psychiatry*, **175**, pp. 526–536.

Csikszentmihalyi, M., Larson, R. & Prescott, S. (1987) The ecology of adolescent activity and experience, *Journal of Youth and Adolescence*, **6**, pp. 281–294.

Hassin, R.R., Bargh, J.A. & Zimerman, S. (2009) Automatic and flexible: The case of nonconscious goal pursuit, *Social Cognition*, **27**, pp. 20–36.

Hoelscher, T.J., Klinger, E. & Barta, S.G. (1981) Incorporation of concern- and nonconcern-related verbal stimuli into dream content, *Journal of Abnormal Psychology*, **49**, pp. 88–91.

Hurlburt, R.T. & Schwitzgebel, E. (2007) *Describing Inner Experience? Proponent Meets Skeptic*, Cambridge, MA: MIT Press.

Hurlburt, R.T. & Sipprelle, C.N. (1978) Random sampling of cognitions in alleviating anxiety attacks, *Cognitive Therapy and Research*, **2**, pp. 165–169.

Johnson, N.F. (1968) Sequential verbal behavior, in Dixon, T.R. & Horton, D.L. (eds.) *Verbal Behavior and General Behavior Theory*, pp. 421–450, Englewood Cliffs, NJ: Prentice-Hall.
Keele, S.W. (1968) Movement control in skilled motor performance, *Psychological Bulletin*, **70**, pp. 387–403.
Klinger, E. (1971) *Structure and Functions of Fantasy*, New York: Wiley.
Klinger, E. (1977) The nature of fantasy and its clinical uses, *Psychotherapy: Theory, Research and Practice*, **14**, pp. 223–231.
Klinger, E. (1978) Modes of normal conscious flow, in Pope, K.S. & Singer, J.L. (eds.) *The Stream of Consciousness: Scientific Investigations into the Flow of Human Experience*, pp. 225–258, New York: Plenum.
Klinger, E. (1978–79) Dimensions of thought and imagery in normal waking states, *Journal of Altered States of Consciousness*, **4**, pp. 97–113.
Klinger, E., Barta, S.G., Mahoney, T.W. et al. (1976) Motivation, mood, and mental events: Patterns and implications for adaptive processes, in Serban, G. (ed.) *Psychopathology of Human Adaptation*, pp. 95–112, New York: Plenum.
Klinger, E. & Cox, W.M. (1987–88) Dimensions of thought flow in everyday life, *Imagination, Cognition and Personality*, **7**, pp. 105–128.
Klinger, E. & Kroll-Mensing, D. (1995) Idiothetic assessment: Experience sampling and motivational analysis, in Butcher, J.N. (ed.) *Clinical Personality Assessment: Practical Approaches*, pp. 267–277, New York: Oxford University Press.
Krauss, R.M. & Weinheimer, S. (1964) Changes in reference phrases as a function of frequency of usage in social interaction: A preliminary study, *Psychonomic Science*, **1**, pp. 113–114.
Kroll-Mensing, D. (1992) *Differentiating Anxiety and Depression: An Experience Sampling Analysis*, Unpublished Ph.D. dissertation, University of Minnesota.
Lamiell, J.T. (1981) Toward an idiothetic psychology of personality, *American Psychologist*, **36** (3), pp. 276–289.
Leuner, H. (1978) Basic principles and therapeutic efficacy of Guided Affective Imagery (GAI), in Singer, J.L. & Pope, K.S. (eds.) *The Power of Human Imagination: New Methods in Psychotherapy*, pp. 125–166, Oxford: Plenum.
Mason, M.F., Norton, M.I., Van Horn, J.D., Wegner, D.M., Grafton, S.T. & Macrae, C.N. (2007) Wandering minds: The default network and stimulus-independent thought, *Science*, **315**, pp. 393–395.
Miller, G.A. (1960) Plans for speaking, in Miller, G.A., Galanter, E. & Pribram, K.H., *Plans and the Structure of Behavior*, pp. 139–158, New York: Henry Holt.
Nikles, C.D.I., Brecht, D.L., Klinger, E. & Bursell, A.L. (1998) The effects of current-concern- and nonconcern-related waking suggestions on nocturnal dream content, *Journal of Personality and Social Psychology*, **75**, pp. 242–255.
Schneider, D.M. & Schmidt, R.A. (1995) Units of action in motor control: Role of response complexity and target speed, *Human Performance*, **8**, pp. 27–49.
Speer, N.K., Reynolds, J.R., Swallow, K.M. & Zacks, J.M. (2009) Reading stories activates neural representations of visual and motor experiences, *Psychological Science*, **20**, pp. 989–999.
Tippett, L.H.C. (1935) A snap reading method of making time studies of machines and operatives in factory surveys, *Journal of the British Textile Institute Transactions*, **26**, pp. 51–55.
Wulf, G., Schmidt, R.A. & Deubel, H. (1993) Reduced feedback frequency enhances generalized motor program learning but not parameterization learning, *Journal of Experimental Psychology: Learning, Memory, and Cognition*, **19**, pp. 1134–1150.

Gualtiero Piccinini

Scientific Methods Must Be Public, and Descriptive Experience Sampling Qualifies[1]

Abstract: *I defend three main conclusions. First, whether a method is public is important, because non-public methods are scientifically illegitimate. Second, there are substantive prescriptive differences between the view that private methods are legitimate and the view that private methods are illegitimate. Third, Descriptive Experience Sampling is a public (and hence legitimate) method.*

1. Must Scientific Methods Be Public?

Hurlburt and Schwitzgebel's groundbreaking book, *Describing Inner Experience? Proponent Meets Skeptic*, examines a research method called Descriptive Experience Sampling (DES). DES, which was developed by Hurlburt and collaborators, works roughly as follows. An investigator gives a subject a random beeper. During the day, as the subject hears a beep, she writes a description of her conscious experience just before the beep. The next day, the investigator interviews the subject, asks for more details, corrects any apparent mistakes made by the subject, and draws conclusions about the subject's mind. Throughout the book, Schwitzgebel challenges some of Hurlburt's

Correspondence:
Email: piccininig@umsl.edu

---

[1] Thanks to Russell Hurlburt, Marcin Miłkowski, Eric Schwitzgebel, and the audience at the 2010 Pacific APA meeting for helpful discussions on this topic and to Brit Brogaard, Jordan Dodd, and Jim Virtel for comments.

specific conclusions. Yet both agree — as I do — that DES is a worthy method.

Why is DES legitimate? In recent years, there's been a serious debate about the legitimacy of methods — such as DES — that rely on so-called 'first-person data'.[2] *Privatists* maintain that such methods are 'first-person' or private, thus different in kind from ordinary scientific methods (Chalmers, 2004; Gertler, 2009; Goldman, 1997; Hatfield, 2005; Varela, 1996; Varela and Shear, 1999). *Publicists* maintain just the opposite: such methods are 'third-person' or public, just like other legitimate scientific methods (Dennett, 2007; Haybron, 2008; Nahmias, 2002; Piccinini, 2003a; 2009).

Surprisingly, Hurlburt and Schwitzgebel assert neutrality on and even indifference to whether DES is public or private:

> Eric [Schwitzgebel]: …This debate has captured the attention of consciousness studies researchers and the interested public, because it seems to concern the fundamentally important question of *how to study consciousness* — what sorts of methods can and cannot, should and should not be implemented. So… the question seems to arise: Are we using here a 'first-person' or a 'third-person' method?
>
> Actually, *I don't know. Nor do I care, much.* The seeming centrality of this debate to the methodology of consciousness studies is an illusion. *One looks in vain for any genuine prescriptive differences, any study or method permitted by Goldman or Chalmers, forbidden by Dennett (as Dennett himself notes).* The dispute really concerns only the *description* of introspective methods. Should we describe the interviews in this book (per Chalmers) as 'irreducibly first-personal' because they depend on Melanie's[3] attunement to her subjective experience? Or should we describe them (per Dennett) as 'third-personal' and 'objective' because what we are doing is analyzing spoken utterances, in principle available to all, and hypothesizing about what might lie behind them?
>
> Each way of speaking highlights important aspects of the study of consciousness. But the more important question for consciousness studies — what *should* be the central methodological question — is *when* and *under what conditions* and *to what extent* people's reports about their experience are trustworthy. That, of course, is the topic of this book.
>
> Russ [Hurlburt]: *I could not agree with you more, Eric!* Fascination with the Goldman-Chalmers-Dennett debate has misdirected

---

[2] Terminological note: the term 'first-person data' is often used to imply that first-person data are private (and the methods using them are private). Here I use 'first-person data' more neutrally, to pick out the relevant type of data without implying that they are either public or private.

[3] Melanie is the fictitious name of the subject interviewed by Hurlburt and Schwitzgebel in their book.

consciousness researchers away from what you rightly call the central question.

Yet let me also say that I consider DES to be a first-person-plural method: *We* (Melanie, you, and I) examined Melanie's inner experience and evaluated her/our characterizations thereof. To be sure, only Melanie had access to the experience we sought to examine. However, only I had experience with a method designed to identify specific moments, focus attention on those moments, bracket presuppositions, avoid faux generalizations, and so on; and you brought your own perspective that changed and illuminated things. But my use of the term 'first-person' here is not intended to imply a position in the Goldman-Chalmers-Dennett debate. I want only to emphasize the value of the skilled investigator-willing participant alliance.

(p. 217, emphasis in second and fourth paragraphs added)[4]

I agree with Hurlburt and Schwitzgebel that the central methodological question is 'when and under what conditions and to what extent people's reports about their experience are trustworthy' (*cf.* Piccinini, 2003a, p. 143).

I also agree that DES is 'a first-person-plural' method, in the sense that it requires an unusual degree of interaction and cooperation between investigators and subjects (*cf.* Jack and Roepstorff's 'second person perspective' in their 2002, Box 2). But as Hurlburt points out (and *contra* Jack and Roepstorff), this is not a way to take a stance in the debate over publicity *vs.* privacy of methods, or a third option in addition to publicism and privatism. Whether DES is public or private (in the relevant sense) remains to be determined.

DES is as good a candidate as any for a method that relies on private data. For not only does DES rely on subjects' private access to their experience; in addition, DES subjects operate in uncontrolled natural environments and describe the most idiosyncratic features of their experiences. In these respects, DES contrasts with methods such as those studied by Ericsson and Simon (1993), in which several subjects verbalize their mental states while performing the same, highly constrained task under controlled environmental conditions. Because of these features of DES, many DES data cannot be validated by reliability studies and validity-checking tests that require comparing multiple subjects (*cf.* p. 33).

Nevertheless, I will argue as follows. First, whether a method is public is important, because non-public methods are scientifically illegitimate. Since Hurlburt and Schwitzgebel care about the science of consciousness (and more generally, of mind), they should care

---

[4] Unless otherwise noted, page numbers refer to Hurlburt and Schwitzgebel (2007).

about method publicity. Second, and contrary to what Schwitzgebel suggests, there are genuine prescriptive differences between privatism and publicism. Third, DES is a public method — and it's (implicitly) treated as such by both Hurlburt and Schwitzgebel.

One caveat. Schwitzgebel is right that, at least in recent years, the debate over publicism *vs.* privatism has been especially heated in the consciousness studies literature. But this is an historical contingency. Whether scientific methods should be public is a question that pertains to all of science. And the legitimacy of methods that rely on subjective reports — and first-person data more generally — pertains not only to the study of consciousness but to the study of the mind in general.[5]

2. Why Method Publicity Matters

We can't afford to remain neutral. The requirement that scientific methods be public is a fundamental aspect of science. I will now argue that if we reject this publicity principle, we open the way for pseudoscience and bad science. So we should accept it. But then, if our proposed methods of investigation — e.g. DES — were private, we should reject *them*. Therefore, it's important to establish that our methods are public.

A method is public just in case different investigators can apply the method to answer the same questions and, when they do, they obtain the same data. Otherwise, a method is private.[6] Now consider what happens if we allow private methods.

The following is a putative method for observing people's *auras*. Place someone against a white background. Focus your attention on the middle of their forehead (their 'Brow Chakra' or 'Third Eye') for 30 seconds or more. Concentrate very hard. Then, with your peripheral

---

[5] In this context, the distinction between mind and consciousness may appear to lack a difference. Someone might argue that if a state is accessible to methods that rely on subjects' reports or other first-person data, it must be a conscious state; therefore, the use of first-person data always belongs in the study of consciousness. But this is a *non sequitur*. Two points. First, studying mental processes, some of whose states are conscious (and hence accessible via first-person data), is not the same as studying 'consciousness'. Researchers rely on first-person data to study problem solving, schizophrenia, subjective well-being, and many other mental phenomena. These studies count as studying consciousness only if the term 'consciousness' is used in such a broad sense as to be virtually synonymous with 'mind'. Second, the concept of consciousness is somewhat nebulous — certainly more nebulous than the concept of mind. There are many things that might be meant by 'consciousness', not all of which are directly related to what can be accessed via first-person data. By contrast, 'mind' is a generic umbrella term that includes the relevant phenomena.

[6] For a defence of this definition of method publicity, and a more detailed defence of method publicity, see Piccinini (2003b).

vision, you will see a coloured halo surrounding the person. That's the aura. (I didn't make this up — there are people making real money with this.)

Why is the study of auras pseudo-scientific? Surely, not for lack of putative methods to observe them or people who claim to observe them. There are plenty of those. Yet most of those who apply the above method would claim not to see any auras, even though the method does not require any special qualifications or expertise. This is the mark of a private method: different investigators, even though they apply the same method to the same questions, get different results. If private methods were legitimate, we should conclude that the study of auras is part of science. All we need to do is rely on those specially gifted individuals who can see auras. Since private methods are illegitimate, however, we may conclude that this putative method for studying auras is spurious.

With publicity comes independent data validation. If different investigators can generate the same data, they can also look for correlations between those data and other data and phenomena, thereby providing independent evidence that the original data are valid. Conversely, with privacy comes lack of public validation. If many investigators cannot generate the same data, they cannot look for independent evidence that such data are valid. Privatists about first-person data are the first to draw the relevant conclusion: first-person data cannot be validated by public means, precisely because others cannot replicate the data (Chalmers, 2004; Gertler, 2009; Goldman, 1997; Hatfield, 2005). The same conclusion holds for the output of other private methods, e.g. data about auras. Since most investigators cannot replicate the data, they cannot establish or investigate any correlation between auras and anything else. The reasonable conclusion is that auras are fictions. By the same token, we should reject any theoretical posit that can only be (putatively) observed via private methods.

First Objection:[7] The publicity requirement is too strong. Scientific experiments are not always repeated or even repeatable. Many data are accepted by the scientific community without anyone else reproducing them. In some cases, obtaining the same data may even be impossible. For instance, a lone astronomer may see a series of events in the sky, which events no other instrument or observer records. But why should this be scientifically illegitimate? It should not. By the

---

[7] This objection was inspired by exchanges with Eric Schwitzgebel and Allan Franklin; an explicit argument along these lines, to the effect that method publicity should be rejected altogether, is in Goldman (1997). My present reply is partially indebted to an exchange with Marcel Weber; see also Piccinini (2003a,b; and 2009).

standard that scientific methods must be public, much of science would be rejected. Therefore, it's the publicity principle that must go.

Reply: The objection misconstrues the publicity principle. The principle is not that all experiments should be repeated and all data reproduced. It's that experiments should be repeat*able* and data reprodu*cible*. Even in the case of lone astronomers and other unique observers of unique events, their data are reproducible in the relevant sense. For nothing prevented other observers from observing the same events, or instruments from recording them. If other observers or instruments had been present, they would have recorded the same events. We believe this because there are enough other skilled observers who share enough knowledge of the relevant methods for us to be confident that, were other skilled observers to have applied the same methods under the same circumstances, they would have obtained the same data. Not so in the case of auras. Although some people claim to observe auras, they cannot teach their method to other unbiased parties. Thus, their method is not public.

Second Objection:[8] Still, first-person data are private, so there must be something wrong with your argument. People's epistemic access to their mental states is *more direct and accurate* than that of external observers. It's epistemically different in kind. In this sense, mental states are private. First-person data are generated by people who rely on their special epistemic access to their mental states. Therefore, first-person data — such as the data DES relies on — are private. In addition, first-person data are too useful to discard; therefore, there is something wrong with the publicity principle.

Reply: There are two claims here, one about directness and one about accuracy. I agree that people have *more direct* epistemic access to (some of) their mental states than external observers do. They are *their* mental states — no one else has them! In this sense, mental states are private and people have private access to them. But that's not the issue. The issue is whether *first-person data*, and *methods relying on them*, are private. The privacy of first-person data and relative methods doesn't follow from the fact that mental states are private.[9] Nor does it follow from the claim that people have *more accurate* access to

---

[8] This objection was inspired by an exchange with Eric Schwitzgebel. *Cf.*: http://consciousnessonline.wordpress.com/2009/02/20/first-person-data-publicity-and-self-measurement/

[9] Unless we identify the data with the mental states. That would make first-person data 'private' by definitional fiat. But that would still be irrelevant to the sense of privacy relevant to our methodological question. For in the ordinary sense of 'data' — i.e. pieces of information about something — data generated through methods that rely on subjective reports are still public. Even mental states are public in the relevant sense, that is, they are

their mental states. But in any case, people do *not* have more accurate access to their mental states than external observers, so long as external observers are allowed to ask people what's in their mind. If they are, then external observers have equal or more accurate access to people's mental states. For in addition to relying on people's reports, external observers may (i) lack some of the biases that subjects have towards themselves and (ii) avail themselves of independent evidence that is unavailable to the subjects. Thanks to (i) and (ii), external observers may be able to correct some of the subjects' mistakes in accessing their mental states. Therefore, depending on the situation, external observers may have more accurate access to other people's mental states. That is one reason many people go to counsellors: to have their misconceptions about themselves corrected by an authoritative external observer (who in turn relies on the subject's first-person reports, among other sources of evidence). This is also how DES works: the investigator interviews the subject; in the course of the interview, the investigator tries to identify and correct any apparent mistakes made by the subject. In the present context, we are discussing the validity of first-person data — data that result from asking subjects about their mind. Therefore, in the present context, external observers have equal or more accurate access to people's minds. Furthermore, nothing in this objection establishes that first-person data are private in the relevant sense.

The second objection helps us see that to avoid a merely verbal dispute, the term 'private' must be used in the relevant sense. Some of what privatists like to stress is consistent with publicism. For instance, privatists point out that (i) mental states are experienced only by one subject, (ii) subjects have more direct access to their mental states than external observers, and (iii) first-person data are produced by subjects by directly accessing their own mental states. But no combination of these theses amounts to what's at issue here. For these theses are consistent with publicism as defined here, i.e. the view that first-person data are public data and that scientists obtain first-person data by following public methods.

In addition to the above, uncontroversial theses, privatists claim that (i) first-person data cannot be replicated by different observers; therefore, (ii) first-person data cannot be publicly validated; and therefore, (iii) methods that rely on first-person data are 'first-person' or private. These theses constitute privatism in the relevant sense.

---

observable by public scientific methods, such as DES, albeit less directly than by the subjects themselves.

The temptation to endorse privatism is of a piece with regarding the subjects (as opposed to those who interview them) as the scientific observers, and the subjects' mental states as the data. Given some people's attachment to their actual or purported self-knowledge, this temptation is understandable. The same temptation is reinforced by the methodologies of old-school introspectionist psychologists, phenomenologists, and assorted philosophers, who advocate privatism more or less explicitly. But we should not translate our introspective pride into a piece of scientific methodology. We should recognize that in science, the role of observer is played by the scientists, and scientific data are pieces of information collected by scientists. Once we see this, we see that scientific data — whether first-person or not — are public and, therefore, can be validated by public means. Thus, methods that use first-person data are as public as other scientific methods.

3. Why Method Publicity Makes a Difference to Experimental Practice

As we saw, Schwitzgebel maintains that '[o]ne looks in vain for any genuine prescriptive differences, any study or method permitted by Goldman or Chalmers, forbidden by Dennett (as Dennett himself notes)'. It will be useful to separate the two claims: first, that there is no prescriptive difference between privatism and publicism; second, that the same set of studies is permitted by privatism and publicism (for a defence of the second claim, see van de Laar, 2008). The second claim is a special case of the first.

Whether a study is permitted is *not* the most pertinent question. It would be pertinent if there were methods that both parties agree are private. If so, privatists would allow the private methods while publicists would reject them. That *would* be a prescriptive difference between the two views. But that's not the situation we're in. For we disagree whether reliance on first-person reports and other first-person data constitute a public or a private method. Still, there are prescriptive differences between the two views.

The questions we should ask are the following. Which view leads to more rigorous, less biased, and more reliable experimental practices? How does each methodology suggest taking precautions against experimental artefacts, searching for and ruling out confounding factors (such as delusion, confabulation, etc.), making explicit assumptions in generating the data, and articulating explicit procedures for encoding the data? Which methodology recommends pursuing research programmes aimed at publicly validating (or invalidating, as the case may be) the data?

Publicism maintains that first-person data are public, like other scientific data. Thus, *ceteris paribus*, given publicism first-person data should be produced with as much rigour, scrutinized as carefully, and validated as much as other scientific data. The burden of doing so falls on the external observers, who should follow the same strategies they would follow when producing any other data (*modulo* the peculiarities of the subject matter).

By contrast, privatism maintains that first-person data are private — no one besides the subject has access to them. Because of this, the only case in which first-person data can be invalidated is when a subject contradicts herself (Goldman, 1997, p. 543). Given privatism, strictly speaking, the only people who can take precautions against experimental artefacts and confounding factors are not the external observers but the subjects. Besides noticing inconsistencies, external observers cannot do anything to either validate or invalidate first-person data (Chalmers, 2004; Gertler, 2009; Goldman, 1997; Hatfield, 2005).

It is *prima facie* doubtful that subjects can be relied on to avoid confounding factors and experimental artefacts. For starters, to anyone but the most committed privatist, there is evidence that people's reports about their experience are often faulty. Both Hurlburt and Schwitzgebel explicitly agree on this point.

In addition, the privatist's self-contradiction test for invalid data is faulty. Subjects who give first-person reports, or at least subjects of DES studies, contradict themselves a lot (Hurlburt, personal communication).[10] It doesn't follow that when they do so they provide no useful information. The correct response to self-contradiction is not to discard the data, but to probe further. One of the contradictory statements is probably more accurate than the other. To determine what happened in the subject's mind — to determine which, if any, of the contradictory statements is more accurate — three things may be done: ask more questions to the subject, appeal to independent evidence, and do more studies of the same kind (e.g. to do more beeping in a DES study). All these actions would be recommended by publicism. They are a clear case of prescriptive differences between privatism and publicism.

How can subjects minimize the risk of experimental artefacts and confounding factors, according to privatists? The most explicit

---

[10] I owe this argument against the self-contradiction test to Russell Hurlburt.

proposal is known as 'neurophenomenology' (Varela, 1996). Neurophenomenology requires that subjects produce reports about their mind only upon performing a 'phenomenological reduction'. Roughly speaking, phenomenological reduction is the suspension of our ordinary beliefs about the relation between our experience and the world. But from a publicist point of view, phenomenological reduction is of dubious utility and may even be harmful.

To begin with, it is not clear that (most) people can suspend their beliefs about the relation between their experience and the world. Since such suspension of belief is a private event, given privatism there is no way to check from the outside whether it occurs. So even if phenomenological reduction did indeed minimize experimental artefacts and confounding factors, there would be no way for external observers to collect evidence that such minimization is in place. This is not a promising way to validate scientific data. In addition, there is little if any reason to believe that phenomenological reduction minimizes the risk of experimental artefacts and confounding factors. Why should it? If anything, it may be a confounding factor itself. For whatever subjects do upon being told to perform a phenomenological reduction, their efforts may drain attentional and cognitive resources *away* from the tasks under investigation, thereby interfering with the tasks themselves. Thus, phenomenological reduction appears of dubious utility and possibly harmful.

Objection: you are taking the privatists' methodological statements too literally. When self-avowed 'neurophenomenologists' perform actual experiments (e.g. Lutz *et al.*, 2002), phenomenological reduction plays no role in their methods. It's not even mentioned. Instead, it's the experimenters (rather than the subjects) who look for confounders, try to avoid experimental artefacts, and perform statistical tests in line with standard scientific methodology. Experimenters may even look for reliable correlations between first-person data and third-person data, thereby offering independent evidence that the first-person data are valid.

Reply: True, at least in some cases. What this shows is that when methodological push comes to experimental shove, at least some privatists do not behave as privatists. Rather than applying their own methodological prescriptions, they follow standard, third-person methodology. This is all the more reason to reject privatism. But there are two caveats. First, there is no guarantee that all privatists will apply standard methodological checks in their studies — especially when their own methodology does not prescribe them because it deems them impossible. To use Hurlburt's nice phrase, there is still plenty of 'armchair introspection' around. Second, methodological rigour comes in degrees. Even if you are a privatist in name only — someone who in fact practises publicist methodology — your background privatism may still incline you towards cavalier reliance on subjective reports, as opposed to checking data as much as you can and striving for public validation. For example, Lutz *et al.*'s study (2002), which is often cited as a paradigmatic example of neurophenomenology, is especially opaque on how the first-person data were collected and clustered. The authors do not say how often subjects described their experience one way or another, what assumptions were made in encoding the data, how many experimenters encoded the data, how much the encoders agreed in their clustering of the data, and whether the encoders were blind to the hypothesis being tested. Ideally, publicism would recommend processing the data so as to maximize their publicity — that is, making explicit assumptions about how to cluster the data and having two encoders, blind to the hypothesis being tested, encode the data independently of one another. These procedures would contribute to maximizing data publicity and minimizing sources of bias during the phases of data collection and encoding. As we have seen, whether or not the authors proceeded in the way recommended by publicism, they did not see the need to inform their readers. This may be a consequence of their self-avowed privatism.

In conclusion, privatism and publicism do differ in their prescriptions — and the publicist prescriptions are the ones that maximize the validity of the data.

4. Descriptive Experience Sampling is a Public Method

By now it should be clear why Descriptive Experience Sampling (DES) is a public method. A public method is a method that can be applied by different investigators to answer the same questions, and that when so used, it yields the same results. DES involves a subject and at least one investigator. The investigator asks the subject to describe her experience when a random beeper beeps, then interviews her in more detail about her descriptions. Anyone with the right training can apply DES to answer the same questions, by interviewing the same subject about the same experiences.

Setting aside Schwitzgebel's lack of prior training in DES, the interviews transcribed in Hurlburt and Schwitzgebel's book are an example of method publicity at work. The two of them work together to investigate the contents of Melanie's mind by jointly interviewing her. They also often disagree about the contents of Melanie's mind. Does this show that DES has at least some element of privacy?

Not quite. There is a difference between a method being public and a method being reliable. Hurlburt and Schwitzgebel's disagreement does not show that DES is private. What it shows is that Hurlburt and Schwitzgebel do not take DES to be reliable to the same extent. They make different assumptions about what can be discovered through DES. While Schwitzgebel agrees that DES can be used to uncover some basic features of people's experience, albeit 'tentatively' and 'pending further evidence' (p. 221), he doubts many of the more detailed conclusions that Hurlburt draws about Melanie's mind. If Schwitzgebel trusted DES as much as Hurlburt and asked the same questions, he would get the same results.

Questioning a method's reliability and the validity of the data obtained through it are important parts of the scientific dialectic. Far from being symptoms of privacy, they lead to further methodological checks — making the method more rigorous — and to data validation studies. In this respect, Schwitzgebel is performing a useful service. By questioning some of Hurlburt's conclusions, he is pushing DES users to make their method more rigorous and uncover independent evidence of data validity.

Looking at the way data are validated (or invalidated) is another way to tell whether a method is public. If the data are validated at best by 'plausibility considerations', without any independent (public) evidence, then the method is private. For instance, privatists sometimes argue that 'introspection' is legitimate because it's a reliable method, but they don't offer public evidence of reliability — indeed, they can't offer any such evidence, on pain of contradicting their privatism (Goldman, 1997; Chalmers, 2004; Hatfield, 2005).[11] By contrast, if data are validated (or invalidated) by appealing to independent (public) evidence, then the method is public. By this standard too, DES is public, and both Hurlburt and Schwitzgebel treat it as such.

To be sure, Hurlburt does present some plausibility arguments in favour of DES, and a few of Hurlburt's considerations are unconvincing. For instance, pointing out that 'DES subjects say they give accurate and complete reports' (p. 28) adds little if any credibility to the reports themselves. But the bulk of Hurlburt's arguments are different from the typical blanket assumption of reliability made by privatists.

---

[11] On the contrary, there is plenty of evidence that introspection is often *un*reliable, and even if there were no evidence one way or the other, this would hardly be enough to conclude that introspection is reliable.

Instead, Hurlburt offers (public) evidence that DES is reliable and methodological prescriptions to ensure that DES data are reproducible. Such prescriptions strive to eliminate many potential sources of bias and error by, among other guidelines, asking subjects to describe experience with little delay, targeting specific experiential episodes, keeping the target experience brief, not asking subjects to infer causation, and separating reports from interpretations (p. 14–20). Other arguments include that DES reports are consistent with independently established aspects of experiences, such as attentional limits (p. 29), and that when more than one investigator interviews the same subject, their conclusions agree (p. 33).

While a few of Hurlburt's arguments are unpersuasive, most of them make the beginning of a good case, based on public evidence and the use of public procedures, that DES is a reliable method producing valid data. And these arguments are not even Hurlburt's main source of support for DES: 'I do not think that arguments based on plausibility are ever an adequate foundation for science. Science must be based on direct observation, not plausibility' (p. 27). The plausibility arguments merely 'set the stage' for 'compelling' or 'convincing idiographic observations' (p. 27). This leads to two questions: who is doing the 'direct' observing? And what makes the idiographic observations 'compelling'? Hurlburt's implicit answers are in line with publicism: the psychologists are the direct observers, and what makes the observations compelling is independent, public evidence of their correctness.

Consider the case of Fran, which Hurlburt briefly describes (pp. 32ff). Fran's DES reports led Hurlburt to conclude that, unlike most people, Fran could experience up to ten visual images simultaneously. Even more strikingly, Fran's images appeared to last for hours or days, without interruption. Finally, based on Fran's reports, Hurlburt concluded that Fran had no figure-ground phenomenon in either her imagination or her external perception.

These observations led to a testable prediction. Hurlburt predicted that Fran would not experience the standard alternation between different interpretations of ambiguous figures (such as the vase/faces or the duck/rabbit). Hurlburt tested and confirmed this prediction. Given Fran's idiosyncratic reports, someone might question whether she understood the question about figure *vs.* ground. Against this worry, Hurlburt points out that Fran was able to describe correctly the difference between her experience and the way other people experience figure *vs.* ground.

The same DES-based conclusions led to explaining some of Fran's unusual behaviours, which were discovered independently of her DES reports. For instance, Fran used to watch three television sets at once, and she was able to count money, participate in a conversation, and listen to one or more other conversations at the same time. This is (public) behavioural evidence that correlates with, and is explained by, the DES-based conclusion that Fran could sustain several streams of conscious cognitive processing at once.

Finally, Fran's reports about her unusual multiple streams of experience correlated with her borderline personality symptoms, i.e. 'exterior disorganization and chaotic psychological fragility' (p. 34). When her symptoms improved, her experiences became 'less complex' and she was able to experience figure-ground phenomena.

In sum, Hurlburt's DES-based conclusions about Fran's experience correlated with her other behaviours, explained unusual features of her behaviour, and were confirmed by a testable prediction. This is remarkable (public) evidence in favour of Hurlburt's DES-based conclusions, which in turn validates the DES data on which the conclusions were based.

As to Schwitzgebel, he explicitly maintains that while validating first-person data publicly is difficult, it is possible. He calls for corroboration of DES data by independent, externally observable evidence (pp. 47, 93, 223, 227). If Schwitzgebel did not take DES data to be public, he should not be calling for their public validation — for as we saw in Section 2, private data cannot be publicly validated.

Many of Hurlburt and Schwitzgebel's discussions bring in independent, public evidence to either bolster or undermine conclusions derived through DES. For example, they discuss how to show that colour experiences are associated with emotions by means of independent evidence (pp. 72–73), independent evidence that Melanie's images are more or less detailed (pp. 96–97, 102), and memory reliability and its role in DES (pp. 149, 235–236). And in his final reflections, to address some of Schwitzgebel's concerns, Hurlburt suggests studies that could be performed to validate DES data (pp. 275–276, 284–285). All of this goes to show not only that DES is a public method, but also that both Hurlburt and Schwitzgebel treat it as such.

5. Conclusion

Whether a putative scientific method is public is not an idle issue. It has practical repercussions on scientific practices. Unlike privatism, method publicity recommends that investigators (i.e. external observers) take precautions against experimental artefacts, search for and minimize the risk of confounding factors, make explicit their assumptions, articulate explicit procedures for encoding the data, and whenever possible, pursue research programmes aimed at publicly validating the data. All of this is part of good science.

Because of this, scientific methods must be public — different investigators must be able to follow the same methods to answer the same questions obtaining the same results. Method publicity is one of the methodological requirements that keep pseudo-science and bad science at bay.

DES is legitimate because it is a public method, yielding public data. While Hurlburt and Schwitzgebel often disagree about which specific conclusions may be legitimately drawn using DES, their discussion is based on independent, public evidence. And the means they identify to resolve their disagreement also rely on public evidence. In spite of their professed neutrality on whether DES is public, commendably, they treat DES as the public method that it is.

References

Chalmers, D.J. (2004) How can we construct a science of consciousness?, in Gazzaniga, M.S. (ed.) *The Cognitive Neurosciences III*, pp. 1111–1119, Cambridge, MA: MIT Press.

Dennett, D.C. (2007) Heterophenomenology reconsidered, *Phenomenology and the Cognitive Sciences*, **6**, pp. 247–270.

Ericsson, K.A. & Simon, H.A. (1993) *Protocol Analysis: Verbal Reports as Data*, Cambridge, MA: MIT Press.

Gertler, B. (2009) Introspection, in Bayne, T., Cleeremans, A. & Wilken, P. (eds.) *The Oxford Companion to Consciousness*, Oxford: Oxford University Press.

Goldman, A. (1997) Science, publicity, and consciousness, *Philosophy of Science*, **64**, pp. 525–545.

Hatfield, G. (2005) Instrospective evidence in psychology, in Achinstein, P. (ed.) *Scientific Evidence: Philosophical Theories and Applications*, pp. 259–286, Baltimore, MD: Johns Hopkins University Press.

Haybron, D. (2008) *The Pursuit of Unhappiness: The Elusive Psychology of Well-Being*, Oxford: Oxford University Press.

Hurlburt, R. & Schwitzgebel, E. (2007) *Describing Inner Experience? Proponent Meets Skeptic*, Cambridge, MA: MIT Press.

Jack, A.I. & Roepstorff, A. (2002) Introspection and cognitive brain mapping: From stimulus-response to script-report, *Trends in Cognitive Sciences*, **6**, pp. 333–339.

Lutz, A., Lachaux, J.-P., Martinerie, J. & Varela, F. (2002) Guiding the study of brain dynamics by using first-person data: Synchrony patterns correlate with ongoing conscious states during a simple visual task, *Proceedings of the National Academy of Sciences USA*, **99**, pp. 1586–1591.

Nahmias, E.A. (2002) Verbal reports on the contents of consciousness: Reconsidering introspectionist methodology, *Psyche*, **8**, [Online], http://psyche.cs.monash.edu.au/v8/psyche-8-21-nahmias.html

Piccinini, G. (2003a) Data from introspective reports: Upgrading from common-sense to science, *Journal of Consciousness Studies*, **10** (9–10), pp. 141–156.

Piccinini, G. (2003b) Epistemic divergence and the publicity of scientific methods, *Studies in the History and Philosophy of Science*, **34**, pp. 597–612.

Piccinini, G. (2009), First-person data, publicity, and self-measurement, *Philosophers' Imprint*, **9** (9), pp. 1–16.

van de Laar, T. (2008) Mind the methodology: Comparing heterophenomenology and neurophenomenology as methodologies for the scientific study of consciousness, *Theory and Psychology*, **18**, pp. 365–379.

Varela, F. (1996) Neurophenomenology: A methodological remedy for the Hard Problem, *Journal of Consciousness Studies*, **3** (4), pp. 330–349.

Varela, F. & Shear, J. (1999) First person methodologies: What, why, how?, *Journal of Consciousness Studies*, **6** (2–3), pp. 1–14.

John Sutton

Time, Experience, and Descriptive Experience Sampling

Abstract: *Descriptive Experience Sampling (DES) rightly encourages concrete, experience-near description of specific psychological states. But it needs to be further connected and opened up, both to the search for converging methods and objective corroborating evidence for the reports of subjective experience, and to more temporally-extended sequences in experience. I criticize DES for deliberately eradicating the dynamics of conscious experience by providing only a flash snapshot of 'the last undisturbed moment before the beep'. This restriction rules out certain significant experiential phenomena, and renders the kind of 'personal truth' revealed strangely thin, by neglecting the fact that we are creatures whose present experience is often animated in many distinctive ways by our past. I query the distinction between recalling and reconstructing, and re-examine parts of two reports discussed by Hurlburt and Schwitzgebel. These examples reveal rich cross-temporal interactions that should encourage us to explore, in ways DES officially rules out, how kinaesthetic memory and autobiographical memory respectively animate present experience. A slightly extended experience-sampling practice could take a central place among other methods for investigating experience.*

This rich book, the best I've read in consciousness studies, offers more at each encounter. It was a brilliant idea to evaluate Hurlburt's

Correspondence:
John Sutton, Macquarie Centre for Cognitive Science, Macquarie University, Sydney, NSW 2109, Australia   Email: john.sutton@mq.edu.au
http://www.phil.mq.edu.au/staff/jsutton

Descriptive Experience Sampling (DES) method through concrete sceptical enquiry by Schwitzgebel, whose role as open-minded but hard-nosed interlocutor makes the debate an intriguing, even gripping read. The radically different views about introspective reports held by the two authors (hereafter Russ and Eric, following the book's informality) are put to the test in the concrete context of 'an examination, in unprecedented detail, of random moments of one person's experience' (p. 11).[1] In addition to the ongoing central pursuit of the general question 'Can we believe people's reports about their inner experience?', a raft of more specific issues (from the speed of an 'inner voice', through theories of emotion, to the indeterminacy of images) are addressed as they arise in the sampling interviews. The book's excellent organization, using in-text boxes linked by detailed cross-referencing into indexed threads, reinforces the thrilling sense that our access to the inner life of one person, 'Melanie', is bringing real progress on a number of fronts at once. Eric's robust scepticism remains, but is tempered somewhat by being forced to confront the real constraints and opportunities of gathering information from a live subject. By the end of the project, he accepts that Russ's 'beep-and-interview methods' deserve a central role in introspective science (p. 250), and that from the interviews 'we do have at least *some* tentative sense of Melanie's experience and how it might differ from the experiences of others' (p. 296). In this commentary, rather than again going over the central points of difference between Russ and Eric, or rehearsing my own Schwitzgebelean scepticisms, I focus on a central set of issues, about time and the dynamics of experience, on which I'd like to see DES liberalized or opened up. Being now wholly convinced about the general utility of the method as one among others, and ready to deal with my methodological worries by trying DES myself, the concerns I raise here are rather about its exclusive use and its exclusive focus on the 'flash snapshot' of 'the millisecond before the beep began' (p. 22).

Much work on mind and action in both philosophy and psychology remains at some distance from concrete experience. Many philosophers trade or (now) collect intuitions, discuss what experience is like *in general*, or worry about how it can possibly emerge in or from the brain: many psychologists take student subjects out of their natural habitats into odd little rooms to test their responses to highly controlled stimuli. Russ's complaint that graduates are just not taught 'how to observe people accurately' (p. 258) is spot on. Although he

---

[1] Page references are to *Describing Inner Experience* unless otherwise specified.

doesn't here consider traditions of participant observation in social sciences like anthropology, I suspect that he's equally unhappy with the typical rush to symbolic, narrative, or ideological interpretation of complex social practices and interactions. Too many discussions of the *habitus* or of cultural norms remain at a level of abstraction from the experience-near description of practices and activities, thinking and feeling in particular contexts.

So DES is refreshing just because it aims (fallibly but honestly) at catching concrete, structured experience in the wild. Its idealizations lie, in the main, in its hopes about the fidelity of trained access to its phenomena, rather than in any artificial limitation to toy versions of reality (save for the one shortcoming to which I come in a moment): as when cognitive ethologists watch animals interacting in the wild, the risks are less about curtailing ordinary behaviour than about misinterpreting it or missing some of its internal complexity. There should still be a complementary place for intervention and manipulation: by tweaking particular elements in an interconnected panoply, we then hope to move step-by-step back to the phenomena to see how the organization of those elements grounds and shapes the processes of interest. Despite his pluralist protestations, Russ hasn't sought much to integrate DES with alternatives, to seek the objective corroborating evidence he says he wants, or to build multi-stranded convergent research methods: though I hope this book changes things, DES perhaps as yet remains too isolated, more a 'hairy' or jazz science than the genuinely mixed 'Marsalis-like' programme that Russ officially advocates (p. 259). One promising line of integration should be with the kind of experimental ethnography developed in cognitive and linguistic anthropology by students of multimodal interaction like Charles Goodwin (2000) and Ed Hutchins (2010), whose microstudies of short communicative sequences (of three girls in a hopscotch game, or a frigate's navigation crew) span gesture, tool- or technology-use, eye gaze, posture, and so on as well as verbal interaction (see also Enfield and Levinson, 2006). Both Russ and Eric may respond that DES is studying ordinary individual *conscious experience*, not more extended cognitive processes, or communication, or social interaction, or expert skills, or collaborative problem-solving. I think it would be wrong to push this too hard, because we want to maintain attention to the many links between consciousness and cognition. Real individual conscious experience is sometimes also part of, and embedded in, such extended activities: the exclusivity of consciousness-purism, as we might call it, should be resisted, and we should join the difficult task of integrating DES into a battery of related research tools.

I pursue this point here by pushing on one particular, striking problem with the subject-matter of DES. Russ takes it that his target — concrete, structured experience in the wild — is a momentary phenomenon. The method deliberately sets out to eradicate any dynamic features of experience by providing 'a flash snapshot', discarding anything other than 'the last undisturbed moment before the beep'. By asking both subjects and interviewers 'to focus on one moment', DES encourages a kind of Humean temporal atomism in which we study only 'a precise moment, perhaps measured to a fraction of a second' (pp. 21–23). But on the face of it, ordinary conscious experience is temporally extended and continuous, even though of course — as Eric often points out — it is more gappy and fleeting than most things in the external world. Russ and Eric have added a brief discussion of how DES loses access to 'the dynamics of experience' (Box 4.10, p. 76), but it fails to quell this concern. Russ says there that flow or dynamics can't be captured because trying to do so would lose the desirable, neutral randomness of DES: he complains that a series of instants would be selected only 'because they seem to cohere with the flow', and that thus departing from the moment of the beep would leave us 'shrouded in the murk of presuppositional self-theory'. This is a false dichotomy. As Russ acknowledges (more when in the midst of the hard interviewing work than when reflecting broadly on the virtues of DES), access to pristine or unsullied single moments of experience is anyway imperfect and fallible: and there's no reason to believe (at least before trying) that attempts at careful extensions of DES to address both slightly longer experiential sequences and the broader temporal interanimation of distinct moments must inevitably be swamped by the chaff of confabulatory self-characterizations and faux generalizations. Many desirable features of DES could be retained while being (fallibly) applied to more extended experiential phenomena. Certain things might be lost, such as (perhaps) access to the multiple simultaneity of distinct components of experience at a time (Hurlburt and Heavey, 2004, p. 121): I'm not suggesting that the focus on single moments should be forever dropped, only that after 30 years some DES work could fruitfully stretch to sequences as well as snapshots. To justify this suggestion, I first discuss Russ's definite lack of interest in the dynamics of experience, and then point to a range of experiential phenomena of interest to Russ and Eric which to my mind require attention to temporal contexts.

Russ quotes William James complaining that introspective analysis often leaves us having caught 'some substantive thing... statically taken, and with its function, tendency, and particular meaning... quite evaporated' (p. 17; Hurlburt and Heavey, 2006, p. 51). He sees James as worried here about our disturbance of experience, and thinks DES answers this concern by using open-ended methods and privileging description over attempted explanation: but he does not respond here to the direct challenge about rendering experience static. However, he discusses the issue elsewhere as a potential criticism of DES, in a passage worth quoting in full:

> *Criticism 3: Inner experience is a stream, but the beeper approach makes it appear like a series of moments.* It is certainly true that most reports of DES subjects make it appear that experience is saltatory, more like a series of beads on a string than a continuous stream. Whether that is an artefact of the method or whether that is the way experience is needs further clarification. It is certainly possible that for some, perhaps most people, awareness jumps from one experience to the next with little or nothing in between. It is also possible that DES is by its nature unable to observe the actual stream-like characteristics of awareness. Further investigation is necessary here. (Hurlburt and Heavey, 2004, p. 123)

To my knowledge, this further investigation has not yet been undertaken. Yet since DES is intended to be theory-neutral, and to allow for dramatic individual differences, it should *investigate* the nature of temporal experience, rather than assuming or enforcing the view that the form and content of experience can be spelled out 'simply by looking at what is the case at an isolated instant' (Hoerl, 1998, p. 156): perhaps experience (sometimes, or for some subjects) 'can comprise a sequence of events' rather than a precise single moment (*ibid.*; on temporal experience see also Le Poidevin, 2009). Russ and Eric engage in productive discussions about the visuospatial content of Melanie's experience, in which Russ rightly insists that subjects may differ substantially and surprisingly: so we should likewise allow subjects to report a range of possibilities with regard to the temporal content of their experience, their experiences of duration, temporal passage, and succession, and with regard to the many ways in which their present experience may be coloured or animated by recent or more distant past experience. It's true that memory demands, and thus sources of potential error, increase as we seek (or even simply permit) reports of more extended sequences of experience: but subjects will gradually improve with training in describing slightly longer stretches before the beep, just as they do in describing the immediate moment before.

Further, DES is intended to illuminate the nature of experience in certain psychopathologies. But some pathologies (such as certain forms of trauma) involve particular experiential sequences, with particular thoughts or images tending to bring other particular images or feelings. Others involve odder ways of inhabiting time, such as an over-abundance or a scarcity of mental time travel. DES could in principle contribute powerfully to our understanding of such temporal pathologies: but its present form rules this out by banning attention to experiential flow and to the mnemonic (or future-oriented) periphery and reference of present experience.

It is as if Russ sees no middle ground between the 'flash snapshot' and the full-scale, problematic causal narrative. But we can reasonably explore such a middle ground even while agreeing with him that many interpretations (both self-interpretations and those offered in clinical contexts) do go awry, when attempts to *explain* experience, or locate its hidden sources and mechanisms, become schema-driven confabulations. This is why Russ resists his subjects' initial expectation that a DES interviewer 'would want a mini-story about each beep and maybe even an explanation', as Sarah Akhter put it in her sampling journal (Akhter and Hurlburt, 2006, p. 136): she was surprised when 'Dr. Hurlburt's questions didn't probe the story or context' of the experience (p. 144). Russ's comment is telling:

> I do usually avoid the story aspect of a person's report. I regard stories as being at least partially, and usually largely, a public mask, as practiced attempts at explaining part of one's world while simultaneously hiding other parts... I find story accounts nearly always to be unsatisfying — I can never figure out which part is real, which part is misleading, which part is public, which part is personal. By contrast, I think sampled experiences are largely true and only in minor ways the result of public masking... for the most part, sampled experiences are far more satisfying to me than are the accompanying stories. I therefore listen to the experiences and avoid the stories. (Akhter and Hurlburt, 2006, p. 145)

This passionately felt preference for the true pristine moments of experience over misleading narratives also influences the particular way Russ seeks to combine personal truth with general theory, and idiographic with nomothetic science. The idiographic conclusions about a particular individual like Melanie which DES permits are indeed drawn from her concrete experiences: she attends to the sensory aspects of her environment, she has detailed visual images, she has a range of feelings which are often not directly experienced, she rarely experiences inner speech, and she is unusually self-analytical. These DES observations are 'truly personal', and allow 'Melanie to emerge as Melanie really is' (p. 259): only on the basis of many such personal truths can we then identify similarities and differences *across* people (Hurlburt and Heavey, 2006, p. 249). But from another point of view the kind of 'personal truth' revealed in these '17 moments of Melanie's existence' is strangely thin. Because these 'very short moments, as close to instants as possible' (Heavey and Hurlburt, 2008, p. 805) have their histories and contexts stripped from them, Melanie herself is here history-less. This is of course deliberate — as Russ says, 'our major aim was *not* to find out something about Melanie as a particular individual' (p. 257). This seems appropriately modest given the nature of DES. But for many people, what matters about experience is not only its synchronic form, but also the way it arises out of, is coloured by, and goes on to shape both individual and shared history. We are, arguably, creatures with a particular kind of past, that is experienced in signature ways: many of our activities and experiences (both solo and shared) are more revealing, more significant, or more fun just because they incorporate that past in various ways and have consequences for the future.

Russ's alternative synchronic and 'saltatory' vision of personal experience is reminiscent of Galen Strawson's (2004) 'Episodics', who do not (as compared to 'Diachronics') see their present experiences as intrinsically connected to their past (or their future). Like Strawson, Russ is hostile to the narrative and form-finding tendencies to which some Diachronics are prone: he would I think agree with Strawson's assessment that 'the aspiration to explicit Narrative self-articulation... almost always does more harm than good... [and] is, in general, a gross hindrance to self-understanding: to a just, general, practically real sense, implicit or explicit, of one's nature' (Strawson, 2004, p. 447). My point here is not to argue against Russ or Strawson, but rather to reiterate that space must be found not only for distinctive forms of momentary experience, but also for distinctive forms of experience in time: for Narratives and Diachronics as well as for Episodics.

Russ is, I think, acknowledging the limitations of a history-free approach to 'personal truth' when he reminds us that 'Melanie herself, really, means little to the reader' (p. 257). But this is in some tension with other claims for DES as a route to personal truths. He suggests that DES can open up those subjects and investigators who 'give themselves over to communicating fearlessly about all aspects of experience' to potentially 'foundation-shattering' discoveries and 'a substantial amount of personal deconstruction/reconstruction' (Hurlburt and Akhter, 2006, pp. 295–299). This is the domination of the subject's diachronic or historical sense by the newly-discovered peculiarities of momentary experience revealed in DES. It is as if Russ expects DES subjects — at least those willing to take 'an elevator into the crypts of inner experience' (Hurlburt and Akhter, 2006, p. 296) — to revise their embedded, interpersonally-grounded self-understanding in light of a batch of flash snapshots, and to let 17 episodes trump an accumulated life. I agree with Russ that 'our culture has encouraged people to be sloppy in their observation of and claims about inner experience' (p. 62), but I deny that only *momentary* inner experience deserves careful observation.

But perhaps I'm way over-emphasizing Russ's episodic purism here. There's one point in the book at which he seems significantly — and in my view correctly — to relax it: I can use this point to underline my suggestion that temporal interanimations are ordinary, not intrinsically distorting, and should be welcomed and studied rather than dismissed. Russ and Eric have a number of acute exchanges about whether Melanie is making novel inferences during the interviews to fill out putative details of her before-the-beep experience. On one occasion, Russ divides the DES interview's 'discovery of Melanie's experience' into three components: Melanie's experience before the beep, 'Melanie's incorrect reconstruction during the interview', and 'our own presuppositionally mistaken overlay over Melanie's reports'. Much of the book concerns the attempt to keep the third, experimenter-induced intrusions and interpretations at bay. But here Russ makes the striking concession that even the extensive intrusion of subsequent reconstruction by the DES subject herself into reports of her experience is 'not terribly important': even if what Melanie says in interview is dominated significantly by, for example, a 'newly (re)created image in place of an original image', this combination 'is still uniquely Melanie' (Box 7.6, p. 151). Russ is here admitting legitimate temporal-experiential interanimations between the time of the beep and the time of the interview.

I stress this for two reasons. Firstly, both Russ and Eric (like most of us who accept the pervasive and persuasive evidence for the constructive nature of remembering) tend wrongly sometimes simply to *equate* construction with distortion. But influence is not inevitably error, nor is memory's malleability inevitably also unreliability (Campbell, 2004; Barnier, Sutton, Harris and Wilson, 2008). Veridical remembering too is the result of the same mechanisms and processes: no matter how much trained subjects use a 'sampling intention' to try to fix and insulate their event-specific knowledge, insulating their memory of the moment before the beep by some combination of inner techniques and supporting external notes, even their successful descriptions of inner experience are compilations. As Eric has noted, 'imagination, inference, the application of pre-existing schemata, and other cognitive processes are not separable from the process of remembering but rather an integral part of it. They are not interfering or aiding forces from which an act of "pure" remembering could be isolated' (Schwitzgebel, 2009). But this means that the distinction between 'recalling and reconstructing' (p. 151) on which much discussion in the book hinges is just not sharp, and that even true DES descriptions of before-the-beep experiences may legitimately draw on an uneven array of resources. This means that 'flash snapshot' purism should be resisted, even if it is a useful training motif or 'instructional nudge' (Sutton, 2007) to help subjects gradually discriminate among better and worse sources for the compilation.

Secondly, the availability and legitimacy of this kind of temporal interanimation — between pre-beep and interview — can alert us to the ubiquity of other ways in which history animates experience in dynamical systems like the embodied person at different levels and timescales (Sutton, 2009). We can take two distinctive examples from Melanie's reports. The case which gave rise to the discussion just mentioned was one in which Melanie claimed that (just before beep 4.1) alongside (or as part of) a strong desire or craving to go scuba diving, she was also experiencing a kind of bodily twisting or yearning which took the form of a sense of her body leaning or reaching forward. Eric was initially sceptical about this, because he thought that, despite her protestations, Melanie was probably now recreating the experience (at the time of the interview) and reporting on her present sensations. This is the mixing or co-presence of times I've already addressed, between beep and interview. But in this case Eric comes in retrospect to relent on his scepticism: on reflection, he realizes that 'a strong yearning might sometimes be accompanied by something like a feeling of forward impetus, or a readiness to move forward — perhaps as a kind of broadly distributed motor imagery of moving forward' (p. 147). This seems entirely plausible: what I want to note is that accepting Melanie's report on such grounds is to introduce and legitimize the animating presence within her experience of a whole history of activity. Melanie has this motor imagery because of her substantial past experience of diving: it is, in part, a form of embodied memory, combining skill-related and kinaesthetic aspects of procedural memory in a kind of experienced bodily tension 'like there's something inside me trying to reach out for something... in a forward direction' (p. 143). Although at the time of the beep this was only imagery, Melanie is nonetheless experiencing what Elizabeth Behnke (1997) calls a 'ghost gesture', a schematic inner vector or tendency towards movement that persists even without the larger, visible implied movements. Much of our kinaesthetic experience, at the level of micromovements as well as kinaesthetic imagery, exists as this kind of bodily sedimentation of the effective presence of past experience, often shrunken but still traceable to larger routines and bodily practices. Behnke's phenomenology of kinaesthetic micromovements, whether inadvertent or reclaimed, exhibits just the precise taste for concrete experience which Russ requires, but rightly admits both melodic stretches of experience and the larger frame of embodied history in order better to describe and understand the nature of specific corporeal-experiential sequences. The temporal interanimations animating Melanie's motor imagery are between the whole history of her scuba diving experience and the moment of the beep, and will, I suggest, be best understood by a framework which explicitly acknowledges such complex relationships between past and present experience.

Moving from the traceless influence of embodied memory to the explicit way in which past experiences are available in personal or autobiographical remembering, we can briefly examine a different case of temporal interanimation. This is a relation between a single and *specific* past event and the moment before the beep (as well as, again, the time of the interview). Just before beep 1.3, Melanie was experiencing a mental image of a shed in the country which she had visited just once, remembering it 'as if you've opened the front door and you're standing just inside' (p. 82). Much of the discussion between Melanie, Russ, and Eric about this report concerns the surprising visual clarity of her entire image, and the surprising amount of visual detail which Melanie describes in the interior of her imaged shed (such as the relative length of the sleeves of a rumpled jacket hanging on a hook on the wall to her left): on this point, Russ reminds us that this is Melanie's first sampling day. I want to pick up on a different issue, because this is the only report in which Melanie's pre-beep experience was a case of autobiographical remembering. Russ expertly helps her try to distinguish between what she was seeing at the moment of the beep and what she is seeing 'as we're talking about it now' (p. 86). But neither he nor Melanie manages so successfully to distinguish between what she was seeing at the precise pre-beep moment and the surrounding, temporally-related elements of her memory: nor should they do so, save for the violation of the official 'flash snapshot' rules of DES. At first Melanie describes her pre-beep image of the shed in DES-friendly terms as 'a snapshot memory of the first time that I saw the shed, or the inside of it', with 'nothing moving'. But this static snapshot is immediately permeated by motion and time, by the real history of her past experience, which bleeds through again now into the present of the interview (p. 85):

> Melanie: No, but it's still. There's nothing moving. It's a snapshot in that it's one moment out of time.
>
> Russ: Okay.
>
> Melanie: And I only stood there for a couple of seconds and then someone came up next to me and I walked inside and everything like that.

Because she's getting the hang of the DES ideology of the instant, Melanie does then snap back to 'just that first moment when the door was opened': but in the two passages quoted, we see that her experience is porous, as she is suddenly talking about the actual experienced past rather than the pre-beep image. We don't know whether this bleeding through — the very medium of mundane remembering — also occurred in the conversation she was having about the shed with her boyfriend at the time of the beep, or whether the beep and accompanying sampling intention cut that off. But there's no reason this interanimation or layering of moments shouldn't be explicitly thematized.

There are many other issues to which the preceding discussion relates tangentially that deserve more space. I'm particularly pleased and intrigued by the analogy between the idea that describing inner experience is a sophisticated skill, only gradually acquired, and David Foulkes' (1999) work on children's dreaming as a cognitive achievement (p. 274). Again, I'd like to see more urgent attempts to identify ways to gather external corroboration of DES reports: recordings and other tests which offer converging access to the same phenomena will be easier to calibrate if our targets are more extended sequences of experience rather than isolated instants. Finally, experience sampling should be reconnected to research on motor skill and expertise: performers with long histories of high-level practice do sometimes confabulate just as wildly as the rest of us about their experience, but on other occasions they can reflect on extraordinary kinaesthetic experience, or on precise decision-making under severe stress or time pressure, in rich and surprising language 'beyond the easy flow of everyday speech' (Sheets-Johnstone, 2005, p. 217). I hope that many philosophers and cognitive scientists alike might look forward to confronting these challenges, and all kinds of unexpected hard-but-ordinary scientific problems, in the course of trying to forge a robust and slightly extended experience-sampling practice.

References

Akhter, S.A. & Hurlburt, R.T. (2006) A sampling journal: Learning about DES, in Hurlburt, R.T. & Heavey, C.L. *Exploring Inner Experience: The Descriptive Experience Sampling Method*, pp. 133–149, Amsterdam: John Benjamins.

Barnier, A.J., Sutton, J., Harris, C.B. & Wilson, R.A. (2008) A conceptual and empirical framework for the social distribution of cognition: The case of memory, *Cognitive Systems Research*, **9**, pp. 33–51.

Behnke, E.A. (1997) Ghost gestures: Phenomenological investigations of bodily micromovements and their intercorporeal implications, *Human Studies*, **20**, pp. 181–201.

Campbell, S. (2004) Models of mind and memory activities, in DesAutels, P. & Walker, M.U. (eds.) *Moral Psychology: Feminist Ethics and Social Theory*, pp. 119–137, Lanham, MD: Rowman & Littlefield.

Enfield, N.J. & Levinson, S.C. (eds.) (2006) *Roots of Human Sociality: Culture, Cognition, and Interaction*, Oxford: Berg.

Foulkes, D. (1999) *Children's Dreaming and the Development of Consciousness*, Cambridge, MA: Harvard University Press.

Goodwin, C. (2000) Action and embodiment within situated human interaction, *Journal of Pragmatics*, **32**, pp. 1489–1522.

Heavey, C.L. & Hurlburt, R.T. (2008) The phenomena of inner experience, *Consciousness and Cognition*, **17**, pp. 798–810.

Hoerl, C. (1998) The perception of time and the notion of a point of view, *European Journal of Philosophy*, **6**, pp. 156–171.

Hurlburt, R.T. & Akhter, S.A. (2006) The Descriptive Experience Sampling method, *Phenomenology and the Cognitive Sciences*, **5**, pp. 271–301.

Hurlburt, R.T. & Heavey, C.L. (2004) To beep or not to beep: Obtaining accurate reports about awareness, *Journal of Consciousness Studies*, **11** (7–8), pp. 113–128.

Hurlburt, R.T. & Heavey, C.L. (2006) *Exploring Inner Experience: The Descriptive Experience Sampling Method*, Amsterdam: John Benjamins.

Hutchins, E. (2010) Imagining the cognitive life of things, in Malafouris, L. & Renfrew, C. (eds.) *The Cognitive Life of Things: Recasting the Boundaries of the Mind*, pp. 91–101, Cambridge: McDonald Institute for Archeological Research.

Le Poidevin, R. (2004) The experience and perception of time, in Zalta, E.N. (ed.) *Stanford Encyclopedia of Philosophy*, (Winter 2009 edition), [Online], http://plato.stanford.edu/archives/win2009/entries/time-experience/

Schwitzgebel, E. (2009) Reconstructive memory, Blog entry *The Splintered Mind*, [Online], http://schwitzsplinters.blogspot.com/2009/08/reconstructive-memory-vs-storage-and.html [27 Aug 2009].

Sheets-Johnstone, M. (2005) What are we naming?, in De Preester, H. & Knockaert, V. (eds.) *Body Image and Body Schema*, pp. 211–231, Amsterdam: John Benjamins.

Strawson, G. (2004) Against narrativity, *Ratio 17*, **XVII**, pp. 428–452.

Sutton, J. (2007) Batting, habit, and memory: The embodied mind and the nature of skill, *Sport in Society*, **10**, pp. 763–786.

Sutton, J. (2009) Exograms, habits, and the confusion of types of memory, in Kania, A. (ed.) *Memento: Philosophers on Film*, pp. 65–86, London: Routledge.

Mark Engelbert and
Peter Carruthers

Descriptive Experience Sampling: What is it good for?

Abstract: We defend the reliability of Hurlburt's Descriptive Experience Sampling method against some of Schwitzgebel's attacks. But we agree with Schwitzgebel that the method could be used much more widely than it has been, helping to answer questions about the nature and structure of consciousness in addition to cataloguing the latter's contents. We sketch a number of potential lines of further enquiry.

1. Introduction

What can the method of Descriptive Experience Sampling (DES) tell us about the human mind? What sorts of questions can it be used to investigate with any degree of reliability? This is the central question addressed in Hurlburt and Schwitzgebel (2007),[1] and it is the question on which we propose to focus this essay. Specifically, in addition to commenting on the reliability of the DES method for the purposes discussed in the book, we are interested in exploring ways of using DES to shed light on a wider variety of psychological and philosophical questions. We will, therefore, be sketching a number of proposals for research strategies that utilize DES, both in the method's current form and with modifications.

Correspondence:
Mark Engelbert, University of Maryland   Email: marke@umd.edu
Peter Carruthers, University of Maryland   Email: pcarruth@umd.edu

---

[1] Hereafter page numbers without a date refer to pages within Hurlburt and Schwitzgebel (2007), and references to either Hurlburt or Schwitzgebel by name alone should be understood to refer to their individual views as expressed in the book. When we refer to any of their other individual writings we use the usual author/date method.

One sort of modification would be as follows. Hurlburt counts among the virtues of DES its 'ecological validity', or the fact that it captures subjects' experience in their natural, everyday environments. The commitment to ecological validity precludes beeping subjects in the laboratory, and also rules out instructing them to focus their reports on particular kinds or aspects of experience. While we recognize the value of this ecological validity for some purposes — particularly when forming generalizations about the prevalence and variability across individuals of different modes of experience — we feel that the DES method has the potential to help answer important psychological and philosophical questions, some of which may require dropping the commitment to ecological validity. Although these aren't questions that have interested Hurlburt himself, they may be of interest to others, and we would urge other investigators to take them up, modifying the DES method as appropriate. As we explore various ways of putting the DES method to use, some of our suggestions will sacrifice ecological validity for the sake of other virtues that are derived from traditional psychological methods, especially the use of experimental controls.

2. Is DES reliable at all?

First, however, we address the question whether experience sampling is appropriate for the main use that Hurlburt has made of it over his career — namely, examining the patterning and diversity of conscious experience in daily life (both within and between individuals). Hurlburt (pp. 21, 27–31) provides a list of features that, to his thinking, make DES a method far superior to 'armchair introspection' for obtaining reliable data about conscious experience. Subjects are beeped randomly, which reduces the complications that accompany attempts to introspect with an intention to introspect (Schwitzgebel experiences precisely this difficulty when trying to capture the phenomenology of his own inner speech). Furthermore, subjects produce written notes immediately upon being beeped and are later debriefed by an experienced interviewer. In order to reduce experimenter bias, subjects are permitted and encouraged to report whatever features of their experience they find salient and important; they are allowed to decline to answer any question that they wish; and interview questions are exploratory and open-ended. Subjects are also trained by the experimenter during the first couple of days of sampling, during which time they become comfortable with the introspection process and are taught to avoid common pitfalls.

Schwitzgebel acknowledges these virtues but thinks that attempts at introspection under the DES paradigm may still be subject to systematic inadequacies. Indeed, Schwitzgebel (2008) challenges the accuracy of introspection itself. He questions, for example, whether emotional states like joy have a distinctive common phenomenology that can be identified introspectively across instances. Note that such worries are irrelevant to the reliability of the DES method, however (and to the reliability of real-time introspection generally — see Engelbert and Carruthers, 2009). This is because accuracy in this respect would require *generalizing* about one's experience over a significant number of occurrences, comparing one's experience from one instance to the next.[2] This isn't something that introspection can accomplish unaided. Plainly it also requires memory. But there is reason to think that memories of introspected experiences may not be preserved on a routine basis, as we explain shortly. In contrast, DES, as practised by Hurlburt, specifically shies away from such '*faux* generalizations'. It instead focuses only on subjects' statements about their experiences at the moment of a particular beep. The generalizations can then be provided by the experimenter, without needing to rely on the subject's memory.

Why should one think that memories for introspected experiences are unlikely to be retained? The most common suggestion for why we possess a capacity for introspection in the first place is that it has a monitoring function (e.g. Shallice, 1988). On this account, we monitor our own mental processes in order to intervene in them when they go awry, or to trouble-shoot when they get blocked. This plainly requires that some sort of short-term record of one's mental states should be retained, so that the monitoring mechanism can represent each stage as an event in an ongoing process. Hence subjects should be capable of reporting their immediately past mental states. But we should predict that representations of one's own mental states will *not* be stored in long-term memory, unless for some reason they are rehearsed and/or consciously attended to and revisited. For this isn't necessary to support the trouble-shooting function, and would serve no useful purpose. Rather, knowledge of our immediately past mental events should fade away rapidly, just as dreams do. And indeed, consistent with this prediction, many of Hurlburt's subjects make discoveries about the patterns in their inner experience that surprise them,

---

[2] By no means do all of the arguments in Schwitzgebel (2008) require generalizing across experiences, however. For some discussion and critique of his other arguments, see Engelbert and Carruthers (2009).

suggesting that long-term memories of such experience aren't routinely created.

As regards the DES method in particular, Schwitzgebel worries considerably about the extent to which subjects' reports are influenced by their own self-theories and the metaphors they employ in describing hard-to-capture features of experience. He also raises issues about memory: subjects may forget such features as the level of detail that is present in their visual images, and whether or not there was any experience represented within a particular sense modality. Furthermore, subjects' reports may be distorted by their revisitations of their beeped experiences during the time between the beep and the follow-up interview.

Our own view is intermediate. We believe that there is every reason to trust the results obtained through DES, but only (on current evidence) when the method is addressed towards the presence or absence of fairly gross categories such as inner speech, visual imagery, and so forth, together with their approximate contents (i.e. what they are about). Since such features (or lack thereof) can be noted within seconds of the beep, and will generally be recorded in the subject's own notes, worries about the reliability of memory, situational demands, and so on, appear to be only minimally applicable.

The more fine-grained the categories employed, however, the more scope there is for scepticism of the above sorts. But relatively straightforward manipulations of the DES method itself should be able to test for such distorting effects. Schwitzgebel himself (2007) was able to address the issue of biasing by subjects' background theories and expectations through the simple expedient of asking subjects about these in advance. He was able to discover no such effects. Likewise, if one were concerned that much of the richness and detail in subjects' descriptions of their experience might be a product, either of the constructive nature of memory following a 24-hour delay (during which time subjects will no doubt have revisited the beeped moment numerous times in their thoughts), or of the pragmatic demands of extended questioning by an experimenter, then these factors could be controlled for. One might have subjects interviewed at varying intervals after the beep (one hour, four hours, eight hours, and so on) to see whether those interviewed following longer intervals tend to produce greater richness and detail in their descriptions of their experience. And one might have interviewers adopt a pair of strategies, one of which would be the usual extended probing, but the other of which would be just a single request to a subject (following initial training) to tell everything that they can remember about the experience in question, perhaps even having them speak privately into a tape recorder rather than to an interviewer (this manipulation could also be performed with both trained and untrained DES subjects, to help answer questions about the effects of training).

Such controls and manipulations would not completely eliminate concerns about confabulation and elaboration, since there may be individual differences in how susceptible subjects are to situational and memory demands. But the experimental controls should reduce such concerns to acceptable levels. It is an empirical matter what effect such manipulations might have, but our tentative prediction after reading Hurlburt and Schwitzgebel's book is that they will not be large.

3. What do current DES findings tell us?

Hurlburt's main finding over his career has been that people's inner experiences are extremely diverse. Some people seem to spend much of their time engaged in inner speech, some in manipulating visual images; some experience unsymbolized thinking, some don't; some report emotional feelings, some don't; a handful report rich multi-modal experience, most don't; and so on. Is this an additional source of scepticism about the reliability of the DES method, as Schwitzgebel alleges? He claims that the biological commonalities between all (or almost all) humans should lead us to expect that their inner lives will be basically similar, just as their digestive systems and respiratory systems are similar. We disagree. Even if there is in some sense a default preference for assuming similarity among individuals, there is more than enough evidence in the present case to indicate that individual variation should come as no surprise. Or so we will now argue.

For one thing, although this is by no means uncontroversial, most psychologists believe that the contents of consciousness are products of *attention* (e.g. Dehaene *et al.*, 2006). One form of attention is stimulus driven, or 'bottom-up'. Thus a sudden loud sound or a snake-like shape in the grass can *grab* our attention, forcing the contents in question into consciousness. But another form of attention is top-down and varies depending upon our current goals and ongoing executive functions. Attending in this latter sense is something that we *do* — although not necessarily deliberately or consciously, of course. People with exactly the same biological and cognitive systems might therefore develop very different habits of top-down attention, which might lead some to undergo frequent emotional experiences while others have frequent visual experiences. Both sets of people might equally be undergoing *emotions*, and both will possess visual perceptions of the environment on a routine basis, just as their common biology and cognitive architecture would lead one to predict. But the groups will differ in whether states of the two kinds are likely to achieve the 'global broadcast' necessary for conscious status (in the sense of Baars, 1988),[3] resulting from their different habits of attention.

Moreover, many of the kinds of items reported by DES subjects (particularly inner speech and visual imagery) are best thought of as belonging to so-called 'System 2' cognitive processes. Scientists who study human reasoning abilities have increasingly converged on the hypothesis that we possess a set of swift and automatic systems that are largely immutable and universal (and frequently shared with other animals), which produce initial intuitions and intuitive answers to reasoning questions (System 1). But we also have a slow, limited capacity, consciousness-involving system (System 2), which operates under intentional control (see Evans and Over, 1996; Sloman, 1996; 2002; Stanovich, 1999; Kahneman and Frederick, 2002; Kahneman, 2003). System 2 utilizes the centralized working memory system investigated over the years by Baddeley and colleagues (Baddeley and Hitch, 1974; Baddeley and Logie, 1999; Baddeley, 2006), and frequently employs visual and auditory imagery (especially inner speech). It is already known that the character and extent of use of System 2 varies widely between individuals (Stanovich, 1999). Moreover, Carruthers (2006; 2009a) argues that System 2 depends crucially upon mental rehearsals of action-schemata (thereby explaining how System 2 processes are under intentional control). So in our view, the discovery that some subjects spend most of their waking lives engaged in inner speech whereas others occupy most of their time manipulating visual images should be no more surprising than the fact that some people spend much of the day engaged in physical activity whereas others are mostly sedentary, or that some people gesture with their hands a lot while speaking whereas others don't. And certainly this discovery isn't grounds for scepticism about the reliability of the experience sampling method itself.

Although Schwitzgebel is sceptical of the patterning of Hurlburt's results, he is actually more interested in the question whether experience sampling can be used to answer deeper questions about the

---

[3] For some more recent evidence supporting the global broadcasting account of consciousness, see Dehaene and Naccache (2001), Baars (2002), Baars *et al.* (2003), Dehaene *et al.* (2003). The framework is now widely accepted among consciousness theorists. Even those like Chalmers (1996) who deny that it provides us with an *explanation* of the phenomenal properties of consciousness nevertheless accept that global broadcast is causally necessary and sufficient for consciousness.

character of consciousness, such as whether people's experience frequently has multimodal contents (tactile experience at the same time as visual and auditory experience, and so on), and whether there is generally a rich background of conscious experience at the periphery of attention. Thus Schwitzgebel wants to know whether one generally has conscious experiences of one's feet in one's shoes, or of the upper left quadrant in one's visual field beyond the window of current attention. We applaud the spirit of Schwitzgebel's approach. We, too, think that DES is an under-utilized and under-appreciated resource, which could be used or adapted to answer a much wider array of questions. But on this specific issue (richness *versus* sparseness) we are inclined to side with Hurlburt, as we will now explain.

Hurlburt tells us that the vast majority of his subjects deny the richness of their inner experience. In general, a sampled moment contains only one or a few experiences at a time. Schwitzgebel is sceptical. For the fact that randomly sampled reports are mostly sparse is consistent with richness plus quick fading. Although this is conceivable, we don't think that the suggestion is a plausible one. For in that case one would at least expect subjects to report that they have the *sense* that there was a lot more going on, but they can't remember what. Compare the way in which dreams tend to fade almost immediately upon waking. Even if one can report very little of the content of the dream, one generally has the sense that it faded rapidly, and that it actually contained much more than one can now recall. Schwitzgebel therefore needs to explain why waking experience should be so different. If experience is characteristically rich, why is it that subjects don't have an introspective sense of that richness rapidly fading away? While one might adduce other evidence for the richness of conscious experience, we think that Hurlburt's results using the DES method provide plausible *prima facie* evidence for the sparseness view.

It is important to distinguish between two different senses in which experience can be rich, however. The first is the one that we have just been discussing, which depends upon the extent to which conscious experience is multimodal in character, as well as on the extent to which there are conscious experiences outside of the window of focal attention. Let us call this 'peripheral richness', to be contrasted with what might be described as 'focal richness'. The latter concerns the richness of experience *within* the window of focal attention (which is both spatially and temporally smeared, it should be noted). The two forms of richness are independent of one another. This enables us to preserve Hurlburt's DES finding of peripheral sparseness in the face of evidence of focal richness. Subjects who briefly view a complex array on which they focus their attention (e.g. three rows of three different numbers) can characteristically only report a small proportion of the items thereafter. But they also report having *seen* all of the items in detail. And if any one row of items is signalled immediately following the removal of the stimulus, subjects are at ceiling in their reports, suggesting that all of the relevant visual information was initially represented in consciousness, just as the subjects themselves claim, but that it fades rapidly (Sperling, 1960; Landman *et al.*, 2003).

Schwitzgebel (2007) himself set out to find evidence on the question of peripheral richness by devising an adaption of the DES methodology. What he found would support a moderate position if taken at face value, containing significantly more riches than Hurlburt's subjects characteristically report. So the question now becomes: can we trust *Schwitzgebel's* experience sampling method? We believe there are good reasons to think that one can't. The crucial feature of the new methodology is that some subjects receive instructions to report specifically on a particular aspect of their peripheral experience at the moment of the beep (e.g. the upper left quadrant of the visual field, or somatic experience in the left foot). But the problem with the new method is this: there is good reason to believe that perceptual contents that are preconscious are held briefly in an iconic memory store, and that those contents can *become* conscious if attended to (Dehaene *et al.*, 2006). Even if a subject has *no* conscious experience of his foot at the time of the beep, information from the foot will have been processed up to a certain level, and might be reverberating in a preconscious iconic memory system. As soon as the beep goes off the subject will direct attention towards that system as instructed, and its contents will thereby *become* conscious. We conclude, therefore, that Hurlburt's finding of the peripheral sparseness of subjects' experience can be allowed to stand.

4. Some possibilities for expanding the use of DES

As we noted above, Hurlburt's main interest is in the character and variety of people's conscious experience itself. But it should be obvious that the DES methodology (whether modified or unmodified) can be applied much more widely (here we are firmly in agreement with Schwitzgebel). One obvious application of the method would be to investigate correlations between patterns of conscious experience and other cognitive traits and abilities (this could in turn be a springboard to more structured sorts of investigation of the cognitive architecture underlying various forms of conscious experience, or indeed consciousness itself). The method has obvious advantages over more traditional survey methods, such as asking people whether their experience is generally rich or not (Hurlburt is surely correct that all you can really get from such questioning are unreliable *faux* generalizations).

For example, Hurlburt himself (Hurlburt et al., 2002) has recently investigated whether faster speakers tend to report more detail in their inner experience generally, finding that they do. This is an intriguing result. It is natural to wonder whether the discovered correlation might be mediated by individual differences in the capacity for fast attention switching. This would have an obvious effect on speed of speech generation. And it would likewise enable multiple contents to enter the temporally extended window of conscious experience. There is reason to think that conscious visual experience, in particular, is built up serially over a period of a second or two through multiple saccades. But something similar might also be at work across different sensory modalities, enabling people to juggle with visual and auditory imagery within the same time-window, while also devoting attention to their emotional feelings, and so on. One can imagine various ways in which the hypothesized differences in fast attention switching might be tested.

In addition, we think that experience sampling might be used to investigate whether the richness and detail of people's reported images correlates with ability in some of the standard psychological tasks requiring imagery, such as mental rotation. Schwitzgebel (2002) assumes, very naturally, that there should be a correlation, and Hurlburt (p. 275) seems inclined to agree. But since the existing studies have for the most part failed to find any, Schwitzgebel (2002) uses this as grounds for suspecting the reliability of introspection itself. The studies in question did not use DES, however. They relied upon more traditional forms of instrospective report, with all of the latter's drawbacks. If one can find a way to quantify the richness in imagery reported by DES subjects, then it would be worth re-examining the issue by conducting batteries of imagery-related tasks with individuals who report varying levels of richness and detail in their images.

We are not entirely convinced of Schwitzgebel's (2002) assumption that differences in experience should correlate with differences in task performance, however. For whether there should be such a correlation depends, at least in part, on whether images are constructed serially and actively or whether they can, rather, spring into consciousness fully-formed (this question is raised at various points in Hurlburt and Schwitzgebel's book).[4] If the former is the case then we might expect to find a correlation with image manipulation tasks, since there will be close parallels between the processes employed in subjects' everyday imagistic thinking and deliberate image manipulation. But if images can arrive instantaneously, then there would be no reason to expect such a correlation. For it would then seem that the capacity to *manipulate* images is something quite different. Anecdotally, at least (warning: we are about to make a *faux* generalization), it appears that images can often arrive fully-detailed, especially in the case of memory images. It seems that an evocative smell or word can sometimes bring to mind an image of a scene from one's past in a single flash.

More ambitiously, then, one might try to adapt the experience sampling method to address this very question. We could (in randomly distributed trials) beep at specified intervals of time following the experimenter's instruction to imagine a particular object. If the object has a known number of basic features, we could compare the results against a baseline for each subject. If images arrive fully formed then we should expect to find no correlation between richness and elapsed time, or even perhaps a negative correlation, as aspects of the initial image are forgotten. If images are constructed serially, in contrast, then we should expect to find a positive correlation with elapsed time. Note that the methodology needed here might be burdensome, however. For the test trials would need to be distributed with sufficient infrequency that subjects aren't continually 'on the watch out' for the occurrence of the beep. And it might be hard to combine the method with probes of *evoked* memory images, as opposed to ones that are formed on command. Our larger point, however, is that until researchers interested in the structure and functioning of cognition take up the DES method and adapt it for their purposes, it is hard to know what its limits might be.

5. DES and the introspectability of attitudes

We think that DES could also be used to investigate a quite separate issue, which isn't discussed directly by Hurlburt and Schwitzgebel. This is the question whether there is any such thing as introspection for attitudes. There is an extensive literature in psychology suggesting that we often engage in self-interpretation when attributing propositional

---

Note that serial construction of images might provide an explanation of the otherwise puzzling phenomenon of images that violate rules of perspective (p. 86). If it turns out that images are *constructed*, and constructed serially, then it wouldn't be surprising if subjects might sometimes combine together image components that presuppose different and conflicting perspectives.

attitudes to ourselves (see Festinger, 1957; Bem, 1967; 1972; Wicklund and Brehm, 1976; Nisbett and Wilson, 1977; Eagly and Chaiken, 1993; Gazzaniga, 1995; 2000; Wegner, 2002; Wilson, 2002; Briñol and Petty, 2003). While most agree that such confabulation data are successful in showing that we *sometimes* engage in self-interpretation, there is considerable debate over whether this is the *only* method of self-attribution, or if we sometimes have direct introspective access to our own attitude states as well.

In recent contributions to this debate, Carruthers (2009b; 2010) has argued that there is no such thing as introspection for propositional attitudes. Perceptual experiences (e.g. visual, auditory, proprioceptory, and somatosensory) and quasi-perceptual experiences (such as visual imagery and inner speech and/or hearing) can be introspected, on Carruthers' model. This is because (and to the extent that) they are globally broadcast, hence being made available as input to the mindreading faculty. But propositional attitudes like beliefs, desires, judgments, decisions, wonderings, and supposings must be self-attributed via processes of self-interpretation, similar to the processes that are employed when we attribute attitudes to other people. But in one's own case the mindreading faculty can not only use information about one's own behaviour and circumstances, it can also utilize 'internal' data in the form of visual imagery, inner speech, and so on, enabling it to make an (unconscious) inference as to the current mental state of the agent even in the absence of overt behaviour.

Here we offer some suggestions for how the DES method might be used to gather additional evidence for or against the existence of introspective access to attitudes. All of these suggestions are tentative, and none of them would be expected to settle the issue decisively. Rather, data from the experiments we propose would be useful supplements to the large corpus of experimental work on the prevalence of confabulation. We focus first on two areas where robust confabulation effects have been reported: split brain subjects and subjects who have undergone hypnosis.

Split brain subjects have had their corpus collosum (which is the structure connecting the two brain hemispheres) severed as a treatment for epilepsy. Because the hemispheres of split brain patients cannot communicate with one another, stimuli presented in the right visual field (which feeds into the left hemisphere) are not perceived in the right hemisphere and *vice versa*. Since language is usually lateralized to the left hemisphere, any decisions taken or intentions formed in response to information presented to the right brain will not be available to the subject's language comprehension and production systems. When queried about actions they have performed in response to information presented to the right brain, these subjects often offer verbal reports that suggest they are engaging in unconscious self-interpretation. For example, Gazzaniga (1995) reports an episode in which the instruction 'Walk!' was presented in a subject's left visual field (and hence to the right brain), which the subject proceeded to follow: he got up and began to leave the testing van. When asked what he was doing, the speech-controlling left brain replied, 'I'm going to get a Coke from the house'. This report is plainly confabulated, but seemingly with all of the apparent-introspective-obviousness as normal.

Similarly, Wegner (2002) documents a number of instances of post-hypnotic behaviour to show that when asked about their intentions in performing an action for which they were given instructions under hypnosis, subjects will often confabulate a reason. For example, one subject was hypnotized and instructed to pick up a book from the table and place it on a shelf, and when asked why she did it she responded, 'I don't like to see things untidy; the bookshelf is the place for books, so that is why I am placing it there' (Wegner, 2002, p. 149). A plausible interpretation of such cases is that since the subject has no knowledge of her *real* intention (that is, to follow the hypnotist's instructions, which she does not remember), she interprets her own behaviour to devise a likely explanation: that she is tidying the room.

Some have argued against drawing strong conclusions about the prevalence of self-interpretation on the basis of such experiments. Critics point to a variety of issues with these experiments that purportedly weaken the force of their results. One worry is that interrupting subjects mid-action and requesting an explanation of their behaviour introduces a pragmatic demand on them to *justify* their behaviour or make it appear *rational* (Rey, 2008). Subjects in such situations might thereby be pushed into self-interpretative mode as a result of the situational demands, which wouldn't impugn the introspective nature of spontaneous, unsolicited self-attributions. The DES method could therefore be used in the context of such an experiment to reduce or eliminate such pragmatic demands by providing a more indirect way of having subjects report their intentions. It could be arranged so that the beep goes off just as a subject is performing an action prompted by post-hypnotic suggestion or by an instruction flashed to the right brain of a split brain subject (it would be best if this could be done using already-trained subjects as part of a larger sampling exercise, for purposes of ecological validity). Subjects could then note the contents of their experience, either to an experimenter present in the laboratory or using a notebook or tape recorder.

The conditions of this experiment could vary, with some subjects left simply to report whatever is 'in their awareness' at the time of the beep and others being explicitly asked to report their intentions. Those in the former condition may well not report any intentions at all, in which case their responses would not be relevant to the hypothesis under investigation. For the subject's intentions might well be *introspectable* even if they aren't actively being introspected at the time of the beep. Instructing subjects beforehand to report their intentions at the time of the beep, however, runs the risk of introducing the very pragmatic demands that the proposed use of the DES method seeks to avoid. For subjects may feel pressured to confabulate an intention that makes their behaviour appear rational. This risk might be mitigated, however, by using trained DES interviewers together with subjects who have already undergone DES training. For Hurlburt is adamant that the open-ended and unstructured nature of DES questioning makes it transparent to subjects that it is perfectly OK to report nothing if there is nothing to report.[5]

Experiments with hypnotized subjects would be especially informative if they could be designed to involve *ambiguous* actions. For example, subjects might be given a post-hypnotic suggestion that when a designated individual (who is known to the subject) walks into the room, they are to move their right hand back and forth in the air, palm outward, to wave away any bugs. Subjects could then be beeped just as they begin to wave, to see what sort of intention is reported. If intentions are introspectable, subjects in such circumstances should report that they are intending to move away any bugs. But if, as Carruthers suggests, intentions are attributed to oneself by interpretation, then subjects ought to reach for the most reasonable interpretation of their own behaviour — which in this instance is that they are waving to greet the person who has just walked into the room. Using the DES beeper to solicit subjects' reports would, again, remove most of the pragmatic and memory demands that are alleged to have contributed to confabulation effects in previous experiments.[6]

---

[5] Note that if subjects are operating under a general instruction to introspect their intentions at the time of the beep, then it would have to be made clear to them whether they are supposed to report a local intention, like placing a book on a shelf, or a more global one, like tidying the room (depending on the details of the experiment).

[6] We admit that the example described here is not ideal. For even if there is introspection and subjects do have access to their bug-removing intentions, they might get pushed into self-interpretation mode when they find themselves waving as if to deter bugs and yet they can plainly see *that there are no bugs*. The example is merely meant to illustrate the general strategy of using ambiguous actions in hypnotism cases. Since subjects differ in their degrees of suggestibility, moreover, we would need to take care that they have no recall of

Another worry about many confabulation experiments is that subjects are often asked to report their intention in performing an action *retrospectively* (i.e. they are asked, 'why *did* you do that?'). One might, therefore, argue that subjects' real intentions were *introspectable* at the time but didn't happen to be *introspected*. That is, it could be that the introspective faculty is only capable of detecting occurrent or very recently past attitudes, and that unless one directs one's attention to an attitude while or shortly after it occurs, no record is thereafter stored in memory. Beeping subjects in the midst of an action for which a confabulated explanation might be expected would allow us to test this hypothesis. If subjects still offer confabulated explanations even when they are beeped *during* an action, it would suggest that confabulation data cannot be dismissed by invoking the introspectable/introspected distinction.

Beyond these suggestions for further research, we should briefly address evidence from existing DES studies that bears on the issue of introspection for attitudes. Two closely related bodies of data are the existence of what Hurlburt calls 'partially unworded speech', on the one hand, and 'unsymbolized thinking', on the other (p. 141). The former is comparatively rare, Hurlburt tells us, whereas the latter occurs commonly in some subjects (while being absent in others). Nevertheless, the mere existence of either one might seem to count against Carruthers' self-interpretational account of self-knowledge. We will discuss them in turn.

In cases of partially unworded speech, subjects report fragmented inner speech tokens at the time of the beep, but nevertheless feel that they know the complete content of the underlying thought or speech intention (i.e. they have a conscious sense of what words belong in the missing parts of the token). For example, when one of Melanie's inner-hearing tokens was interrupted by a beep, she reported having a clear sense of how the sentence was going to end. She had just realized that she had forgotten to take off the parking brake and heard, 'Why can't I...' just at the moment of the beep. She reported knowing that the sentence was going to end with '...remember about the parking brake?' (pp. 135–136). Do cases like this suggest, as Schwitzgebel (p. 137) claims, that there is introspective access to one's thoughts beyond the imagery that one experiences?

Not necessarily. Carruthers argues that self-interpretation is a global affair, drawing on evidence not just from internal imagery but

---

the conditions involved in their hypnosis. Otherwise we will get the contrary problem: subjects may report their real intention from memory rather than from introspection.

also facts about the agent's behaviour and situation (in the latter regard operating much like third-person mindreading). Thus, just as a third party observing Melanie might predict, given her situation, that her inner speech token would involve the parking brake, so Melanie is able to make that prediction about her own experience. Hence as long as the content of an inner speech token could be inferred from a subject's situation, partially unworded speech poses no threat to Carruthers' model. And indeed, consistent with that model, Hurlburt reports that 'the most frequent experience of inner speech involves simply the speech itself with no conscious sense of what is about to be said' (p. 138). Moreover, he tells us that when people are beeped in the midst of speaking they generally have no conscious awareness of what they are intending to say.

In cases of unsymbolized thinking, in contrast, subjects report propositional thoughts in the absence any mental symbols like visual imagery or inner speech. It happens that Melanie is one of the many subjects who report no instances of this phenomenon. But unsymbolized thinking is by no means uncommon, and Hurlburt and Akhter (2008) describe a number of cases in some detail. Many instances can be handled by Carruthers in the manner just outlined above. For there will often be features of the context, and/or the agent's own behaviour, that would make self-attribution of the thought in question entirely natural (and something that a third party, too, might hit upon as an interpretation), independently of any imagistic cues. But this is by no means true of all cases of unsymbolized thinking. For example, Hurlburt and Akhter describe how Abigail was wondering, at the time of the beep, whether her friend Julio would be driving his car or his pickup truck when he came to collect her. Not only was this thought not symbolized in inner speech or other imagery, but there was nothing in Abigail's physical or behavioural context to suggest it.

Hurlburt himself (2009) suggests that unsymbolized thinking is consistent with Carruthers' self-interpretational model, however.[7] For to say that someone is undergoing unsymbolized thinking is to say that

---

[7] Indeed, Hurlburt (2009) goes further, claiming that DES data actually *supports* Carruthers' self-interpretational model. But here we think he oversteps the mark. His reasoning is that DES subjects never report any awareness of an attitude at the moment of the beep (except in the early stages of training, in which case they are inclined to back off such claims in discussion with the interviewer). But in making this claim Hurlburt must have in mind medium-term or standing attitudes like *intending to go out to dinner this evening*, or *believing that the economy will soon turn around*. For DES subjects *do* report *momentary* attitudes in cases of unsymbolized thinking, and they *don't* back off these claims. One will report *wondering* something (as in the case of Abigail, described above), whereas another will report *urging* herself to do something, and so on. But Carruthers (2009b) doesn't claim only that *standing* attitudes are self-attributed through self-interpretation. On the

there is no sensory awareness of any imagistic symbols at the time of a self-attributed thought. But 'sensory awareness', for Hurlburt, is a technical term, referring to sensory information that is at the focus of attention. He therefore suggests that 'the apprehension of an unsymbolized thought may involve the apprehension of some sensory bits, so long as those sensory bits are not organized into a coherent, central, thematized sensory awareness' of the sort that would be revealed in a standard DES interview (2009, p. 30). It is quite possible, therefore, that unsymbolized thinkers do have fragmentary imagistic awareness at the moment of the beep that could aid in a process of self-interpretation, leading to the attribution to themselves of a particular thought. Since subjects are unaware of the self-interpretation process, but find themselves inclined to attribute a specific thought to themselves, they will have the sense that they are consciously thinking that thought in an unsymbolized way.

Carruthers (2009b) proposes an alternative way of responding to the challenge posed to his views by instances of unsymbolized thinking.[8] This involves noticing that even if there is *no* imagery or other sensory information available in consciousness at the time of the beep, such information may nevertheless have been available just a moment previously. Since the DES method focuses only on the moment of the beep, and subjects are urged to ignore everything that came before it or after it, we (presently) have no way of knowing. So for all we know, there may have been visual or other images occurring shortly before any reported instance of unsymbolized thinking, which would have been sufficient for the mindreading faculty to construct the reported (unsymbolized) thought through the usual process of self-interpretation. And again, since subjects are unaware of the self-interpretation process, but find themselves inclined to attribute a specific thought to themselves at the time of the beep, they will have the sense that they are thinking that thought in an unsymbolized manner.

This leads us to our final experimental suggestions, the first of which is to adapt DES to probe the explanations of unsymbolized thinking outlined above. Subjects who are already known to have a high proportion of unsymbolized thoughts could be asked to sit quietly in a dimly lit room allowing their minds to wander, thus ensuring that there will be no overt behaviour or aspects of the context

---

contrary, the thesis extends also to momentary ones like wondering, supposing, and urging.

[8] The two suggestions are consistent with one another, it should be stressed. Some instances of unsymbolized thought might be arrived at in the manner suggested by Hurlburt (2009) and others in the manner outlined by Carruthers (2009b).

sufficient to issue in self-interpretation of specific thoughts. Intervals between beeps would have to be adjusted so that subjects aren't continually 'on the lookout' for them. In these circumstances one might hope to get a high number of reports of unsymbolized thinking. The background instructions would deviate from normal DES protocols, however, and could take one of two forms. In one condition subjects could be asked to note any sensory aspects at the moment of the beep, no matter how peripheral. If these are always found to be paired with reports of unsymbolized thinking in ways that are relevant to the content of the latter, then it would support Hurlburt's (2009) account. In another condition subjects could be asked to note, not just what is at the focus of their attention at the time of the beep, but to try to recall as much as they can of their experience in the immediately preceding moments. Naturally, this task might be quite demanding. But if even some subjects report relevant imagery in the moments before the occurrence of an unsymbolized thought, then it would provide some support for Carruthers' (2009b) proposal.[9]

Another sort of suggestion would be to probe the correlates of individual differences in reports of unsymbolized thinking. If Carruthers is right that self-attributions of unsymbolized thought are the result of swift and unconscious processes of self-interpretation, then one might predict that subjects who score high in unsymbolized thinking should perform better on other measures of mindreading capability, especially those requiring swift and intuitive (unreflective) forms of interpretation. Such data would need to be interpreted in the light of individual differences in rates of reporting visual imagery and inner speech, however. For while one reason why some subjects report unsymbolized thinking more often than others could be that they interpret current and recent sensory and imagistic data more swiftly and smoothly, another might be that some subjects simply have more such data to interpret.

6. Conclusion

We have sought to address two main issues. The first is the extent to which DES is a sound and reliable method for gathering data about ongoing conscious experience. While we share many of Schwitzgebel's doubts about the ability of subjects to report accurately on finely-detailed features of their experience, we also share Hurlburt's optimism about the reliability

---

[9] Ideally, of course, one would like to combine the two conditions into one, since the proposals made by Hurlburt and Carruthers are consistent with one another. But we fear that this would almost certainly exceed what it is possible for a normal individual to notice and describe in the space of just a few seconds.

of DES in allowing subjects to accurately apprehend broad, coarse-grained, features. The second issue builds upon the first: given that DES is a reliable source of data about at least many features of ongoing conscious experience, how can we put this method to use in answering outstanding psychological and philosophical questions? We suggest that DES embodies a useful method for clustering subjects into groups based on shared traits of inner experience (in terms of frequency and detail of particular sensory modalities, say), who can then be subjected to testing for correlations with other cognitive abilities. In addition, we are hopeful that the DES method might be adapted to help settle the question whether propositional attitudes can be directly introspected, or whether they must always be self-attributed based on a process of self-interpretation.[10]

References

Baars, B. (1988) *A Cognitive Theory of Consciousness*, Cambridge: Cambridge University Press.
Baars, B. (2002) The conscious access hypothesis: Origins and recent evidence, *Trends in Cognitive Science*, **6**, pp. 47–52.
Baars, B., Ramsoy, T. & Laureys, S. (2003) Brain, consciousness, and the observing self, *Trends in Neurosciences*, **26**, pp. 671–675.
Baddeley, A. (2006) *Working Memory, Thought, and Action*, Oxford: Oxford University Press.
Baddeley, A. & Hitch, G. (1974) Working memory, in Bower, G. (ed.) *Recent Advances in Learning and Motivation*, vol. 8, Maryland Heights, MO: Academic Press.
Baddeley, A. & Logie, R. (1999) Working memory: The multiple-component model, in Miyake, A. & Shah, P. (eds.) *Models of Working Memory*, Cambridge: Cambridge University Press.
Bem, D. (1967) Self-perception: An alternative interpretation of cognitive dissonance phenomena, *Psychological Review*, **74**, pp. 183–200.
Bem, D. (1972) Self-perception theory, in Berkowitz, L. (ed.) *Advances in Experimental Social Psychology*, vol. 6, Maryland Heights, MO: Academic Press.
Briñol, P. & Petty, R. (2003) Overt head movements and persuasion: A self-validation analysis, *Journal of Personality and Social Psychology*, **84**, pp. 1123–1139.
Carruthers, P. (2006) *The Architecture of the Mind*, Oxford: Oxford University Press.
Carruthers, P. (2009a) An architecture for dual reasoning, in Evans, J. & Frankish, K. (eds.) *In Two Minds*, Oxford: Oxford University Press.
Carruthers, P. (2009b) How we know our own minds: The relationship between mindreading and metacognition, *Behavioral and Brain Sciences*, **32**, pp. 121–138.
Carruthers, P. (2010) Introspection: Divided and partly eliminated, *Philosophy and Phenomenological Research*, **80**, pp. 76–111.
Chalmers, D. (1996) *The Conscious Mind*, Oxford: Oxford University Press.

---

[10] We are grateful to Russ Hurlburt and Eric Schwitzgebel for their respective comments and corrections on an earlier draft of this essay.

Dehaene, S. & Naccache, L. (2001) Towards a cognitive neuroscience of consciousness: Basic evidence and a workspace framework, *Cognition*, **79**, pp. 1–37.

Dehaene, S., Changeux, J.-P., Naccache, L., Sackur, J. & Sergent, C. (2006) Conscious, preconscious, and subliminal processing: A testable taxonomy, *Trends in Cognitive Sciences*, **10**, pp. 204–211.

Dehaene, S., Sergent, C. & Changeux, J.-P. (2003) A neuronal network model linking subjective reports and objective physiological data during conscious perception, *Proceedings of the National Academy of Science*, **100**, pp. 8520–8525.

Eagly, A. & Chaiken, S. (1993) *The Psychology of Attitudes*, San Diego, CA: Harcourt Brace Jovanovich.

Engelbert, M. & Carruthers, P. (2009) Introspection, in Nadel, L. (ed.) *Wiley Interdisciplinary Reviews: Cognitive Science*, Hoboken, NJ: John Wiley & Sons.

Evans, J. & Over, D. (1996) *Rationality and Reasoning*, London: Psychology Press.

Festinger, L. (1957) *A Theory of Cognitive Dissonance*, Palo Alto, CA: Stanford University Press.

Gazzaniga, M. (1995) Consciousness and the cerebral hemispheres, in Gazzaniga, M. (ed.) *The Cognitive Neurosciences*, Cambridge, MA: MIT Press.

Gazzaniga, M. (2000) Cerebral specialization and inter-hemispheric communication: Does the corpus callosum enable the human condition?, *Brain*, **123**, pp. 1293–1326.

Hurlburt, R. (2009) Unsymbolized thinking, sensory awareness, and mindreading, *Behavioral and Brain Sciences*, **32**, pp. 149–150.

Hurlburt, R. & Akhter, S. (2008) Unsymbolized thinking, *Consciousness and Cognition*, **17**, pp. 1364–1374.

Hurlburt, R. & Schwitzgebel, E. (2007) *Describing Inner Experience? Proponent Meets Skeptic*, Cambridge, MA: MIT Press.

Hurlburt, R., Koch, M. & Heavey, C. (2002) Descriptive experience sampling demonstrates the connection of thinking to externally observable behavior, *Cognitive Therapy and Research*, **26**, pp. 117–134.

Kahneman, D. (2003) A perspective on judgment and choice: Mapping bounded rationality, *American Psychologist*, **58**, pp. 697–720.

Kahneman, D. & Frederick, S. (2002) Representativeness revisited: Attribute substitution in intuitive judgment, in Gilovich, T., Griffin, D. & Kahneman, D. (eds.) *Heuristics and Biases*, Cambridge: Cambridge University Press.

Landman, R., Spekreijse, H. & Lamme, V. (2003) Large capacity storage of integrated objects before change blindness, *Vision Research*, **43**, pp. 149–164.

Nisbett, R. & Wilson, T. (1977) Telling more than we can know, *Psychological Review*, **84**, pp. 231–295.

Rey, G. (2008) (Even higher-order) intentionality without consciousness, *Review Internationale de Philosophie*, **62**, pp. 51–78.

Schwitzgebel, E. (2002) How well do we know our own conscious experience? The case of visual imagery, *Journal of Consciousness Studies*, **9** (5–6), pp. 35–53.

Schwitzgebel, E. (2007) Do you have constant tactile experience of your feet in your shoes? Or is experience limited to what's in attention?, *Journal of Consciousness Studies*, **14** (3), pp. 5–35.

Schwitzgebel, E. (2008) The unreliability of naïve introspection, *Philosophical Review*, **117**, pp. 245–273.

Shallice, T. (1988) *From Neuropsychology to Mental Structure*, Cambridge: Cambridge University Press.

Sloman, S. (1996) The empirical case for two systems of reasoning, *Psychological Bulletin*, **119**, pp. 3–22.
Sloman, S. (2002) Two systems of reasoning, in Gilovich, T., Griffin, D. & Kahneman, D. (eds.) *Heuristics and Biases*, Cambridge: Cambridge University Press.
Sperling, G. (1960) The information available in brief visual presentations, *Psychological Monographs: General and Applied*, **74**, pp. 1–29.
Stanovich, K. (1999) *Who is Rational? Studies of Individual Differences in Reasoning*, Mahwah, NJ: Lawrence Erlbaum Associates.
Wegner, D. (2002) *The Illusion of Conscious Will*, Cambridge, MA: MIT Press.
Wicklund, R. & Brehm, J. (1976) *Perspectives on Cognitive Dissonance*, Mahwah, NJ: Lawrence Erlbaum Associates.
Wilson, T. (2002) *Strangers to Ourselves*, Cambridge, MA: Harvard University Press.

Michael J. Kane

Describing, Debating, and Discovering Inner Experience

Review of Hurlburt and Schwitzgebel (2007),
'Describing Inner Experience?
Proponent Meets Skeptic'

Abstract: In the spirit of the competitive-collaborative approach that Russ Hurlburt and Eric Schwitzgebel take to examining the Descriptive Experience Sampling (DES) method, I review 'Describing Inner Experience? Proponent Meets Skeptic' — and consider the scientific potential of DES — from the inside, in light of my own subjective experience as a DES subject, as a person who lives with the unusual symptoms of Tourette Syndrome, and as a cognitive psychologist who conducts idiographic and experience-sampling work on volitional control and mind-wandering experiences.

This is an unusual review of an unusual book.

In *Describing Inner Experience? Proponent Meets Skeptic*, authors Russell Hurlburt (a psychologist; hereafter, 'Russ') and Eric Schwitzgebel (a philosopher; hereafter, 'Eric') debate the possibility of faithfully — or, 'pretty faithfully' — assessing people's momentary conscious experiences. What makes their discussion so engaging, and so novel, is not simply that Russ's and Eric's arguments and counter-arguments are remarkably clear, compelling, and thoughtful; rather, the bounty is in the discussion's form and target. First, the reader experiences the debate playing out as a 'real time' conversational

Correspondence:
Michael J. Kane, Department of Psychology, 321 McIver St., University of North Carolina at Greensboro, Greensboro, NC 27412, Phone: 336.256.1022
Email: mjkane@uncg.edu

exchange, in the forms of interview transcripts and boxed-off discussions about those transcripts; in this way, the book harks back to the 'old days' of published conference proceedings that included verbatim text of the question-and-answer periods, thereby humanizing the participants and conveying the excitement of the scientific process. But second, and most critically, Russ's and Eric's dialogue focuses on the intensive examination of a single subject's actual conscious experiences, as data gathered by all three of them via the 'Descriptive Experience Sampling' (DES) method (Hurlburt, 1990; 1993).

The DES subject, 'Melanie' (a pseudonym), wore a device with an earpiece over several days, which beeped her at random intervals as a cue for her to apprehend the contents, features, qualities, and extent of her conscious experience at that beeped moment (in Russ's words, 'the truth, the whole truth, and nothing but the truth' about the experience); she then took notes to help her recall the details of that moment when subsequently interviewed by Russ and Eric. These DES interviews, where Melanie describes her inner experiences and Russ and Eric interrogate them, form the bulk of the book and the grist for the mill of the debate. Russ, the DES proponent, hopes to use the Melanie interviews to convince Eric, the sceptic, (and the reader, as well) that DES avoids most of the pitfalls of other introspective methods and therefore should take a prominent place in advancing the science of consciousness studies.

This academic text is unusual, then, because it features not only a probing dialogue among two researchers and their research participant, but also a vigorous (yet exceedingly civil) *meta*-dialogue between the researchers about the discussion. This review, however, is pretty conventional so far. Where it diverges somewhat from the ordinary is that, in the same way that Russ and Eric anchored their arguments to Melanie's reported experiences, I will consider both Melanie's and my own DES data in my comments on *Describing Inner Experience*.

With Eric's blessing, I wore the beeper and served as a DES subject for three sampling days with Russ as the interviewer (by phone). I had two purposes. First, as a researcher who uses the normative form of beeper-cued, experience-sampling methodology (ESM; Csikszentmihalyi, Larson and Prescott, 1977) in my cognitive-psychology research on individual differences in attention, memory, and mind-wandering, and as a prospective reviewer of *Describing Inner Experience*, I thought that 'doing' DES from the inside might provide me with insights unavailable through second-hand accounts. Second, I have Tourette Syndrome (TS) and, based on my observation of my own experience and the reports of others, I once proposed a framework for understanding TS that made phenomenological claims about the bodily (somatosensory, kinaesthetic, and proprioceptive) experiences that seemed to precede and even precipitate tics (Kane, 1994). Although this TS framework was consistent with previously and subsequently published research (e.g. Bliss, 1980; Prado *et al.*, 2008), and although it was anecdotally supported by periodic 'thank you' notes I received from lay readers with TS, it was based on subjective, introspective evidence and so it might be fundamentally wrong. I speculated that DES might eventually provide a novel, rigorous means of testing whether my claims had merit.

Thoughts About DES, and the Book, Before Sampling

On Russ's recommendation, I made careful notes about my reactions to *Describing Inner Experience* before undergoing DES, in order to prevent my DES experience from retroactively biasing my original responses. I should note, however, that my knowledge of DES was not limited to the book, for I'd previously or contemporaneously read other reports about the method and its results (e.g. Heavey and Hurlburt, 2008; Hurlburt, 1997; Hurlburt and Heavey, 2001; 2006; Hurlburt, Koch and Heavey, 2002; Scwhitzgebel, 2007); my pre-DES views were thus informed by this broader literature.

Objective Corroboration of Inner Experience

From the outset, I was sympathetic to Eric's concerns about corroboration and external validation of DES reports, at least about the specific details of Melanie's reports, and especially about those details that were drawn out of the interview-exposed reports not present in the raw reports offered by Melanie before questioning. Should we really trust, given the hours elapsed between Melanie's experiences and her reports, that she felt the yearning to scuba dive as a tension-like, and forward-moving, feeling throughout her *entire* body, from her head to her toes (Beep 4.1; pp. 139–165)? Or that the Greek woman in Melanie's complex, sprawling image while reading was looking to Melanie's right and 'gesturing a little bit' with her hands (Beep 2.1; pp. 95–108)? Or that, while driving, Melanie experienced an awareness, or a knowledge, of being anxious about keeping an appointment as being located in the back of her head (Beep 5.1; pp. 167–189)?

Russ, himself, also seems to appreciate the value of corroborated self-reports, for his impressive case of Fran, a woman with borderline personality disorder and no demonstrable figure-ground sense in vision or imagery, has been recounted in many of his books and papers, including this one (e.g. Hurlburt, 1993; 1997; Hurlburt and Heavey, 2001; 2004; Hurlburt and Schwitzgebel, 2007; see also Russ's explicit discussion of the desirability of objective corroboration on pp. 274–276). My own sympathy for Eric's call for corroboration probably reflects my training in experimental cognitive psychology, where mental processes are typically observed indirectly, or inferred, via outward behaviours (such as response latency, or recall accuracy) and in response to controlled environmental conditions. It is thus rare that one finds introspective data published in cognitive psychology journals that are not systematically validated against convincing behavioural evidence.

Indeed, take the inner-experience example of mind-wandering, which has inspired a modest but growing laboratory-based empirical literature since Antrobus and Singer began studying 'stimulus-independent thought' in the 1960s (e.g. Antrobus, 1968; Antrobus and Singer, 1964; Antrobus, Singer and Greenberg, 1966), and which recently has been revived as the study of 'task-unrelated thought' or 'mind-wandering' (e.g. Giambra, 1989; 1995; Grodsky and Giambra, 1990–91; Smallwood, McSpadden and Schooler, 2007; Smallwood and Schooler, 2006). As Russ notes regarding Melanie's tooth-brushing sample, where she claimed to have let her mind wander (Beep 2.4; see pp. 123–126), the concept and phenomenology of 'mind-wandering' might be understood quite differently by different people. Moreover, most lab studies provide minimal instruction to subjects about how to accurately apprehend and report off- versus on-task thoughts or experiences. Russ thus argues that a DES procedure that iteratively trains subjects to observe their experiences might be critical to obtaining accurate reports about mind-wandering and related phenomena (see also Heavey and Hurlburt, 2008; Hurlburt and Akhter, 2006).

Yet, despite Russ's concerns (and Eric's likely scepticism, as well), the empirical data make plain that laboratory mind-wandering reports are impressively verifiable: They vary systematically with task practice and fatigue (e.g. Antrobus, Coleman and Singer, 1967; McVay and Kane, 2009; Smallwood et al., 2004; Teasdale et al., 1995), with task difficulty (e.g. Antrobus, 1968; Antrobus et al., 1966; Giambra, 1995; Grodsky and Giambra, 1990–91; Teasdale et al., 1993), with alcohol consumption (Finnigan, Schulze and Smallwood, 2007; Sayette, Reichle and Schooler, 2009), with individual-differences characteristics, such as adult age, psychopathology, and objectively measured cognitive abilities (Giambra, 1989; McVay and Kane, 2009;

Shaw and Giambra, 1993; Smallwood, O'Connor and Heim, 2006), and even with neuroimaging signatures (Christoff *et al.*, 2009; Mason *et al.*, 2007; Smallwood *et al.*, 2008). Mind-wandering reports also reliably predict objective measures of ongoing task performance (e.g. McVay and Kane, 2009; Schooler, Reichle and Halpern, 2004; Smallwood *et al.*, 2004). My claim, then, is that simple — even simple-minded — probes of people's ongoing conscious experiences can provide incredibly convincing and useful data, both descriptively and theoretically. Time- and labour-intensive DES procedures are simply not necessary to learn *some* important things about people's inner experiences. And, while Russ's suggestions (pp. 274–276) for DES validation methods are interesting and worth pursuing, it seems that the intricate details yielded by DES methods will be much more difficult to verify objectively than are 'one-shot', gross assessments of particular types of theoretically relevant, common subjective experiences, such as mind-wandering.

Idiographic and Descriptive Versus Nomothetic and Hypothetico-Deductive Psychology

I make my living conducting individual-differences research, and so I resonated with Russ's stated desire for Psychology to take greater care in examining the individuals that make up our typically studied groups (pp. 257–260; see also Cronbach, 1957; Underwood, 1975; Vogel and Awh, 2008). As well, and unlike Eric (e.g. pp. 147–148, 187–189, 294–295), I have no difficulty accepting Russ's findings that some people's conscious experiences may be dramatically different from others': consider people who experience (to a greater or lesser degree, for they may be *dimensional*, rather than categorical) schizophrenia, synaesthesia, amnesia, autism, or spiritual ecstasy, to name just a few striking but uncommon flavours of human experience. As well, regarding Russ's and Eric's discussion about the Flavell's work with children (pp. 45–47, 271–274), I find it arbitrary that, on one hand, Eric is willing to accept that children are remarkably different from adults in their introspective ability to apprehend their own experiences, and yet, on the other hand, he is unwilling to accept that children are remarkably different from adults in their lived experiences themselves. In either case, we have an apparent developmental chasm that separates children from adults in brain functioning. I don't see why — in the absence of some compelling evidence (which there may well be) — we should consider, *a priori*, one kind of developmental or individual difference to be so much more probable than the other.

At the same time, I do not believe that all of psychological science must be as 'personally true' and 'truly personal' as Russ might be interpreted as advocating (e.g. pp. 257–260). Whereas getting to 'truly personal truths' does seem critical to good psychotherapy, compelling oral history, or a solid DES interview, there is surely a meaningful distinction to be made between scientific psychology and biography. To the extent that case studies contribute to psychological knowledge and discovery, they do so by going beyond themselves to point out new phenomena, questions, or directions for further research; the particular must contribute to the general. Although Russ does explicitly call for a science '…that starts with personal truths and builds toward the general/theoretical' (p. 259), a reader could be forgiven for interpreting the bulk of Russ's argument to be that theoretical generalizations beyond individuals are overwhelmingly premature and potentially obfuscating.

This would be a shame, for DES not only has the potential to contribute generalizable, scientific knowledge about consciousness (and individual differences therein), but it already has! Unfortunately, you really wouldn't know it from reading *Describing Inner Experience*, which gives short shrift to some of the most exciting and compelling findings from DES research. This recent research (which must be considered provisional, given the small samples involved) has been conducted by Russ and his colleagues in three broad areas, and some of it was published before *Describing Inner Experience* (see also Schwitzgebel, 2007). First, people who differ along objectively verifiable dimensions, such as overt speech rate, or psychopathological symptoms of schizophrenia, depression, Asperger's syndrome, hypomania, anxiety, or bulimia, also differ systematically from each other in particular aspects of their inner experiences (Doucette and Hurlburt, 1993; Hebert and Hurlburt, 1993; Hurlburt, 1990; 1993; Hurlburt, Happé and Frith, 1994; Hurlburt *et al.*, 2002). Note that only some of these dimensions (e.g. schizophrenia) might be expected to correlate with irregularities of language and communication, and so it is unlikely that all of these apparent group differences in conscious experience can be explained away as reflecting differences in *reporting on* conscious experience. Second, the testing of modest-sized, stratified samples of young adults (Heavey and Hurlburt, 2008) has suggested quantitative base rates of five broad categories of frequently occurring inner-experience phenomena: inner speech, inner seeing, unsymbolized thinking, feeling, and sensory awareness, all of which occur in about 20–30% of samples, overall, but with dramatic individual differences around the median rates. Third, by aggregating across the reports of hundreds of subjects who have undergone DES, Russ and colleagues have begun to intensively describe and characterize various categories of conscious phenomena that have been unknown to, or ignored by, mainstream consciousness research, such as unsymbolized thinking (Hurlburt and Akhter, 2008) and sensory awareness (Hurlburt, Heavey and Bensaheb, in press). Where I'd love to see this research go next, while replicating the findings above, is to use DES protocols that also ask subjects, after they've taken their notes about their inner experiences, to provide information about their context (where they were, who they were with, what activities they were engaged in) in order to discover whether individuals' experiences vary systematically with context, and further whether any such individual experience-by-context variation is generalizable to groups.

For now, though, the importance of these more nomothetic lines of DES work, these examples of Russ's 'hairy' science (p. 259) that builds from the particular to the general, derives partly from their providing means to validate DES reports. That is, if groups identified via some objective criteria, such as observable speech rate or psychiatric symptoms, consistently report different varieties of experience, and those varying reports are unlikely to be traced to mere language, biases, or folk beliefs, then Russ's case becomes stronger that DES pretty faithfully captures some aspects of inner experience. As well, if statistical regularities in the frequency of particular experience categories (such as inner speech or unsymbolized thinking) emerge from DES reports from different samples and, again, systematic influences of bias or folk belief can be provisionally ruled out, then DES rests on still firmer ground. I would, therefore, have appreciated Russ and Eric debating the merits and potential promise of these individual-within-group studies of DES; perhaps they might in their reply to this review.

Notes on My Sampling Experience

I had several concerns about acting as a DES subject, and some of them were quite similar to those of subjects who had gone before me (e.g. Akhter and Hurlburt, 2006), from '*Will sampling reveal personal information I am uncomfortable sharing?*' to '*Will I even be able to do this at all?*' Beyond these, however, my primary worry was that I wouldn't be able, in Russ's words, to 'bracket my presuppositions' about my experiences, given that I have published an introspective case study that makes claims about the everyday conscious experiences of people, like me, with TS (Kane, 1994). It wasn't that I was concerned about deliberately deceiving Russ or myself about my experiences, but instead that I might be more subtly biased, over-attending to any theory-confirming tactile or somatosensory experiences *as a response to the beeper* rather than simply apprehending those experiences *in light of the beeper*. Russ acknowledged my concerns and noted that I might or might not be able to overcome such biases, if I had them; we could only find out by giving DES a shot. I agreed.

Like some DES subjects, I found the sampling process to be very difficult (I believe that I told Russ I was 'despairing' on sampling Day 1). Whether it was due to the nature of my inner experiences, to my scientific knowledge about consciousness, to my fears of being biased, to particular aspects of my cognitive machinery, to my sampling for only three days, or to some combination of these factors (I believe that Russ would argue for the first of these), I never felt that I'd mastered the ability to apprehend my experience, and I rarely felt as confident about many details of my experiences as I thought that I should (or as confident as Melanie often seemed to be in her interviews). I certainly didn't feel confident about reporting the kinds of experiences, or the variety of experiences, that Melanie seemed to have had.

One apparently unusual reaction I had to sampling was that I found the beeper to be overwhelmingly disruptive. Before sampling began, I understood, cognitively, that the beeper would continue sounding until I physically switched it off by pressing a button on the unit I kept in my pocket. Yet I was unready for its impact. In fact, I was convinced, after the first few beeps on the first day, that I was losing *almost everything* about my momentary experiences when I subsequently turned my attention to fumbling with the device. My informal notes to myself following Day 1's Beep 4 ('Beep 1.4') reflect the difficulties I was having: 'Beep is killing me — that it keeps going and I have to turn it off. I'm having trouble apprehending. Need to "let go" of beep issue.' What subsequently worked better (but imperfectly) for me was to simply let the beep continue while I 'gathered up' my experiences and started note-taking; once I felt that I'd mentally solidified the experience, I shut the beeper off and finished my notes.[1]

---

[1] My significant difficulties with the beep lead me to wonder about others' experiences, and whether a controlled test comparing subjects whose beepers stayed on until disabled versus subjects whose beepers sounded briefly before going silent, might yield meaningfully discrepant rates or qualities of different experiential categories. Although Russ has apparently conducted some informal assessments of variations in the DES method, my sense is that it is time to engage in some more formal experimental tests and reports.

Although I won't dwell here on too many of the particulars of my experiences, as revealed by DES, some are worth sharing. Let me preface this discussion by noting how I would have characterized my inner experiences before sampling: (1) I am relatively introverted and introspective, spending a lot of time 'in my head', thinking about personal, political, and professional issues via inner-speech and inner-seeing simulations of events and exchanges; (2) As someone with TS, I am generally (i.e. when awake, almost always) 'hyper-aware' of bodily sensations and find myself producing tics as a means to quell the intensity of those sensations (Kane, 1994); (3) I almost always, even upon waking in the middle of the night, have a song running through my head.

So, how did DES characterize my experiences? To my surprise, I rarely reported inner speech, visual imagery, or anything else that most people (including me) would recognize as 'thoughts'. In fact, upon the conclusion of my sampling and the review of my reports with Russ, my inner life seemed so devoid of meaningful, semantic content that I found it a bit distressing. I don't fancy myself an intellectual or an artist, but shouldn't a professor and active scientist, one who's written at least pedestrian poetry and songs, muster an *occasional* thought about an abstract idea — or even a concrete one? My distress also likely followed from the simple, surprising conflict between what I'd thought about my inner world and the portrait of it painted by DES.

What I actually found — what DES found — was that the majority of my experiences were sensory, with most of these being either visual or auditory and only some somatosensory.[2] For example, at beep 1.5, I seemed most aware of the red markings on a white board (without considering their meaning; they were written words) behind the person I was speaking to, along with the feeling of my gesturing hands moving up and down together; at beep 2.2, I was watching the cascading honey mustard that I was pouring onto my son's plate and hearing myself ask him — as I often do — to say 'thank you' (*'What d'you sa-ay?'*); at beep 2.6, I watched the pattern of faucet water pouring into a bowl of moose-tracks ice cream while I swirled and cleaned it, hearing myself innerly singing the opening guitar riff from Alice Cooper's *'School's Out'*, and feeling my lips pursed tightly; at beep 3.1, I

---

[2] I should also note here that, despite my never quite understanding or believing the published DES-revealed experiences that Russ calls 'unsymbolized thinking', I had two likely unsymbolized-thinking experiences in my second sampling day (beeps 2.4 and 2.5); I didn't use this label at the time, but to the extent that I accurately apprehended those experiences, they very much seemed to involve clear semantic content yet no visual or verbal imagery or symbols.

was primarily engaged by the deep pink blooms of a Tonto Crape Myrtle tree I was walking past (noticing its visually 'popping' against the deep-grey brick wall behind it), along with an inner hearing of the chorus of Paul Simon's *'Mother and Child Reunion'*. In all of these cases (and in several others), the primacy of sensory phenomena reflected my own initial interpretations of the experiences, being explicitly present in my notes and in my raw reports to Russ, prior to his questioning.

Those experiences thus seemed pretty clear and compelling to me. At the same time, I could not shake the concern that at least some of my reported sensory experiences during sampling resulted from my inferring them as a result of the beep. Even on the second and third sampling days, I sometimes felt jolted by the beep and left to put the pieces back together by noting my experience subsequent to the beep. That is, I was not always sure that I had been aware of a visual stimulus at the moment of the beep, rather than simply looking at it once I 'came to' from the beeping.[3] Perhaps my sensory observations on these occasions were compromised somewhat by facts of the situation (*I am now looking at a Crape Myrtle*), which DES pushed me to rapidly fashion into an experience that made sense to me (*I was 'seeing' the Crape Myrtle*). Moreover, on at least five of 12 occasions on the second and third sampling days, I felt a nagging certainty that I'd been having a semantic, non-sensory thought experience in the moment before the beep, but the beep seemed to have wiped it out entirely (beeps 2.1, 2.6, 3.2, 3.4, 3.6). Best I can tell, this wasn't just 'wishful thinking'; I experienced it as a tip-of-the-tongue kind of phenomenon (see Brown, 1991). It is therefore possible, I think, that my experiences, as they are normally lived, often have more semantic content than DES revealed. But even if that is, in fact, the case (it may well not be), I must remain surprised by how fleeting and ephemeral those semantic thoughts are and how poorly I'm able to access them. They have seemed so robust to me in my normal daily life, for example while I absentmindedly shampoo my hair in the shower or mow my lawn, or while I purposefully compose arguments against political blog posts or for formal papers like these. Interesting!

---

[3] These experiences of difficulty in isolating the pre-beep experience caused me to become much more sceptical of the reports in Eric's (2007) rich-versus-thin DES study than I had been before sampling. Recall that Eric's subjects were asked to report on peripheral, non-salient aspects of their experience, such as awareness of their left foot; my experiences tell me that I would have had terrible difficulties knowing whether any such experiences had actually been occurring in the absence of the beeping cue to attend to them.

Thoughts About DES, and the Book, After Sampling

How do I then consider Melanie's — and my — DES reports? As a reader, and a research psychologist who studies attention, memory, and conscious experience in the laboratory, I found it reasonable to trust the broad strokes of Melanie's raw reports, but I felt more sceptical about the surprising (at least, to me and to Eric) level of detail she was able to convey in response to Russ's and Eric's questions. In the same way, I trust some of my reports about some of my experiences, but I remain a bit more sceptical of others. As a DES veteran, my general evaluation of the method's promise is probably about the same as it was before (which is pretty optimistic), but like Russ's and Eric's separate positions after completing their book project, I feel as though I have gained a richer, deeper understanding of the issues at hand.

If I'm sure of one thing, it's that DES reports may sometimes come as a surprise to the subject making those very reports. Russ has mentioned this fact before (e.g. pp. 266–268; Hurlburt *et al.*, in press) and I reiterate it here to suggest that it might count to Eric as a decidedly modest sort of validation for the method: these occasions demonstrate that, at the very least, DES subjects are not driven entirely to confirm their folk beliefs about inner experience, and their memories (and reports) of experience aren't spoiled rotten by schema-consistent inferences. In my case, one might be reasonably sceptical of my frequent reports of bodily awareness, given that I have a dog in the theoretical hunt concerning TS (Kane, 1994). At the same time, I don't see a similar reason to doubt my general reports of visual or auditory awareness. I had absolutely no prior sense that I paid particular attention to such sensory details of external events; in fact, I would have denied, and I'm still astonished by, these apparent facts. Yet I have found myself (mostly) believing (many of) them because they simply seemed self-evident, in an informal sense, too straightforward and obvious to ignore or explain away.

Another reason I've come to believe at least some of my sensory-experience reports as 'pretty accurate' is that they are provisionally corroborated by similar reports of sensory awareness in the literature. As I noted above, Russ and his colleagues have recently begun to generalize from their subjects' 'truly personal' reports some broad descriptions of particular varieties of common but underappreciated inner experiences, such as unsymbolized thinking and sensory awareness. After my DES sampling was complete, Russ thought my sensory awareness experiences to be so strikingly dominant in my reports that he shared with me the Hurlburt *et al.* (in press) paper on sensory awareness. Although I am mindful of the snare of so-called 'P.T. Barnum effects' (e.g. Dickson and Kelly, 1985; Forer, 1949), I can't help but see strong parallels between my own DES experiences and those described by other subjects, beyond their obvious concern with the qualities of sensory phenomena (see also Akhter and Hurlburt, 2006): people who frequently experience sensory awareness are often especially confused (or disheartened) about their sampling on the first DES days, in part because they don't recognize such phenomena as 'counting' as inner experience; reports of sensory awareness are thus overlooked or denied early on in sampling; people with frequent sensory awareness also tend to be surprised at the extent of it that emerges from DES, perhaps because these phenomena are so fleeting, nonverbal, seemingly trivial, or personal, they are not much reflected upon in daily life (Hurlburt *et al.*, in press). Indeed, after my last DES interview, before discussing with Russ his interpretation of my samples, I took the following notes to myself:

> I don't think I'm very good at this; I'm not getting the semantic stuff that I know is there at other times... All I'm getting is the obvious, the basic, the perceptual; I'm missing all the interesting stuff!

Finally, with respect to the validity of my own DES reports, I wonder whether my frequent sensory awareness might provide a clue to my strong reactions to the beep. If, as studies of 'perceptual masking' seem to indicate (e.g. Turvey, 1973), brief sensory phenomena are especially vulnerable to interference from other perceptual events (such as shifts of visual attention to the buttons on the beeper unit), and if auditory stimuli (like the beep) are especially powerful in capturing attention (see Johnson and Proctor, 2004), then one might expect that people with frequent sensory-awareness reports in DES might have particular difficulty apprehending those experiences in the wake of the beeper. I cannot say whether anecdotal reports of DES subjects support this conjecture, but it seems possible, albeit difficult, to test empirically.

Indeed, through the processes of considering carefully the contents of *Describing Inner Experience*, as well as through my own DES experience, I am optimistic that DES has opened, and will continue to open, many interesting and important questions about consciousness to empirical test, particularly those about the broader characteristics of various domains of inner experience. I therefore find that DES deserves a proper place at the scientific table of consciousness studies, and that it may someday, as I had hoped, provide useful data on those questions that are nearest my own heart, regarding TS phenomenology and perhaps, used along with more prototypical experience-sampling techniques that assess the influence of contextual variables, regarding the nature of mind-wandering experiences, too.

References

Akhter, S. & Hurlburt, R.T. (2006) A sampling journal: Learning about DES, in Hurlburt, R.T. & Heavey, C.L., *Exploring Inner Experience: The Descriptive Experience Sampling Method*, pp. 133–149, Amsterdam: John Benjamins.

Antrobus, J.S. (1968) Information theory and stimulus-independent thought, *British Journal of Psychology*, **59**, pp. 423–430.

Antrobus, J.S., Coleman, R. & Singer, J.L. (1967) Signal-detection performance by subjects differing in predisposition to daydreaming, *Journal of Consulting Psychology*, **31**, pp. 487–491.

Antrobus, J.S. & Singer, J.L. (1964) Visual signal detection as a function of sequential variability of simultaneous speech, *Journal of Experimental Psychology*, **68**, pp. 603–610.

Antrobus, J.S., Singer, J.L. & Greenberg, S. (1966) Studies in the stream of consciousness: Experimental enhancement and suppression of spontaneous cognitive processes, *Perceptual and Motor Skills*, **23**, pp. 399–417.

Bliss, J. (1980) Sensory experiences of Gilles de la Tourette syndrome, *Archives of General Psychiatry*, **37**, pp. 1343–1347.

Brown, A.S. (1991) A review of the tip of the tongue experience, *Psychological Bulletin*, **109**, pp. 204–223.

Christoff, K., Gordon, A.M., Smallwood, J., Smith, R. & Schooler, J.W. (2009) Experience sampling during fMRI reveals default network and executive system contributions to mind wandering, *Proceedings of the National Academy of Sciences*, **106**, pp. 8719–8724.

Cronbach, L.J. (1957) The two disciplines of scientific psychology, *American Psychologist*, **12**, pp. 671–684.

Csikszentmihalyi, M., Larson, R. & Prescott, S. (1977) The ecology of adolescent activity and experience, *Journal of Youth and Adolescence*, **6**, pp. 281–294.

Dickson, D.H. & Kelly, I.W. (1985) The 'Barnum Effect' in personality assessment: A review of the literature, *Psychological Reports*, **57**, pp. 367–382.

Doucette, S. & Hurlburt, R.T. (1993) Inner experience in bulimia, in Hurlburt, R.T., *Inner Experience in Disordered Affect*, pp. 153–164, New York: Plenum Press.

Finnigan, F., Schulze, D. & Smallwood, J. (2007) Alcohol and the wandering mind: A new direction in the study of alcohol on attentional lapses, *International Journal on Disability and Human Development*, **6**, pp. 189–199.

Forer, B.R. (1949) The fallacy of personal validation: A classroom demonstration of gullibility, *Journal of Abnormal and Social Psychology*, **44**, pp. 118–123.

Giambra, L.M. (1989) Task-unrelated thought frequency as a function of age: A laboratory study, *Psychology and Aging*, **4**, pp. 136–143.

Giambra, L.M. (1995) A laboratory method for investigating influences on switching attention to task-unrelated imagery and thought, *Consciousness and Cognition*, **4**, pp. 1–21.

Grodsky, A. & Giambra, L.M. (1990–91) The consistency across vigilance and reading tasks of individual differences in the occurrence of task-unrelated and task-related images and thoughts, *Imagination, Cognition and Personality*, **10**, pp. 39–52.

Heavey, C.L. & Hurlburt, R.T. (2008) The phenomena of inner experience, *Consciousness and Cognition*, **17**, pp. 798–810.

Hebert, J. & Hurlburt, R.T. (1993) Inner experience in anxiety, in Hurlburt, R.T., *Inner Experience in Disordered Affect*, pp. 189–196, New York: Plenum Press.

Hurlburt, R.T. (1990) *Sampling Normal and Schizophrenic Inner Experience*, New York: Plenum Press.

Hurlburt, R.T. (1993) *Sampling Inner Experience in Disturbed Affect*, New York: Plenum Press.

Hurlburt, R.T. (1997) Randomly sampling thinking in the natural environment, *Journal of Counseling and Clinical Psychology*, **65**, pp. 941–949.

Hurlburt, R.T. & Akhter, S.A. (2006) The Descriptive Experience Sampling method, *Phenomenology and the Cognitive Sciences*, **5**, pp. 271–301.

Hurlburt, R.T. & Akhter, S.A. (2008) Unsymbolized thinking, *Consciousness and Cognition*, **17**, pp. 1364–1374.

Hurlburt, R.T., Happé, F. & Frith, U. (1994) Sampling the form of inner experience in three adults with Asperger's syndrome, *Psychological Medicine*, **24**, pp. 385–395.

Hurlburt, R.T. & Heavey, C.L. (2001) Telling what we know: Describing inner experience, *Trends in Cognitive Sciences*, **5**, pp. 400–403.

Hurlburt, R.T. & Heavey, C.L. (2004) To beep or not to beep: Obtaining accurate reports about awareness, *Journal of Consciousness Studies*, **11** (7–8), pp. 113–128.

Hurlburt, R.T. & Heavey, C.L. (2006) *Exploring Inner Experience: The Descriptive Experience Sampling Method*, Amsterdam: John Benjamins.

Hurlburt, R.T., Heavey, C.L. & Bensaheb, A. (in press) Sensory awareness, *Journal of Consciousness Studies*.

Hurlburt, R.T., Koch, M. & Heavey, C.L. (2002) Descriptive Experience Sampling demonstrates the connection of thinking to externally observable behavior, *Cognitive Therapy and Research*, **26**, pp. 117–134.

Hurlburt, R.T. & Schwitzgebel, E. (2007) *Describing Inner Experience? Proponent Meets Skeptic*, Cambridge, MA: MIT Press.

Johnson, A. & Proctor, R.W. (2004) *Attention: Theory and Practice*, Thousand Oaks, CA: Sage.

Kane, M.J. (1994) Premonitory urges as 'attentional tics' in Tourette's Syndrome, *Journal of the American Academy of Child and Adolescent Psychiatry*, **33**, pp. 805–808.

Mason, M.F., Norton, M.I., Van Horn, J.D., Wegner, D.M., Grafton, S.T. & Macrae, C.N. (2007) Wandering minds: The default network and stimulus-independent thought, *Science*, **315**, pp. 393–395.

McVay, J.C. & Kane, M.J. (2009) Conducting the train of thought: Working memory capacity, goal neglect, and mind wandering in an executive-control task, *Journal of Experimental Psychology: Learning, Memory, and Cognition*, **35**, pp. 196–204.

Prado, H.D., do Rosario, M.C., Lee, J., Hounie, A.G., Shavitt, R.G. & Miguel, E.C. (2008) Sensory phenomena in obsessive-compulsive disorder and tic disorders: A review of the literature, *CNS Spectrums*, **13**, pp. 425–432.

Sayette, M.A., Reichle, E.D. & Schooler, J.W. (2009) Lost in the sauce: The effects of alcohol on mind-wandering, *Psychological Science*, **20**, pp. 747–752.

Schooler, J.W., Reichle, E.D. & Halpern, D.V. (2004) Zoning out while reading: Evidence for dissociations between experience and metaconsciousness, in

Levin, D. (ed.) *Thinking and Seeing: Visual Metacognition in Adults and Children*, pp. 203–226, Cambridge, MA: MIT Press.

Schwitzgebel, E. (2007) Do you have constant tactile experience in your feet in your shoes? Or is experience limited to what's in attention?, *Journal of Consciousness Studies*, **14** (3), pp. 5–35.

Shaw, G.A. & Giambra, L.M. (1993) Task unrelated thoughts of college students diagnosed as hyperactive in childhood, *Developmental Neuropsychology*, **9**, pp. 17–30.

Smallwood, J., Beach, E., Schooler, J.W. & Handy, T.C. (2008) Going AWOL in the brain: Mind wandering reduces cortical analysis of external events, *Journal of Cognitive Neuroscience*, **20**, pp. 458–469.

Smallwood, J., Davies, J.B., Heim, D., Finnigan, F., Sudberry, M.V., O Connor, R.C. & Obonsawain, M.C. (2004) Subjective experience and the attentional lapse: Task engagement and disengagement during sustained attention, *Consciousness and Cognition*, **4**, pp. 657–690.

Smallwood, J.M., McSpadden, M. & Schooler, J.W. (2007) The lights are on but no one's home: Meta-awareness and the decoupling of attention when the mind wanders, *Psychonomic Bulletin and Review*, **14**, pp. 527–533.

Smallwood, J.M., O'Connor, R.C. & Heim, D. (2006) Rumination, dysphoria, and subjective experience, *Imagination, Cognition, and Personality*, **24**, pp. 355–367.

Smallwood, J.M. & Schooler, J.W. (2006) The restless mind, *Psychological Bulletin*, **132**, pp. 946–958.

Teasdale, J.D., Dritschel, B.H., Taylor, M.J., Proctor, L., Lloyd, C.A., Nimmo-Smith, I. & Baddeley, A.D. (1995) Stimulus-independent thought depends on central executive resources, *Memory and Cognition*, **23**, pp. 551–559.

Teasdale, J.D., Proctor, L., Lloyd, C.A. & Baddeley, A.D. (1993) Working memory and stimulus-independent thought: Effects of memory load and presentation rate, *European Journal of Cognitive Psychology*, **5**, pp. 417–433.

Turvey, M.T. (1973) On peripheral and central processes in vision, *Psychological Review*, **80**, pp. 1–52.

Underwood, B.J. (1975) Individual differences as a crucible in theory construction, *American Psychologist*, **30**, pp. 128–134.

Vogel, E. & Awh, E. (2008) How to exploit diversity for scientific gain: Using individual differences to constrain cognitive theory, *Current Directions in Psychological Science*, **17**, pp. 171–176.

Maja Spener

Using First-Person Data About Consciousness

Abstract: In Describing Inner Experience, *Hurlburt and Schwitzgebel explore the proper limits of scepticism about consciousness and the prospect of a scientific investigation of consciousness. Their debate with each other focuses on the question about whether we can trust people's reports about their inner experiences and on Hurlburt's introspective method, DES. I point out that their discussion leaves unclear the crucial question of the aims and objectives of DES. This makes it difficult genuinely to assess DES's merits and the problems for theorizing that might be created by inaccuracy in the introspective data. I then provide a taxonomy of different introspective methods, depending on different roles played by introspective data and on the kinds of questions that are being asked. I suggest that introspective methods tasked to answer a certain group of questions — certain philosophical questions about experience — are more vulnerable to the possibility of introspective error than others.*

In *Describing Inner Experience*, Russ Hurlburt and Eric Schwitzgebel set out on a joint project to investigate DES, a method to collect data about our conscious states and episodes via subjects' introspective reports about them. DES requires subjects to wear an alarm as they go about their normal lives, which beeps at random intervals. Subjects are instructed to introspect and record their experiences when the beep goes off. The target is the last undisturbed experiential moment immediately before the beeper sound. An interview about these introspected experiences is conducted by a trained interviewer within 24 hours.

Correspondence:
Email: maja.spener@philosophy.ox.ac.uk

The two co-investigators come with very different perspectives: psychologist Hurlburt has developed, practised and defended DES over the past twenty years, philosopher Schwitzgebel has spent the last decade or so arguing for scepticism about introspective access to our conscious lives and he is accordingly critical about introspection-based methodologies to explore consciousness. What unites them in this project is an earnest desire to advance their own thinking by submitting their views to the critical scrutiny of the opposite camp. In pursuing this project, they both aspire to give their opponent's arguments due consideration and to be open-minded about the outcome of the project. Neither of them considers themselves radical in their respective views: acknowledgment of serious problems with introspective methodologies on the one hand, and the thought that introspection must deliver *something* of value on the other, is common ground between them. However, Hurlburt is optimistic that DES overcomes most of the well-documented problems that besets other introspective methodologies and that, via DES, valuable data about consciousness can be secured. Schwitzgebel, by contrast, is doubtful that there is such a method to be found. Correspondingly, he is less positive about finding a rational basis for his belief that introspection cannot sensibly be held a total disaster. In this way, Hurlburt and Schwitzgebel both emphasize, their investigation is not just about the merits of DES, but about the proper limits of scepticism concerning our introspective access to consciousness and the prospect of a fruitful scientific investigation of consciousness.

It is hard to see how much progress Hurlburt and Schwitzgebel make towards these goals. At the end of the book, neither of them has shifted their original perspective in serious ways. If anything, they have become more confident in their divergent views about core issues. One might expect genuine, sustained dialogue to produce more agreement than that. But while the dialogue between them in the book certainly is sustained, there is a lack of real engagement in crucial places. When it comes to key issues, Hurlburt and Schwitzgebel often talk past each other.

The main reason for this is that Hurlburt's and Schwitzgebel's interest in conscious experience is different and consequently they place different demands on an introspective methodology. This divergence of interest never gets discussed in detail — although both do touch upon this issue, they do not do so until at the very end of the book in their respective *Reflections*. It would have helped to have the question of aims and objectives out in the open right up front. After all, DES cannot reasonably be criticized for failure to help with debate on a given topic if DES is not designed to provide results bearing on the issues involved.

One reason the question of aims and objectives is not discussed up front is probably that DES, as practised by Hurlburt, does not actually have a clearly defined objective. At a given beep, Hurlburt says that DES subjects are instructed to tell 'the truth, the whole truth and nothing but the truth' in describing their experiences. DES interviewers, in turn, aim to 'discover the complete truth' (p. 22). Moreover, in some interviews, Hurlburt asks Melanie whether she has reported everything about her experience at the moment of the beep with questions like 'Is there anything else in this beep?' (first interview); p. 78: 'Is there anything else in your awareness [at the moment of the beep]?; and p. 123: 'And is that it, in your awareness?' This suggests that DES tries to elicit accurate and exhaustive descriptions of each subject's experience at the moment of each beep, leaving no aspect of experience unreported. Yet, Hurlburt cautions readers not to expect too much from DES, saying that 'the aim of DES is not to be exhaustive but to be accurate about as much of experience as possible' (p. 74, see also p. 255). And even in this modified statement of DES's aim, the standard of accuracy involved must be further moderated. Hurlburt acknowledges that DES will frequently yield observations and reports that are likely incorrect, especially in specific details. He is open about distorting interference from subjects' faulty memory and susceptibility to confabulation, as well as interviewers' bias in asking questions. But he nonetheless thinks that DES results in observations about conscious experience that are broadly accurate, with the (trained) subject's reports being 'pretty good' (p. 262) or 'pretty darn good' (p. 253).

So, what do these broadly accurate reports about experience elicited by DES do for us? What can we learn about conscious experience with the help of DES? According to Hurlburt, a science of conscious experience must start with randomly sampled reports of individual subjects, gathered while bracketing presuppositions on the part of both interviewer and interviewee. Bracketing guarantees whatever accuracy there is to be had from introspective reports. But the extent of presuppositions to be bracketed is rather wide-ranging, including particular theoretical questions one might have about conscious experience. In other words, the scientist must begin merely with a general interest in conscious experience when she starts sampling to collect data. Starting with a particular theoretical focus in mind would warp the phenomenon to be investigated. This is the main mistake, according to Hurlburt, to which early introspectionist psychologists fell prey

(p. 269): they engaged in what he calls 'theory-driven objective studies' (pp. 274ff). By contrast, he says, a proper science of conscious experience ought to undertake 'experiential-phenomenon-driven objective studies'. Roughly, the idea is that our theoretical interest in specific aspects of conscious experience ought to be guided by characteristics emerging from a large enough randomly sampled pool of data about conscious experience which in turn is collected in an interest-free manner by DES. Once we have a picture of what the various conscious phenomena are like as one actually finds them among individuals, one can start developing a theoretical interest investigating them further.

Hurlburt's point here is that the science of consciousness has to concern itself with what is actually there and not go on a wild goose chase, collecting expectation-driven data which misrepresents conscious experience. His complaint seems to be that usually scientists roll what ought to be two steps into one step, they collect data and construct theories at the same time, thereby forming the data to suit their needs and missing the actual phenomenon. This suggests that DES is meant to be merely the first step in a proper procedure, namely collecting data in an interest-free way, not driven by expectation. The debate between Hurlburt and Schwitzgebel on this point is merely whether, and to what extent, DES is successful in collecting accurate data about conscious experience. As we have seen, even Hurlburt thinks that DES cannot overcome all limitations, but that the observations are overall accurate. Schwitzgebel concedes that DES probably tells us something accurate about experience, but he has little faith in the specific information contained in the data. Considered on its own, their disagreement and extent of agreement on this point is of little interest. The difference between them is a matter of degree. Not much is at stake unless the data is put to theoretical use.

But what of the theorizing? Once the data are collected in an interest-free way, can the scientist ask her questions just as before? This is where the dispute between Hurlburt and Schwitzgebel becomes substantive. For this is where Hurlburt's DES might make promises it does not deliver, or where Schwitzgebel's scepticism might be shown to be mistaken. Unfortunately it is unclear what Hurlburt's position is. On the one hand, he seems to think that certain questions that have been asked by scientists in the field simply cannot be answered with the help of DES (or any other currently available introspective method). He gives different reasons for this limitation. Sometimes he says that those questions themselves are misguided in that they do not track anything in the experiential phenomena they are allegedly about. Instead, he proposes that the actual characteristics of a given experiential phenomenon as revealed by DES prompt a set of different questions altogether (see, e.g. his discussion of mental imagery studies, p. 275). At other times, Hurlburt insists that certain questions cannot be answered by DES because while there is a fact of the matter tracked by these questions, DES does not deliver the level of detail/clarity to be able to settle these questions (e.g. p. 278) — and it should not be expected to do so. He uses questions from the early introspectionist literature (Titchener *vs.* the Würtzberg School) as an example.

In other places again, though, when it comes to questions that demand a level of detail/clarity beyond the reach of DES, Hurlburt is less pessimistic about limitations inherent in DES. Even in such circumstances, he suggests that DES-based observations about experience can 'incline' one to a particular answer, or support reasonable speculation. While this sort of support should not be taken to be confirmation beyond doubt, it is at least a species of *prima facie* confirmation that needs compelling reason to the contrary to be overturned (p. 278).

So before one can evaluate the data collected by DES with respect to a particular theoretical task, one first has to know whether the question is one that DES is designed to deal with and how. Moreover, if Schwitzgebel criticizes DES with a particular question about conscious experience in mind, Hurlburt's response presumably depends on his view of what sort of question it is. The trouble is that there is often not enough clarity on this point and this seriously hampers understanding of DES as well as preventing genuine progress in Hurlburt and Schwitzgebel's project. In particular DES's lack of precise objective makes it difficult for Schwitzgebel to connect with Hurlburt and to make headway with his own concerns. *Describing Inner Experience*'s recurring theme of the debate between rich *versus* thin views of consciousness is a case in point. This topic has been a focus of critique in Schwitzgebel's work, where the general thrust of his sceptical stance is that introspection cannot help settle the matter and that this failure indicates the disastrous state of the science of consciousness. Unsurprisingly, Schwitzgebel ties assessment of DES's success *inter alia* to this question about rich and thin views of consciousness. And, throughout the book he worries that DES does not particularly advance the position. Schwitzgebel rightly notes that in response to his concerns, Hurlburt 'waver[s] between restraint when pushed... and a stronger denial of the rich view when [he's] not on guard...' (p. 75).

While it is relatively easy to point out that someone else does not give due attention to a certain issue, it is typically much harder to figure out what positively doing so involves exactly. The key issue as I see it is this. Hurlburt and Schwitzgebel frame the book as an attempt to address the question 'Can we believe people's reports about their inner experiences?' (p. 13). But, without further specification, this question has not much bite. For the intuitive answer is: sometimes yes, sometimes no. Most, those of us with a sceptical bent included, would accept that one can believe a subject's report that she is having a conscious experience of some sort right now, or that she is currently in pain, or that she is having a visual experience. This is because we assume that people are not radically mistaken about their conscious lives and that they get the basic stuff right a lot of the time. The uninformative answer above reflects this minimal common ground. What we really want to know is whether we can trust people's introspective reports *enough* — enough to do some theorizing, that is. In order to make the question relevant to a discussion of the soundness of introspective methodology, then, we need to be more specific about the role of subject's reports in the affair. There are several aspects to consider.

One is that we need to specify what question or questions the reports are supposed to help answer. The accuracy of introspective reports can properly only be evaluated with respect to a specific question that the introspective method employed is tasked to answer. Of course, since the general purpose of introspection-based methods is to investigate the mind, the reports are to be accurate about mental states, episodes and processes. But this general gloss makes room for a whole manner of different questions about the mind concerning different levels of description. Not all of these should be expected to be within, or near enough within, introspection's ken and thus introspective reports should not be expected to be accurate about them. For example, we should not, and nobody presumably would, expect subject's introspective reports about painful experiences to be accurate with respect to questions about the evolutionary origin of pain. On the other hand, as I said above, we would expect such reports to be accurate with respect to the presence of a painful experience. These two examples constitute extreme ends of a whole range of possible questions. The difficulty is to decide which questions inside these extremes are in and which are out. I will return to this issue later.

A second aspect to consider when thinking about the role of introspective reports in one's introspective methodology is that there are different ways to conceive of the evidential import of subjects' reports, resulting in different ways of using the data to support one's conclusions. Let us distinguish first between introspection as a mental activity on the one hand, and introspection as a procedure of investigation on the other. By the former I mean a kind of mental activity, namely first-person reflection upon one's mental condition.[1] By the latter I mean a particular technique in conducting a theoretical enquiry. In both cases one might speak of a method, but I will reserve the terms 'introspective methodology' and 'introspective method' for the latter and 'introspection' for the former. A given methodology is introspective in so far as it employs data delivered by introspection to derive its hypotheses. This employment can take different forms, resulting in different types of introspective methodologies.

Firstly, there are different ways of handling the data, what I will call third-person and first-person uses of introspective data. Some theorists collect introspective data from an independent pool of subjects (for example, scientists conducting experiments designed to elicit such data from a group of subjects). This constitutes a third-person use of introspective data. Other theorists collect introspective data by introspecting their own experiences (for example, philosophers reasoning on the basis of reflection on their experience). This constitutes a first-person use of introspective data.

Secondly, there are potential differences depending on the generalizing moves involved. In the first instance, first-person reflection concerns a particular mental token of the individual subject. However, theorists using introspection to investigate about the mind generalize in either or both of two ways: (i) the data delivered is held to support conclusions about the individual subject's mind in general, about her mental types and features, or (ii) it is held to support such conclusions beyond the individual subject about the human mind in general (*cf.* Hatfield, 2005). Arguably most theorists endeavour to make claims about the human mind in general and not just about individual subjects.

Thirdly, there are various possibilities as to what sort of hypothesis-confirming information the introspective data is supposed to provide. Most straightforwardly, one might hold that the deliverance of introspection enables one to 'read off' the hypothesis in question. Short of this, one might still hold that it provides conclusive or near conclusive evidence in favour of one's hypothesis. Another possibility for instance is to hold that the deliverance of introspection provides the basis for an inference to the best explanation, where this inference can vary

---

[1] I do not want to suggest here that there is an underlying process in common to all and only instances of introspection or that there is a distinct mental faculty, introspection. Different kinds of processes might be involved for different mental targets, for instance (see, e.g. Prinz, 2004).

in strength, depending in part on other theoretical commitments and additional evidence from other sources.

In view of these three variables we can see that introspective methodologies might take very different shapes, depending on the role that introspective data play in establishing a given hypothesis. But clearly, different introspective methodologies are subject to different worries concerning their reliability and they are amenable to different ways of being patched up. Consider first the difference between introspective methodologies involving first-person and third-person uses of introspective data. It has been suggested that while the introspecting subject herself is plausibly *prima facie* warranted believing her introspective reports, the scientist who wants to use her introspective report in his theorizing faces higher standards of warrant *vis-à-vis* her report. In part this difference in standards stems from different epistemic requirements on laypersons' and scientists' respective enquiries. But also the scientist's relation to the introspective report is via testimony and this, too, introduces further reliability-compromising factors (Goldman, 2004, p. 6). Thus, introspective methodologies involving third-person uses may be vulnerable in ways that those involving first-person uses are not. This is particularly so if introspective methodologies involving first-person uses of introspective data can exploit any of the *prima facie* warrant attached to ordinary introspective judgments. Conversely, introspective methodologies involving third-person uses of introspective data have been defended in several places as capable of neutralizing various factors contributing to the unreliability of introspection itself. For example, Piccinini (2003; forthcoming) argues that given an appropriate conception of introspective data as output of a measurement instrument, such data meets the requirements for serving in a *bona fide* scientific methodology, namely that of being publicly available and subject to public validation procedures. Haybron (2007) shows that our introspective access to affective experience leaves us open to pervasive and gross error about such experience. If he is right, this casts doubt on the use of introspective data concerning affective experience and Haybron consequently claims that an individual ought to be rather wary of accepting her introspective judgments about her own current state of happiness. However, he also suggests that third-person use of introspective data in empirical studies can adapt and compensate in various ways (for instance by correcting for known biases, by focusing on information conveyed by the compromised reports rather than on what is directly reported on by the subject, or by sampling a large enough pool of subjects to ensure that certain idiosyncratic inaccuracies 'wash out'). This sort of defence is obviously not open to introspective methodologies involving first-person uses.

Moreover, worries and solutions about an introspective methodology differ according to how the evidential relation between introspective data and hypothesis is conceived. Reading the hypothesis off the introspective data means that the latter provides direct, and in that sense very strong, support for the former, certainly stronger than support on the basis of an inference to the best explanation does. But an inference to the best explanation allows for a looser and more flexible connection between introspective evidence and hypothesis. This makes the immediate case for the hypothesis less strong — and the introspective methodology less powerful — but at the same time it protects the methodology from certain objections based on denying that the features mentioned in the hypothesis are introspectable. For, those features do not have to be introspectable themselves; they merely have to figure relevantly in the most plausible explanation of what is in fact introspectable.

Let me now return to the issue of which questions one can and which one cannot reasonably attempt with an introspective methodology. Setting aside the clear 'ins and outs' I mentioned above, it should be evident that the decision concerning a given question depends in part on the kind of introspective methodology employed — not all are suitable, or equally suitable, to tackle the same questions. Consider questions about the cognitive architecture underlying certain kinds of mental states, e.g. what sort of processes and cognitive mechanisms are responsible for producing visual depth perception. We should not expect introspective data to be directly revealing about them; after all, introspective data consist in a personal-level description of experience, processes responsible for producing visual depth perception are sub-personal processes. Rather, introspective data hopefully provide valuable evidence about what depth experience is like which then can be used as a constraint on the explanatory hypothesis formulated in terms of underlying cognitive processes. None of these terms would show up in an introspective report in such experiences. Most likely, too, such introspective evidence is not the only constraint on theorizing; other behavioural evidence and perhaps evidence from non-behavioural sources have an important role to play as well. Thus, 'cognitive architecture questions' of this sort are not sensibly pursued by an introspective methodology that envisages introspective data to provide direct evidence for the favoured hypothesis (see also Goldman, 2004). It also seems that introspective methodologies involving third-person uses of introspective data are preferable. The goal is a theory of cognitive processes underlying depth perception in humans and introspective data is supposed to provide evidence for it, along with, or at least on a par with, other kinds of evidence. Drawing data from a large sample of subjects helps ensure that the data is relevant and representative of human cognitive architecture in general. This sample of data can include the theorist's own introspective report, of course. But if a theorist collected her data by merely observing her own behaviour and reporting on her own experience, the resulting theory would be less powerful (everything else being equal) than if she had collected data from a large pool of subjects.

So, returning to Hurlburt's and Schwitzgebel's framing worry — whether people's reports about their inner experiences are accurate — there is some good news for those introspective methodologies that involve third-person use of introspective data and inferences to the best explanation. For although cognitive-architecture-questions are not straightforwardly within the ken of introspection, introspective data is plausibly thought relevant to investigating some of them. And, given that methods involving third-person uses of introspective data allow for different ways to adjust in light of individual's introspective inaccuracies, introspective reports can be taken to be overall reliable indicators of various features of the mind. This can plausibly be maintained, albeit to a lesser extent, even if one shares Schwitzgebel's view that introspective reports about the conscious character of experience are very likely to be inaccurate about the details. On the one hand, general introspectively available features and regularities will suffice to use as indicators for underlying processes. On the other hand, the precise personal-level description of the feature might not matter too much in this context.

Let me turn now to a different group of questions, namely broadly speaking 'philosophical questions' about phenomenal consciousness. Examples are: is the character of visual experience exhausted by representational content? Does conscious thought have a *sui generis* phenomenology? Is perceptual experience fundamentally representational or relational? Is consciousness unified at a given moment? What are the objects (if any) of sound experience? Do we project colour onto the world? What kinds of properties does visual experience present to us? Theorists interested in these sorts of questions have long held, implicitly or explicitly, that introspective data plays a central role in tackling them. It is also fair to say, I think, that the introspective methodologies that they have employed and are currently employing typically involve first-person uses of introspective data.[2] One might wonder whether this prevalence of first-person use is due to circumstantial facts like convenience, an absence of appropriate labs in the work environment, etc. and whether third-person use could be substituted easily without changing the nature of the enquiry. In principle I don't see why not; however, in practice this might be difficult for some cases where a great amount of detail and subtlety is required. In fact, DES is a good example of the kind of time-consuming and exacting effort that this would require and Schwitzgebel's worries about it concerning memory and interviewer-biases are some of the obstacles that would need to be addressed.

More significantly, some of these broadly philosophical questions differ from cognitive architecture questions in that they seem to relate differently to conscious experience itself. As I have said above, introspective data can be thought to reveal something about conscious experience that in turn functions as a reliable indicator of whatever the sub-personal mental aspect is under investigation. So, introspective data can serve a useful purpose even if nothing in the content of the introspective reports actually literally says anything about that mental aspect. In fact, since cognitive architecture is something that is supposed to underlie conscious experience, and since the deliverance of introspection is as of conscious experience, we do not expect the character of the latter literally to reveal the former. But consider a question such as: what are the objects, if any, of auditory experience — do we perhaps hear sources of sounds like cars roaring by or sounds themselves? On the face of it, this is a question about the character of conscious auditory experience itself, about how auditory experience presents things to the subject in consciousness. We are here not asking for sub-personal psychological processes. In using introspective data to answer this question, it may thus seem hard to see how there could be much daylight between the content of the deliverance of introspection and what it is to indicate reliably. It does not seem that we can make much sense of introspective data that reliably indicates features of the content of conscious experience but where the deliverance of introspection itself has an entirely different subject-matter. In sum, concerning some questions of the broadly philosophical type there seems to be a closeness between introspective data and theories

---

[2] Although, of course, some of these questions have also been studied by means of third-person uses of introspective data, most prominently perhaps the question about whether conscious thought has a *sui generis* phenomenology. I am also not saying that they are exclusively investigated by philosophers.

putatively supported by the data which there is not in relation to the cognitive architecture questions.

This perceived closeness bolsters existing optimism that such philosophical questions can be successfully investigated by means of an introspective methodology: closeness of data to theory is generally held to be a good thing. Yet, that closeness makes introspective methodologies designed to answer some of these philosophical questions vulnerable to worries about introspective error in a special way. Given that I find myself at Schwitzgebel's end of the spectrum when it comes to an assessment of the possibility and pervasiveness of introspective error, on my view such worries warrant a somewhat less positive outlook than the one alluded to above (see, e.g. Spener, 2010; 2011).

Consider introspective methodologies that aim to read off the answer from the introspective data itself. In these cases there is no room to accommodate introspective error: if introspection delivers bad data, it delivers a bad theory. Suppose now we have good reason to be sceptical about people's capacity to report accurately most of the details of the conscious character of experience. Then, employing this method to draw anything but fairly trivial and general conclusions about conscious experience will yield conclusions that are ill-grounded (unless one has an independent argument to show that the introspective reports used in a given case are *bona fide*).

In fact, though, theorists dealing with these broadly philosophical questions do not always assume that their hypothesis can be more or less read off the introspective data. Some theorists are more modest about the power of introspective evidence. Instead, their idea is that introspective data can be used to give strong reason to endorse a given theory, or even more weakly, to strongly motivate that theory. Consider, for instance, Michael Tye's appeal to transparency (Tye, 2003). He concedes that the introspective evidence from reflection on ordinary perceptual experience does not positively show that representationalism about perceptual experience is true (he does think it positively shows that qualia theory is false, though). But, he maintains, it does provide the basis for an inference to the best explanation in favour of representationalism in conjunction with other arguments and background commitments. The representational nature of experience is not taken to be directly written in its introspectively available phenomenology, but it is taken to be illuminating that phenomenology in offering an adequate account of it. So, on the one hand, this sort of approach makes room for a gap between the content of the deliverance of introspection and the theory supported by that deliverance. On the other hand, though, the approach aspires to keep a close connection between introspected features and the properties by the theory. In some vague sense, this connection is supposed to bear significant explanatory weight.

One can find some motivation both for a gap and for a close connection between introspective data and theory. I said above that a philosophical question such as whether conscious experience is representational is more directly about conscious experience itself than typical sub-personal level questions about the processes underlying visual depth perception. But then again, what reason do we have to think that the former is a straightforwardly *personal*-level question, if by that we mean something that is part of the subject's conscious awareness in having the experience or reflecting on it? After all, it is a question about the metaphysical structure of experience. Perhaps we should not expect all metaphysical matters pertaining to experience, say about its causal nature or about its temporal nature, to be open to introspective reflection. We should not take for granted that experience wears its metaphysics on its sleeve. This thought creates some space between the introspective data and the theory it is serve as evidence for, if the philosophical question concerns metaphysical aspects of conscious experience.[3]

A close connection between them, however, can also be motivated. An important and widely accepted requirement on a philosophical theory of the nature of experience is that it is phenomenally adequate. Minimally, this is taken to mean that the theory must respect or not distort the phenomenal character of the experience. More substantially, though, phenomenal adequacy is taken sometimes to require that a theory renders intelligible what phenomenal character is, that it provides an explanation of it. If that is the aim, there cannot be too great a gap between the metaphysical structure posited by the theory and the introspective data about the conscious character of experience. This thought tightens the connection between introspective data and the theory it is to serve as evidence for.

To return to the main issue, is this sort of introspective methodology vulnerable to special worries of introspective error in the same way that the 'read-off' introspective methodology is? Recall that I am asking this question from Schwitzgebel's side of the divide: suppose one believes that we are very prone to making introspective mistakes about many of the details concerning the conscious character of our experience. The two thoughts just considered allow for a more nuanced

---

[3] As often, though, the issue is not likely to be clear-cut. The question about the objects of auditory experience, for example, does seem more appropriately concerned with the personal-level characterization of experience delivered by introspection.

judgment. To the extent that phenomenal adequacy tightens the connection between introspective data and theory, the vulnerability of the introspective methodology to worries about introspective error increases.[4] This is because the details about conscious character of experience delivered by introspection are taken to be reflective of the features postulated by the theory in a more direct way. Different details would dictate a different theory and importantly, introspective mistakes turn into theoretical mistakes. Against the background assumption that the chances of introspective error are high, this should lead one to be highly doubtful about the soundness of such an introspective methodology.

But to the extent that the first thought leads one to accept that there is a gap between introspective data and theory, the vulnerability of introspective methodology to worries about introspective error decreases. If metaphysical features, such as being representational or being relational are not expected to be directly reflected in the relevant introspective data, one might be able to allow for some mistakes in the exact details of the introspective report because these details do not determine one's choice of theory. Theorizing can be held to be more or less independent of the precise details introspectively reported, depending on how big a gap one thinks there is. When seen in this light, one should be hopeful that introspective data can provide some useful constraining evidence, even against the background assumption that the chances of introspective error are high. Of course, the bigger the gap, the less powerful introspective evidence becomes *vis-à-vis* other sources of evidence and the less heavy lifting such an introspective methodology can do all on its own.

There is good news and bad news, then, when it comes to assessing whether we can trust people's introspective reports enough to use them to investigate what I called 'broadly philosophical questions'. The good news is that I think we can — and should — find a useful role for introspective data in our theorizing even if we worry about pervasive introspective error. The bad news is that introspective data is not as powerful a constraint as thought by some, not even a *primus inter pares* when it comes to theorizing about conscious experience. In putting this forward I consider myself to be very much in agreement with Schwitzgebel's own views. Figuring out exactly how much of a constraint introspective data can provide given its limitations, even

---

[4] Unless we are talking about very general, uncontroversial features of conscious experience, such as that experience presents colour in some way or other to us. But many divergent theories about experience can account for that datum.

merely for those philosophical questions about the nature of experience I mentioned is, of course, far from easy.[5]

References

Goldman, A. (2004) Epistemology and evidential status of introspective reports, in Jack, A. & Roepstorff, A. (eds.) *Trusting the Subject? The Use of Introspective Evidence In Cognitive Science*, Vol. 2, Exeter: Imprint Academic.

Hatfield, G. (2005) Introspective evidence in psychology, in Achinstein, P. (ed.) *Scientific Evidence: Philosophical Theories & Applications*, Baltimore, MD: Johns Hopkins University Press.

Haybron, D. (2007) How do we know how happy we are?, *Nous*, **42** (3), pp. 394–428.

Hurlburt, R. & Schwitzgebel, E. (2007) *Describing Inner Experience? Proponent Meets Skeptic*, Cambridge, MA: MIT Press.

Piccinini, G. (2003) Data from introspective reports: Upgrading from common sense to science, in Jack, A. & Roepstorff, A. (eds.) *Trusting the Subject? The Use of Introspective Evidence In Cognitive Science*, Vol. 1, Exeter: Imprint Academic.

Piccinini, G. (forthcoming) First-person data, publicity, and self-measurement, *Philosopher's Imprint*.

Prinz, J. (2004) The fractination of introspection, in Jack, A. & Roepstorff, A. (eds.) *Trusting the Subject? The Use of Introspective Evidence In Cognitive Science*, Vol. 2, Exeter: Imprint Academic.

Spener, M. (2010) Introspective humility, co-authored with Bayne, T., *Philosophical Issues*, **20**.

Spener, M. (2011) Disagreement about cognitive phenomenology, in Bayne, T. & Montague, M. (eds.) *Cognitive Phenomenology*, Oxford: Oxford University Press.

Tye, M. (2003) Representationalism and the transparency of experience, in Gertler, B. (ed.) *Privileged Access*, Farnham: Ashgate.

---

[5] I am grateful to David Chalmers and Susanna Siegel for very helpful comments and suggestions.

Terry Horgan and
Mark Timmons

Introspection and the Phenomenology of Free Will: Problems and Prospects

Abstract: Inspired and informed by the work of Russ Hurlburt and Eric Schwitzgebel in their 'Describing Inner Experience', we do two things in this commentary. First, we discuss the degree of reliability that introspective methods might be expected to deliver across a range of types of experience. Second, we explore the phenomenology of agency as it bears on the topic of free will. We pose a number of potential problems for attempts to use introspective methods to answer various questions about the phenomenology of free-will experience — questions such as this: does such experience have metaphysical-libertarian satisfaction conditions? We then discuss the prospects for overcoming some of these problems via approaches such as Hurlburt's DES methodology, the so-called 'talk aloud' protocol, and forms of abduction that combine introspection with non-introspection-based forms of evidence.

> [V]oluntary actions, though generally neglected in psychology, have a distinctive phenomenology which can be studied both qualitatively and quantitatively. (Haggard and Johnson, 2003)

The work of Russ Hurlburt and Eric Schwitzgebel in their *Describing Inner Experience* represents a welcome interdisciplinary collaboration resulting in a series of fruitful exchanges which thereby advances

Correspondence:
Terry Horgan, University of Arizona   Email: thorgan@email.arizona.edu
Mark Timmons, University of Arizona   Email: mtimmons@u.arizona.edu

understanding of the prospects and challenges for Hurlburt's Descriptive Experience Sampling (DES) method in particular and introspectionist methodology in general.[1] We appreciate the invitation from the editors of the *Journal of Consciousness Studies* to participate in this book symposium, particularly in light of some of our recent work that makes contact with the sorts of issues Hurlburt and Schwitzgebel discuss.

Inspired and informed by their discussion, we would like to do two things in our commentary. First, we wish to say something about introspection and the degree of reliability any such method might be expected to deliver across a range of types of experience. Second, because, as philosophers, we are particularly interested in the reliability of introspectionist methodology for answering questions about phenomenology that are relevant to certain philosophical debates, we wish to explore, even if briefly, the phenomenology of agency as it bears on the topic of free will. In particular, we wish to raise and clarify certain difficulties that make the probing of agentive experiences a matter of some delicacy, and then explore (again, briefly) the prospects for successful introspectionist probing of such phenomenology. Clarification with the aim of posing certain questions that might guide enquiry is what, as philosophers, we think we can usefully contribute to issues that are largely (but not entirely) empirical.

I. Introspection and Impotence

How reliable might one expect any (known) method of introspection to be with respect to the details of one's experiences?[2] Speaking very generally and (we think) uncontroversially, the answer to this question is that there is a range of types of experience with respect to which the reliability of introspection varies from being infallible or nearly so to being completely impotent or nearly so, with many cases in between. We are particularly interested in questions about the limits of introspectionist enquiry as it bears on certain philosophical questions. And we propose to (tentatively) probe its limits by considering the prospects of introspection being able to deliver answers to questions about rather subtle aspects of one's agentive phenomenology. We

---

[1] All unchaperoned page references in the text are to *Describing Inner Experience*.

[2] We should note that henceforth we will use the term 'experience' to refer to those occurrent mental states — states of phenomenal consciousness — that constitute the subject matter of introspectionist enquiry. Hurlburt prefers the term 'inner experience' while Schwitzgebel prefers 'conscious experience' or just 'experience' for the subject matter of their joint enquiry. They briefly discuss this terminological issue on p. 15.

suspect that introspection alone will prove to be largely impotent in this regard. And if we are right, this fact would bear importantly on the philosophical controversy over free will, given the evidential role of introspection in this debate. In order to approach this issue, it will be useful to begin with some general remarks about the reliability of introspection.

If one considers the range of cases with respect to which introspection might be more or less reliable in revealing answers to questions about the contents of one's experiences, then toward one end of the spectrum, one would expect carefully guarded introspective beliefs — beliefs about certain aspects of the contents of one's occurrent experiences — to approach infallibility. Suppose one is well rested, not drunk, sick, or suffering from any maladies that would interfere with one's capacity to attend to one's own occurrent mental states, and suppose that one is staring at a uniformly red circle painted on a white sheet and is standing close enough so that one's visual awareness is completely filled by an experience of the red circle. And suppose as one attends carefully to one's visual experience, one forms the following belief about one's ongoing (subjective) experience: *I am now having an experience of reddishness*. This belief predicates a phenomenal property (reddishness) of one's occurrent experience, which, under the specified conditions, seems extremely unlikely to be mistaken.[3] In such cases, the room for error in one's introspective belief is quite narrow.

Melanie's introspective reports span the range from the admittedly narrow realm of the (nearly) infallible introspective beliefs to the realm of the highly fallible. Melanie's reports are not reports of simultaneous ongoing experience (a good deal of recall is involved), nor are the experiences being reported all perceptual (outer sensory) experiences involving a single sense modality, nor do they all involve simple, easy to classify gross features of experience that are nearly unmistakable upon careful attention. Now the general thought that any method of enquiry (including DES) will vary in its reliability under varying conditions is certainly not a bone of contention between our authors. Both agree that DES and perhaps all existing methods of introspection are very unreliable when subjects are asked to report (on the basis of introspection) the cognitive processes that led up to and produced some occurrent mental state, though subjects may be very

---

[3] Are such beliefs infallible? Well, it depends on how guarded the belief about one's experience is. Horgan and Kriegel (2007) argue that very carefully bracketed introspective beliefs about certain aspects of one's occurrent experience are or can be infallible.

reliable in describing certain aspects of the contents of those states.[4] Considering then just the contents of one's occurrent mental states, one main point of disagreement between Hurlburt and Schwitzgebel concerns the degree to which DES[5] can reliably help reveal aspects of phenomenological detail. Both are inclined to accept the 'exposed' reports[6] of their subject Melanie in which she is describing the grosser, more salient aspects of her sampled experiences. But Schwitzgebel is far more sceptical than is Hurlburt in trusting Melanie's exposed reports that concern matters of detail.[7]

We do not wish to weigh in on this particular dispute between our authors over their subject's exposed reports. But we are especially interested in questions about the limits of introspection concerning aspects of experience that are of particular concern to philosophers. For instance, at various places in the book the authors discuss the question of the relative 'richness' of one's total overall experience at a time. If one distinguishes types of experience according to a typical scheme of classification specifying various 'modes' of experience (e.g. visual, auditory, emotional, cognitive, agentive, etc.) one can ask with respect to the totality of one's conscious experience at a time how rich it is with respect to one's having experiences of the various types at the time in question. Call this the question of *inter-modal* richness. Advocates of inter-modal richness claim that at any time one's conscious experience is liable to *far* exceed any aspects of one's overall experience to which one is paying attention and is thus a focal point of attention at that time. Advocates of thin inter-modal views *restrict* conscious experience to what one is attending to at any moment, though they allow that there may be non-conscious occurrent processes related to various modalities that can have an effect on, for example, one's behaviour at the time in question. For instance, as one is sitting at one's desk absorbed in reading *Describing Inner Experience*, the unnoticed (and thus, on the thinness account, non-experienced) stimulus resulting from having a small rock in one's shoe may cause one to spontaneously move one's foot slightly so that the rock is no longer impinging upon one's skin. In between the rich and thin

---

[4] The widely held scepticism about the reliability of introspection with respect to the causes of one's experiences is largely owing to the famous paper by Nisbett and Wilson (1977) which is briefly discussed by our authors on pp. 26–27.

[5] The same question can be raised about any method of introspective enquiry.

[6] Exposed reports are those that result from employing DES methodology, and are contrasted with 'raw' reports that a subject offers without the aid of DES or other introspectionist methodology. See pp. 254–255.

[7] See Schwitzgebel's summary of such differences on pp. 293–294.

views are moderate views according to which experiences one is having at any time are liable to *somewhat* outrun one's focal attention. Hurlburt apparently embraces inter-modal thinness, while Schwitzgebel is more inclined toward a richer view.[8]

But in addition to disputes over inter-modal richness, there can be disputes over the relative richness of experiences of a single type. Call this *intra-modal* richness. This too comes up in the book in a number of places where, for example, Melanie is attempting to describe some of her (past) visual imagery experiences and where the issue under discussion is the extent to which these imagery experiences did include at the time they were being had the rich detail that she reports them as having.[9] The authors do not dispute whether or not various types of experience, particularly those associated with the five senses, can be rich in detail (though speaking for ourselves, our 'external' sensory experiences in any one mode tend to be far richer than any of our associated imagery experiences). They do dispute the extent to which Melanie's exposed reports accurately characterize the exact character of the experience she is attempting to describe. And, of course, if one is attempting to describe as much of one's experience as possible that occurs during a very brief time interval, one is not likely to be able to accurately report in detail those experiences with rich content. But in such cases, the problem may be due to the fact that the experience is both rich in detail and fleeting. Perhaps if one could somehow freeze the experience under scrutiny, one could provide a more thorough and more accurate description of its rich phenomenal characteristics, in which case the characteristics in question would be subject to introspective detection.

In addition to questions about the inter- and intra-modal richness of experience and the ability of introspection to reliably detect rich phenomenological detail, there are related questions about subtle features of various types of experience. That is, there may be experiences that possess a certain phenomenal character that resists reliable introspective detection because the character itself is a very subtle feature of the experience, or because the question one is asking about the character in question is itself a subtle question, or because the concepts figuring in the question one is asking are themselves subtle. Any one or a combination of these features may severely limit the power of

---

[8] See Schwitzgebel's discussion (pp. 228–234) of his DES inspired study on the issue of richness, and his (2007) article for extensive discussion.

[9] See, for instance, the discussion of Melanie's reports of her experiences at beep 2.1 on pp. 95–108.

known methods of introspection to answer some particular question about the phenomenal character of experience.

Consider the phenomenology of moral experience, for example. One main focus of philosophical interest in this topic is whether such experience has (as an aspect of its intrinsic nature) ontological objectivist purport — i.e. whether the experience is as-of objective, attitude-independent, in-the-world moral properties and relations. In recent years, we two have collaborated on a series of essays about moral phenomenology (Horgan and Timmons, 2005; 2007; 2008a; 2008b), and one claim we have defended is that unaided introspection cannot reliably answer this question about ontological objectivist purport (see especially Horgan and Timmons, 2008a).

Another case in point, which will be our focus here, involves certain questions about ordinary agentive experience — questions that are relevant to philosophical debates about free will. The issue we are interested in is whether introspectionist methodology alone can answer these questions.

II. Agentive Phenomenology and Free Will: Questions and Problems

Free will libertarians make two fundamental claims about the nature and reality of free choice and action.

> L.1. A particular action (or choice) of an agent A at a time t is truly free only if it was metaphysically possible at some slightly earlier time t-δ, consistently with the total actual situation that existed at t-δ and the total internal state of A at t-δ and the prevailing laws of nature, for A to refrain from performing that action (or making that choice) at t.

> L.2. Some actions and choices are (truly) free.

We will call claim L.1 the thesis of *metaphysical indeterminism for agency* (for short, just *metaphysical indeterminism*), and we will call claim L.2 the thesis of the *reality of freedom*. The core libertarian position is the conjunction of these two theses (the core 'hard incompatibilist' position is the conjunction of L.1 with the *negation* of L.2). Many libertarians (and also many hard incompatibilists) accept a further thesis:

> L.3. In so far as an agent freely acts (or freely chooses), the agent herself is a metaphysically fundamental determinative source of the action, above and beyond any internal states

(mental or non-mental) the agent is in; she exercises determinative control over action and choice in the manner of a godlike 'unmoved mover'.

We'll call this latter claim the thesis of *godlike metaphysical sourcehood*. Those who are committed to L.3 are also committed to L.1, and so any evidence for L.3 is also evidence for L.1.

Free will compatibilists embrace L.2, but repudiate both L.1 and L.3. As regards L.1 *vis-à-vis* L.2, they claim that an action or choice can be genuinely free even if determinism is true. Some compatibilists hold that genuine freedom simply does not require the ability to do otherwise — not in fanciful thought-experimental 'Frankfurt-style scenarios', and not in ordinary cases either. Others hold that genuine freedom normally does require the ability to do otherwise (except perhaps in unusual circumstances, such as Frankfurt-style cases), but that the relevant kind of ability is conditional — it involves the fact that the agent *would* do otherwise (or choose otherwise) if certain factors *were* different from what they actually are (e.g. different desires, different comparative strengths of desires, or the like). Still others (e.g. Horgan, 1979) hold that genuine freedom normally requires (Frankfurt cases aside, perhaps) a categorical ability to do otherwise that is not readily expressible by a counterfactual conditional, but that this categorical ability to do otherwise is nonetheless compatible with determinism.

As regards L.3 *vis-à-vis* L.2, free will compatibilists deny that free agency requires the agent to be a godlike unmoved mover. Although talk of agents as 'sources' of their actions may well be appropriate as a way to mark certain important distinctions — e.g. the distinction between full-fledged actions and other kinds of behaviours such as involuntary startle-reactions to unexpected loud noises — the relevant kind of sourcehood is entirely compatible with determinism. It also is entirely compatible with the claim that every action (and every choice) is fully causally determined (to the extent that indeterministic randomness does not intrude) by prior states and events; thus, agentive sourcehood, whatever exactly it is, is not a matter of the agent's exerting some kind of determinative influence that transcends the world's state-causal nexus.

Now as anyone acquainted with the philosophical issue knows, one main argument marshalled by libertarians (and also to some extent by hard incompatibilists) is the apparent evidence of introspection. Those who accept L.1 and L.3 often make two claims about agentive phenomenology. First, the phenomenology of agency as revealed by introspection possesses libertarian purport. That is to say, experiences of agency possess, as part of their intrinsic nature, phenomenal characteristics that present oneself to oneself as possessing an ability to do otherwise that is incompatible with determinism, as well as presenting oneself to oneself as a godlike, causal-nexus transcending, source of one's choices and actions. Second, (assuming the methodological claim that the better a theory about free will is at accommodating the data of experience the more plausible the theory) this introspective evidence provides some support for the metaphysical position that free will both genuinely exists and genuinely involves these very attributes.[10] Here are two particularly clear examples of this mode of argument from John Searle and Timothy O'Conner respectively, both of whom are claiming that introspection reveals that agentive phenomenology has libertarian purport:

> Reflect very carefully on the character of the experiences you have as you engage in normal, everyday human actions... You will sense the possibility of alternative courses of action built into these experiences... that we could be doing something else right here and now, that is all other conditions remaining the same. This, I submit is the source of our own unshakeable conviction of our own free will. (Searle, 1984, p. 95)

> It does not seem to me (at least ordinarily) that I am caused to act by the reasons which favor doing so; it seems to be the case, rather, that I produce my own decisions in view of those reasons, and could have, in an unconditional sense, decided differently. (O'Connor, 1995, p. 196)

O'Connor, in this same passage, points to this phenomenological data as evidence for L.3 because, as he says, that thesis 'captures the way we experience our own activity' (*ibid.*).

But such appeals to introspection are contentious. One worry about these various phenomenological claims is that perhaps they are theory-laden. As Nahmias *et al.* (2004) point out in reviewing these conflicting appeals to introspection, the armchair phenomenological data being reported might be tainted by the philosopher's philosophical views about the free will issue. They write:

> Introspective reports [by philosophers] about the relevant experiences are likely influenced by theoretical commitments of the philosopher doing the introspection. Introspection does not simply present 'pure' content to be analysed, rather, by the time philosophers develop theories of free will, they introspect through the lens of their theoretical commitments. (*ibid.*, p. 163)

---

[10] Hard incompatibilists, however, hold that there is decisive countervailing evidence against the existence claim. Phenomenology reveals what free will would have to be like in order to be real, but people's experiences as-of actually possessing free will are illusory.

A second worry, related in some ways to the first but also importantly different from it, is that although the phenomenology itself may well have aspects that are aptly characterized in the manner of Searle and O'Connor, a problematic element of theory-ladenness enters in if one takes that phenomenology, thus described, to have libertarian purport. It is one thing for the phenomenology to be aptly described as 'an experience as-of the act's emanating from me myself' (and likewise, to be aptly described negatively as 'not an experience as-of my bodily motion being caused by *states* of me'); it is another thing for phenomenology that is aptly described this way to have libertarian *satisfaction conditions* involving one's being a godlike unmoved mover. Likewise, it is one thing for the phenomenology to be aptly described as 'an experience as-of having an unconditional ability to do otherwise in my actual circumstances'; it is another thing for phenomenology that is thus aptly described to have libertarian satisfaction conditions involving the falsity of determinism. Problematic theory-ladenness might intrude itself not in the use of the phenomenological descriptions themselves, and not in the aptness of these descriptions in characterizing the phenomenology of freedom, but rather in one's construal of the intentional content of the pertinent phenomenology as thus described — its satisfaction conditions. I.e. even if the phenomenological descriptions are quite apt rather than being tendentiously theory-laden, libertarian-style *interpretations* of those descriptions nonetheless might be tendentiously theory-laden: such interpretations might misconstrue the intentional content of the phenomenology, its representational purport.

Nahmias *et al.* (2004) do not seem to notice the possibility of the second, more subtle, kind of theory-ladenness. They clearly suspect authors like Searle and O'Connor of the first putative mistake, and they clearly believe that the language deployed by such authors is not apt to describe the actual phenomenology of agency. We ourselves think, however, that it is introspectively *just obvious* that actions are normally experienced as emanating from oneself as source, and also are normally experienced as being such that one could have done otherwise in the actual circumstances. If tendentious theory-ladenness intrudes at all — and we believe it does — this happens not in the mere deployment of these phenomenologically apt descriptions, but rather in one's interpretation of the representational purport of such phenomenology as thus described. This more subtle kind of theory-ladenness, we would maintain, is operative not only in arguments (like Searle's and O'Connor's) to the effect that libertarian purport as an aspect of agentive experience is clearly evident introspectively, but also —

ironically — in the assumption by Nahmias *et al.* (2004) that phenomenological descriptions in terms of 'self as source', or 'unconditional ability to do otherwise in the actual circumstances', could be aptly applied only if the phenomenology of free will has libertarian satisfaction conditions (we have in mind the possibility that phenomenology that is aptly described this way actually has compatibilist satisfaction conditions — a theme we return to below).

Worries about theory-ladenness notwithstanding, Nahmias *et al.* (2004) do not think that appeals to evidence gathered by introspection in grappling with the free will issue is hopeless. They propose that it is the pre-philosophical, relatively theory-free phenomenology of ordinary folk (philosophers excluded) that should serve as the real data that a philosophical theory about free will ought to accommodate. And they see some hope of being able to get at the relevant phenomenological data through careful introspective methodology.

We ourselves wish Nahmias and company much luck in that optimistic endeavour, but we also think there are serious obstacles that stand in the way of any method of introspection (or combination of such methods) being powerful enough to reveal decisively whether experiences of choice and action possess libertarian purport. And we have the same misgivings about any method of introspection (or combination of them) with respect to delivering reliable verdicts to the effect that the phenomenology of freedom has compatibilist satisfaction conditions — e.g. conditions that require one's behaviours to be caused by certain kinds of psychological *states* of oneself, such as occurrent beliefs and occurrent desires.[11] That is, contrary to what Nahmias *et al.* (2004) claim, we think that it is quite unlikely that introspection can reveal a decisive answer to the question of whether the satisfaction conditions for agentive experience require certain choices and actions to be caused by the sorts of psychological states that precede and are cited in folk psychological explanations of various choices and actions. We are thus inclined to think that introspection alone cannot reliably answer all the questions about the psychology of

---

[11] We ourselves do think it is introspectively obvious both (1) that paradigmatic agentive experience is as-of self as source, and (2) that such experience is *not* as-of one's behaviour being caused by mental *states* of oneself. But this leaves the question of satisfaction conditions largely open. Self-as-source experience could have satisfaction conditions involving mental state-causation of behaviour, even though such experience does not *overtly represent* one's behaviours, to oneself, as being state-causally necessitated by one's occurrent mental states. One way this could happen, for instance, would be that the satisfaction conditions are partly fixed by extra-phenomenological empirical facts involving the normal operation — whatever that might be — of one's act-generating cognitive architecture. For further related discussion, see Horgan, Tienson and Graham (2003; 2004) and Horgan (2007a; 2007b).

choice and action that interest philosophers. Let us explain, beginning with a series of questions about the topic at hand that need to be addressed if progress is to be made.

(1) Aptness. Do expressions like 'emanating from the self as their source', and 'being such that one could have done otherwise in the actual circumstances' aptly characterize certain genuine aspects of the phenomenology of action and choice? On this matter, at least, we ourselves are optimistic that the answer is affirmative. But one needs to exercise great caution in two correlative respects — *viz.* in interpreting the representational purport of the phenomenology thus described (on the one hand), and in avoiding theory-laden construals of the descriptions themselves (on the other hand). The descriptive aptness of such characterizations does not, by itself, settle the issue of whether the pertinent phenomenology has libertarian purport.

(2) Determinacy. Do philosophically inspired questions about the phenomenology of agency — and, more specifically, about the representational intentional content of its 'self-as-source' aspects and its 'could have done otherwise in the circumstances' aspects — have answers that are determinate, given the intrinsic character of agentive phenomenology itself?[12] Those who appeal to the phenomenology of agency in support of their favoured position on free will seem to take for granted that the answer to this question is yes. But as made clear in discussions by our authors about Melanie's reports of visual imagery, it may be that with respect to certain questions about matters of phenomenological detail, there simply is no fact of the matter that is determined by the intrinsic phenomenal nature of the experience itself.[13] So, perhaps no determinate satisfaction conditions accrue to agentive

---

[12] There are two potential ways that determinate satisfaction conditions could accrue to these aspects of phenomenology. First, the satisfaction conditions might be *fully* determined by the intrinsic character of the phenomenology itself, independently of any non-phenomenological facts about the experiencing agent or about the agent's external environment. Alternatively, second, the satisfaction conditions might be determined by two factors in combination: (a) the intrinsic character of the phenomenology, and (b) certain non-phenomenological features of the agent or the agent's environment. One version of this second possibility was mentioned in the preceding note: (a) the intrinsic character of the phenomenology imposes as a satisfaction condition that the given act or choice results from the normal operation of the agent's act/choice-generating cognitive architecture; and (b) the non-phenomenal facts about the agent's cognitive architecture figure in the overall satisfaction conditions as the 'filler' for the 'role-slot' that is determined by the intrinsic phenomenology itself.

[13] See, for example, Boxes 7.7 and 7.8 on pp. 153–154.

phenomenology, given its intrinsic character — neither determinate libertarian conditions nor determinate compatibilist conditions.

(3) Libertarian purport. Assuming a yes answer to the determinacy question, are agentive experiences such that their theoretically untainted representational contents have veridicality conditions requiring metaphysical-libertarian freedom? In other words, do all, or many, or at least some experiences of agency have libertarian purport?

(4) Causal compatibilist purport. Again, assuming a yes answer to the determinacy question, do the untainted representational contents of agentive experiences have veridicality conditions requiring that choices and actions be causally determined by antecedent psychological causes and in a way that is not compatible with libertarian purport?

(5) Potency of introspection. Finally, is any method or combination of methods of introspection powerful enough to yield answers to questions such as 2–4 above?

We are, of course, particularly interested in the fifth question, and we will have more to say about it in the next section. For the remainder of this section, we wish to call attention to four types of difficulty that any attempt to answer questions about the phenomenology of free agency will have to face, and which make getting reliable answers by any method of enquiry particularly difficult. In the following section we address the prospects for any method of introspection (including DES) for overcoming these problems.

A. Motley subject matter

Consider the motley assortment of types of agentive experience that are mentioned by Nahmias *et al.* (2004) as falling under the term 'phenomenology of free will': experiences of deliberating, making decisions, feeling free, feeling responsible, voluntariness, efforts of will, authorship, intention formation. We would add to this list ordinary experiences of performing goal-directed actions that arguably one experiences as freely performed. Now (assuming a yes answer to the determinacy question) the obvious thing to say here is that some of these forms of agentive experience may be much more likely to possess libertarian purport than others, and indeed some may possess such purport while other types of agentive experience may not. The point we are making here is important for those doing empirical research on the phenomenology of free will. For instance, in 1957, C.A. Campbell, a noted libertarian, argued that it is only in cases where one must expend moral effort of will to overcome the urges of conflicting desires and aversions that one is introspectively aware of any libertarian pretensions one's actions possess. He furthermore claimed that only such actions enjoyed metaphysical libertarian freedom; all other actions he thought are causally determined.

So, one important methodological point for those investigating the phenomenology of free will is that different types of agentive experience might enjoy importantly different veridicality conditions bearing on freedom. And here are two related points. First, it may be that many agentive experiences are relatively 'thin' and representationally indeterminate, and so do not possess veridicality conditions that are either determinately libertarian or determinately causal-compatibilist. As Haggard and Johnson (2003, p. 76) point out, many psychologists, reflecting on actions that are 'automatic' (walking, eating, etc.), often suppose that there is very little content to normal experiences of our own agency.[14] Second, it may be that even fairly automatic actions, such as the one Melanie describes at beep 6.4 where she is picking flower petals out of a sink, do enjoy either libertarian or causal compatibilist veridicality conditions, but that those aspects of her phenomenology are part of the experiential background and not part of her focal agentive experience. This point about what is focal and what may be in the background of one's agentive experience engages of course the dispute between Hurlburt and Schwitzgebel over intramodality richness, which we return to briefly in the next section.

B. Conceptual problems

Among the leading concepts that figure in philosophical discussion of agency and free will are, as we have noted, such concepts as 'able to do otherwise' and 'self as source'. It is a philosophically difficult and tendentious matter to get clear about the semantic workings of 'could do otherwise', both with respect to how this and related locutions are *actually* employed in contexts of agency ascription, moral-responsibility attribution, and the like, and also with respect to how these locutions *should* be employed in such contexts. Compatibilists traditionally have

---

[14] In opposition to those who think this, Haggard and Johnson comment: 'On the one hand the phenomenology of action is often thin… On the other hand, when we wish to, we can report in considerable detail the processes of preparation and execution of our actions… Moreover, when our actions go wrong, the phenomenology is often very strong indeed…' (2004, p. 76). So-called thinness may be more a matter of inattention to rich agentive phenomenology than absence of it.

tended to try analysing such locutions in terms of subjunctive conditionals — e.g. construing 'I could have done otherwise' as equivalent to 'I would have done otherwise if I had chosen to do otherwise'. But there are other approaches that compatibilists can pursue too, some of which are arguably much more plausible and attractive than conditional analyses of 'could'-locutions. One little-explored suggestion, which both of us find plausible and appealing, is the following (*cf.* Horgan, 1979): repudiate hypothetical analyses, and construe categorical 'could'-statements as governed by implicit contextual parameters that normally render such statements compatible with determinism but can take on limit-case settings under which such statements become incompatible with determinism (the implicit parameters determine, contextually, the relation called 'accessibility' in modal logic — where a statement 'Person P *could have* performed action A at time t' is true just in case there is some *accessible* possible world in which P *does* perform A at t).

So, in light of the subtlety and possible context-sensitivity of 'could do otherwise' in everyday discourse, those probing agentive phenomenology for answers to the question of whether, for example, such experiences have libertarian purport must be careful to design experiments or to frame interview questions that are sensitive to such matters. They must be *especially* careful in light of contextualism, since that approach strongly suggests that the explicit posing of freedom/determinism quandaries is apt to create a context that favours limit-case settings of contextual parameters under which 'could do otherwise' becomes incompatible with determinism.[15]

What is perhaps not as often noticed is that similar conceptual subtlety and potential context-sensitivity arise for the concept of self as source, because this concept too admits of stronger and weaker construals. According to a weak reading, one is the source of one's behaviour as long as the behaviour is caused by internal states of oneself such as occurrent wants and beliefs — as opposed, say, to having one's arm moved by someone else, or having one's leg involuntarily jerk upwards in response to a physician's tapping one's knee with a rubber mallet.[16] But the veridicality conditions associated with

---

[15] A pertinent analogy to bear in mind is contextualist treatments of the concept of *knowledge*, which strongly suggest that the very posing of Cartesian radical-deception scenarios is apt to create a context that favours limit-cases settings of implicit parameters under which, for instance, 'I know I have hands' becomes incompatible with the possibility that one is a handless brain in a vat.

[16] Movements analogous to such reflex actions are instances of 'Penfield motion' in which the movement of a subject's body is triggered by an electrode implanted in the subject's

sourcehood plausibly 'swing together' with the veridicality conditions for 'could do otherwise' — which would mean that varying potential uses of the latter would bring in their wake varying potential uses of the former, and implicit contextual parameters governing the latter would also govern the former.

And so in probing agentive phenomenology for answers to questions about the veridicality conditions for free will experiences — particularly if one is probing for libertarian veridicality conditions — one must be careful to design experiments or frame interview questions mindful of the stronger and weaker ways of understanding self as source. But again, is any method of introspectionist enquiry (or any combination of such methods) sufficiently powerful to reveal reliable answers to questions about whether or not experiences of agency have satisfaction conditions of the *libertarian* kind, i.e. satisfaction conditions requiring the experiencer to be a godlike unmoved mover? We doubt it.

C. Interpretative problems

Related to conceptual problems are those of interpretation. And here it is particularly important to be careful of how one interprets certain negative reports about first-person agentive experience. For example, there may be a temptation to suppose that lack of an experience as-of being a godlike unmoved mover is positive evidence for a phenomenology of state causation.[17] It is one thing for one's agentive phenomenology to *lack* any trace of representing oneself as being an unmoved mover, but it is quite another to hold that one's agentive phenomenology does indeed represent one's choices and actions, positively to oneself, *as being state caused*. Suppose one is thirsty for a cold beer and believes there is one in the next room and so walks to the room in

---

brain. Penfield bodily motion is *not* experienced by subjects as something they do. For relevant discussion, see Wakefield and Dreyfus (1991).

[17] We suspect Nahmias *et al.* (2004) of committing this error or coming close to doing so. They contrast (i) phenomenological reports ascribing libertarian self-as-source purport to agentive experiences, with (ii) the remarks of philosophers who appeal to their own agentive experiences in defending compatibilist theories of free will. But of the four authors in the latter camp that they quote, none of them report what would clearly count as experiences as of one's choices or actions being state caused. For instance, they quote Joseph Priestly who reports that 'all that a man can possibly be conscious of... [is] that nothing hinders his choosing or taking whichsoever of the fruits appears to him more desirable'. But in this short passage Priestly does not report experiences of choices or actions being state caused. Their quote from W.T. Stace is not about phenomenology. Their quote from Hume about the origins of the idea of power is a negative point Hume is making against Reid's theory of agency. And the quote from Dennett is about what the phenomenology of agency lacks, not what it positively contains.

question, opens the refrigerator door, looks for the bottle, spies it, reaches for it, grabs it, closes the fridge door, twists off the cap, and begins to drink. This goal-directed series of actions (or at least some of them) may well include as part of one's agentive phenomenology the idea or representation of one acting *because* one is thirsty. If so, is that an instance in which at least part of one's agentive experience is one's action being *state-caused* by one's thirst? The compatibilist, remember, is someone who thinks that all events (including choices and actions) are causally determined by antecedent conditions but who also thinks that a proper understanding of the very notion of free action is compatible with such determination. So, in the beer-getting example just mentioned (and supposing that it is part of one's overall agentive phenomenology that one experiences what one is doing as a doing because one is thirsty), does one experience any of the actions in question *as being causally necessitated* by one's thirst together with other conditions? We think not. And we strongly suspect that those who think otherwise are over-interpreting what is actually, reliably, introspectible in their agentive phenomenology. It is perhaps easy to go from the thought, *My phenomenology presents me to myself as making choices and performing actions **because** I have thus and so desires and beliefs* to *My phenomenology presents me to myself as making choices and performing actions that are **causally necessitated** by thus and so desires and beliefs*. It is very plausible that the phenomenology of agency often includes representational content whose veridicality conditions require the former statement to be true (and also makes this fact introspectively obvious), but we ourselves think it is very far from introspectively obvious whether or not the representational content of the phenomenology requires the latter statement to be true.

A related observation about possible interpretive errors, this time about reading too much pro-libertarian purport into one's agentive phenomenology, has been made recently by Horgan (2007a; 2007b). It is an easy but fallacious inference or conflation to go from *My experience does **not** present my actions **as** state-caused* to *My experience presents my actions **as not** state caused*.

Yet another possible interpretive error, again about reading too much pro-libertarian purport into one's agentive phenomenology, has also been stressed recently by Horgan (2007a; 2007b). Suppose that the following contentions, adverted to above, are all correct: (1) both the concept expressible by 'could do otherwise', and also the concept expressible by 'self as source' are governed by implicit contextual parameters; (2) the satisfaction conditions for agentive 'could'-

statements and self-as-source statements therefore swing in tandem, across discourse contexts; and (3) there are limit-case settings of the contextual parameters under which (i) an agentive 'could'-statement is true only if determinism is false and (ii) the corresponding self-as-source statement is true only if the agent functioned as a godlike unmoved mover with respect to the given act or choice. If indeed these three claims are all true (as we ourselves are inclined to think), then it would be quite easy to form mistaken, excessively libertarian, beliefs about the satisfaction conditions that accrue to one's agentive phenomenology — not because of the nature of the phenomenology itself, but rather because one characterizes this phenomenology using *concepts* expressible linguistically by 'could do otherwise' and by 'self as source'. The thought is this: merely raising the general issue of freedom and determinism is apt to create a context of enquiry and discourse in which the implicit contextual parameters governing those concepts take on their limit-case, libertarian, settings; thus, since one deploys those very concepts in describing the pertinent aspects of agentive phenomenology that one is introspectively attending to, one might easily come to think that these phenomenological features *themselves* have libertarian satisfaction conditions. This would be an interpretive mistake, but a very subtle one indeed — *viz.* wrongly construing the contextually invariant representational content of agentive experience as having libertarian satisfaction conditions, where one imposes this construal on the experience because one is describing that experience in terms of *concepts* which, in context, have acquired limit-case, libertarian, satisfaction conditions.

D. Probing problems

Whether one is engaged in armchair introspection or engaged in the kind of collaborative process characteristic of DES, there is much delicacy in how one conducts the probing of one's own or another's experiences. This matter of how to conduct an interview is crucial to Hurlburt's DES methodology. For instance, he insists on avoiding questions that ask subjects about the processes leading up to the experience being probed (DES guideline 10 on pp. 18–19), and as he says, the interview 'asks essentially one and only one question: "What were you experiencing at the time of the beep?" The object is to get as complete and detailed an answer to that question as is possible, while at the same time avoiding confabulation' (p. 21). But as he is well aware, the probing that follows this opening question can be a tricky matter when trying to get the subject to reveal not only nothing but the truth, but the whole truth as well. Avoiding confabulation seems especially worrisome when probing agentive phenomenology for answers to questions about experiences of free will. If, as we ourselves think, any phenomenological aspects of one's agentive experiences that bear on such questions are likely rather subtle and hard to get at through introspection because of the motley array of types of agentive experience, as well as subtle conceptual and interpretive matters that we have just mentioned, then one ought to expect serious obstacles standing in the way of using introspection alone to get at answers to free will questions about agentive phenomenology.

III. Prospects

But obstacles can be overcome, as in the advances that Hurlburt's DES methodology arguably enjoys over methods that do not heed his fifteen guidelines that he sets forth in chapter 2 of *Describing Inner Experience*. And even if introspection (no matter the associated methodology) cannot alone yield reliable answers to free will questions about agentive phenomenology, it may well yield valuable data that can play a role in broadly abductive arguments about certain aspects of the phenomenal character of agentive experiences. What, then, are the likely prospects for accurately and thoroughly describing one's agentive experiences (getting at the whole truth about them, or anyway a lot of it)?

Consider first the use of introspection alone, beginning with the DES method. We note that in the Hurlburt and Schwitzgebel book there is almost nothing said that bears directly on questions about agentive phenomenology, even though in all of the beeps Melanie is engaged in some doing or other (unpacking a chair, walking from hallway to kitchen, eating dinner, talking, reading, and so on). Indeed, in one place in the text, Box 9.7: 'Melanie's experience of activity' (p. 209), the authors agree that they failed to probe Melanie's experience of picking up rose petals from the sink — her doing. Rather they focused on aspects of what she was thinking at the time. But commenting on having not further probed this aspect of Melanie's beeped experience, Hurlburt remarks that doings are difficult or impossible to describe in more detail than we find in Melanie's unprobed initial description of the experience: 'I was leaning over the sink and picking up the remaining petals and collecting them in my hand to throw them in the trash' (p. 206). Hurlburt seems to have concluded over the years that there is nothing more to common, everyday agentive phenomenology than the sort of elements of experience that are featured in

Melanie's report. But if this speculation is correct (and here we are inviting Russ to comment), it may be that the DES method is too narrowly focused on the non-subtle and easily introspectible aspects of one's phenomenology at a very 'thin' time slice of one's ongoing experience to really reveal much about agentive phenomenology. The focus on non-subtle, most easily introspectible aspects of experience is something Hurlburt emphasizes. But note also that because the DES method focuses on a *very* brief time slice (what was going on experientially at the moment of the beep), the method may cut the subject off from the diachronic flow of experience over time in which any libertarian or causal-compatibilist purport would most likely be introspectible.[18] So it may be that although DES is the best available method of introspectionist enquiry for getting an accurate description of the gross features of an experiential time slice, it may not be the best method now available for probing agentive phenomenology.

Again, because DES is aimed at guarding against subjects' interpretations (rather than mere descriptions) of their experiences,[19] subjects are not primed in the way they are in Schwitzgebels's DES-like 'richness' study that he describes on pp. 228–234. But without some priming of subjects in which the libertarian/compatibilist dispute over agentive phenomenology is explained, one worries that the more subtle aspects of such phenomenology will be missed by indiscriminate introspective reporting. The matter is delicate of course, since priming subjects and having them respond to specific questions may have a distorting influence on one's phenomenology.[20]

In light of these worries (time slice, non-priming, and non-targeted questioning), one might look to other introspectionist methods of enquiry that could be used for purposes of probing agentive experience. One such approach is the so-called 'talk aloud' method in which (roughly) subjects are asked to say aloud what they are thinking during the time they are engaged in a particular task.[21] This method was in fact employed by Nahmias and his associates in a decision making task in which subjects were presented with descriptions of three apartments and told to choose among them on the assumption that they

---

[18] Schwitzgebel brings up the general issue about DES as focusing only on a thin time slice in Box 4.10, 'Focusing on a single moment and the dynamics of experience', p. 76.

[19] See DES guideline 12: Separate reports from introspection (p. 19).

[20] See similar remarks by Nahmias *et al.* (2004, p. 172).

[21] On p. 16 (Box 2.2, 'Summary of Sampling Methods'), Hurlburt briefly describes six sampling methods (including DES and the talk aloud, verbal protocol analyses) that are used to probe people's experiences. See Ericsson and Simon (1993) and Ericsson (2003) for elaboration and discussion of verbal protocol analysis.

would be living in one of them the following year. Here is how they describe what happened:

> Following the basic talk-aloud protocol, we asked subjects to verbalize any thoughts (and feelings) they have as they performed practice tasks and the experimental task. Among our (twelve) subjects the general trend was simply to mention the features of the apartments they liked and disliked. As they read descriptions and while they deliberated, they simply said aloud things like, 'Hardwood floors — I like that', 'Five minutes from campus — that's too far', 'I'm choosing apartment C because it has a washer/dryer', etc. (Nahmias *et al.*, 2004, pp. 175–176)

With some guarded misgivings about whether to understand subjects as reporting their thoughts or explaining their decisions (or perhaps both), Nahmias *et al.* suggest that in their study the subjects were aware of their own reactions to the presented information about apartments and that they by and large chose on the basis of what they found most attractive about one of the choices. Nahmias and associates take the fact that the subjects tended to describe their deliberating and choosing experiences in passive terms and did not mention anything about or suggestive of a self as source as favouring a compatibilist construal of these experiences.

In commenting on the significance of this study, Nahmias *et al.* remark that the talk-aloud methodology employed in their study may itself be impotent in getting at any details of agentive phenomenology that would bear on the free will issue. They worry that subjects who are not primed to pay attention to aspects of their agentive phenomenology may be missing important detail. They go on to suggest a kind of phenomenological interview which, like DES, treats subjects and scientists as co-investigators. So one might consider combining the talk-aloud method with a particular kind of phenomenological interview that would sidestep the problem of relying on memory, would avoid the time slice worry that besets DES for this kind of enquiry, and would involve subjects who are primed by being informed of the free will debate, and would feature scientists conducting such studies who strove to be careful in the manner of Hurlburt in questioning subjects about the details of their agentive experiences and interpreting their responses. But suppose that for whatever reasons the methods of introspection either alone or in combination are not powerful enough to yield decisive answers to questions about those aspects of agentive phenomenology that presumably bear on the free will debate. This might be because such phenomenology is indeterminate with regard to the free will issue. But if one has reason to suppose that the phenomenology is (at least some of the time) determinate with respect to this issue, then one might appeal to other types of enquiry, the results of which one might bring to bear on the issue of whether people's agentive experiences are likely to have one sort of freedom-relevant purport or not.[22]

For instance, our colleague Shaun Nichols (2004) conducted a study whose purpose was to explore the question whether young children around the ages of 4 and 5 possessed the concept of agent-as-cause. Based on his own results together with relevant results from certain other psychological studies on young children, he concluded that children at that age do possess the concept in question, which prompted him to speculate about how they might come to have it. His tentative suggestion is that children acquire the concept, and also a belief in agent-causation, as a result of a prior belief in obligation.[23]

Suppose that Nichols is right about children having the relevant concept. Surely this bears, even if indirectly, on whether individuals possessing this concept have self-as-source agentive *phenomenology* at least some of the time — regardless whether they introspectively *report* that they do.[24] One could reasonably expect that one's 'naturally' having the *concept* of agent-as-cause would be in part a reflection of one's agentive phenomenology, at least some of the time. Suppose, then, that one grants that one's typical agentive phenomenology as revealed by introspection is *not* that of one's choices and actions being causally necessitated by one's choice and action-relevant desires, aversions, or intentions. And suppose also that children possess the relevant notions of 'self as source' and 'could have done otherwise'. Together these claims (if true) might be a sound enough basis (barring countervailing evidence) that people's agentive phenomenology (at least some of the time) possesses full-fledged

---

[22] Keep in mind the possibility that people may differ in their agentive phenomenologies and that some people may have libertarian-like agentive experiences some of the time while having non-libertarian and even causal-compatibilist-like agentive experiences at other times.

[23] Nichols assumes throughout his paper that the concept of agent as cause has libertarian satisfaction conditions, as do statements that one 'could do otherwise in the circumstances'. By our own lights, these assumptions are much too quick, and reflect the subtle kind of theory-ladenness that we said above is also operative in Nahmias *et al.* (2004). But as far as we can see, his principal arguments and conclusions do not require those assumptions.

[24] As we said earlier, we ourselves find it introspectively obvious that there is self-as-source phenomenology, even though it is far from introspectively obvious what its satisfaction conditions might be. But some people (e.g. Nahmias *et al.*, 2004) profess doubts about whether experiences of free agency have a phenomenological aspect that is aptly described this way — which makes other, non-introspective, kinds of evidence and data especially germane to the issue.

self-as-source phenomenology — regardless of what various people might say about the matter on the basis of their own introspection.

What about the issue of satisfaction conditions for the phenomenology of free agency? This we think is a much trickier matter, in part because we claim that introspection alone cannot effectively address it. Still, Nichols' results, and his tentative suggestion about how the concept of agent-causation arises in children, both seem to us to provide some degree of non-introspection-based support for compatibilism about satisfaction conditions. This is because there is just no evident reason why the concept of agent-causation itself, or the phenomenology that corresponds to it, would need to have libertarian satisfaction conditions in order to play the role in cognitive economy that Nichols ascribes to it — a role that involves the close intertwining of agent-causation and obligation, both conceptually and experientially. As long as one refrains (as one should) from a tendentiously theory-laden construal of descriptions like 'self as source' and 'could do otherwise in the circumstances', there is no particularly good reason to think that experiences of obligation and of free agency represent oneself, to oneself, as a godlike unmoved mover that transcends the world's state-causal nexus. Rather, given that the satisfaction conditions for agentive phenomenology are not directly ascertainable by introspection, and given that libertarian satisfactions are much more metaphysically extravagant than compatibilist ones, the default hypothesis should be that the relevant phenomenology has compatibilist satisfaction conditions.

There are various kinds of non-introspectionist empirical evidence which, together with whatever evidence may be revealed by introspection (no matter how limited in themselves), may support an abductive inference about the veridicality conditions of agentive experience.[25] Such an argument is strongly suggested in, for example, the writings of C.A. Campbell with regard to agentive experiences other than experiences involving moral effort of will. As mentioned earlier, Campbell held that introspection reveals that in cases where one must exert moral effort of will to overcome the force of contrary desire, one's experiences represent oneself as being a godlike metaphysical source of one's action (L.3). He calls the kind of self-activity that such agentive experiences of moral effort represent one as having, 'creative self-activity', which he contrasts with what he calls 'expressive self-activity' (Campbell, 1957, pp. 148–157). Expressive

---

[25] Several kinds of evidence to this effect, which we will not rehearse here, are set forth in sections 3.5 and 3.6 of Horgan (forthcoming).

self-activity is characteristic of those agentive experiences in all other cases of willed action[26] where one's experiences are *compatible* with those actions being causally determined, although those experiences do not themselves *overtly represent* one's actions as being state-caused. He writes:

> If self-activity did not reach beyond the expressive mode, then so far as I can see, man's power of self-determination would be of very limited significance indeed. His choices would, no doubt, still be self-determining, in the sense that whatever end a self-conscious subject chooses he accepts as his *own* end. But such self-determination is formal rather than real, and is consistent with the effective determination of his choices coming from factors external to him. (*ibid.*, pp. 155–156)

So, according to Campbell, the phenomenology of this class of agentive experiences, characterized by a kind of self-activity, is consistent with causal compatibilist purport, although such experiences do not themselves represent one's actions as being causally necessitated by one's desires and other mental states.[27] However, he also held that non-introspective empirical facts about a person's inherited nature and her environment provide evidence that the veridicality conditions for ascriptions of freedom in such cases are causal-compatibilist. In such cases one acts according to one's strongest desires 'and [he writes] I cannot see to what else we can point as determinant of the man's strongest desires (and accordingly of his choices) save the particular kind and degree of his congenital impulses *plus* the environmental situation by which they are in varying degrees fostered or discouraged' (*ibid.*, p. 156). For Campbell, then, the evidence of introspection in these cases is consistent with one's self-expressive actions being state-causally necessitated. And when combined with evidence about the formation of desires and character generally, Campbell thought one may infer that cases of ordinary willed action have causal-compatibilist veridicality conditions.

---

[26] Campbell distinguishes willed from impulsive 'action' and holds that it is only with respect to the former type of action that a sense of one's own self activity is present (1957, p. 147).

[27] One way for this to happen would be for the phenomenology of expressive-mode agency to only partially determine its satisfaction conditions, in a way that allows a further constitutive role for extra-phenomenological facts about the agent (e.g. facts about how one's cognitive architecture normally operates to produce actions expressive of one's ends). *Cf.* notes 11 and 12 above.

IV. Conclusion

We ourselves are fairly pessimistic about the power of any known method of introspection (or combined introspectionist methods) to reliably deliver answers to questions about the phenomenology of agency that would either favour or disfavour (even for a restricted range of types of agentive experience) the hypothesis that such experiences possess libertarian satisfaction conditions. We are likewise sceptical that introspection can reliably deliver answers to questions about whether, for a range of agentive experiences, such experiences possess the kind of satisfaction conditions that require state-causal determination. And we have explained what we take to be among the main conceptual, interpretive, and methodological problems to be confronted in conducting introspectionist enquiry into matters of agentive experience and free will. If introspection is impotent with respect to answering such questions, this may be due to outright indeterminacy of satisfaction conditions, given the phenomenology. But it may also be due entirely to the limits of the power of introspection itself, granting that phenomenology does have satisfaction conditions that are either libertarian or compatibilist.

We offer these negative remarks not on the basis of any experimental evidence, but on the basis of our own understanding of the complex free will controversy, plus our belief in the pertinence of various non-introspection-based kinds of evidence both experimental and non-experimental, plus what we have learned about the challenges to introspectionist methodology from reading our authors' book. However, we do think there is such a thing as agentive phenomenology, with rich and distinctive phenomenal aspects. And we wonder to what extent that phenomenology may be fruitfully investigated via introspection. So, we end with some questions for our authors about this matter. Our questions are not meant to challenge any of the claims made by either of our authors; rather, they are questions whose answers we ourselves are unsure about, and about which we would like to hear what our authors have to say.

First, as noted earlier, DES does not seem particularly well-suited to explore this kind of phenomenology, since it focuses exclusively on a very thin time slice of experience. Still, might this method, perhaps with proper questioning focused on reported experiences that involve doings, enable subjects to accurately describe aspects of their experiences of doing? Perhaps if experiences of ordinary doings of the sort that Melanie reports in beep 6.4 (picking up the rose petals) are phenomenologically thin (or appear to be so), then probing cases where subjects experience having to exert self-control are better for probing any intra-modal richness possessed by at least some sorts of agentive experience.

Second, might other methods of introspection, including verbal protocol analysis (talk-aloud) or something like it, be better suited, perhaps in combination with DES-like probing, for reliably revealing whatever phenomenological features there are to agentive experiences of at least some types that can be accessed via introspection?

Because any such non-DES methodology might involve both priming and targeted probing, our second question leads to a third. Is the sort of priming whereby subjects are made aware of issues regarding agency or free will, and then asked to report on any aspects of sampled experiences that have to do with the issue in question, likely to greatly distort any reports about their experience that subjects offer, making them more suspect than the reports by Melanie that Hurlburt thinks are reliable?

Fourth, Hurlburt is extremely critical of premature hypothesis testing in psychology because he claims that such testing 'elevates the status of presuppositions rather than diminishes it: A hypothesis is entirely (or almost entirely) shaped by the presuppositions that lie behind it'. But might there be a way of generating descriptive data about people's agentive experiences that involves relatively presupposition-free questioning *vis-à-vis* views about free will and agentive experience generally? We don't see why not (not that Hurlburt would say otherwise). In fact, the observations we have made about the conceptual, interpretive, and methodological obstacles to overcome and pitfalls to avoid in the investigation of agentive phenomenology should serve, we think, in helping investigators avoid the bracketing issue that Hurlburt claims is the central issue of consciousness studies and the science of psychology (p. 263).

References

Campbell, C.A. (1957) *Selfhood and Godhood*, New York & London: George Allen & Unwin.
Ericsson, K.A. (2003) Valid and non-reactive verbalization of thoughts during performance tasks, *Journal of Consciousness Studies*, **10** (9–10), pp. 1–18.
Ericsson, K.A. & Simon, H.A. (1993) *Protocol Analysis: Verbal Reports as Data*, revised ed., Cambridge, MA: Bradford books/MIT Press.
Ginet, C. (1990) *On Action*, Cambridge: Cambridge University Press.
Haggard, P. & Johnson, H. (2003) Experiences of voluntary action, *Journal of Consciousness Studies*, **10** (9–10), pp. 72–84.
Horgan, T. (1979) 'Could', possible worlds, and moral responsibility, *Southern Journal of Philosophy*, **17**, pp. 345–358.

Horgan, T. (2007a) Agentive phenomenal intentionality and the limits of introspection, *Psyche*, **13**, pp. 1–29.
Horgan, T. (2007b) Mental causation and the agent-exclusion problem, *Erkenntnis*, **67**, pp. 183–200.
Horgan, T. (forthcoming) Causal compatibilism about agentive phenomenology, for a *festschrift for Jaegwon Kim*, Horgan, T., Sabates, M. and Sosa, D. (eds.), Cambridge, MA: MIT Press.
Horgan, T. & Kriegel, U. (2007) Phenomenal epistemology: What is phenomenal consciousness that we may know it so well?, *Philosophical Issues*, **17**, pp. 123–144.
Horgan, T., Tienson, J. & Graham, G. (2003) The phenomenology of first-person agency, in Walter, S. & Heckman, H.D. (eds.) *Physicalism and Mental Causation: The Metaphysics of Mind and Action*, pp. 323–340, Exeter: Imprint Academic.
Horgan, T., Tienson, J. & Graham, G. (2004) Phenomenal intentionality and the brain in a vat, in Schantz, R. (ed.) *The Externalist Challenge*, pp. 297–317, Berlin: Walter de Gruyter.
Horgan, T. & Timmons, M. (2005) Moral phenomenology and moral theory, *Philosophical Issues*, **15**, pp. 56–77.
Horgan, T. & Timmons, M. (2007) Morphological rationalism: Making room for moral principles, *Ethical Theory and Moral Practice*, **10**, pp. 279–295.
Horgan, T. & Timmons, M. (2008a) Prolegomena to a future phenomenology of moral, *Phenomenology and the Cognitive Sciences*, **7**, pp. 115–131.
Horgan, T. & Timmons, M. (2008b) What does moral phenomenology tell us about moral objectivity?, *Social Philosophy & Policy*, **25**, pp. 267–300. Reprinted in Paul, E.F., Miller, F.D. & Paul, J. (eds.) *Objectivism, Subjectivism, and Relativism in Ethics*, pp. 267–300, Cambridge: Cambridge University Press.
Nahmias, E., Morris, S., Nadelhoffer, T. & Turner, S. (2004) The phenomenology of free will, *Journal of Consciousness Studies*, **11** (7–8), pp. 162–179.
Nichols, S. (2004) The folk psychology of free will: Fits and starts, *Mind & Language*, **19**, pp. 473–502.
Nisbett, R.E. & Wilson, T.D. (1977) Telling more than we can know: Verbal reports on mental processes, *Psychological Review*, **84**, pp. 231–259.
O'Connor, T. (1995) Agent causation, in O'Connor, T. (ed.) *Agents, Causes, and Events*, New York: Oxford University Press.
Schwitzgebel, E. (2007) Do you have constant tactile experience of your feet in your shoes? Or is experience limited to what's in attention?, *Journal of Consciousness Studies*, **14** (3), pp. 5–35.
Searle, J. (1984) *Minds, Brains, and Science*, Cambridge: Cambridge University Press.
Wakefield, J. & Dreyfus, H. (1991) Intentionality and the phenomenology of action, in Lepore, E. & van Gulick, R. (eds.) *John Searle and His Critics*, Oxford: Blackwell.

Russell T. Hurlburt
and Eric Schwitzgebel

Presuppositions and Background Assumptions

ERIC

Christopher S. Hill[1] argues that 'It is futile to seek a *presupposition-less* method of studying introspection' because 'we inevitably use concepts that are associated with a theory when we attempt to characterize the objects of introspective awareness and also when we attempt to characterize introspection itself' (p. 31). Thus, 'every method has substantial presuppositions' (p. 33). Hill therefore recommends that rather than trying to bracket presuppositions in collecting subjective reports, researchers should offer subjects an improved, scientific conceptual framework, where there is good evidence that it is superior to the conceptual frameworks of folk psychology.

Russ and I have decided to start our reaction to the commentaries with the issue of bracketing presuppositions both because Russ thinks bracketing presuppositions is crucial to the study of experience and because it is the issue on which Russ and I have been least satisfied that we have understood each other.

I am approximately in agreement with **Hill** on the futility of seeking presuppositionless methods, though I might recommend a lighter touch with the scientific vocabulary than **Hill** seems to want — perhaps offering scientific vocabulary to the subject as a possibility rather than requiring the subject to use it.

Correspondence:
R.T. Hurlburt: *russ@unlv.nevada.edu* ; E. Schwitzgebel: *eschwitz@ucr.edu*

---

[1] 'H&S' refers to Hurlburt & Schwitzgebel (2007), the target book of this symposium. Items in bold face refer to contributions appearing in this symposium: bold face names identify authored contributions; bold face titles refer to contributions written by Russ and or Eric. All bare page numbers refer to this volume.

PRESUPPOSITIONS AND ASSUMPTIONS

Presuppositions both necessary and good

Let me develop the point a little farther. Contra what Russ seems to be saying (which **Claire Petitmengin** also apparently endorses), presuppositions are both *necessary* and *good*. They are necessary and good because presuppositions are built into the very having of concepts, into every action, and into every perceptual, theoretical, memorial, and introspective judgment. When I walk into a building, I presuppose that the floor will support me. When I sit on a bus, I presuppose that the person next to me won't punch me in the nose for no reason. Walking past an orchard, the splashes of red I see among the trees I assume more likely to be apples than coffee mugs. It will take more evidence — rightly so — to convince me of the latter than the former.

In both cognitive science and folk psychology, the dominant metaphor for memory — a metaphor than both reflects and reinforces a certain way of thinking about it — is the metaphor of storage and retrieval, often with a search in the middle. This metaphor is misleading in a number of ways, but there's one aspect I wish to highlight here: on the storage-and-retrieval view, memory is a process that, once initiated, can and typically should operate largely independently of other cognitive processes. Processes like inferring, imagining, and perceiving *interfere* with pure remembering. To the extent such processes influence one's final judgment about some remembered fact or event, one isn't really quite *remembering* it.

Bartlett (1932), Neisser (1967), Roediger (1980), and Sutton (1998) have ably described various infelicities of this storage-and-retrieval view. If I tell you a story about, say, a cricket match and ask you to recall it later, you will not reproduce the story verbatim. Nor will you produce gappy but otherwise verbatim pieces of the story. Rather, you will produce a new version of the story, in light of your general background knowledge of cricket. This partially-inventive process is especially revealed by plausible mistakes and interpolations, but there's no reason to suppose that it would *only* be mistakes and interpolations that arise from the heavy influence of background knowledge. Someone without a background knowledge of cricket, or with a much better background knowledge of cricket, would both digest and retell the story differently. Memorial judgments, especially of complex events, arise from a confluence of cognitive processes, not a single search-and-retrieval mechanism. They are necessarily reconstructive. Imagination, inference, the application of pre-existing schemata, and other cognitive processes are not separable from the process of remembering but rather an integral part of it. They are not interfering or aiding forces

Memories necessarily reconstructive

from which a 'pure' act of remembering could be isolated. Background beliefs or presuppositions — working assumptions about what kinds of things are relatively likely and unlikely, how the world divides up and fits together — thus play an ineliminable role in memory, including the memory of 'beeped' moments of experience.

An event transpires in your stream of experience — an image of warplanes in flight, say — and then the Descriptive Experience Sampling (DES) beep occurs. That event is now gone. There's no reason to think your brain would have stored a detailed and enduring record of that event as it was ongoing. You might try to retain that image of warplanes over the duration of the beep and the post-beep reflection, using the retained image as a model for the image as it existed at the moment of the beep; but surely it's plausible to suppose that the image might be transformed, elaborated, or rendered artificial in the course of retention, and it might be very difficult to detect such changes reliably, accurately accounting for them and subtracting them when reaching judgments about the target experience. You might, as **Petitmengin** recommends, try to replay or re-enact the image, if it was momentarily lost, which would appear to invite all the same risks if not more (risks that make me even more nervous about **Petitmengin**'s method than about DES). Or you might try to recall the image, without retaining or replaying it — perhaps purely linguistically? — but this too will be a constructive or reconstructive act, involving for example one's knowledge of warplanes, how you take them generally to look, knowledge of the outward event that inspired the image (a passage in a book, say), and probably also one's general opinions about imagery. It will not be the simple retrieval of a recorded trace, in high or low pixilation, but rather elaborative, constructive, and plausibility-and-schemata-grounded, like the subjects' recollections of written stories in Bartlett's classic (1932) study.

Hours later, you are interviewed and the reconstructive process begins again, with the target even less fresh but — perhaps compensatingly — with more available bases for the reconstruction: all the general knowledge (or opinions), schemata, and skills that were originally available (except literal retention); plus one's knowledge of or best recollection of the other processes that occurred after the beep; plus one's written notes; plus cues (maybe subtle) from the interviewer; plus one's knowledge of the intervening beeps and interviews. From this confluence of forces issues an utterance, 'they're jet planes with a tapered nose and that kind of dark gray steel with a...' (H&S, p. 108), which the interviewer

Confluence of influences on DES reports

interprets in accord with his own system of schemata and prejudices.

That, I think, is the cognitive process underlying interviews about sampled experience — both in DES and in **Petitmengin**'s explicitation. It should be evident then: (1) that there is plenty of room for error, and (2) that background beliefs, assumptions, schemata, and categories are inseparable from the process, with all of their attendant risks and benefits. It is incoherent to suppose that one could suspend all presuppositions and do anything like ordinary cognition.

RUSS

> A presupposition is a preconception, something that is taken for granted. It is a notion about the world that is so fundamental that it exists prior to critical examination. It is something accepted without controversy as being true, something that shapes perception, behavior, and affect without the fact of that shaping being noticed or recognized. It is an unquestioned manner of relating to the world that chooses what is seen and what is not seen, what is experienced and how it is experienced, so invisibly that what is seen and experienced seems to be the world itself, not aspects of the world selected, shaped, and distorted by the presuppositional process. (Hurlburt & Heavey, 2006, p. 151)

Presuppositions, what they are

A presupposition is a characteristic turning away from evidence that might counter that view, a persistent assumption that one's methods are adequate (and therefore a disinclination to examine or improve those methods or to commit to the practice required to improve the skill with which one uses them). Presuppositions arise from (and at the same time create) a personally-advantageous and self-sustaining mix of prideful, professional, social, economic, and so on influences.

Eric, you lump presuppositions into the 'background beliefs' category ('working assumptions about what kinds of things are relatively likely and unlikely, how the world divides up and fits together'), a distortion similar to lumping the Arab-Israeli situation into the 'disagreements' category: both lumpings overlook the definingly powerful human motivations. Knowledge (or lack thereof) about cricket is similar to a presupposition only to the extent that ignorance is similar to delusion. By emphasizing the similarity between presuppositions and concepts, schemata, and general knowledge, I fear you mask the fact that the failure to try relentlessly to bracket presuppositions can be and often is toxic to science in a way that accepting ordinary reconstructive processes is not.

I will make two preparatory observations and then will provide some examples. First, I agree that being presuppositionless is beyond my reach, and I accept that I have written things that could be interpreted as my advocating being presuppositionless. Therefore when you and **Hill** say that it is impossible or incoherent to bracket all presuppositions, and what you mean is that memory is necessarily reconstructive in this way, then I agree with that, too. However, actually I don't advocate being presuppositionless; I advocate relentlessly trying to bracket all presuppositions that arise, which is quite a different thing.

Second, I agree completely with your and Bartlett's reconstructive view of memory, and I agree with your characterization of DES as relying on constructive or reconstructive memory at the two time frames you identify: the contemporaneous apprehension of experience during the jotting down of notes about the experience (say 10 or 60 seconds after the beep) and the recollection of the experience during the interview (a few hours later). However, there are actually *three* (not two) time frames on which something like memory is required by DES; you overlook the immediate (short term memory) apprehension of the experience (within, say, a second or so after the onset of the beep). There is a lot of evidence to suggest that short term (within a second or so) memory is not reconstructive in the same way as are the longer term memories you discuss. That is an important distinction when you take into consideration the iterative nature of DES (for a more complete discussion see **Clarifications of DES**). For example, on Melanie's first sampling day, we discussed with Melanie her putative self-consciousness. It is likely that that discussion informed and improved her interest/skill in recognizing and discriminating self-consciousness should it appear on the second sampling day, and that recognition/discrimination may then occur at the moment of the experience — that is, within the short-term-memory time frame. Therefore as the iterative process takes effect, short-term-memory apprehensions are probably *not* as coloured by the background assumptions of reconstructive memory as you worry for the other time frames. That is one reason that DES is fundamentally an iterative procedure.

You would like me to give a precise definition of 'presupposition' that makes clear exactly how presuppositions differ from less toxic concepts, schemata, and general knowledge; but I don't think that is possible, just as it is not possible to draw a clear division between disagreements like '*Avatar* is a better movie than *The Hurt Locker;* No it's not!' and 'The Israelis have more right to Jerusalem than do the Palestinians; No they don't!' All presuppositions, concepts, schemata, and general knowings (and disagreements) contain at bottom some kernel of toxicity. Some things, however, are more toxic than others; some toxicities are more specific to the particular investigation at hand than are others. Perhaps I can clarify by providing some examples and analogies.

Example 1: Inner Speech.

For whatever reason, researchers in consciousness studies appear to be especially prone to toxic presuppositions about inner speech. Consider the following quotes:

> Human beings talk to themselves every moment of the waking day. Most readers of this sentence are doing it now. It becomes a little clearer with difficult-to-say words, like 'infundibulum' or 'methylparabine'... Overt speech takes up perhaps a tenth of the waking day; but inner speech goes on all the time. (Baars, 2003, p. 106; cf. H&S, p. 269)

> Human beings...engage in a continual running commentary with the events going on around us. ...It is doubtful if there is a (normal) human being who is unaware of an internal dialogue which silently voices sentiments like, 'Isn't he ever going to stop talking?', 'Careful, that truck's pulling out', or, 'I can't face that again.' Moreover, we all also know that these are not just idle commentaries. ...Since this experience is so universal and continuous to human beings, and also one of which they are acutely if not infallibly aware, one wonders why it has suffered such considerable neglect (Archer, 2000, pp. 193–94).

> [Inner speech] shows a tendency toward an altogether specific form of abbreviation, namely: omitting the subject of a sentence and all words connected with it, while preserving the predicate [Vygotsky calls this predication]. This tendency toward predication appears in all our experiments with such regularity that we must assume it to be the basic form of syntax of inner speech....
>
> This tendency [predication], never found in written speech and only sometimes in oral speech, arises in inner speech always. Predication is the natural form of inner speech; psychologically, it consists of predicates only. It is as much a law of inner speech to omit subjects as it is a law of written speech to contain both subjects and predicates (Vygotsky, 1986, p. 236–37, 243).

> When we utter a word, we cannot help but mentally see an image of its written version. In our heads, what we have said ... is that sequence of written symbols. When we say 'dog,' a little picture of that word flashes through our minds, Sesame Street-style.... Imagine saying 'dog' and only thinking of a canine, but not thinking of the written word. If you're reading this book, it follows that you couldn't pull this off even at gunpoint (McWhorter, 2003, p. 3).

Presuppositions about inner speech

Not all these writers can be correct, and our DES work shows to my satisfaction that *none* is correct. Regarding

Archer and Baars, Heavey and Hurlburt (2008) showed that inner speech occurs in (normal) human beings about a quarter of the time, and in some people never or hardly ever. Regarding Vygotsky, my own extensive but unpublished observations show that predication is no more common in inner speech than in external speech. Regarding McWhorter, images of written words are very rare, perhaps less than one percent of samples, and *more* rare while uttering words aloud than when silent.

What makes these significant from the standpoint of presuppositions is not that they (at least some of them) are mistaken — that's merely ignorance — but the unquestioned assumption that apparently lies behind their mistakes: the ubiquity of inner speech. Each apparently took it as his task to explain some aspect of that ubiquitous inner speech without considering the possibility that that ubiquity was itself nonexistent. It is that assuming without question that makes this kind of presupposing toxic to consciousness science; the blindness, the systematic vigorous turning away from phenomena is revealed by the dogmatic nature of their own writings: 'It is doubtful it there is a (normal) human being who is unaware'; 'acutely if not infallibly aware'; '[predication] arises in inner speech always'; 'It is ... a law'; 'you couldn't pull this off even at gunpoint.' Mere ignorance is easy to correct; unquestioned assumptions are deeply rooted and stubborn.

It is possible that Archer himself does in fact have non-stop inner speech, that Vygotsky himself did in fact constantly predicate, and that McWhorter himself constantly sees pictures of words when he talks. But (a) I'd bet against it and (b) even if true, they have no warrant dogmatically to generalize from their own experience (see **Methodological Pluralism**). Getting inner speech right is pretty central to consciousness science, and, in my view, presuppositions toxically interfere with science's getting it right.

The remaining examples are drawn, one by one, from the contributors to this symposium, starting with you, Eric. If toxic presuppositions are a problem for them, it seems likely that presuppositions are widely problematic in consciousness studies.

Example 2: Eric.

Eric gave several subjects beepers and asked them to report on whether, at the moment of the beep, they were having tactile experience in their left foot (H&S, Ch. 10.3; Schwitzgebel, 2007). Eric asked other subjects to report on their tactile experience more generally, or on their visual experience, or on their visual experience in the right periphery of their visual field. While Eric's interviews of his subjects were fairly even-handed (to judge from the samples he shared with me), his prompting them to consider the issue important to *Eric* and the type of experience *Eric* is interested in, privileges *Eric*'s distinctions and interests over all others. He thus coerces his subjects into looking more directly at *his model* than at their own experience. We should expect subjects' reports not to reflect faithfully their experience, but rather to reflect, just as much, their response to the pressures and framework that Eric imposes upon them. (See also **Mark Engelbert and Peter Carruthers** for a different criticism of Eric's rich–thin study.)

Example 3: Kane.

Michael J. Kane published in 1994 a view of the inner experience in Tourette Syndrome based on his own introspections, in which he characterized himself as having frequent inner speech, inner seeings, and general hyper-awareness of bodily sensations. He freely acknowledged that he was quite attached, personally and professionally, to this view. His DES sampling as part of this symposium showed, to his surprise, that inner speech and visual imagery were rare for him. He did experience frequent sensations, but those were predominately of the external world rather than bodily. Thus in my view, for decades **Kane** has held powerful but incorrect presuppositional views of the inner experience in Tourette Syndrome that could be exposed by an adequate bracketing of presuppositions in DES interviews.

Example 4: Hill.

Hill (p. 33) implies that there is some scientific consensus about his three-kinds-of-pain-experience view, according to which there is 'peripheral pain' ('peripheral bodily disturbance'), 'somatosensory pain' ('somatosensory representation of that type of disturbance'), and 'pain affect' ('a complex pattern of activity in the anterior cingulate cortex and certain other parts of the limbic system'). He holds that subjects should be trained in this three-aspect system as a way of improving the accuracy of their reports. **Hill** attributes the three-kinds-of-pain-experience view to Price (1999). Price does indeed discuss three aspects of pain, but they seem to be three *different* aspects from **Hill**'s: a bodily sensation, an experienced threat, and a feeling of unpleasantness (Price, 1999, pp. 1–2). So I do not accept **Hill**'s premise that there is a scientific consensus about pain phenomena.

Hill on training pain reports

If **Hill**'s view of the phenomena of pain is not absolutely correct (which seems a live possibility given Price's view), training subjects in his view is likely to *decrease* the fidelity of their reports about pain. It will make it difficult for them to focus on *their own* pain experience because they will be encouraged to focus on one or another aspect of **Hill**'s (possibly incorrect) view. As a result, **Hill**'s subjects would likely give reports aligned with his theory at the expense of fidelity to their own experience. Because **Hill**'s subjects focus on **Hill**'s theory rather than on their experience, **Hill**'s failure to bracket presuppositions is toxic to his endeavour: it undermines his ability to validate his theory.

Example 5: Petitmengin.

As you pointed out above, Eric, **Petitmengin** helps her subjects to replay or re-enact experiences from the perhaps distant past. That procedure rests on the presupposition that such replaying/re-enacting is possible and that the replaying/re-enacting process does *not* inject its own substantial new material based on current interests, the current social situations, current cognitive development, current state, and other well known heuristics. I think all that is doubtful (Hurlburt & Akhter, 2006), largely because I think you, Bartlett, Neisser, Roediger, and **Sutton** are right about the reconstructive nature of recollection, and I presume it is that same concern that makes you 'nervous' about **Petitmengin**'s method. There may well be some phenomena and some situations where **Petitmengin**'s assumptions are correct, but rather than explore which phenomena and which situations, she seems quite sure that replaying/re-enacting is possible. It is that surety-without-examination that I call presuppositional, and which I fear is toxic to her endeavour, a fear which you, Eric, apparently share.

Example 6: Siewert.

Charles Siewert relies on what I called in H&S 'armchair introspection', which rests on the presupposition that one's own self-targeted, self-occasioned, theory-informed introspections do not unduly influence the pristine phenomena, a position I argue against in **Methodological Pluralism**. I note that **Siewert**'s contribution to this symposium does *not* counter my H&S criticisms of armchair introspection; instead, Siewert argues that DES has its own inadequacies, a position I freely accept but which does nothing to defend armchair introspection. I take that as evidence that **Siewert**'s view of self-targeted, self-occasioned, theory-informed introspection is presuppositionally rooted: **Siewert** seems to be saying that *of course* self-targeted, self-occasioned, theory-informed introspection has a central place in consciousness science. I accept that it does have some circumscribed place, but its current use is, I think, toxic: it's likely that Baars, Archer, Vygotsky, and McWhorter arrived at their (I think) faulty understandings courtesy of armchair introspection. See **Methodological Pluralism.**

Example 7: Horgan and Timmons.

Terry Horgan and Mark Timmons write, 'Might there be a way of generating descriptive data about people's agentive experiences that involves relatively presupposition-free questioning vis-à-vis views about free will and agentive experience generally? We don't see why not' (p. 204). That question reveals a presupposition that I think has two equally bad ramifications. It is difficult to ask presupposition-free questions that specifically single out the experience of free will, because the singling-out question itself strongly tilts the playing field towards reporting the experience of free will, whether or not that experience exists. That is, **Horgan and Timmons** appear to be suggesting a study that forces the subject into a preconceived frame, as would **Hill**'s study (and as does Eric's tactile-left-foot study discussed above). Even if **Horgan and Timmons** are genuinely open about what kind of agentive experiences might be discovered, entering the experiment with a model that subjects' reports are held against, and privileging reports of one type over another, already poisons the well. Similar risks attend **Engelbert and Carruthers**'s otherwise welcome suggestions for directions to expand DES methodology.

<small>Forcing into a preconceived frame</small>

As a result, a study such as **Horgan and Timmons** suggest is highly *un*likely to discover what they seek. This is unfortunate, because if they asked truly presupposition-bracketed questions, inquiring about experience *whatever that experience might be*, including the experience of free will *or not*, they might discover something fascinating about the experience of agency. In 1993 I wrote about the phenomenon of the 'doing of understanding,' suggesting that when some of my anxious subjects were engaged in conversation when another was speaking, they experienced a powerful direct-in-experience *necessity* to work hard at, actively reach out for, purposefully assemble their understandings of the other's speech. That is in distinct contrast with non-anxious subjects, for whom understanding is experienced as occurring with no sense of agency, work, or effort whatever — as if understanding happens automatically. Since 1993 I've corroborated that view, although I have not written about it since. The point here is that I'm pretty sure that if one sets out specifically to explore agency in the way **Horgan and Timmons** seem to suggest, *one will overlook entirely the doing of understanding phenomenon*, and such overlooking would deprive the investigator of a potentially fruitful slant on agency. Neda Raymond and I amplify this point in **Agency: A Case Study.**

Example 8: Klinger.

Eric Klinger, like most scientists of imagery, apparently believes that everyone has visual imagery, and that the differences in vividness of imagery 'arise from individual differences in the varying thresholds for admitting anything — sensory, cognitive, and emotional properties — into focal consciousness' (p. 93). That is possible but unlikely, I think, because there are large individual differences between people, and those differences are not threshold differences. Iman Abdulmajid could not be a National Football League lineman because of her body type, *not* because she has some differing threshold. I think it reasonable that inner differences are just as different as exterior differences.

<small>Presuppositions of universalism about imagery</small>

Klinger seems, like most imagery scientists, to hold a universalist position, as if everyone has the same kind of imagery to which some people have easier access. He writes, 'I have applied the classic window-counting exercise to numerous people, …[and] everyone…uses some variation of imagining walking around the house or, alternatively, walking into each room, and counting the windows' (p. 93). That statement is, I think, quite typical of exploration of phenomena in the science of imagery, and it suffers from all the disadvantages of armchair introspection (see **Methodological Pluralism)** plus social pressure from the interviewer, and therefore deserves substantial scepticism. Here's a kind of study that has *not* been performed: train a group of subjects in the DES procedure in their natural environments for enough days that they become adequately skilled at the method. Then engage them in the classic window-counting exercise and deliver a seemingly random DES beep during that event. Do that often enough, and one could discover what indeed occurs in the experience of a variety of individuals as they deal with that task. Such studies have not been undertaken, largely, I think, because consciousness science shares the (I think) toxic presupposition that imagery is universal with varying thresholds, so such studies are not necessary.

Example 9: Engelbert and Carruthers.

Carruthers's presuppositions about unsymbolized thinking

The case of **Carruthers** and presuppositions about unsymbolized thinking is especially instructive. Fifteen years ago, Carruthers argued against the existence of unsymbolized thinking (1996). I thought that argument was based on faulty presuppositions and said so in Hurlburt & Akhter (2008). As a result, Carruthers (2009) accepted the existence of unsymbolized thinking but mischaracterized it (by my lights) as 'purely propositional'. Thus it seems that **Carruthers** rolled back one presupposition and replaced it with another. I pointed out that mischaracterization in Hurlburt (2009), suggesting that unsymbolized thinking was a directly observed phenomenon, not a behind-the-scenes proposition. As result, in this symposium **Engelbert and Carruthers** accept the phenomenal nature of unsymbolized thinking and suggest the following experiment: 'Subjects who are already known [from prior sampling] to have a high proportion of unsymbolized thoughts could be asked to sit quietly in a dimly lit room allowing their minds to wander…. In these circumstances one might hope to get a high number of reports of unsymbolized thinking' (pp. 145–46). But there is nothing that I know of about unsymbolized thinking that suggests that unsymbolized thinking is more frequent while sitting quietly in dimly lit rooms — that apparently reflects some presupposition of **Engelbert and Carruthers**. Thus it seems that **Carruthers** rolled back the second presupposition and replaced it with a third.

To his credit, **Carruthers** has evolved his view of unsymbolized thinking. But at every step of the way, his newly emerging presuppositions have toxically interfered with his ability to grasp this phenomenon with fidelity: at first he presupposed that unsymbolized thinking couldn't exist; then he presupposed that if it existed, it must be purely propositional; then he accepted that it was phenomenal, but presupposed that it must occur most frequently in dimly lit rooms. Such a sequence is highly typical: presuppositions don't give up without a fight.

Example 10: Spener.

Many scientists would agree with **Maja Spener**'s statement, 'Most, those of us with a sceptical bent included, would accept that one can believe a subject's report that she is having a conscious experience of some sort right now, or that she is currently in pain, or that she is having a visual experience. This is because we assume that it is highly unlikely that people can be radically mistaken about their conscious lives' (p. 170). However, I have observed that many people are radically mistaken about their conscious lives. For example, **Kane**, in this symposium, had no knowledge, prior to sampling, that his experience consisted of much visual sensory awareness. Kane is not an exception; most people are to some degree mistaken, many radically.

That presupposition that it is 'unlikely that people can be radically mistaken about their conscious lives' is, I think, toxic to the science of experience. It lies behind the not-sufficiently-critical acceptance of self-report and armchair introspection, and discourages science from developing (or at least trying to develop) methods that might in fact reduce the frequency of such radical mistakes.

Examples 11 and 12: Sutton and Piccinini.

My presupposition detectors are quite silent in reading **Sutton**'s and **Gualtiero Piccinini**'s contributions. They jangle really only on one small detail. **Sutton** claims that I expect 17 DES-collected episodes to 'trump an accumulated life'. Actually, I have no such expectation: See **Clarifications of DES.**

Thus, of the 11 contributors to this symposium, my presupposition detectors jangle for 9 or maybe 10, depending on whether you count **Sutton**. I remind the reader that the symposium contributors were selected because of their prominence and the quality of their work; it is reasonable to suppose that presuppositions would be *more* problematic for a non-select group, although that would have to be shown. Thus I think that bracketing presuppositions is a major issue, striking at the heart of consciousness science.

Analogy 1:

Eric, you say, 'I presuppose that the floor will support me.' I also presuppose that. But we presuppose that exactly because the system has created a particular class of individuals ('building inspectors') whose job is precisely *not* to presuppose that. Building inspectors are trained to set aside appearances of solidity and structural adequacy and examine the solidity and structure for themselves. I want the building inspector to try to bracket all presuppositions related to construction adequacy, to try not to be taken in by the surface appearance, or by the adequacy of the drawings, or by the reputation of the builder, or by anything that you or I would take for granted when we step out of the elevator. I want the building inspector to look for herself: to take her own core samples, X-rays, ultrasounds, whatever it takes to establish for herself that the construction is adequate.

Analogy 2:

We're stranded in the deep forest. Russ sets out with his gun to get food.

Charles: What are you hunting for?

Russ: I don't limit myself with such predefined intentions — I'm going to shoot whatever I see that looks like food. Once I see something, then I'll invoke appropriate distinctions: if it has feathers I'll aim high; if it has antlers on one end, I'll aim nearer that end, and so on.

We're stranded in the deep forest. Charles sets out with his gun to get food.

Russ: What are you hunting for?

Charles: Squirrel. I have researched the habits of black squirrels, tree squirrels, Delmarva Fox Squirrels, and American Red Squirrels, and I have developed four hunting techniques, one specialized for each. I examine the foliage to determine which kind of squirrel is likely to be present, and then use the appropriate technique.

Charles's technique is superior if (a) he's right about the squirrel habits; (b) there really are squirrels in the forest; and (c) there aren't deer, turkey, or anything else that might be better to eat than squirrel. I have great faith in random sampling. If there are many squirrels, sooner or later I'll find them and then hire Charles to teach me how to shoot them. But if the forest is teeming with birds, deer, and corn, but not squirrels, Charles will starve to death. (For discussion of whether it is fair to use 'Charles' here — as in **Siewert** — see **Methodological Pluralism.**)

What all these examples and analogies try to illustrate is that a presupposition is a point of view that is so taken for granted that it invisibly affects everything in its range of convenience: it shapes what counts as evidence, specifies what seems necessary and what seems wasteful, dictates the time and energy that seems useful to invest in something, and so on; and in so doing it predetermines the range of possible outcomes of any investigation, blinds the investigator to what is overlooked, and perhaps above all provides an unwarranted sense of confidence in the justness of the cause. All this is difficult or impossible to observe in oneself, and I fear that the current version of consciousness science favours the collusive overlooking of such blindnesses in other scientists.

ERIC

Russ, I'm not going to be able to react to all of the above, but here are a few thoughts:

On **Hill**: I'm inclined to agree, Russ, that **Hill** overstates the degree of consensus about pain, though my impression is that most researchers do think that there are aspects of pain that can be pulled apart, in ways that lay introspectors don't think to do without some prompting, such as 'fast' vs. 'slow' pain or sensory vs. affective dimensions. I agree that it would be problematic to *impose* one of these distinctions on subjects, especially without an appreciation of the risks in doing so. However, it seems potentially helpful to point out to a subject that some researchers have made distinctions along these lines (explaining in some detail if necessary), inviting the subject to employ the distinctions if she finds them useful.

On my own work: I acknowledge that there will be potentially distorting pressures that come from applying any frame or distinction upon the reports, even if one tries to be open to answers of any sort, including answers that reject the frame, as I try to be, and as temperate versions of **Hill** or **Horgan and Timmons** presumably would also try to be. However, there will also be questions that will resist the application of unmodified DES — questions that require some conceptual preparation or that require that the subject try to notice aspects of her experience that might not be the first thing she would think to notice. This is one reason why I recommend trying to find convergence among flawed methods. (See also **Methodological Pluralism**.)

I draw the same pluralistic lesson from the analogy of the hunters. I want both types of hunter in the forest.

Russ, I think when you say that you aim to bracket all presuppositions (or all presuppositions 'that arise'), you evoke the ill-conceived scientific ideals of Bacon (1620/2000) and Descartes (1641/1984) — in particular the ideal of conducting inquiry completely free of background assumptions. The incoherence of that ideal was, I think, amply demonstrated by twentieth-century philosophy of science (especially Popper, 1935/1959, and Kuhn, 1962/1970) and twentieth-century cognitive psychology (including the work on memory I discussed above). Without background assumptions, and the categories and schemata that

[margin: Against Baconian philosophy of science]

depend on and embody them, one is as cognitively naked as the empiricists' baby, all sensory input only a buzz of confusion. This is true, I submit, regardless of temporal span. Contrary to what you seem to be suggesting above, Russ, our perceptions, judgments, and memories are thoroughly theory-laden, category-laden, and constructive or reconstructive from the start — even within one second of the DES beep.

I think we agree that twentieth-century philosophy of science is an improvement, in this respect, over seventeenth-century philosophy of science. And I think we can agree that there are cases in which it is a vice to adhere too rigidly to one's background assumptions and to discount too sharply evidence that conflicts with them. [Russ says: We agree on both.] Consider your hunter analogy. If Charles is right in his assumptions, then he will be better off than Russ. The greater the likelihood that he's not right, the better off we are having Russ-like hunters in the forest. Furthermore, the Russ-like hunter, as I'm imagining him, will not 'bracket' — at least not in any substantial sense of the term — all of his hunting-related knowledge. He will not set aside all his knowledge about squirrel behaviour, his knowledge of the difference between deer tracks and squirrel tracks, his knowledge of the fact that wind can carry odours, his knowledge of how to shoot a gun. Such knowledge, I assume, is well grounded enough that unless there are signs that something is amiss with it (e.g., the deer seem to keep scenting Russ, though Russ would swear he's downwind), he will act with that knowledge as working background. The core problem, then, as I see it — and as it seems to manifest in the dozen examples of presuppositions listed above — is that often what consciousness studies takes for granted *doesn't merit* being taken for granted. The Charles-like hunter has been reading, you think, from a bad manual or a manual that applies only to very different forests. We know far less about the stream of experience than we suppose; many of our working assumptions are false. The problem is not that working assumptions in general are toxic; it's that there are toxic ones in our soup.

<small>Only ill-grounded presuppositions toxic</small>

And thus it pays to be like the building inspector, explicitly examining the theoretical structures we bring to our study of the mind. But contrary to what you say, Russ, the building inspector should not aim to bracket *everything* pertinent to construction adequacy. She checks the strength of the floor at positions A, B, and C, and then, given her knowledge of building principles and the properties of materials, she feels licensed in concluding that it is also sufficiently strong at point D nearby. She assumes that concrete will not dramatically lose its strength over time. Barring any evidence of defect or strange outputs, she assumes that her instruments are working properly — except at certain moments when she is actively testing them. She has only an eight-hour day and she needs to make choices about what to check and what at least tentatively to accept.

It seems that a skilled building inspector will engage in two rather different epistemic activities. The first, it seems to me, we can rightly think of as 'bracketing': Although the rebar looks good, she checks it just to be sure. Although her voltmeter is giving no signs of defect, she checks it occasionally, against known voltages. This kind of active bracketing, I'd suggest, can only be of limited scope: our cognitive boat still needs to float while we remove and check a one or a few boards; we can't suspend everything all at once; we only fool ourselves, and blind ourselves to our biases and deficits, if we think we can hoist ourselves boatless across the sea.

Active bracketing vs. nose for trouble

The inspector's second skill is a nose for signs of trouble — a skill much harder, perhaps, to codify and a skill only acquired through long experience. Maybe although the floor at A, B, and C tests out okay, there's something a little weird or funny-looking about the floor at point D that calls out for testing. Maybe although the rebar generally passes, it sags slightly in one corner, or maybe there's something peculiar-seeming about how the windows are installed. The skilled building inspector will be attuned to such anomalies, so that even though she cannot actively check and explicitly test everything, as she looks around and uses her instruments, she is sensitive to a vast array of details — and that attunement seems to require deploying a large array of implicit assumptions, background knowledge, schemata, and prototypes.

So also in DES. I don't think it makes sense to try to bracket all assumptions pertinent to conscious experience: That would be like the hunter bracketing his knowledge of which end of the gun to point toward the animal or the building inspector bracketing her knowledge of whether the voltmeter tests voltage or amperage or ectoplasmic vibration. Unless there are signs of trouble, unless the interviewer's nose picks up something funny, the DES interviewer will, I think, tend to assume that when someone says 'I experienced it as physically inside my head' that that person has a relatively normal body-map according to which the head is not enclosed like the heart in the middle of the chest. The interviewer will not bracket the assumption of a relatively normal body map, I think, as much as hold it lightly, implicitly attuned to signs of trouble. Barring indications of something unusual in the subject's time experience, the DES interviewer will not think to ask the subject if she experiences time in one dimension or two different independent dimensions. In interviewing Melanie, I don't think you, Russ, were bracketing the presupposition or background belief that Melanie was speaking English as opposed to a weird possible language that sounds just like English but in which the words all mean something else entirely. Maybe you were holding that assumption lightly; maybe you were sensitively alert for places where she might be using words differently than most people do; but that attunement or holding lightly seems to me epistemically and cognitively very different from active bracketing of the sort the building inspector does when she runs her tests or the Russ-like hunter does when he says he is open to the possibility of lots of different types of game.

Even to hear a subject's report and to classify it in one's mind as an instance of inner speech, say, involves the deployment of categories, involves situating it in a web of knowledge. That's what we need to do in order to think about it, and in order to know what questions to ask and where to probe. It's the hunter seeing feathers (even though he wasn't assuming he would find birds) and knowing how to use his gun. I've noticed that you're pretty consistent in your interviewing about trying to distinguish (passive) inner hearing from (active) inner speaking (H&S, Box 6.5, p. 137). That's your background knowledge at work, directing your probing, probably with good cause and rightfully, getting at something possibly important in a way that most of us wouldn't have, as a result of long experience with open-minded DES interviewing; but if you're wrong about this distinction — if it's just an artifact and inner speech and inner hearing are really the same thing, only reported differently — then your interview and conclusions will be fouled up as a result. That's the upside and downside of background assumptions. We can't think without assumptions; but assumptions carry risk.

Thus the recommendation 'bracket all presuppositions' has, I think, at best a heuristic value, like the yoga teacher's instruction to 'reach up to touch the stars'. Maybe, given that most of us are hunched over with toxic background assumptions, it helps move us in a good direction, but you neither can touch the stars nor would want to do so if you could.

RUSS

Eric, we agree about much. In particular, we agree that 'The core problem... is that often what consciousness studies takes for granted *doesn't merit* being taken for granted,' and that is hugely important.

But we disagree about how science should proceed from there, and that disagreement has, I fear, serious consequences. I say 'presuppositions'; you say 'background assumptions.' I say 'bracket presuppositions'; you say 'hold presuppositions lightly.' I say 'bracket all presuppositions that arise'; you say 'bracket one or a few presuppositions.' I spend much time trying to develop a method that aids in the bracketing of presuppositions and trying to develop my own skill (and that of others) in applying that method; you do not see it as necessary to invest substantially in skill building before interviewing subjects. I'm willing to be somewhat casual about whether 'all that arise' means '*absolutely all* that arise' or just the first few hundred; you think that determining whether 'all' is meant ontologically or heuristically is of consequence.

It is not the words themselves that matter to me, it is their ramifications. I would be happy to say, for example, 'Fine! Go ahead and call it 'holding presuppositions lightly'!' except that I think those words encourage consciousness studies to remain stuck in the unwarranted-taking-for-granteds that we both decry. That is, I think you unintentionally *contribute* to the *continuation* of what you and I agree is its 'core problem,' so I will contest your word choices.

(1) 'Background assumptions' is too neutral, too free of human motivations, as discussed above.

(2) By 'hold presuppositions lightly' you mean that an investigator should be 'implicitly attuned to signs of trouble' and change her position if such signs occur. That is not relentless enough. For example, Baars, Archer, Vygotsky, and McWhorter would probably insist that *of course* they are attuned to signs of trouble in their theories of inner speech, and *of course* if they spotted such signs they would change their ways. *But they don't spot such signs of trouble* because it is the nature of presuppositions to blind one to such trouble spots.

'Hold presuppositions lightly' too wimpy

A presupposition is a skill (or set of skills), a dextrous coordination of learned tasks. That skill is perhaps counterproductive or self-defeating, but it is a skill nonetheless. A presupposition is a skillfully built, elaborated, and maintained coordinated, self-amplifying system of beliefs, fears, professional advantages, anxieties, economic incentives, narcissisms, and the like, each aspect supporting and defending itself and the other aspects. Part of that skill is to spot potential disconfirming evidence and, to turn away, defocus, aim attention elsewhere, whatever it takes to defuse the potential disconfirmation. An obvious example is the conservative who turns away from MSNBC and turns toward Fox News, whereas a liberal would do the opposite.

But presuppositions are high skills, practised across a lifetime, so this turning-away is usually not obvious. The skill is to turn away, defocus, aim attention elsewhere, do whatever it takes to undermine disconfirmation *when there is only a trivial hint of it,* at its first whiff, when it is a mere speck on the horizon. At the same time, one learns, with the same level of at-the-first-whiff subtlety, to spot potential confirmations when they appear and to turn toward them. Because the first whiffs, in either direction, are probably not explicitly recognized (and if they are recognized they are dismissed as trivial), the *world itself* seems full of confirmations and devoid of disconfirmations, and there is no appreciation for the highly refined (albeit self-defeating) skill that warps the view of the world.

The bracketing of presuppositions is also a skill, a personal set of coordinations that must be relentlessly sensitive and powerful enough to be able to counter the deeply rooted and taken for granted presupposition skill. It is an ongoing battle, pitching one set of coordinations against another set within the same individual. I'm pretty sure it is possible for the bracketing-skill to make progress against the presupposition-skill; I don't know whether the bracketing-skill can win once and for all (perhaps that is what is called nirvana, about which I have no personal knowledge).

'Hold presuppositions lightly' simply does not connote an activity that is energetic enough, relentless enough to penetrate the presuppositional self-containment; it does not acknowledge the difficulties presented or the courage required; it contains the implication that of-course!-I'm-already-doing-that; it implies that skill and practice is not required; it does not undermine the overconfidence that people have in their own positions. Most scientists, it seems to me, believe that they hold their presuppositions lightly, so if I were to exhort my colleagues to hold presuppositions lightly, as you suggest, I think I would be *de facto* saying to them: *Stay the course! No big deal here! Everything will be cool, just as now!*

But I don't want to communicate that. I want to say: *It's not good enough, and it is a huge deal! We have to do better! Consciousness science is full of unwarranted presuppositions, and we have persistently, continually, aggressively, fearlessly to fight to get them under control.* My attempt at conveying that is to say 'bracket presuppositions.' I'd be delighted if someone could suggest better words.

> Bracket more than 'one of a few'

(3) Your 'bracket one or a few presuppositions' is problematic for two main reasons. First, it is the nature of presuppositions that investigators *are blind* to which are the important presuppositions that should be bracketed.

Second, even if an investigator does know which one presupposition should be bracketed, the singling out of that one presupposition focuses *extra* attention on precisely that region of interest, and that makes the bracketing of that one presupposition *more difficult, not easier*, than the attempt to bracket many or all presuppositions. In your left foot study, for example (Schwitzgebel, 2007; H&S, Ch. 10.3, and the discussion above), you instructed the subjects in the tactile-left-foot condition that they were specifically to notice whether they were experiencing tactile sensations in their left foot, but instructed them *not* to pay any *special* attention to their left foot. Subjects so instructed reported more left-foot experience than did subjects who were instructed to report tactile experiences anywhere in their bodies (including but not limited to the left foot). There are obviously many potential explanations for why a part could be greater than the whole, but a likely one, in my view, is that when you tell someone (a) that you'll be asking in particular about their left foot and also (b) that they are not to pay any special attention to their left foot (that is, they are to bracket any special effect of instruction (a)), instruction (a) overwhelms instruction (b).

Thus, Eric, you seem to think it would be easier to bracket one or a few presuppositions than to bracket many presuppositions, whereas I think that is easier to bracket many than one. I accept that the bracketing of many presuppositions simultaneously is a complex, virtuosic skill, but there's nothing magical or metaphysical about that — it is merely the result of honing and rehoning a skill in many different situations.

(4) You consider my 'bracket all presuppositions that arise' as 'at best a heuristic..., like the yoga teacher's instruction to "reach up to touch the stars",' but that is misleading. 'Reach up and touch the stars' implies that the entire enterprise is a pretending — you never *actually* touch any single star. By distinct contrast, I want you *actually* to bracket one presupposition; and then while continuing to bracket that presuppositions bracket another; and then while continuing to bracket those presuppositions bracket another; and so on. There is no pretending involved; this is *not* a mere heuristic.

Not a heuristic

You list a series of things that you assume I take for granted, but I think I do *not* take such things for granted: I relentlessly probe to ensure that I understand what the subject is saying. For example, you say I presuppose 'that that person has a relatively normal body-map according to which the head is not enclosed like the heart in the middle of the chest.' However, I *don't* presuppose normal body maps. For example, I sampled with 'Emma', who said that at the moment of the beep she experienced anger in her head. Relentless examination revealed that by 'in her head' she actually meant a region began inside her physical head behind her forehead *but extended three or four inches into the space in front* of her forehead. Thus I discovered that the normal body map did not apply in her case, and I think I *would* similarly discover that the head was experienced to be in the chest next to the heart, if that is what was experienced. You say 'the DES interviewer will not think to ask the subject if she experiences time in one dimension or two different independent dimensions.' I fully accept that I might be presuppositionally blind to the multidimensionality of time, but I *do* relentlessly press time distinctions that seem pretty close to that. Last week, for instance, 'Adam' said that at the moment of the beep he was innerly seeing himself punch 'Bill' in the face and was watching the shock wave ripple across the skin of Bill's face. Careful questioning revealed that the first part of this seeing (the punch) was in real time, whereas the second part of the seeing (the ripples) was in substantially slow motion. It was only because we relentlessly did *not* take the experience of time for granted that we were able to make this discovery. You say I presupposed that 'Melanie was speaking English as opposed to a weird possible language that sounds just like English but in which the words all mean something else entirely.' However, I *don't* presuppose that I understand the language use; I investigate relentlessly to ensure that I understand the language that is being spoken, and that relentless investigation is what has allowed me to discover, for example, that 'thinking', when applied to one's own experience often does not mean something cognitive (see H&S, Box 4.1).

You say I merely lightly hold those presuppositions, and that when something fishy arises I investigate, but that substantially underappreciates the relentless checking, insistent probing, redundant questioning that I undertake to expose potential fishynesses. I probe in a variety of ways so that trivial hints, first whiffs, horizon specks *might appear*, and then relentlessly turn toward, seek out, track down the experience that created (or might have created) those hints/whiffs/specks.

Perhaps you would still say, 'Even so it is impossible to bracket *all* presuppositions that arise.' But I think that betrays your lack of the appreciation for skill. Some years ago I was a pretty good (I thought) self-taught classical guitarist when Ricardo Cobo, the internationally acclaimed virtuoso guitarist, moved to town. Cobo was also known as an excellent teacher, so I

Skills involve simultaneous doings: guitar example

decided to take some lessons. Cobo thought my right-hand technique was crummy: I needed to adjust my wrist so the ulnar bones were aligned; I needed to prepare each pluck by setting the fingertip on the string before initiating the pluck; I needed to follow through until my fingertips touch the palm; and so on. He thought my posture was crummy: I needed to hold the neck of the guitar lower; I needed to support my back just so; and so on. He thought my left-hand technique was crummy: I needed to see the new position *before* I moved my fingers; I needed to let the weight of my forearm do more of the work (rather than squeezing with the muscles of my fingers); and so on. So he had me slow my performances *way* down. I asked him which of these he wanted me to focus on, and he said '*All* of them: play slow enough so you can focus on *all of them*.' I replied that that was not possible — I could focus on only one or maybe a few. He said that I had to learn to control all of them simultaneously.

At first, I focused on only one at a time, but as I became more skillful, I could focus on two at a time, and as I became even more skillful I could focus on more and more at a time, and as my level of skill increased, I became able to play at faster tempos and increase my ability to focus on multiple tasks.

Perhaps you would say that I am not performing *all* these skills simultaneously, but rather am performing one new skill that has incorporated all the subskills into one organic whole. But it seems to me that by the time we get to this point, the distinction between *all as separate entities* and *all as facets of a single skill* is no longer important. Bracketing presuppositions is a skill closer to the virtuosic than to the pedestrian, acquired by relentless and long-term practice along hundreds of dimensions, always aiming at incorporating multiple dimensions in an active looking-for-and-controlling rather than a passive I'll-do-something-about-it-if-it-arises manner.

(5) You worry that I rule out prior knowledge, but I don't rule it out, I bracket it, and those are two very different things. For example, you said in your comment about **Hill** that 'it seems potentially helpful to point out to a subject that some researchers have made distinctions along these [three kinds of pain] lines (explaining in some detail if necessary), inviting the subject to employ the distinctions if she finds them useful.' If pain *arises* in the course of an interview —that is, the subject, *on her own*, describes pain — then I think it is okay, if it can be conveyed dispassionately, to point out to a subject 'that some researchers have made distinctions along these lines,' and invite the subject *to see whether or not that distinction helps her describe her experience with fidelity*. By contrast, **Hill** seemed to say, Make these

distinctions and *then* see if your experience can be fit (Procrusteanly or not) into *those distinctions*. That is far different from saying, Look at *your experience* and see if these distinctions help you describe *that experience*.

Here's a DES example. Aadee Mizrachi and I are exploring the inner experience of left-handed individuals (Mizrachi, 2010). There is a literature that *might* be related to the pristine experience of left-handers; for example, there are studies (Martin & Jones, 1999) about people's drawings that conclude that right-handed people draw action mostly headed to the left whereas left-handed people draw action mostly headed to the right. For example, if you ask people to draw a person in profile, the right-handed person's drawing will more often have the nose headed to the left, whereas the left-hander's drawing will more often have the nose headed to the right. The issue here is how or whether that knowledge should be used by a DES investigator.

_{Bracketing left-handedness theory in DES}

Yesterday's sampling of a left-hander included an experience in which left-handed 'Jill' was innerly seeing one of a series of images representing the idea of all the things she can do with her left-hand (apparently the result of a discussion she had had with us earlier as part of her volunteering for the study of left-handed individuals). At the moment of the beep, Jill was innerly seeing herself brushing her hair with her left hand. She innerly saw herself and her reflection in a mirror, seeing the right side of the directly observed Jill's body from the shoulders up looking at the reflected Jill in the mirror. The centre of her interest was on her left hand brushing her hair. This hand was seen in the reflected Jill, not in the unreflected Jill; Jill's unreflected head obstructed the view of her left hand.

This sample may have some significance from the prior-research-on-drawing perspective. Jill creates an inner seeing aimed at her left hand, but the way she constructs that seeing, she can't see her left hand because it is hidden by her head, which she sees from the right side, nose to the right as the literature would suggest. *Hmm. That's interesting.* It seems it would have been easier had she simply seen the left side of her head so that her left hand could be clearly seen (no mirror required); but no, Jill creates a more complex seeing that must involve two Jills. Does she do that because of a strong penchant to see action moving to the right? *Don't know. But we will make a note of it on the possibility that later sampling may reveal some regularities along this line.*

Thus the literature provides potentially interesting ways to understand this sample. But we have bracketed the way that literature will influence our research. First, we did *not* set out to validate the nose-direction-in-drawing literature. (Had we done so, we probably would have focused on drawing and missed entirely the inner seeing evidence.) As a result, the inner-seeing-to-the-right observation is even more interesting — we didn't go fishing for it. Second, we do *not* take this sample as evidence for or against the nose-direction view. Instead, it is potentially the beginning of something that might count as evidence, but also potentially merely a random occurrence that has nothing to do with the motion-to-the-right view.

The bracketing of the action-direction presupposition does *not* require that we stubbornly ignore (or, actually, that we *pretend* to ignore) everything that we know from other sources. Instead, it requires cultivating whatever skills are required to be genuinely even handed with respect to action direction, requires genuinely maintaining a level playing field with respect to action direction. The prior knowledge is *not inert*: it is only because we have the prior knowledge of the literature on handedness that we can have the interesting thoughts that we do have. And yet there's still a way of handling that prior knowledge skillfully, so that if the tempting thought precipitated by that literature is false — if the imagery experience of lefties isn't, in fact, typically right-directed — our ability to observe accurately remains uncompromised.

Eric, our conversation here about presuppositions and their bracketing has been abstract and general: we have argued for and against notions about what presuppositions are and what to do about them. But presuppositions are never abstract or general; my presuppositions are my own personal, idiosyncratic way of exaggerating, minimizing, avoiding, defending my own sensitivities. Therefore I fear our abstract/general discussion is itself a symptom of the disease rather than a step toward the cure. We have spent hundreds of hours debating the desirability of bracketing presuppositions and approximately zero hours actually building the skills of bracketing presuppositions.

Let's be personal

Presuppositions are stubborn and devious. Developing the bracketing-of-presuppositions skill requires commitment, effort, courage, and time, and it risks pain and decompensation. People avoid that development, it seems to me, using whatever highest-power defensive strategies they have at their disposal: they create a diversion, they preoccupy themselves elsewhere, they shut down, they feign weakness, they preach some Truth. In your case, your highest-power strategies include skilled argumentation, so a main impediment to your bracketing of presuppositions is likely to be seemingly sincere argumentation about whether such bracketing is necessary: the more energy you spend wondering whether it is necessary to attack presuppositions, the less energy you have actually to attack presuppositions. If I'm right about that, and if you want to apprehend experience in high fidelity, you will have to scale back your faith in the power of argument, and that will take substantial courage and commitment, because that faith is central to your philosophy, your everyday being, your job security, your financial situation, your collegiality, and doubtless many other substantially important features that send roots down to your very core.

Eric, your presuppositions are your own private property, your own skills and core beliefs ganging up to protect your own core beliefs, presuppositionally irrational or not. Bracketing your presuppositions is your task (if you choose to undertake it) and yours alone. It is not given to me to know whether you should undertake such a task, how successful you might be, or to prescribe how you should go about it if you do undertake it — there are doubtless many ways of confronting presuppositions. However, I remain convinced that 'If you let it, the randomness of the beep will break you, one presupposition at a time' (Hurlburt & Akhter, 2006, p. 284). If you apply your considerable skill and energy to the genuine attempt to apprehend randomly selected pristine experiences from randomly selected individuals, and as you do so you genuinely attempt neither to exaggerate nor minimize the fidelity of your apprehensions, and you do that for as long as is required, and you enlist the aid of fair-minded individuals who have presuppositions different from your own, you may be able substantially to refine your ability to apprehend pristine experience with fidelity and may become substantially more differentiated and acute in your scepticism thereabouts.

I happily accept that I may be wrong about all this — that it is *my* presuppositions, not yours, that are primarily at play here, that it is possible that I have engaged in this analytic exchange with you as *my* way of avoiding/defending *my own* irrationalities. Short of omniscience, I have no standing, no right, no ability to diagnose your presuppositions. The most I can say is that my presupposition detectors jangle, rightly or wrongly; forthrightly considered, that is a statement about *me*, not about you. That is the best that can be done: me on my side of the chasm suggesting a possibility about what might be taking place on the other side of the chasm.

Presuppositions are a challenge for consciousness science: they promote the status quo, which is problematic for a field whose status is contradictory and uncertain. I have suggested (Hurlburt, in press) ways that aid the bracketing of presuppositions: openbeginningedness, random sampling, joint-interviewing-with-sceptics, and so on. I expect that if science grasped the importance of the bracketing presuppositions, it could develop more and better ways than I have suggested. But the genuine attempt at bracketing is arduous; you have to 'be willing to see your own unbridled greed as well as the neurotic fallout that seems inevitably to follow the exposure of greed, be willing to be deconstructed (a process, which, if you want to avoid complete disorganization, requires varying periods of digestion, integration, maturation) with no guarantees about what gets reconstructed in its place and no guarantees about how long and deep the process has to go' (Hurlburt & Akhter, 2006, p. 296). In my optimistic moments, I think consciousness science can figure out how to support such efforts.

References

Archer, M.S. (2000) *Being Human: The Problem of Agency*, West Nyack, NY: Cambridge University Press.

Baars, B.J. (2003) How brain reveals mind: Neural studies support the fundamental role of conscious experience, *Journal of Consciousness Studies*, **10** (9–10), pp. 100–114.

Bacon, F. (1620/2000) *The New Organon*, Jardine, L. & Silverthorne, M. (eds.) Cambridge: Cambridge University Press.

Bartlett, F.C. (1932) *Remembering*, Cambridge: Cambridge University Press.

Carruthers, P. (1996) *Language, Thought and Consciousness*, Cambridge: Cambridge University Press.

Carruthers, P. (2009) How we know our own minds: The relationship between mindreading and metacognition, *Behavioral and Brain Sciences*, **32**, pp. 121–138.

Descartes, R. (1641/1984) Meditations on first philosophy, in Cottingham, J., Stoothoff, R. & Murdoch, D. (eds.) *The Philosophical Writings of Descartes*, Cambridge: Cambridge University Press.

Engelbert, M. & Carruthers, P. (this symposium) Descriptive Experience Sampling: What is it good for?, *Journal of Consciousness Studies*, **18** (1).

Heavey, C.L. & Hurlburt, R.T. (2008) The phenomena of inner experience, *Consciousness and Cognition*, **17**, pp. 798–810.

Hill, C. (this symposium) How to study introspection, *Journal of Consciousness Studies*, **18** (1).

Horgan, T. & Timmons, M. (this symposium) Introspection and the phenomenology of free will: Problems and prospects, *Journal of Consciousness Studies*, **18** (1).

Hurlburt, R.T. (1993) *Sampling Inner Experience in Disturbed Affect*, New York: Plenum Press.

Hurlburt, R.T. (2009) Iteratively apprehending pristine experience, *Journal of Consciousness Studies*, **16** (10–12), pp. 156–188.

Hurlburt, R.T. (this symposium) Nine clarifications of Descriptive Experience Sampling, *Journal of Consciousness Studies*, **18** (1).

Hurlburt, R.T. (in press) *Investigating Pristine Inner Experience: Moments of Truth*, Cambridge: Cambridge University Press.

Hurlburt, R.T. & Akhter, S.A. (2006) The Descriptive Experience Sampling method, *Phenomenology and the Cognitive Sciences*, **5**, pp. 271–301.

Hurlburt, R.T. & Akhter, S.A. (2008) Unsymbolized thinking, *Consciousness and Cognition*, **17**, pp. 1364–1374.

Hurlburt, R.T. & Heavey, C.L. (2006) *Exploring Inner Experience: The Descriptive Experience Sampling Method*, Amsterdam and Philadelphia: John Benjamins.

Hurlburt, R.T. & Raymond, N. (this symposium) A case study in bracketing presuppositions: Agency, *Journal of Consciousness Studies*, **18** (1).

Hurlburt, R.T. & Schwitzgebel, E. (2007) *Describing Inner Experience? Proponent Meets Skeptic*, Cambridge, MA: MIT Press.

Hurlburt, R.T & Schwitzgebel, E. (this symposium) Methodological pluralism, armchair introspection, and DES as the epistemic tribunal, *Journal of Consciousness Studies*, **18** (1).

Kane, M.J. (this symposium) Describing, debating, and discovering inner experience, *Journal of Consciousness Studies*, **18** (1).

Kane, M.J. (1994) Premonitory urges as 'attentional tics' in Tourette's Syndrome, *Journal of the American Academy of Child and Adolescent Psychiatry*, **33**, pp. 805–808.

Klinger, E. (this symposium) Response organization of mental imagery, evaluation of Descriptive Experience Sampling, and alternatives, *Journal of Consciousness Studies*, **18** (1).

Kuhn, T.S. (1962/1970) *The Structure of Scientific Revolutions*, 2nd ed., Chicago, IL: University of Chicago Press.

Martin, M. & Jones, G. (1999) Motor imagery theory of a contralateral handedness effect in recognition memory: Toward a chiral psychology of cognition, *Journal of Experimental Psychology: General*, **128** (3), pp. 265–282.

McWhorter, J. (2003) *Doing Our Own Thing*, New York: Gotham.

Mizrachi, A. (2010) *Examining the Inner Experience of Left-Handers Using Descriptive Experience Sampling*, unpublished Masters thesis, University of Nevada, Las Vegas.

Neisser, U. (1967) *Cognitive Psychology*, East Norwalk, CT: Appleton-Century-Crofts.

Petitmengin, C. (this symposium) Describing the experience of describing?, *Journal of Consciousness Studies*, **18** (1).

Piccinini, G. (this symposium) Scientific methods ought to be public, and Descriptive Experience Sampling is one of them, *Journal of Consciousness Studies*, **18** (1).

Popper, K. (1935/1959) *The Logic of Scientific Discovery*, London: Routledge.

Price, D.D. (1999) Psychological mechanisms of pain and analgesia, *Progress in Pain Research and Management*, Vol. 15, Seattle, WA: IASP Press.

Roediger, H.L. (1980) Memory metaphors in cognitive psychology, *Journal of Experimental Psychology: Human Learning and Memory*, **6**, pp. 558–567.

Schwitzgebel, E. (2007) Do you have constant tactile experience of your feet in your shoes? Or is experience limited to what's in attention?, *Journal of Consciousness Studies*, **14** (3), pp. 5–35.

Siewert, C. (this symposium) Socratic introspection and the abundance of experience, *Journal of Consciousness Studies*, **18** (1).

Spener, M. (this symposium) Using first-person data about consciousness, *Journal of Consciousness Studies*, **18** (1).

Sutton, J. (1998) *Philosophy and Memory Traces*, Cambridge: Cambridge University Press.

Sutton, J. (this symposium) Time, experience, and Descriptive Experience Sampling, *Journal of Consciousness Studies*, **18** (1).

Vygotsky, L. (1986) *Thought and Language*, Cambridge, MA: MIT Press.

Russell T. Hurlburt
and Eric Schwitzgebel

Little or No Experience Outside of Attention?

Some of the things [Hurlburt] says suggest he thinks that it is fairly common for DES subjects to believe correctly they just saw and were looking at something, even while lacking visual experience *entirely*. More astonishingly still, he suggests that they (and we) are ordinarily actually like this for much of our day. For if I usually don't have visual experience while reading and talking, it's unclear to me when I do — but surely it can't be *very often*. Hurlburt's view of visual experience is radically 'thin'. (**Siewert**, p. 66)

When a subject denies that an experience of a certain sort occurred on a particular occasion, it may be that, as a result of the limits of attention, the subject has simply overlooked an experience that was present but not prominent. As a result, *negative* introspective reports should be accorded much less weight than positive reports. (**Hill**, p. 29)

Hurlburt tells us that the vast majority of his subjects deny the richness of their inner experience. In general, a sampled moment contains only one or a few experiences at a time. Schwitzgebel is sceptical. For the fact that randomly sampled reports are mostly sparse is consistent with richness plus quick fading. Although this is conceivable, we don't think that the suggestion is a plausible one. For in that case one would at least expect subjects to report that they have the *sense* that there was a lot more going on, but they can't remember what. (**Engelbert and Carruthers**, p. 136)

ERIC

In H&S[1] and in Schwitzgebel (2007) I expressed an inclination toward the rich view of experience, according to which, for example, we have constant tactile experience of our feet in our shoes and constant visual experience of the scene before our eyes even when our

---

[1] See note and correspondence details on page 206 above.

attention is directed elsewhere — though I endorsed that view with a substantial helping of doubt. Several of our commentators address the issue. **Charles Siewert** finds it incredible to suppose that we often entirely lack visual experience. **Mark Engelbert and Peter Carruthers**, in contrast, accept a thin view according to which inner experience is relatively sparse. **Christopher S. Hill** views the question as open, but argues that negative results (the denial of experience) should be accorded much less weight than positive results (the assertion of experience).

<small>Engelbert & Carruthers *contra* the rich view</small>

In more recent work (Schwitzgebel, in press) I find myself more even-handedly sceptical, in part because I feel the force of **Engelbert and Carruthers**'s criticism of my view. I find especially interesting their argument about 'iconic memory' as a possible explanation of why those of us intuitively attracted to the rich view might think we have sensory experience of unattended events. My favourite example here is the chiming clock tower: you are paying no attention to the clock tower until you hear the fourth chime. Immediately after you hear the fourth chime you count back chimes in memory and correctly conclude that there have been four. But does this show that you experienced those first three chimes when they occurred? Not necessarily. As **Engelbert and Carruthers** say, information from those chimes will have been processed to some degree and might still be 'reverberating' in some nonconscious memory system; as soon as attention is directed to the matter, that information might become conscious for the first time. I'm not endorsing that view; but neither do I feel comfortable dismissing it.

Engelbert and Carruthers's positive argument for the thin view, that people don't report having a sense that a lot was going on, I find less convincing. Some people do report such a sense, I've found, when questioned directly about it. And as I mentioned in H&S (Ch. 10.3), I think that the Descriptive Experience Sampling (DES) interview situation creates pressures against reporting richness: DES explicitly focuses on what is central, subjects may have the sense that reports on what is peripheral and not swiftly considered after the beep may not have much value, and asking for about six samples conveys the expectation that each sample shouldn't normally take more than about ten minutes to discuss. And **Engelbert and Carruthers** are more sanguine than I about the accuracy of introspection if they think that the theory-laden retrospective judgments of subjects who lean toward a thin view (or who are nudged, as I think DES does nudge them a bit, toward thinnish reports) should count as evidence strong enough to dismount a proponent of a rich view.

Here's why I think the issue is important: if the rich view is correct, then consciousness is very abundant. That should have a big impact on any general theory of consciousness — on any theory of the functional role of consciousness and of the kinds of brain structures in which it's instantiated. If the thin view is correct, then consciousness is sparse, with a consequent impact in the opposite direction on theories about the functional role and brain structures of consciousness. Or maybe experience is moderately abundant or moderately sparse. To some people — **Siewert**, perhaps — it seems obvious that consciousness (or visual consciousness specifically) is abundant. To others, I've found, it seems obvious the other way around. Attempts to settle the question by concurrent introspection founder on the possibility of the refrigerator light illusion (e.g., the possibility that attention to whether you have experience in your feet causes experience in your feet, where none was before; H&S, Box 4.18, p. 90). So immediate retrospection seems like the way to go — possibly through DES or some DES-like method, like I tried in my 2007 article. So the question becomes to what extent we should trust such retrospective reports.

RUSS

Imagine the following scenario:

Example: looking without attention

A person named Mark is sitting across the restaurant booth table from his friend/colleague Eric during an APA meeting. The conversation lulls at time t_1, and Mark looks at Eric's hat, closely inspecting the pattern of its stitching. Mark does indeed have a visual experience of its stitching and pattern. While so looking, Mark overhears a conversation in the booth behind him, recognizes the voices to be Dan's and David's, and notices that their conversation concerns an evaluation of Mark's own work. Mark is interested in this seemingly confidential conversation, so he freezes, not wishing to add any creak of the booth or rustling of his own clothing to the ambient restaurant noise, and he strains to hear what Dan is saying to David. During this intent listening, at time t_2, Mark's eyes happen to remain aimed at Eric's hat (the same hat is projected onto Mark's retinas at time t_2 as at time t_1).

Now suppose that Mark undergoes a state-of-the-art interview about his experience at t_2. Mark might say that he was entirely absorbed in what Dan was saying to David. If asked about the hat, he might say that *experientially* the hat ceased to exist — that of course in reality it persisted, but his experience of it had vanished. If pressed, he might say that yes, he understands that his eyes were aimed at the hat, but it certainly seemed that he had no experience of it whatsoever.

Now imagine a parallel universe identical to the one just described except that it is a person named Charles, not Mark, who happens to be sitting across from Eric. If asked to report on his experience at t_2, he might not even think to mention seeing the hat. If pressed, he might say that yes, there probably was some slight or secondary or peripheral experience of it.

It seems to me that *if a state-of-the-art interview has been employed,* we can say the following with substantial confidence:

(1) Mark had substantial visual experience (of the hat) at t_1; same for Charles.
(2) Mark had little or no visual experience (of the hat or anything else) at t_2; same for Charles.
(3) Mark had substantially more visual experience at t_1 than he did at t_2; same for Charles.

It further seems to me that *even* if a state-of-the-art interview has been employed, we *cannot* say *any* of these with confidence:

(4) Mark had *no* visual experience at t_2; same for Charles.
(5) Mark had *a little* visual experience at time t_2; same for Charles.
(6) Charles had more visual experience at t_2 than Mark had at t_2; or vice versa.

Perhaps if science can substantially improve the introspection art, the present analysis can be scrapped. But for now, it is not possible confidently to determine whether there is a difference in pristine experience — experience unaffected by beeping or other for-the-subject unusual form of self-examination (see **Clarifications of DES**) — between what one person (say, Mark) characterizes as 'seemingly no inner experience' and another person (say, Charles) characterizes as something like 'probably a little inner experience'. The skilled DES interviewer, knowing that it is practically impossible to tease apart the 'seemingly no' from the 'probably a little' experience, *does not try* to do so, and therefore settles for concluding that Mark and Charles each had 'little or no' experience. If I say, about a DES subject, that she had 'no inner experience' of a particular kind at a particular moment, that is a relaxed (some might say sloppy) way of saying that the subject had 'little or no inner experience' of that kind at the time.

DES does not try to distinguish 'little' from 'no'

By setting aside the distinction between 'little' and 'no' experience, I am setting aside a distracting issue that we don't (yet) have the tools to address adequately. Instead of trying to distinguish between things that are impossible (or nearly so) to distinguish, I seek instead to distinguish between things *that are straightforwardly possible to distinguish* (that are easily observed *with the right method and skills*) but which have been overlooked by those who have not used an adequate method (and by those who have been distracted by trying to distinguish between things that are (nearly) impossible to distinguish). For example, most modern introspection has overlooked unsymbolized thinking (Hurlburt & Akhter, 2008; though Siewert, 1998 is a notable exception) and sensory awareness (Hurlburt, Heavey, & Bensaheb, 2009), despite the DES fact that each occurs in about a quarter of all pristine experiences (Heavey & Hurlburt, 2008). Unsymbolized thinking and sensory awareness are, I think, robust phenomena, close to the centre of the experiential target, but paying too much attention to difficult-if-not-impossible-to-distinguish fringes (such as rich/thin and no/little) can cause and probably has caused robust phenomena to be overlooked (Hurlburt, in press).

ERIC

I wouldn't entirely disagree with your cautious attitude, Russ, but I think you're missing the merit in **Hill**'s and **Siewert**'s criticisms.

Hill on overlooking experiences

Hill doesn't flesh out exactly what he means when he says that a subject might 'overlook an experience that was present but not prominent,' so let me develop the idea just a bit further. At the last undisturbed moment of experience before the beep, there might be N different types of experience ongoing. (I'm nervous about counting up types of experience, but I don't think the argument turns on strict countability.) If consciousness is thin, N might be one or a few, or even zero; if consciousness is rich, N might be a dozen or more, depending on how finely one individuates experience types. Then the beep occurs and the subject starts reflecting on what her experience was. She will think, first, of one particular experience — say a vivid image. What makes her think first of this experience might depend on any number of competing and co-operating factors, including: the vividness of the experience, her interest in that type of experience, her theory-driven expectation that such experience would be found, the fact that that experience has persisted (or not) into the moment after the beep, environmental cues, the ease with which that aspect of experience is conceptualized, the distinctiveness or appeal of the experience, habits governing what kinds of experience she tends to look for first, and so on. After at least a brief preliminary judgment about the presence of that type of experience, and presumably a few of its features, she will think about another one of the N experiences, or she will try to reach a judgment about the presence or absence of some particular type of experience — that is, whether that type of experience was among the N. And so on. At some point, probably pretty quickly, she will lose patience or her memory will have faded too much for her to feel like it's worthwhile to continue the process.

On this model of what's going on after the beep, one might expect regular denials of experience of various types, even if the rich view is correct. And since the vividness of the experience is only one factor influencing whether it is noticed, we cannot, I think, assume that the denial of experience implies that the experience was not vivid; we cannot assume (if this makes sense — see my comments on **Siewert** shortly to come) that there was only a 'little' of that experience, or that there was 'more' visual experience at t_1 than at t_2 in your example. Perhaps big elements of experience are regularly missed simply because they're not the kinds of things that the subject is inclined to look for, or to attend to, in the moment immediately after the beep. Thus, I'm inclined to agree with **Hill** that we should be especially cautious about negative reports.

RUSS

Eric, I agree that DES may overlook some types of experience, perhaps including some important types and perhaps including many types. But that is true of *all* forms of introspection, and I think arguably *less* damning for DES than for other introspections because of the iterative and collaborative nature of DES (see **Clarifications of DES**). Consider **Michael J. Kane**'s lack of inner speech in the DES sampling he did for this symposium. Mike believed about himself, prior to sampling, that he 'spend[s] a lot of time "in my head", thinking about personal, political, and professional issues via inner-speech and inner-seeing simulations of events and exchanges' (p. 158). However, sampling revealed *no* confidently apprehended inner speech. Here is Mike's sample that includes his *most* confident report about inner speech:

Iterative procedure reduces risk of overlooking

> Sample 3.1 Mike is walking from his office to the bus stop and has three simultaneous aspects of his experience:

1. He has a sensory awareness of the pink of a crape myrtle bloom against the slate-gray of the building behind it. The pink was 'popping' at him. He is confident that his focus was on the *contrast between* the pink and the gray. That is, his experience was pink-against-gray, not merely of strong pink that happened to be against a gray background.

2. He is innerly hearing the chorus from Paul Simon's 'Mother and Child Reunion,' apparently just like hearing it on the CD. As best he can tell it is an accurate rehearing, probably including the accompaniment, but he is focused on the singing, not the accompaniment. However, he is confident that it's not like an *a cappella* version of the song — it sounds just like the original, as far as he can tell. This phenomenon is clearly an inner *hearing*, not a *speaking*.

3. He has little confidence about this third aspect: he thinks he was innerly talking to himself, or maybe hearing himself talk, but he's not sure. The topic was how to explain the beeper's earpiece to his neighbor Wesley if Wesley stops, as he sometimes does, to pick Mike up at the bus stop and give him a ride home. Mike had the sense that he was 'just missing' catching fragments of a conversation he imagined having with Wesley, but he couldn't apprehend the words at all. He is pretty sure that the general topic was what to say about the earpiece.

The question here is whether Mike is experiencing inner speech about (or to) Wesley in sample 3.1; I think it is not possible to answer that with confidence. Maybe Mike experienced clear inner speech but forgot it when beeped. Maybe Mike experienced only a very vague inner speech which was overrun by the clear sensory awareness. Maybe he experienced an intimation of inner speech but not speech itself. Maybe Mike's presupposition of frequent inner speech led him to believe he experienced a hinty inner speech when none is there. About this particular sample, we must concede that we can*not* tease those alternatives apart with confidence.

Consulting your list of factors, Eric, Mike's inner speech is just the kind of experience that Mike should *not* be expected to have overlooked: inner speech is easily conceptualized; Mike was interested in and expected to find inner speech; it seems strange that he would tend first to consider the sensory awareness of colour (about which he had no prior interest) before inner speech; it seems strange that inner speech would evaporate for Mike while it easily continues to be present for other subjects; and inner speech is certainly distinctive and appealing. That is, the factors you list (except, perhaps, environmental cues, and even they seem likely to wash out across multiple randomly selected occasions) seem to suggest that Mike *would easily* spot inner speech if it were present. I accept, as you say, that surely there are other factors that might be invoked, but your own analysis seems to suggest that the most likely explanation is that Mike had little or no inner speech experience at the moment of this beep.

But more importantly, you and **Hill** seem to overlook that a DES *iteratively refined* report is substantially different from a one-shot (= first-day) report (see the discussion of iteration in **Clarifications of DES** and in Hurlburt, 2009; in press). I agree with you and **Hill** that if this were an unpractised, first-day report, it would be of highly questionable validity.

But in the first sampling interview, Mike and I discussed his seeming lack of inner speech. (*Hmm! I have no inner speech! Is that really possible?!? I was sure I had frequent inner speech! I'll look closer next time!*) On the second sampling day, Mike still did not directly experience inner speech. (*Hmm! That's wild! I'll look really closely now!*) Third sampling day; still no inner speech; the closest we get to inner speech is sample 3.1 above.

Now we have a series of what might still be called 'negative introspective reports', but these *iteratively refined* negative reports are *not*, as it seems to me, on an epistemological par with the first-day (= one-shot) negative introspective reports. Mike might have simply forgotten to report inner speech (because of the demands of working memory, as **Hill** suggests) on the *first* sampling day, but such a claim seems absurd about Mike's *third* day.

I fully accept that it remains possible that something about the beeping process scares away Mike's inner speech (on the third day as well as on the first day). But if one accepts that possibility, then it seems that one should accept about equally the possibility that the beep *creates* the sensory awareness that dominated Mike's experience on all sampling days. So I conclude that whereas DES reports (as probably all introspective reports) have limitations, iteratively refined negative reports do not deserve less credence than positive reports, and both deserve more credence than one-shot introspections. I don't place great faith in any one report (positive or negative), but instead rely on a randomly generated, iteratively improved group of reports which I continue to collect and examine as long as a particular issue is in play (e.g., Is there inner speech or isn't there?).

ERIC

I like that example, Russ, and for the reasons you suggest I'm inclined tentatively to accept that Mike doesn't have nearly as much inner speech as he expected. However, the factors governing the credibility of the reports might play out differently when it's peripheral sensory experience at issue, especially if the subject is disinclined to expect such experience and the interview is not designed to bring it out. [Russ says: I agree.]

<small>What does 'a little' experience mean?</small>

Siewert is critical not only of your use of 'no' experience but also of your use of 'a little' experience, and, like Siewert, I'm not sure, really, what you mean by 'a little' experience. Siewert mentions three possible interpretations of what someone might mean by saying she had a little visual experience of something. One possibility is that one had only a brief glance at that thing. A second possibility is that things looked relatively homogenous and undifferentiated (in the extreme case, like an evenly gray 'Ganzfeld') — possibly because of poor lighting or visual defect. A third possibility is that there are few items that '*you can identify in the course of that experience*' — for example, only a few of the shapes or patterns in a complex Persian rug that you are appreciating well enough to be able to identify, retrospectively, after the rug has been removed (p. 76). I might add a fourth possibility to Siewert's list: that the size of the experienced visual field is small, say ten degrees of visual arc, with blankness outside of that, as opposed to (say) 160 degrees of visual arc.

It seems, Russ, that you must mean something different by 'a little' than any of those things. It seems that you are saying that at any particular moment, with respect to any particular part of the visual field or any particular object in the visual field, there is a quantity of consciousness pertaining to it, ranging from zero to a lot, with 'a little' in the middle. I see some of the theoretical attractions in this view. For example, it seems doubtful that there is a single moment in evolution or in human development when we suddenly change from experienceless creatures to experiencing creatures. And if that's the case, then there must be some way for it to be a vague or in-between matter whether one has experiences, for transitional creatures; and if that is so for them, maybe it's also so for us, perhaps instantiated in a vagueness or in-betweenness in the perceptual experience of unattended objects. But despite my theoretical attraction to that view I can't wrap my mind around the concept of vagueness in experience. I can only conceptualize experience as on/off, as determinately present or absent. However tiny you make the experience — maybe it's visual experience of plain grayness over half a degree of visual arc, or maybe it's the fleetingest experience of an indistinct form I can say virtually nothing about in retrospect — that experience is either there or not there. I can't seem to conceive of its being a vague or in-between matter whether I had visual experience in such a case or not. While degrees of visually experienced arc is a scalable predicate, as is

> Experience not scalable

amount of memorable detail, as is temporal duration, as is degree of homogeneity, I don't see how 'experienced' itself is a scalable predicate in that way. I don't see, then, how you can have only 'a little' experience of a visual scene, except in one of the ways that **Siewert** and I have articulated, or a similar way. Either you had some visual experience, or you had none. (See also H&S Box 9.1, pp. 194–95; Antony, 2008.)

I readily admit that this might be a limitation only in my conceptualization of experience, or a flaw in my criteria of conceivability, not reflecting any fact about the world. As I said, it seems plausible evolutionarily and developmentally that there would be a scalable range of vague cases between having visual experience and not having it. But if so, I can't wrap my mind around that.

RUSS

Eric, let me first address one of **Siewert**'s arguments against my 'little or none' view, then I will reply to your concern about the coherence of my view.

Siewert says that if a DES subject denies having visual experience, then he wants to ask, 'Right before the beep, did things look to you just the way they look to you when you are in a tightly sealed lightless room — i.e., *not any way at all*?' And he says that he would interpret the subject as denying having visual experience if she said '*yes, that's exactly how it was in the moment before the beep*' (p. 71). He then states that he would be surprised if a DES subject like Melanie would say this; so he seems to think that DES reports, properly collected, would not provide evidence for the thin view.

I agree that DES reports, properly collected, do not provide evidence for the thin view (nor for the rich view), for the reasons discussed above. But in any case, **Siewert**'s question is a deceptive question, for two reasons. (1) It implies, probably incorrectly, that Melanie is familiar with the details of her experience in lightless rooms. (2) It presupposes what experience in lightless rooms is like as if it were a simple thing; but I think it is not at all simple. Certainly there is visual experience in lightless rooms, of blackness, of flashing lights, and so on (in fact, Eric discusses this issue at length in Schwitzgebel, in press, Ch. 8).

Eric, you and **Siewert** apparently imagine that I distinguish three ranges of experience (a lot, a little, and no) when actually I distinguish only two (some, and little-or-no). So I do not think it necessary (or possible) to define what I mean by 'a little' because in fact I do not mean *anything* by 'a little' separate from little-or-no.

I accept that there are some arenas where a disjunction between 'a little' and 'no' applies — money, for example. There is an ontological distinction between having 'no money' and 'a little money': if you have one penny, you are in the 'a little money' category (even if it is *practically* indistinguishable from being in the 'no money' category). But there are other arenas where terms do not reflect ontological distinctions but instead have limited ranges of convenience — 'mountain' for example. How many mountains are there in Figure 1? One reasonable answer is 'One — the one labeled "1".' Another reasonable answer is 'Two — the one labeled "1" and the one labeled "2".' Yet another reasonable answer is 'Four — the ones labeled "1", "2", "3", and "4".' In fact, depending on the length of your ruler, the closeness of the inspection, and the flatness of the surrounding landscape, answers that range from 'one' to 'hundreds' can be defended as reasonable. It is *not* the case that there is a region of mountains, another region of little mountains, and another region of no mountains. Instead, there are peaks that everyone would always call mountains, and there are peaks that it wouldn't typically occur to anyone to invoke the term mountains (or, for that matter, not-mountains), not because there are two ontologically distinct landscape types but because the term mountain has a limited range of convenience.

> The experiential landscape

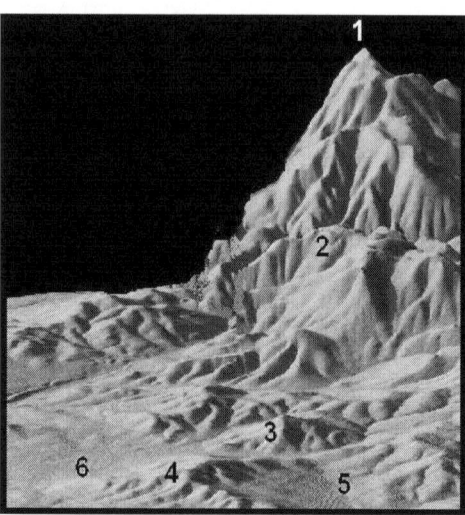

Figure 1. How many mountain peaks?

I take the landscape of Figure 1 to be a reasonable schematic of typical pristine (undisturbed) inner experience, where the height represents salience (whatever that is) and the two horizontal axes represent only that there is more than one dimension where experience might occur. Figure 1 as experience-schematic illustrates that there are a welter of things (potential experiences or 'experience-lets') clamoring or competing or jostling or whatever (the peaks in Figure 1) for <salience> (or <experiencedness>, <power>, <focus>, <attention>; I do not claim to know what I'm talking about here; hereafter I'll call it salience for short). I've numbered a few of these experiencelets (1 through 6), but there are hundreds more I could have numbered. At time t, the experience that I have numbered 1 has (for whatever reason) become highly salient — that is, *far* higher than any of the other potential (or actual but small) experiences. As I have gleaned from hundreds of very careful and iteratively refined interviews, most people, at most pristine moments, experience *one* (or a very few) dominances, and little or nothing else is experienced. Not all people are like this; Fran (H&S, Ch. 2.3.2.1) is a notable exception, as are the bulimic women of Hurlburt & Jones-Forrester (in press). That is, in typical everyday pristine experience, out of the hundreds or thousands of things in the welter of experience-lets or potential experiences that *could* rise to salience, most *don't* get very salient (the peaks don't get very 'high') at any given moment.

The picture I'm trying to paint here is of an experiential 'landscape' that is, in all its features, constantly changing, more or less like a three-dimensional version of the bars on the equalizer of your stereo. A few moments after the Figure 1 snapshot, peak #1 shrinks and (say) #4 grows dramatically. All the peaks are moving up and down, growing and shrinking, widening and narrowing, more or less independently of each other.

This experiential landscape illustrates why I think trying to distinguish between 'rich' and 'thin,' and between 'no' and 'a little' is impossible. How many experiences are illustrated in this figure? Answers that range from 'one' to 'hundreds' can be defended as reasonable. How salient does an experience-let have to be (how high does a peak have to be) before we stop saying 'a little experience' and start saying 'no experience'? That dividing line is entirely arbitrary. Some would say this schematic gives evidence for 'rich' — there are *lots* of peaks. But that ignores that some peaks are *far* higher than others. I can see no way out. My solution has been to try to develop a method that gets all (or almost all) of the 1s and nearly all of the 2s, and accept that it may well overlook the 3s, 4s, 5s, and 6s. Whether that is adequate depends on one's point of view. Most methods of introspection miss many of the 1s (unsymbolized thinking and sensory awareness, for example).

Thus I think **Siewert** has it wrong when he says, 'I don't think DES supports — or has any prospect of supporting — the radical denials of [visual] experience suggested by many of Hurlburt's remarks' (p. 77). I have not radically denied visual experience. Radical implies absolute, and that is not what I have thought or said. Visual experience is *often* a small peak (like a #3, 4, 5, or 6 in the Figure 1 schematic), or perhaps a number of such peaks, or perhaps no peak at all, far overshadowed by some other non-visual experience (peak #1). Visual experience often exists in the 'little-or-no' minorly hillocky flatland along with lots of other experience-lets.

ERIC

Russ, I think you probably mischaracterize the issue when you imply that it's a matter of linguistic choice, like the matter of choosing what to label a mountain peak, given that we agree about the actual topology. We don't agree about the topology. And there's a real difference, it seems to me, between *potential* experiences, which are literally unexperienced, and *actual* experiences, regardless how 'little' or un-'salient' the latter are. So I might adjust your schematization as follows: There is a threshold height — perhaps a vague and ill-defined threshold — above which those hillocks are actually experienced and below which they represent only cognitive processes that could be experienced but are in fact not experienced. It is then a difficult empirical question how high that threshold is. Perhaps we can imagine this as a sea level. Advocates of a thin view say that sea level is very high, so that only one or a few prominences cross it; advocates of a rich view say it's much lower, so that many prominences cross it. But it's not merely a matter of convention or linguistic decision whether there is only a little bit of dry land or whether there's a lot. It's a matter of how plentiful the stream of experience is. For example, as **Siewert** illustrates, those who think we have a constant stream of rich visual experience have a radically different view of our phenomenology than do those who think we often have little or no visual experience.

It looks, Russ, like you and I agree that a DES-type project can't, at least in the near term, adjudicate the rich vs. thin question. So unless there's some more suitable concurrent or immediately retrospective method for addressing this question, I think we're left without

Difference between actual and potential experiences not a linguistic choice

knowing the answer to a fundamental question about consciousness — or rather, we're left without knowing unless we can justify that answer theoretically, by some means other than concurrent introspection or immediate retrospection. But, like you, I worry that no such theoretical answer is possible. A general theory of consciousness cannot, I suspect, be well justified independently of a prior answer to the question of how broadly consciousness spreads. If we don't know whether most visual input is conscious or almost none of it is, how can we ground a general theory of visual consciousness?

<small>Rich/thin issue possibly irresolvable</small>

Possibly, then, there's a tight little vicious circle here, which will frustrate any near-term attempts at a general theory of consciousness: no well-justified general theory of consciousness without prior knowledge of roughly how abundant consciousness is; no knowledge of roughly how abundant consciousness is without a prior, well-justified general theory of consciousness. (I develop this argument in more detail in Schwitzgebel, in press, Ch. 6.)

RUSS

<small>Self-defeat in trying to imagine unclarity</small>

Eric, you say that you are amenable to a gradualist theory in principle but simply have trouble conceiving of a what it would be to have a little experience. If that's really true, then maybe the following is the root of your problem: it is inherently self-defeating to try to visually imagine, in a clear way, a vague case of visual experience — sort of like looking down the barrel of a gun to see what a bullet looks like on the way out or, in William James's (1890/1981) famous metaphor, turning up the light quickly enough to see the darkness. The problem is not specific to vision: it is inherently self-defeating to try to imagine in a clear way vague experience. The *trying* does you in. If you have to *try* to observe unclarity in yourself, then you will not be able to observe it because *trying* involves bringing together all your clarity resources and aiming them at the target. It is no more possible to try to observe unclarity in yourself than to try to observe not-trying in yourself. It *is* possible, however, to try to observe not-trying and unclarity in *someone else*. There is no self-defeat in that manoeuvre.

The problem (which is one reason I oppose armchair introspection; see **Methodological Pluralism**) is that most people, including apparently you, Eric, decline to observe unclarity in others *because they don't see it in themselves*. That is, they unwarrantedly generalize their self-defeat to other-defeat. It's like the opposite of the refrigerator light illusion. You're inside the refrigerator, and you say, 'Man, it's dark in here. I can't see a thing. Therefore nobody anywhere can see anything.'

I think you could learn to appreciate unclarity in others if you applied yourself assiduously to the task (instead of applying yourself assiduously to arguing against the necessity of the task), and then, perhaps, you could see it in yourself too because you would no longer have to *try* to see it. You would *know how* to see it when it presents itself without having to try.

Here's an example to illustrate how we can find unclarity by starting with others. Doucette, Jones-Forrester, and I have undertaken three DES explorations of the experience of women with bulimia nervosa. We have observed the phenomenon I call 'tails' or 'sensed thoughts or feelings: the "tail" [is] the knowledge present in awareness that the particular thought or feeling was ongoing' (Hurlburt, 1993, p. 125–26). That is, the tail is the directly-in-experience-but-small intimation that a thought is somehow 'parked' or 'waiting', while the thought itself is *not* in experience. Eric, you and I don't do this. If we think of A, and then for whatever reason turn our attention to B, A disappears entirely from our direct experience. At some later time, we may again think directly of A, and in the meantime some processing of A might have occurred. Our bulimic women, by contrast, think of A, and then think of B while *at the same time continuing to think, a little bit that is directly in experience, about A.*

'Tails' in the experience of bulimic women

To grasp the concept of the tail requires the clear distinction between something that is indeed *a little* in experience (the tail), and something about which there is *little or no* experience (the thought itself). My claim in the bulimia studies is that the bulimic women and we *can* make that distinction with confidence.

As a practical matter, I think it is possible to make that distinction *only* if we accept the practical impossibility of distinguishing between a little and none. If we *always* press for the distinction between a little and none when that distinction is practically impossible to make, we will either learn a helplessness in the face of such distinctions or we will allow ourselves to impose a presuppositional (rich or thin) view that obliterates the actual phenomenon.

One final example will illustrate that 'just like' is a corollary of our analysis of 'little or none'. At Melanie's beep 5.1 she described her inner seeing experience as being 'just like' her visual experience of being in a real car. **Siewert** questioned what that meant, so let me clarify. Suppose I present you with Figure 1 for a second or so and then take it away. Then I present

'Just like' means 'little or no discernible difference'

another figure (say, Figure X) for a second or so and take it away. Figure X in reality has basically the same mountain #1 but may have some discrepancies in details — perhaps the shape of #1 is not quite identical, perhaps #5 or #6 is missing, and so on. I ask you whether the two figures are the same. You might say, 'As far as I could tell, Figure X was *just like* Figure 1.' The 'as far as I could tell' portion of that locution is fundamentally important: it acknowledges that Figures 1 and X may have been different, but if so it was in ways you were not able to (or at least did not adequately) discern. By analogy, when Melanie said that her visual imagery was 'just like' real driving experience, I understood her to mean, 'as far as I could tell, there was little or no difference between my imagery experience and a real driving experience.'

When Melanie is in a real car, there are lots of things ongoing in her inner and outer environment, that is, a welter of experience-lets or potential experiences: seeing the road, seeing the steering wheel, seeing the instruments, feeling the steering wheel, feeling the seat against her back side, hearing the engine noise, hearing the wind noise, smelling the leather, thinking about the appointment she is going to, being angry at her landlord, recalling her birthday party three years ago, seeking a new solution to Fermat's last theorem, and so on. She does *not* attend to *all* of the details of *all* of those experience-lets all the time — out of that welter, one or a few experience-lets become salient (peak 1), while about the remaining potentialities she has little or no experience (3, 4, 5, 6 or even smaller or nonexistent peaks). A bit later some other experience-let will become the high-mountain salience, and mountain 1 will more-or-less vanish (that equalizer bar will shorten into the 3, 4, 5, 6 range). That is, at some moment, her in-the-car experience is predominately visual — seeing the road beyond her hands on the steering wheel — and she has little or no experience of anything else, including the pressure of the gas pedal, the smell of the leather, and so on; at the next moment she's angry at her landlord, and she has little or no experience of anything else, including the road, the leather, and so on. At any moment, *none* of those predominant experiences is a complete experience of being in the car. In fact, Melanie probably *never* (or at most rarely) *has the experience of being in the car*. She has a series of experiences that are consonant with being in the car, but 'consonant with' is far-reaching, extending to landlords, birthday parties, theorems, and so on. So it would not be possible for Melanie to compare in detail her imagery experience with her typical driving experience: there is no typical driving experience. Furthermore, there is no reason to believe that

Melanie (like most other people) has a high fidelity understanding of her own actual experiences while driving. For example, it is likely that Mike has frequent specific and vivid sensory awarenesses of visual aspects of his surroundings while driving his car, but does not know it (or at least did not know it prior to his DES encounter). People often don't know some important characteristics of their real experience (Hurlburt, in press).

Differentiating imagining from seeing

Perhaps Siewert would reply that Melanie 'can, after all, … generally tell when she's seeing a traffic light, and when she's just imagining one. And it just may be that part of what makes the experiences distinguishable is that the one in some sense contains a level and type of "detail" that the other does not.' Perhaps so. But I think it likely that there is often *little or nothing* about the seeing/imagery *experiences themselves* that lets Melanie tell whether she's really seeing or innerly seeing a traffic light. Real experience is not as detailed as the real object; imaginary experience is not as detailed as the real object. I think there is no reason to believe that real experience is more or less detailed than imaginary experience. How, then, does Melanie tell that she is only *imagining* being in the car, and is not *really* in the car? The real Melanie is a complex bag of coordinations: one process coordinating her heart rate, another process coordinating the motion of her left foot, another process coordinating her eyeball movement, another process coordinating her smellings, another her hearings, another her secretion of thyroxine, and so on — a huge number of such processes that are to some degree independent, to some degree dependent (sharing the same bones, sinews, blood), to some degree inter-coordinated. All of these are experience-lets; some have the potential for becoming the main-mountain experiences, some (like the thyroxine coordinator) probably don't. When Melanie is in a real car, every one of these is to some degree coordinated with the facticity of being in the car: the heart rate coordinator is attuned to the driving task coordinator, the left foot coordinator recognizes the solidity of the adjacent door, and so on. That is, the heart rate coordinator is attuned to being in the car, the left-foot coordinator is attuned to being in the car. In fact, every fibre of Melanie's being is, more or less closely, more or less directly, attuned to being in the car. But at the moments of most beeps, Melanie would not be particularly interested in her heart rate or left foot coordinator or her smell coordinator, so they would remain in the little-or-no experience realm.

At the actual moment of beep 5.1, Melanie is at her breakfast table. Melanie can tell that she is *imagining*, rather than seeing, the road, because every fibre of her being is attuned, more or less closely, more or less directly, to the facticity of her sitting at the *breakfast table*, not in her car. Her left foot coordinator, under the influence of the tile floor and the table leg, is not in the slightest duped by her imagining of the road.

So I think it likely that Melanie's ability to distinguish imagining from seeing comes from the complex constellation of Melanie's processes, most of which are little-or-no-experience-lets that are so slight as to be overlooked along with all the other experience-lets that may exist at any given time.

In my view, the stakes of recognizing the difficulty or impossibility of distinguishing little-or-no from no experience are high. I think there are large individual differences in inner experience, many of which are not recognized by current consciousness science. Once science has firmly established those large differences, distinguishing little-or-no from no experience may well be the most important remaining task; but until then, it is a distraction that may well inhibit science's advance.

References

Antony, M.V. (2008) Are our concepts CONSCIOUS STATE and CONSCIOUS CREATURE vague?, *Erkenntnis*, **68**, pp. 239–263.

Engelbert, M. & Carruthers, P. (this symposium) Descriptive Experience Sampling: What is it good for?, *Journal of Consciousness Studies*, **18** (1).

Heavey, C.L. & Hurlburt, R.T. (2008) The phenomena of inner experience, *Consciousness and Cognition*, **17**, pp. 798–810.

Hill, C. (this symposium) How to study introspection, *Journal of Consciousness Studies*, **18** (1).

Hurlburt, R.T. (1993) *Sampling Inner Experience in Disturbed Affect*, New York: Plenum Press.

Hurlburt, R.T. (2009) Unsymbolized thinking, sensory awareness, and mindreading, *Behavioral and Brain Sciences*, **32**, pp. 149–150. (doi:10.1017/S0140525X09000673.)

Hurlburt, R.T. (this symposium) Nine clarifications of Descriptive Experience Sampling, *Journal of Consciousness Studies*, **18** (1).

Hurlburt, R.T. (in press) *Investigating Pristine Inner Experience: Moments of Truth*, Cambridge: Cambridge University Press.

Hurlburt, R.T. & Akhter, S.A. (2008) Unsymbolized thinking, *Consciousness and Cognition*, **17**, pp. 1364–1374.

Hurlburt, R.T., Heavey, C.L. & Bensaheb, A. (2009) Sensory awareness, *Journal of Consciousness Studies*, **16** (10–12), pp. 231–251.

Hurlburt, R.T. & Jones-Forrester, S. (in press) Fragmented experience in bulimia nervosa, in Hurlburt, R.T., *Investigating Pristine Inner Experience: Moments of Truth*, New York: Cambridge.

Hurlburt, R.T. & Schwitzgebel, E. (2007) *Describing Inner Experience? Proponent Meets Skeptic*, Cambridge, MA: MIT Press.

James, W. (1890/1981) *The Principles of Psychology*, Cambridge, MA: Harvard University Press.

Kane, M. (this symposium) Describing, debating, and discovering inner experience, *Journal of Consciousness Studies*, **18** (1).

Schwitzgebel, E. (2007) Do you have constant tactile experience of your feet in your shoes? Or is experience limited to what's in attention?, *Journal of Consciousness Studies*, **14** (3), pp. 5–35.

Schwitzgebel, E. (in press) *Perplexities of Consciousness*, Cambridge, MA: MIT Press.

Siewert, C. (1998) *The Significance of Consciousness*, Princeton, NJ: Princeton University Press.

Siewert, C. (this symposium) Socratic introspection and the abundance of experience, *Journal of Consciousness Studies*, **18** (1).

Spener, M. (this symposium) Using first-person data about consciousness, *Journal of Consciousness Studies*, **18** (1).

Russell T. Hurlburt
and Eric Schwitzgebel

Methodological Pluralism, Armchair Introspection, and DES as the Epistemic Tribunal

ERIC

Seek[ing] to minimize many of the sources of error and distortion in first-person judgments ... doesn't justify according to beeper reports a place of such high *epistemic privilege* that these should serve as a sort of tribunal, before which *present* tense judgments, and those made in response to more *targeted* questions, can be tried. ... Insufficient reasons have been offered to think other reports are overall inferior to [beeper reports]. Nor is it even clear the court Hurlburt convenes would yield the harsh verdicts he suggests, were it furnished with appropriate rules of evidence. (**Siewert**, p. 80)

I heartily encourage a pluralism of method. Therefore I agree with **Charles Siewert**[1] that Descriptive Experience Sampling (DES) does not deserve a uniquely high position (see H&S, ch. 10.1). Let a thousand flowers bloom, then let those flowers fight it out in vitriolic journal articles. Russ has nicely articulated some of the advantages of DES (see esp. H&S, Ch. 2), but DES, as he acknowledges, is also flawed and limited in various ways. Among the weaknesses of DES, it seems to me, are:

- in its inability to examine questions other than those that arise naturally in the DES interview (see also **Engelbert and Carruthers**, **Horgan and Timmons**);
- in the unsystematic incomparability of subjects' responses (see also **Klinger**);

---

[1] See note and correspondence details on page 206 above.

- in its dependence on the interviewer's possession of unusual skills — including an ability to ask even-handed questions, an ability to know what direction to steer inquiry, and an ability accurately to interpret the subject's perhaps infelicitous statements in real time (see also **Horgan and Timmons, Siewert**);
- in its labour-intensiveness, which severely limits the feasible number of subjects (see also **Klinger, Spener**);
- in its lack of transparency (except when full transcripts of the entire series of interviews are provided);
- in the difficulty of manipulating the context and content of the target experience;
- in its high level of dependence on memory (see also **Klinger, Siewert, Sutton**);
- in the difficulty of correlating reported experience with other simultaneous measures of cognition, behaviour, or physiology (see also **Engelbert and Carruthers**);
- in its reliance on what aspects of experience the subject happens to attend to after the beep – which, if experience is rich, may involve a high degree of idiosyncratic selection (see also **Hill, Petitmengin, Siewert**);
- in the potential disruptiveness of the beep itself (see also **Kane, Petitmengin**);
- in its dependence on the categories and classifications attractive to the subject, which may be laden with problematic assumptions or map poorly onto the target experiences or onto interesting aspects of the target experience (see also **Hill, Horgan and Timmons**);
- in its creation of an interview situation with a particular array of pressures on the subject — including time pressures, pressures to satisfy the interviewer's apparent demands, pressures to look like a good subject who reports accurately, and pressures to seek out phenomena that appear to evoke interesting discussion (see also **Klinger**);
- in the problems that follow from the interviewer's dual role as both introspective report solicitor and introspective report evaluator — for example, the pressure to be collaborative and supportive as a solicitor may interfere with being sufficiently critical as an evaluator, and the evaluator and solicitor will share the same quirks and possibly toxic background assumptions.

To be clear, I mean these bullet-points as a list of weaknesses or limitations of DES *in addition to* the intrinsic difficulties of the introspective task common to all introspective methods (difficulties like the complexity and evasiveness of experience, our lack of practice in assessing our experience, and the outward-object orientation of our linguistic categories; see H&S, Ch. 3.3). Also, as I have said elsewhere (H&S, Chs. 3.4 and 10.1), I think every competing method also has a serious array of weaknesses — though their weaknesses may differ from the weaknesses of DES. This situation compels consciousness studies to employ a variety of competing methods, with complementary strengths and weaknesses, *even though those methods do have the weaknesses Russ attributes to them.* Among the legitimate methods are, I think, 'armchair' methods of the sort **Siewert** favours. Ideally, we should seek a triangulation of flawed methods, the results of which all point toward a single interpretation, while we recognize the competing advantages and disadvantages of different approaches. (On some major issues, however — like the rich/thin issue, as I argue in Chapter 6 of Schwitzgebel, in press — intermediate-term convergence might be beyond our reach. See also **Little or No**.)

Necessity of methodological pluralism in consciousness studies

RUSS

I accept your characterization of methodological pluralism, Eric: 'recogniz[ing] the competing advantages and disadvantages of different approaches,' so long as by 'recognizing' you imply action coherent with that recognition. That is, I do *not* think it is okay to *recognize* the disadvantages of method *X* but then to *act as if* the disadvantages don't exist; I do *not* think it is okay to recognize that the advantages of method *X* outweigh the advantages of method *Y* but then to weight the results of *X* and *Y* equally. That understood, I see myself as an enthusiastic methodological pluralist, and I think I have earned my bona fides in that claim. Eric, we agree that the exploration of experience is difficult and has a highly problematic history. My work has always been about trying to figure out the advantages and disadvantages of available explorational methods and then trying to act accordingly. Early on, I concluded that it was advantageous to explore experience contemporaneously in natural environments, so in 1973 I invented the random beepers (Hurlburt, 1976) that made that possible and in 1974 launched the method I called 'random sampling of cognitions' or 'thought sampling'. In 1974 I recognized the advantages to structured questionnaires in which all subjects receive the same prompts, and I acted accordingly: I instructed thought

Russ's early questionnaire methods

sampling subjects to fill out Likert-scale questionnaires when randomly signaled in their natural environments.

But in debriefing my thought-sampling subjects, I discovered that subjects had widely different interpretations of seemingly simple questionnaire prompts (e.g., 'To what extent was this thought about the past?') and how they used the Likert scales to quantify those responses. Eventually I was forced to accept that I simply didn't know what subject *A* meant by checking *4* on Likert scale *X*, except that I was pretty sure that at least sometimes, what subject *A* meant was quite likely much *different* from what subject *B* meant by checking *4* on Likert scale *X*. That seemed a pretty major disadvantage, and I tried to act accordingly: I started being more and more careful in the training of subjects and in the debriefing interviews.

As I did so, I discovered that subjects often couldn't remember the details of samples that had occurred several days earlier; that seemed a disadvantage, so I started scheduling a *series* of debriefing interviews rather than just one, which turned out to be an advantage — subjects seemed much better able to remember within hours than within days. Now that I was performing serial debriefing interviews, I found that a subject on the first day of sampling might report inner speech, but on the subsequent five days of sampling, her reports included *no* inner speech. And similarly for imagery, and so on. Did I scare her out of reporting inner speech? That didn't seem likely — I found inner speech frequently on other subjects' first, middle, and last sampling days. That inconsistency at first seemed like a disadvantage, but eventually I became neutral about it: it's just the way sampling is: early in sampling, presuppositions about experience frequently outweigh the introspection of experience (see **Presuppositions and Background Assumptions**), and no amount of pre-sampling training, no matter how carefully I tried to administer it, could deter such presuppositions. This was the beginning of my recognition of the advantage, if not the necessity, of iteration; see **Clarifications of DES** and Hurlburt (2009; in press).

DES not the ultimate tribunal

Thus the development of DES was, in my view, the straightforward application of genuine methodological pluralism: I have conducted lots of different kinds of research about inner experience, evaluated the advantages and disadvantages of each, and then tried to do better. Therefore it is backwards to say that I think that DES is the ultimate tribunal against which other methods should be judged. There is no tribunal; there are only the genuinely methodologically pluralistic judgments about advantages and disadvantages. DES is a *defendant* before that methodologically plural tribunal, as should be thought sampling, armchair introspection, **Claire Petitmengin**'s explicitation interview, **Eric Klinger**'s idiothetic experience sampling, and all other methods of exploring experience. So rather than DES *being* the tribunal, DES was instead *created by* the tribunal: DES was my response to considering the advantages and disadvantages I encountered while struggling with the tribunal throughout a succession of different methods for exploring inner experience.

I turn now to armchair introspection. I was in H&S critical of armchair introspection not because I am opposed to armchair introspection per se; I am happy to use armchair introspection (and do myself use it) *on the condition that it's advantages and disadvantages are kept clearly in mind*. I intend here to criticize armchair introspection because consciousness science (as I see it) often (perhaps usually) fails to acknowledge the disadvantages of armchair introspection (or at least fails to act in accordance with those disadvantages), and as a result I think armchair introspection is a central actor in the stymied progress of consciousness science.

Siewert disagrees strongly with my comments on armchair introspection, offering the occasion for me to elaborate my views. Preliminarily I note that broadly speaking there are two different activities that might be called armchair introspection, which I will call the serious and the casual. By serious armchair introspection I refer to assiduous, usually repeated, highly motivated endeavours such as **Siewert** and a relatively few others (dozens? hundreds?) engage in. By casual armchair introspection I refer to the mélange of ad hoc, often one-shot, often relatively unmotivated, often theoretically influenced introspection that many (thousands?) engage in (including you and, occasionally, me). As an example of casual introspection, you, Eric, ask acquaintances to 'form a visual image of some familiar object, such as the front of your house' (Schwitzgebel, 2002, p. 38). For many of your subjects, this request may be the first formal introspection they have undertaken. Therefore, I think your subjects' introspections deserve to be called casual, by comparison to **Siewert's** repeated introspective efforts. Clearly there are gradations of seriousness and casualness, but I think nothing hinges on the details of this division (that is, in close cases it matters little whether introspection *X* is held to be serious or casual) because, as we shall see, many of the disadvantages apply to both ends of the spectrum and everywhere in between. But it seems a mistake to lump Siewert's introspections and those of your acquaintances into the same bucket without at least noticing the distinction.

[margin note: Serious vs. casual armchair introspection]

Here's the plan: first I will meet **Siewert's** objections; then I will discuss the limitations of armchair introspection; and then I will return to give an example of how the advantages and disadvantages of armchair introspection are often not adequately recognized by science.

When **Siewert** defends armchair introspection, I presume he is referring to 'serious' introspection — that is, I don't think he intends to defend introspectors who make pronouncements based on a quick glance at their experience. At the outset, **Siewert** objects to the label 'armchair introspection' because it sounds pejorative. As an alternative, he seems to propose 'self-initiated present-tense first-person targeted judgments,' which he intends to contrast with DES, which he labels as 'near-term retrospective judgments in response to an open-ended prompt' (p. 87). However, I think these labels are misleading in two ways. First, in drawing a contrast between his own 'targeted' approach and the DES 'open-ended' approach, **Siewert** misleadingly suggests that DES is not targeted. Second, **Siewert**'s labels misleadingly suggest that his own method is less retrospective than is DES.

First, DES is targeted in its way. From the beginning, it targets pristine experience (see **Clarifications of DES**), specifically, relentlessly training the subject to focus on pristine experience and to avoid non-pristine-experience reports. It is true that DES starts out, on the first sampling day, broadly, even chaotically, open-beginninged, so that neither interviewer nor subject knows in advance what particular characteristics of pristine experience will be discussed; for example, before sampling with Melanie we had not a clue that we would be discussing bodily self-consciousness. However, as the iterative process takes its effect across sampling days, the interviews can become, in a manner of speaking, as specifically targeted as are **Siewert**'s 'first-person targeted judgments'. For example, in H&S, Melanie, Eric and I all became specifically motivated to sort through Melanie's putative bodily self-consciousness. Similarly, the **Michael J. Kane** interviews became more and more targeted at the question of the existence of inner speech (see **Little or No**). Thus the distinction is not that one method is targeted and the other is not; it is in the nature of the targeting: a priori specifically self-targeted for **Siewert** and aspects-of-pristine-experience-emergently-brought-into-relief for DES.

<small>a priori targeting</small>

It seems to me that the overwhelming majority of Western scientific methods (excepting a very few such as DES, ethology, and the participant-observation methods of cultural anthropology) involve a priori specific self-targeting, so it is worth repeating why that is risky. As discussed in our dialogue in **Presuppositions and Background Assumptions**, a priori targeting involves forcing the subject into a preconceived frame, and that risk applies whether that subject is oneself, as in **Siewert**'s method, or another person as in Eric's rich-thin study and the approaches suggested by **Christopher S. Hill, Terry Horgan and Mark Timmons, Mark Englebert and Peter Carruthers, Petitmengin**, and **Klinger**. Now if we could know with a high degree of certainty what frame would best capture what is going on in people's experience, setting the frame in advance would be an efficient approach. But we don't yet know. Recall the parable of the hunters in **Presuppositions and Background Assumptions**: going into the unknown woods, it is better not to presuppose what prey you will find; rather, keep alert for any possibility that comes your way.

Second, **Siewert**'s holding that his method is 'present-tense' whereas DES is 'retrospective' is undercut by the iterative nature of DES. I fully agree that Melanie's apprehension, *on the first day*, of her bodily self-consciousness was indeed distantly retrospective (hours later), as **Siewert** states. But by the second day and beyond, because of the iterative procedure (see **Clarifications of DES)**, her bodily self-consciousness was something Melanie was prepared to assess immediately after the beep. Her judgment was no longer a *long-term* retrospection but rather a short-term retrospection. And *all* introspections are at least slightly retrospective, including **Siewert**'s introspections, because at best, all ask, What was going on with me *just then*? So both DES judgments, once the iterative process has taken effect, and **Siewert**'s present-tense judgments are near-term, almost immediate retrospections.

> All methods retrospective

Thus, **Siewert**'s distinction between his method as 'self-initiated present-tense first-person targeted judgments' and DES as 'near-term retrospective judgments in response to an open-ended prompt' is misleading: Both methods are short-term retrospective and both are targeted. So here's my shot at a non-pejorative label for **Siewert**'s first-person (formerly known as armchair) introspections: 'judgments about experience where the target, the occasion, the duration, the introspection, the interpretation, and the generalization are all self-defined, self-initiated, and performed by one person, generally on the basis of an implicit or explicit theory.' For short, let's refer to these as 'self-targeted, self-occasioned, theory-informed introspections'.

Here's my shot at a non-pejorative label for DES: 'characterization of experience based on apprehensions of moments of a subject's experience where: (a) what is apprehended is the result of an open-beginninged and iteratively evolving co-researcher dialogue between a subject and an interviewer; (b) the moments are selected and unambiguously identified by an external signal that is unpredictable by either subject or interviewer; (c) the focus is limited to the subject's directly-apprehended-as-ongoing-at-the-moment-of- the-signal experience; (d) the characterizations are based on truly inductive generalizations of the specifically apprehended moments; and (e) the investigator attempts in some systematic way to bracket his/her own presuppositions and to help the subject bracket his/hers.' For short, let's refer to these as 'open-beginninged, randomly initiated, presupposition-bracketed introspections'.

ERIC

I am more sympathetic with **Siewert**'s characterization of targeting and retrospection than you are, Russ. 'Targeted' means targeted in advance, by the researcher's antecedent plan. As you emphasize, that is a very different approach than your own 'open-beginninged' approach; and there are corresponding advantages and disadvantages. Likewise, in asserting that all methods are retrospective you underplay the differences, as I see it, between concurrent and immediately retrospective methods, which again have corresponding advantages and disadvantages.

Both here and in **Presuppositions and Background Assumptions** you are too hard on a priori targeting and preconceived frames. A researcher might be drawn into an inquiry by interest in a targeted question, like how rich is visual experience? (**Siewert**) or do different dimensions of pain often come apart? (**Hill**) or is there normally an experience of freedom? (**Horgan and Timmons**). Although you are right that a priori targeting can blind us to the unexpected, and that antecedently chosen frames and focuses can create potentially distortive pressures on subjects, if we always refuse to focus inquiry beforehand we lose at least two things (in addition, perhaps, to researchers' enthusiasm): first, we lose the opportunity to explore issues that are theoretically important but that don't tend to arise naturally in ordinary sampling interviews. Perhaps such issues will arise in *unusual* sampling interviews, but then we learn about them only from those unusual interviews and not in the normal case. **Horgan and Timmons**'s proposal about exploring whether people normally experience a feeling of freedom might be an example (though see **Case Study in Bracketing Presuppositions** for an objection to this example). Second, we lose the opportunity to

Advantages of a priori targeting

systematically explore issues across subjects using comparable vocabulary and comparable prompts, rather than just whatever vocabulary the subject finds comfortable and whatever variations the prompt questions take in the DES interview. Although I suspect we might have overlapping criticisms of **Klinger**, Russ, there are advantages to structured questionnaires in which all subjects receive the same prompts — as you of course recognized in your early research. You came to think these advantages were outweighed by competing disadvantages, but others might assess the weights differently, and the ideal, it seems to me, is to see whether these competing approaches converge.

I disagree with you, Russ, that all methods are retrospective. One can, for example, think 'what am I thinking right now?' and discover, presumably, that one is thinking about what one is thinking (perhaps among other things). Or one can reflect on one's currently ongoing emotional experience (e.g., 'am I feeling tense now, or relaxed?'). There are important epistemic differences between introspection of experience as it is ongoing and introspection of experience in the immediate past (e.g., 'what *was* I just thinking, a moment ago?'). As many researchers have noted (going back at least to Comte, 1830), immediate retrospection has one very important advantage over concurrent introspection: since the target experience is over before one starts to reflect on it, the target experience cannot be interfered with by the act of reflecting on it. Thus, in DES, *if* the subject can adequately focus on her experience just before the beep and not confuse it with her experience as affected by the beep, she will avoid the refrigerator light problem and other nuisances (e.g., H&S, pp. 17 and 90–91). On the other hand, however, concurrent introspection has two important advantages over immediate retrospection. First, immediate retrospection requires memory, and it is certainly possible that even within a second much will be forgotten, especially if experience is rich (see also my discussion in **Little or No**). And second — as recently emphasized by Jakob Hohwy (in press) — in concurrent introspection one can manipulate the target experience in a way that might help reveal its features. For example, in thinking about whether one's experience is an experience of thirst, one can imagine drinking a glass of water and notice whether and how it affects that supposed feeling of thirst. One can notice how one's concurrently ongoing emotional state shifts with various shifts in cognitive and bodily attention. Such active exploration is crucial to sensory knowledge and may also be crucial to introspective self-knowledge. **Siewert**, too, seems to utilize the exploratory,

margin note: Advantages of concurrent introspection

manipulative possibilities of concurrent introspection, for example when he invites the reader to consider the changes in her experience as she shifts her angle of view on a coin (Siewert, 2006).

RUSS

I accept that there are important differences between **Siewert**'s targeting in advance and my own 'open-beginninged' targeting, and that there are corresponding advantages and disadvantages. I'm happy to agree that the methodologically plural investigator can tick off *Can manipulate the target* in the Advantages column for self-targeted, self-occasioned, theory-informed introspection. Furthermore, I would add to that Advantages column the *Ability to plan the investigation in advance* and *Ability to focus on one specifically targeted aspect*. However, as I explained in **Presuppositions and Background Assumptions** and below, targeting in advance *increases the difficulty of bracketing presuppositions*, and that counts in the Disadvantage column.

Two more advantages of self-self introspection

If consciousness science were having an open, honest, level-playing-field, spirited, methodologically pluralistic discussion of the advantages and disadvantages of targeting introspections, I wouldn't feel the need to advocate open-beginninged! I don't think that open-beginninged is *always* the best, and I apologize if I imply that. But the current consciousness-science conversation seems to me to be Target in advance! Target in advance!! TARGET IN ADVANCE!!!, and it's difficult to say, even-temperedly above the din, *Y'know, open-beginninged might be better in some or many situations*.

And I accept that there are differences between the immediate retrospection of DES and the concurrent introspection emphasized by **Siewert**, but I think you exaggerate when you say concurrent introspection is 'not hostage' to retrospection. Even concurrent introspection involves some retrospection, across the delay between the concurrent introspection and the writing notes about it.

So I fully accept that the genuinely methodologically plural investigator must understand the advantages and disadvantages of any introspective method. I turn now to discuss five limitations that affect all self-targeted, self-occasioned, theory-informed introspection: pristine, presuppositions, parochial, public, and skill. But even here, I don't really wish to argue that DES is better under all conditions. I wish to support a genuine methodological pluralism. I'm cast in the role of articulating the disadvantages of self-targeted, self-occasioned, theory-informed introspections not because I relish the

1. Serious (self-targeted, self-occasioned, theory-informed) or casual introspection does not apprehend pristine experience (experience as it naturally occurs in usual, everyday environments, not altered or coloured or shaped by the specific intention to apprehend it; see **Clarifications of DES**).

<aside>Self-self introspection does not apprehend pristine experience</aside>

Self-targeted, self-occasioned, theory-informed introspection begins with the specific intention to apprehend experience; thus self-targeted, self-occasioned, theory-informed introspection specifically *excludes* the investigation of pristine experience. There are two problematic aspects of the failure to investigate pristine experience: the interference aspect and the representative aspect.

First, interference. As you point out, Eric, at least as early as Comte (1830) it has been known that people's behaviour may change dramatically when they realize they are being observed. In **Clarifications of DES**, I observed that people's behaviour changes dramatically when they realize they are on TV; by analogy, people's inner experience can be expected to change when they know they are being observed, even by themselves.

It is possible to *act as if* you were not on TV; but carefully considered, that behaviour is substantially different from behaviour that takes place when not on TV. Experienced TV personalities doubtless can 'forget' that they are on TV and act pretty naturally, but that is analogous to forgetting to introspect. I accept that there are some aspects of experience that are largely unchanged by the intention to introspect, and self-targeted, self-occasioned, theory-informed introspected experience and pristine experience will be largely the same in those aspects. But what those aspects are is not known and should not be presumed without being shown. Furthermore, I accept the possibility that some highly skilled introspectors may be able to transcend the self-observational interference and be-as-observed exactly the same as be-without-observation (for example, some adept meditators claim to be able to do that), but (a) that non-interference would have to be demonstrated in some way, not merely claimed; and (b) the experience of people who can consistently non-interfere may well be different in important ways (as is meditators') from everyday folks.

Second, representativeness. If we can solve the interference problem, I note that what one *can* do, when (self-) asked to introspect, is not necessarily what one *does* do in everyday experience. I *can* juggle; I *do* juggle only about once a year, if that. An investigation into my juggling ability would reveal almost nothing about my important characteristics. By analogy, it is quite possible that person X could produce an image when demanded to do so by an investigator (including a self-investigator), but that doesn't necessarily imply that X frequently or ever produces images in pristine experience.

Furthermore, what one *tries to* do, when (self-) asked to introspect, does not necessarily have the same characteristics as what one *does* do in everyday experience. An image created on demand (including self-demand) may or may not resemble an image created pristinely. Let's compare a typical targeted introspection of inner seeing with a haphazardly chosen (and typical) DES apprehension of pristine inner seeing, and see whether it seems reasonable to believe that the two are the same phenomenon. As a typical targeted example of introspection, let's use one of yours, Eric: you instruct an acquaintance (let's call her 'Erica'), 'Reflect … on your own phenomenology as you form and maintain a visual image. Form a visual image of some familiar object, such as the front of your house' (Schwitzgebel, 2002, p. 38). When you ask questions about the details of such an image, Erica, like most of your subjects (Schwitzgebel, 2002), stumbles and becomes uncertain.

Now the DES example. As a haphazardly chosen pristine inner seeing, I simply selected the most recent inner seeing example from my own DES interviews; that happened to be 'Matthew's' first sample from his eighth sampling day (see Raymond, in preparation):

> Sample 8.1 Matthew is driving home from class but has little or no awareness of the driving or the traffic. At the moment of the beep he innerly sees a recreation of a video that he and his political science classmates had watched earlier; he sees the words 'GLOBALIZATION IS GOOD' printed in block white letters below a long-haired guy with hair blowing in the wind — a glamour-shot kind of scene. He had seen what he took to be this same scene a few hours earlier on the TV screen in his political science class, where the professor had led a spirited discussion about one-sided advertising using this video as an example. Matthew had taken an active, passionate role in criticizing the use of such glamour-based-scenes to unfairly influence important non-glamour-based topics such as globalization. Now, at the moment of the beep, he sees just the glamour guy and the words, with most of his attention aimed at the words (that is, he does not see the TV screen, the classroom, etc.). At the same time he is experiencing dislike for this one-sided video, a mental dislike that seems to be a feeling more than a thought, but it is difficult to be sure.

Erica stumbles in uncertainty whereas Matthew describes with substantial detail and confidence. I think there is a huge difference between what Erica is doing and what Matthew is doing. Erica is responding *to you*, Eric; *you* are likely to be at least as important in

Erica's experience as the task you set for her. Erica may not have had an image at all but felt pressured into describing one to please you. Even if we grant that Erica *did* innerly see the front of her house, we should note that Erica doesn't really care about the front-of-house seeing — she's just doing some task to please you, Eric. If you had asked her to stand on her left foot with her finger in her ear, she would have done that, too, *with the same amount of self-directed enthusiasm and personal, self-directed, organismic commitment*, which is to say, nearly none.

By distinct contrast, if we grant that Matthew was innerly seeing a glamour-guy and the words 'GLOBALIZATION IS GOOD,' that inner seeing *is the most important experiential reality in the world* for Matthew at that moment. Matthew is *not* compelled, instructed, cajoled, encouraged to think about glamour-based advertising at that time: he could have been watching the traffic, feeling the itch in his left calf, wondering what to get his girlfriend for her birthday next week, recalling his high school graduation. But, apparently, *none* of those things and *nothing else in the universe* is as experientially relevant as glamour-based advertising to Matthew at that moment. Furthermore, even granting that Matthew was *thinking* about glamour-based advertising, that thinking does not have to involve the *seeing* of anything — he could repeat in inner speech what he had said in the debate, could think in unsymbolized thinking about it, and so on. For whatever reason, *inner seeing* was, out of all the ways he could have been experiencing, the most experientially felicitous at that moment. Thus out of all the possible things Matthew could experience, and out of all the possible ways he could experience it, Matthew created just exactly this particular *inner seeing*, created it exactly the way he himself was inclined to create it, created just exactly that by himself, for himself, without outside intervention (Hurlburt, in press, Ch.1).

Does Erica's created-by-Erica-for-Eric inner seeing (the result of *Eric's* interest, not *Erica's*) have the same characteristics as Matthew's created-by-Matthew-for-Matthew inner seeing (the result of *Matthew's own* most-relevant-at-that-time interest)? Maybe, but it certainly doesn't seem that that should be presumed without examination.

I conclude that self-targeted, self-occasioned, theory-informed introspection cannot investigate pristine experience. I can't see how self-targeted, self-occasioned, theory-informed introspection can avoid that. Because self-targeted, self-occasioned, theory-informed introspection dominates, current consciousness science is an exploration of experience at its *least* pristine. This limitation seems to apply equally to serious self-targeted, self-occasioned, theory-informed introspection or casual introspection.

<small>Self-self introspection may amplify toxic presuppositions</small>

2. Self-targeted, self-occasioned, theory-informed introspection may amplify the toxic role of presuppositions (see **Presuppositions and Background Assumptions**) for at least five reasons: first, because only one person occupies the observer role in the introspective process, there is no possibility for between-observer correctives; no opportunity to compare the details of an observation; no possibility for one observer's hyper-sensitivities to balance another person's avoidances. Second, because the observer is the same person as the subject, there is no possibility for the observer to help the subject discover or describe something that the subject is insensitive to. Whatever the subject overlooks (and of course fails to notice — or if noticed, forgives), the same-person interviewer will overlook in exquisitely unnoticed or forgiven synchrony. Whatever the subject exaggerates (and of course fails to notice — or if noticed, forgives — his own exaggeration) the same-person observer will exaggerate in exquisitely unnoticed or forgiven synchrony. Third, because the observer selects the theory to be explored, the observer is likely to have some attachment to that theory, so it will be difficult to take a dispassionate stance toward that theory (and the same-person subject will have the same attachment). Fourth, because the person who chooses the occasion to observe is the same person who is attached to the theory, occasions may be selected (knowingly or otherwise) that particularly favour the theory without recognizing that those occasions may be peculiar or rare, and without observing occasions that run counter to the theory. Fifth, because the theoretician chooses the duration of the observation, there may be a tendency to shorten or lengthen the observation in favour of the theory. Taken together, one might say that self-targeted, self-occasioned, theory-informed introspections are ripe for confirmation bias.

In all these cases, there is no outside person who can, because of different sensitivities or blindnesses, serve as a corrective influence to the introspector's presuppositions. Most modern guilds recognize the risks of the failure to separate such roles. Modern society doesn't let the prosecutor advise the defendant, the builder be the building inspector, the auctioneer bid on the goods, the home team pay the referee. An exception to that rule is the current financial system, which has let the brokers pay the rating agencies with disastrous results.

In distinct contrast to self-targeted, self-occasioned, theory-informed introspections, the open-beginninged, randomly initiated, presupposition-bracketed introspections of DES are expressly designed to *weaken* the grip of presuppositions. That the interviewer is a different person from the subject means that there can be no exquisite synchrony between the presuppositions of both. (Certainly one person's presuppositions can overwhelm the other's, but that is less insidious.) DES can be (and usually is) performed by two interviewers, allowing the hypersensitivities and blindness of one to temper the other. The separation of interviewer and subject facilitates the clarification and exploration of phenomena that the subject takes for granted or exaggerates — there is no exquisite coordination. A truly open-beginninged investigation allows the theory to emerge if it applies, rather than Procrusteanly to guide the observation. The randomness of the occasions ensures that the theory does not select peculiar or rare opportunities to observe. The focus on the moment of the beep helps focus the interview on actually occurring events rather than favoured proclivities or assumptions.

The difficulty of bracketing presuppositions applies both to serious self-targeted, self-occasioned, theory-informed introspection and to casual introspection.

Self-self introspection parochial

3. Self-targeted, self-occasioned, theory-informed introspection is parochial, by which I mean it has difficulty considering alternatives beyond its own noticings. There are three time frames where parochialism presents a problem for self-targeted, self-occasioned, theory-informed introspection: pre-introspection, during the introspection, and post introspection.

Pre-introspection: Because the individual self-targeted, self-occasioned, theory-informed introspector has only one arena in which to make observations, it may not be obvious what kinds of observations are really the most salient. For example, Doucette and I (Doucette & Hurlburt, 1993), and Jones-Forrester and I (Hurlburt & Jones-Forrester, in press) have used DES to explore the inner experience of women with bulimia nervosa. We have discovered that all these women have fragmentedly multiple inner experience, with as many as ten or twenty simultaneously ongoing things in experience. This is quite unusual in non-bulimics; of the 17 bulimic women sampled in Hurlburt & Jones-Forrester (in press), the woman with the *lowest* frequency of multiple awareness had *eight times* as frequent multiple awareness as the average participant in Heavey and Hurlburt's (2008) normative sample; fragmented multiplicity isn't a needle in the haystack, it is the hay in the haystack. There are about 5000 articles in the bulimia literature; many of them rely to some degree on introspective reports of experience because experience is implicated as a causative factor in most of the leading theories of bulimia. *There is no mention in that literature of fragmented multiplicity.* There are potentially many explanations for this oversight (including that I and my colleagues have been consistently mistaken), but the one that appeals to me is that bulimic women take their multiplicity for granted; to the extent that if they think about it at all, they presume that everyone's experience is multiple, so it wouldn't occur to them to mention it (Hurlburt & Jones-Forrester, in press).

It is very difficult, if not impossible, for a self-targeted, self-occasioned, theory-informed introspector to overcome that everyone-is-like-me bias (in fact, self-targeted, self-occasioned, theory-informed introspectors often seem to elevate that bias to a virtue by claiming universality for their own characteristics). By contrast, when the role of investigator is played by a different person from the role of subject, the difficulty diminishes dramatically if not evaporates completely. It is relatively easy for a DES investigator, who has the luxury of investigating the experience of a wide variety of individuals, to spot the differences between those people who are thinking one thing at a time and those who are thinking ten.

During the introspection: Because of the fundamental privacy of experience, it is highly unlikely that an individual person will have an adequate perspective on how his own experience compares to that of others. Here's a recent example from a DES subject's seventh sampling day. 'Walter' is an experienced DES subject, without doubt motivated to be as forthcoming and accurate as he can. Earlier that day he had had a disagreement with a coworker. At the moment of the beep Walter is driving home, fuming. He is innerly screaming in his own, angrily inflected inner voice a dozen or more simultaneous (or perhaps rapid-fire sequential, the experience is so chaotic that it's difficult or impossible to determine) comments/questions: 'How could she!?!?' 'What's she trying to do!?!?' 'What a bitch!!!' and the like. His hands are gripping the steering wheel like a vice; a wave of heat rises up his back and into his neck. We asked him how angry he was, on a scale from 0 = *no anger* to 10 = *extremely angry*; he said about a 7.

Now if *I* had an experience like that, it would be about a 14 on a 10-point scale — *I* don't scream innerly, I don't death-grip steering wheels, and so on. *At best*, Walter's rating of a 7 should be considered ipsative — more angry *than Walter is* when he rates himself a 4, less angry *than Walter is* when he rates himself a 10. There is *no* justification for believing that Walter's rating of 7 has any comparative across-subjects significance. I use the numerical ratings as an example, but it is not the numbers that are important. There simply is no reason to believe that Walter has a good comparative understanding of how his own experience stacks up with other people's.

Post-introspection: Even if an individual investigator manages successfully to avoid the limitations of non-pristine experience, the difficulty of bracketing presuppositions, and the potential blindness caused by observing only one kind of experience, there is still the problem of generalization of the results. The best self-targeted, self-occasioned, theory-informed introspections are still of only one person, and so can provide no guidance on the issue of whether individual differences exist in important ways. I accept that there may well be universal features of consciousness, and for those features the description of one person's consciousness applies to all. But the universality of any feature of consciousness is entirely at issue at this stage in the progress of consciousness science. Referring to the examples discussed in **Presuppositions and Background Assumptions**, it may well be that McWhorter does indeed see images of words every time he speaks, but that in no way implies that *everyone* does such a thing, his own insistence to the contrary notwithstanding. It may well be that Baars and Archer talk to themselves in inner speech all the time, but that does not make it the universal feature of consciousness that they claim. Self-targeted, self-occasioned, theory-informed introspection may lead to mistaken confidence that one is observing universal features.

An important corollary to the generalization problem is that as the skill of an introspector increases, the representativeness of the experience may decrease. An extreme was mentioned above: we might take an adept meditator as an example of an extremely skilled introspector; she has reached a state where she can observe her experience without interfering with it. If motivated, she could perhaps produce high fidelity introspective descriptions. But those descriptions have only limited (albeit important) representativeness — they may apply only to adept meditators.

It seems reasonable to suppose that self-targeted, self-occasioned, theory-informed introspection is a skill, which, like other skills, requires practice. Someone who undertakes to be a very good introspector might invest thousands of hours into the introspection practice. It is likely, or at least possible, that such an investment would affect the generalizability of the results.

By contrast, the acquisition of the skill of a DES investigator does *not* have this negative feedback, because the roles of investigator and subject are separated. The DES investigator can easily invest thousands of hours in skill acquisition; the subject's iterative skill acquisition is important but is typically on the order of a few hours.

The limitations of parochialism applies both to serious self-targeted, self-occasioned, theory-informed introspection and casual introspection.

Self-self introspection difficult to make public

4. It is difficult to provide a public inspection of the self-targeted, self-occasioned, theory-informed introspection process. In your list of bullet points above, Eric, you criticize DES for 'in its lack of transparency (except when full transcripts of the entire series of interviews are provided)'. Presumably you have in mind that in DES, unlike in standardized questionnaire studies, readers don't normally get to see the exact questions posed and the exact answers given. Such transparency is difficult but *not impossible* for DES. I *have* provided many verbatim transcripts (including in H&S); I have invited a noted sceptic to participate in the process and then discussed every detail of what happened with him (what could be more transparent than that?); nearly all of my DES interviews involve two (sometimes three) interviewers, who ask clarifying questions of and for each other during the interview, and then jointly view videotapes of the interviews; and so on. None of that is perfect public inspection, of course, but I fail to see how self-targeted, self-occasioned, theory-informed introspection can undertake *any* such safeguards. The self-targeted, self-occasioned, theory-informed introspector *might* be able to tell us the exact question he posed to himself, but even that is highly problematic (because the self-presented question might have specific and idiosyncratic meanings that are exquisitely known by the both the investigator and the same-person-subject but by no-one else). And it is very difficult if not impossible for the self-targeted, self-occasioned, theory-informed introspector to make public any aspect of the introspection itself other than the final description of a result. A self-targeted, self-occasioned, theory-informed introspector could engage in something like thinking-aloud, a transcript of which could be made public (with all the attendant limitations of think-aloud methods); or perhaps X could introspect, and Y could introspect, and then X and Y could compare results (but that is ripe for the dangers of presuppositions and is probably not 'transparent' in the sense you mean).

Self-self introspection inhibits skill acquisition

5. Self-targeted, self-occasioned, theory-informed introspection inhibits its own skill acquisition. If it is accepted that introspection is a skill, then like all skills introspection needs to be developed, improved, elaborated. Whereas self-targeted, self-occasioned, theory-informed introspection can certainly be

practised, and probably that practice will afford some improvement, self-targeted, self-occasioned, theory-informed introspection *cannot* provide optimal opportunity for development for at least five reasons. First, all self-targeted, self-occasioned, theory-informed introspection practice always takes place on the same turf — the introspector's own experience. Second, there is no opportunity to correct the self-targeted, self-occasioned, theory-informed introspector's relative weaknesses. Third, there is no opportunity to observe other, potentially superior examples of introspectors at work. Skill-building basketball players watch other players so that they can thereafter emulate and practice new moves. Fourth, there is little opportunity for instruction or coaching. Skill acquisition is not easy because much skill development takes place in one's own areas of weakness, which are likely to exist in one's own blind spots. Everyone accepts that if I were a violinist trying to acquire the violin-playing skill, I would consult a teacher and ask the teacher to point out my weaknesses and provide exercises designed to repair those weaknesses. Those exercises are likely to be unpleasant — if the teacher is correct about my weakness, the exercises will focus me directly at that part of my ability that is the *worst*, which is likely that part of my ability that in the past I have consistently *avoided* trying to improve. To the extent that I have ego involvement, I will therefore resist any attempt to improve — practice makes me seem worse to myself than I'd like to think I am. A good teacher, therefore, provides support and encouragement. Fifth, it is difficult to refine the ability to apprehend and describe what is experienced by comparing and contrasting it with what someone else experiences. For example, the ability to apprehend inner seeings in high fidelity benefits greatly by the opportunity to ask the same kinds of questions to those who do not innerly see at all, to those whose inner seeings are sketchy, to those whose inner seeings are florid, to those who claim to be innerly seeing but are not, and so on. At best, the self-targeted, self-occasioned, theory-informed introspection can compare self to others, a more difficult task than comparing one other to another other.

All self-targeted, self-occasioned, theory-informed or casual introspectors should ask themselves: what have I done to acquire this skill? What effort have I made to repair my own weaknesses and blind spots? What systematic efforts have I undertaken (the analogue of a violinist's scale and arpeggio practice)? How do my efforts at skill acquisition compare to, say, that of a virtuoso violinist?

The difficulty of skill acquisition applies both to serious self-targeted, self-occasioned, theory-informed introspection and to casual introspection, for different reasons. Casual introspection is presumed not to require skill, so skill *building* is not the problem — the problem is the lack of skill.

The five limitations I have just discussed (pristine, presuppositions, parochial, public, and skill) apply (perhaps not entirely equally), it seems to me, to all serious self-targeted, self-occasioned, theory-informed introspection and to casual introspection. I accept the possibility that there are ways that skillful individual self-targeted, self-occasioned, theory-informed introspectors can reduce or overcome some of these limitations in particular situations. However, I note that these are major issues at the centre of the introspective task, and that such reduction or overcoming is difficult. Furthermore, most (perhaps *overwhelmingly* most) introspections that are invoked in the science of consciousness are *not* skillful self-targeted, self-occasioned, theory-informed introspections, but are casual, undisciplined, off-the-cuff introspections; consciousness science relies on them anyway, to its detriment.

Eric, we agree on the desirability of methodological pluralism as you describe it: recognizing and acting on the competing advantages and disadvantages of different approaches. I see myself as being methodologically plural in this sense. I acknowledge, for example, that much of the science of perception rests on self-initiated, self-targeted, theory-informed introspections later confirmed by experimentation; the ability of self-initiated, self-targeted, theory-informed introspection systematically to vary perceptual stimuli was clearly an efficient way of advancing the science of perception. But that strategy hasn't worked well with the science of consciousness, which has relied heavily on casual and self-initiated, self-targeted, theory-informed introspection and yet remains, as you said in H&S (p. 298) 'a pandemonium of theories with little common ground ... not yet a mature or progressing science.' You appear to think, Eric, (as do **Spener** and **Siewert**) that despite its shortcomings we can continue to rely, to a large extent, on self-initiated, self-targeted, theory-informed introspection, as long as it is checked with corroborating measures; I believe we should put more energy into trying to develop new and better paths (DES is my attempt, but there may well be other and better ones) to explore the phenomena of consciousness, limiting self-initiated, self-targeted, theory-informed introspection to those areas where it is best suited.

> Russ not categorically opposed to self-self introspection

References

Comte, A. (1830) *Cours de Philosophie Positive*, vol. 1, Paris: Bachelier.

Doucette, S. & Hurlburt, R.T. (1993) Inner experience in bulimia, in Hurlburt, R.T., *Sampling Inner Experience in Disturbed Affect*, pp. 153–163, New York: Plenum Press.

Engelbert, M. & Carruthers, P. (this symposium) Descriptive Experience Sampling: What is it good for?, *Journal of Consciousness Studies*, **18** (1).

Heavey, C.L. & Hurlburt, R.T. (2008) The phenomena of inner experience, *Consciousness and Cognition*, **17**, pp. 798–810.

Hill, C. (this symposium) How to study introspection, *Journal of Consciousness Studies*, **18** (1).

Hohwy, J. (in press) Phenomenal variability and introspective reliability, *Mind and Language*.

Horgan, T. & Timmons, M. (this symposium) Introspection and the phenomenology of free will: Problems and prospects, *Journal of Consciousness Studies*, **18** (1).

Hurlburt, R.T. (1976) Random interval generators and method of behavior modification using same, US Patent #3,986,136.

Hurlburt, R.T. (2009) Iteratively apprehending pristine experience, *Journal of Consciousness Studies*, **16** (10–12), pp. 156–188.

Hurlburt, R.T. (this symposium) Nine clarifications of Descriptive Experience Sampling, *Journal of Consciousness Studies*, **18** (1).

Hurlburt, R.T. (in press) *Investigating Pristine Inner Experience: Moments of Truth*, Cambridge: Cambridge University Press.

Hurlburt, R.T. & Jones-Forrester, S. (in press) Fragmented experience in bulimia nervosa, in Hurlburt, R. T., *Investigating Pristine Inner Experience: Moments of Truth*, Cambridge: Cambridge University Press.

Hurlburt, R.T. & Schwitzgebel, E. (2007) *Describing Inner Experience? Proponent Meets Skeptic*, Cambridge, MA: MIT Press.

Hurlburt, R.T. & Schwitzgebel, E. (this symposium) Little or no experience outside of attention?, *Journal of Consciousness Studies*, **18** (1).

Hurlburt, R.T. & Schwitzgebel, E. (this symposium) Presuppositions and background assumptions, *Journal of Consciousness Studies*, **18** (1).

Kane, M. (this symposium) Describing, debating, and discovering inner experience, *Journal of Consciousness Studies*, **18** (1).

Klinger, E. (this symposium) Response organization of mental imagery, evaluation of Descriptive Experience Sampling, and alternatives, *Journal of Consciousness Studies*, **18** (1).

Petitmengin, C. (this symposium) Describing the experience of describing?, *Journal of Consciousness Studies*, **18** (1).

Raymond, R. (in preparation) Inner experience in PTSD.

Schwitzgebel, E. (2002) How well do we know our own conscious experience? The case of visual imagery, *Journal of Consciousness Studies*, **9** (5–6), pp. 35–53.

Schwitzgebel, E. (in press) *Perplexities of Consciousness*, Cambridge, MA: MIT Press.

Siewert, C. (2006) Is the appearance of shape Protean?, *Psyche*, **12** (3).

Siewert, C. (this symposium) Socratic introspection and the abundance of experience, *Journal of Consciousness Studies*, **18** (1).

Spener, M. (this symposium) Using first-person data about consciousness, *Journal of Consciousness Studies*, **18** (1).

Sutton, J. (this symposium) Time, experience, and Descriptive Experience Sampling, *Journal of Consciousness Studies*, **18** (1).

Russell T. Hurlburt

Nine Clarifications of Descriptive Experience Sampling

The commentaries in this symposium[1] reveal nine misconceptions about Descriptive Experience Sampling (DES) that the present paper attempts to clear up: about pristine experience, about the iterative nature of DES, about the term of DES retrospection, about the accuracy of DES, about the diachronic abilities of DES, about the inability of DES to target specific questions, about the worry that DES stifles careful observation, about the difficulty/expense of DES, and about the transformative power of DES to trump a lifetime of observations.

Pristine Experience

By *pristine experience* I mean experience as it naturally occurs in usual, everyday environments, *not* altered or coloured or shaped by the specific intention to apprehend it (Hurlburt & Akhter, 2008). I use *pristine* in the same sense as we would say a forest is pristine — before the loggers clear-cut, before the Park Service installs the walkways and the signage, before the visitors leave their plastic bags and bottles. Pristine does not necessarily mean 'clean' or 'tranquil'; much of a pristine forest is mucky, bloody, brutal, and so on.

People alter their behaviour when they discover they are being observed — watch people at the moment they realize that they're on TV and you'll see their behaviour change dramatically. It is therefore reasonable to suppose that people's *inner* experience when they know their *inner experience* is being observed (that is, when they premeditatedly engage in introspection) will differ from their pristine (not premeditatedly observed) experience.

---

[1] See note and correspondence details on page 206 above.

It seems that pristine experience ought to be a central interest of a science of experience. We should, for example, be at least as interested in people's visual experience as it usually is in its everydayness as as we are in their visual experience in those unusual instances of premeditatedly specified concurrent introspection. And contra Wundt, and apparently **Charles Siewert**, the two might not be at all the same (see the GLOBALIZATION IS GOOD example in **Methodological Pluralism**). For example, as discussed in **Little or No**, **Siewert** may be misled into thinking that there is a constant, rich stream of visual experience *in his pristine experience* because there is a constant rich stream of visual experience *whenever he premeditatedly looks for it* — a version of what Eric and others have called the 'refrigerator light illusion'. There may well be some similarity (or even identity) between some aspects of pristine experience and introspected experience, but such similarity/identity should not be assumed.

Iteration

I regret not having given the iterative nature of DES more explicit attention in H&S because the comments of **Siewert, Christopher S. Hill**, and **Eric Klinger**, and perhaps **Michael J. Kane**, Eric, and others seem not to grasp that iteration is an essential feature of DES (Hurlburt, 2009; in press; Hurlburt & Akhter, 2006; Hurlburt & Heavey, 2006).

The DES task sounds simple: report whatever you were experiencing at the moment of the beep. However, as an empirical fact, it is not at all simple for the vast majority of subjects on the first sampling day. On the first day, the subject probably does not adequately discriminate between actual ongoing experience and her presuppositions about it; probably does not adequately discriminate between what is actually ongoing at the moment of the beep and what is before the beep or after it; and so on. As a result, first-day apprehensions are of low fidelity, so the primary aim of the first-day interview is *not* to apprehend experience; the first-day primary aim is to learn to cleave to the moment of the beep, to clarify communication, to expose and reduce presuppositions, and in general to build the skills of apprehending experience. As a result, the first-day interview likely makes the second-day's observations more skillful, which likely makes second day's interview more effective, which likely makes the third day's observations more skillful and its interview more effective, and so on (Hurlburt, 2009).

Thus iteration is *not* mere repetition; it is on-the-job training systematically intercalated between each day's apprehensions. Multiple observations without intercalated training is *not* iteration; whatever presuppositions and skills that existed at the first observation are likely to continue to exist at the last (Hurlburt, in press).

Thus an essential feature of DES is that the first few interviews are primarily intended as iterative training sessions, and gradually over sampling days the emphasis shifts to the earnest attempt to apprehend experience. That may be overlooked by most observers, however, because first-day DES interviews *look* approximately the same as the last-day interviews — the interviewer asks the same fundamental question ('What was in your experience at the moment of the beep?') on all sampling days. It may not be apparent that the interviewer's intention in asking that question on early sampling days is to initiate a conversation during which on-the-job training can take place, whereas the intention of the same question on later days is to elicit a description of experience.

Over the course of iteration, targets emerge, and the expositional interviews allow interviewer and subject to focus, iteratively with more and more acuity, on those targets. For example, in Melanie's first H&S interview, her reports of bodily self-consciousness became central during the discussion of her second and third samples. DES accepts that the first-interview discussion of Melanie's self-consciousness was problematic (as are all DES first-day interviews) because we were asking her to recall the details of events that had happened hours earlier *and in the apprehension of which we had not yet provided adequate training*. When, in the first interview, we pressed her for details about bodily self-consciousness, we cultivated in ourselves and in Melanie an attitude that might be expressed, 'Hmm! I wonder what the deal is on bodily self-consciousness? Was that *really* her/my experience? Am I mistaken? I'll have to pay attention to that!' That contributed to our/her ability to apprehend her experience on her second day in higher fidelity.

Eric would say that such iteration might also amplify problematic self-theories. For example, he suggested (H&S Boxes 8.9 and 9.5) that iteration may have amplified Melanie's view of herself as unusually self-conscious: she mentioned it in passing on the first day and then, perhaps out of a desire to be consistent, might have developed habits of responding to questions, habits of attending to certain aspects of her experience rather than other ones after the beep, habits of classification and conceptualization that are both problematic and entrenched by the iterative process. I agree that those are risks. DES seeks to make that possibility explicit and to subvert it as much as possible (for example, by thoroughly discussing the potential for distortions, as Eric, Melanie, and I did for 25 minutes at the end of day 1; this transcript is not in H&S but the audio and a transcript are available on the MIT Press web site, http://mitpress.mit.edu/inner_experience/). That doesn't eliminate the risk, but it doesn't overlook it, either, and the other alternatives I can think of are worse. For example, we could do one-shot studies, thus eliminating the possibility of the iterative habit-making Eric worries about, but I consider first-day (and therefore one-shot) reports of experience to be untrustworthy (see H&S Boxes 4.1, 4.9, and 4.18), and no amount of training that we have been able to devise, other than on-the-job iterative training, can overcome this.

For a more complete discussion of iteration see Hurlburt (2009; in press).

Retrospection

Some commentators think of the DES retrospective 'term' as measured in hours; for example, **Klinger** (p. 97) says, 'I am still left with grave doubts about the collection of data from interviews that occur up to 24 hours after the experience samples were recorded.' Such a focus is a misleading characterization of DES for two reasons. First, it overlooks the iterative nature of DES; second, the several hour delay is not an essential feature of DES. I discuss each in turn.

First, as we have just seen, because of the iterative nature of DES, subjects may become, across the course of sampling, better and better prepared to apprehend the salient characteristics of their experience immediately at the beep. For example, on her first sampling day, Melanie's apprehension of her bodily self-consciousness was entirely 24-hour retrospective: she did not know that that self-consciousness would be of interest. But on subsequent sampling days, the iterative nature of DES allowed Melanie to be more and more ready to consider her bodily self-consciousness immediately as it occurred, and to jot down notes specifically about that within seconds after the beep. The interview might occur up to 24 hours later, but the iteratively-informed introspection itself was essentially *contemporaneous* with the experience. (See also **Methodological Pluralism**.)

Second, whereas it is indeed the case that DES interviews *customarily* take place several hours after the sampled experience, that is *not an essential feature* of DES. DES interviewers can and often do use dramatically shorter intervals between experience and interview. For example, in some of the interviews with children (e.g., in Akhter, 2008), we sat in the car in front of the subject's house; subjects came to us immediately after each beep and we conducted the expositional interview on the spot. In some of our interviews with the elderly (e.g., in Seibert, 2009), we sat in the next bedroom or the hallway while the subject was in the living room or kitchen; subjects came to us immediately after each beep for the expositional interview about that beep. We have given subjects miniature tape recorders and asked them to audiotape extended descriptions of their experience immediately after the beep. We have asked subjects to telephone us on cell phones for interviews immediately following the beep. And so on.

I'm convinced, on the basis of informal but repeated consideration, that once the iterative training has had its effect, and so long as there is some permanent (written, tape recorded, videotaped, sketched, whatever) unchangeable record made immediately after the beep, it doesn't much matter whether the expositional interview is a few minutes later or a few hours later.

Thus the several-hour delay between the contemporaneous documentation and the interview is not an essential part of DES. If **Klinger** or others are concerned about the delay, they could eliminate those concerns either by conducting DES-type interviews with shorter delays, and/or conducting formal evaluations of the informal consideration of the previous paragraph.

Accuracy vs Fidelity

The interactively informal nature of Eric's and my debates that led to H&S had the unfortunate consequence of leading us to discuss, occasionally, whether DES descriptions were 'accurate'. I regret my usage of 'accurate' because I think *all* introspection, including DES, is inaccurate: inner experience always includes details, fringes, pre-reflective bits (see **Petitmengin**), and so on that are impossible completely to grasp.

What was at stake in H&S and elsewhere is not really the *accuracy* of an introspection but its *faithfulness* (or *fidelity*, terms I used in H&S and elsewhere as synonyms). For example, section 2.3 (H&S pp. 27–39) is titled, 'Does DES-Apprehended Inner Experience Faithfully Mirror Inner Experience?' When I am careful (as, regrettably, I was not always in H&S) I refer to the question of the *faithful* (or high fidelity) *apprehension* of Melanie's experience, *not* to the *accurate introspection* of her experience.

I think inner experience can be more or less faithfully apprehended. For example (as discussed in **Presuppositions**), I think the view of **Kane**'s experience as nearly always including inner speech is of lower fidelity than is the view of his experience as nearly always including sensory awareness; I think McWhorter's view of everyone's always picturing the words they speak aloud is a low fidelity apprehension of experience; I think Baars's and Archer's view of everyone always innerly speaking is a low fidelity apprehension of experience.

DES descriptions always fall short of accuracy, so I agree with **Maja Spener** and Eric (see **Context**) that inaccuracy does not rule out introspection. But I think that DES apprehensions can be of higher fidelity than many other introspections (see **Methodological Pluralism**). Therefore I disagree with any implication from Eric (see **Context**) or **Spener** that all inaccurate introspections should be treated equally (see **Methodological Pluralism**). If there is reason to believe that one apprehension of experience is of higher fidelity than another, then the higher fidelity apprehension should be accorded more weight. A corollary is that science should be on the constant lookout for better and better (that is, higher and higher fidelity) methods to apprehend experience.

Diachronic

John Sutton writes

> [There is] one particular, striking problem with the subject-matter of DES. Russ takes it that his target — concrete, structured experience in the wild — is a momentary phenomenon. The method deliberately sets out to eradicate any dynamic features of experience by providing 'a flash snapshot', discarding anything other than 'the last undisturbed moment before the beep'. (Sutton, this symposium, p. 121)

Terry Horgan and Mark Timmons and **Claire Petitmengin** make similar criticisms, as did Eric briefly in H&S (p. 76). The worry appears to be that the DES relentless focus on the moment of the beep rules out the dynamic situation, rules out experience whose duration is longer than a moment, rules out the diachronic.

I'm not so worried. Perhaps this metaphor will be helpful. Suppose your task is to understand the surface of the earth; your method is to position lasers on geostationary satellites. The software that controls the lasers picks a latitude and longitude at random and shoots a laser at the earth, 'painting' a thin line that is a centimeter wide and 10 metres long. Your task is to describe the slice of the earth surface that is painted by the laser line. That process is repeated; eventually you will collect a sample of descriptions of the planet at randomly selected line hits.

For example, the computer randomly produces a latitude 38°31'35.94"N and longitude 77°21'50.68"W and a line orientation of 80 degrees. What does the line paint? Here is one description:

> *Molecular Description A:* At the west end of the line is a small pebble; heading along the line east from that pebble is a bit of concrete with a rubbery residue on it; continuing east is another bit of concrete, also with a rubbery residue; ... continuing east there is a once-centimeter step down and then a patch of asphalt; ... continuing east there is a blade of coarse grass; now another blade, ... etc.

Such a description provides many details of a very narrow slice of the earth. By contrast, here is another description of the same (38°31'35.94"N, 77°21'50.68"W, 80°) laser line:

> *Referential Description B:* The laser hits Interstate 95, the highway that connects Florida and Maine and points in between. The west end of the laser line is on the right-most lane of the northbound side of the interstate at a point just west of Quantico, Virginia; Interstate 95 is a six-lane highway at this point. The line starts at the right-hand lane, which is concrete; then there is a one centimeter step down to an asphalt shoulder lane; once off the shoulder that line hits the weeds that grow wild alongside the roadway.

Description A could be called a 'molecular' description because it seeks to confine itself entirely to those bits of material that exist within the slice. Description B could be called a 'referential' description because it seeks to describe what exists within the slice with the help of references to things outside the slice. The referential Description B therefore mentions that the I95 goes from Florida to Maine, not because Florida and Maine are *in* the slice, but because to understand what *is* in the slice, one needs references. From a referential point of view, what is in the slice is *not* merely bits of concrete but a snippet of a long superhighway.

It seems to me that all descriptions — even molecular Description A — are referential descriptions to some degree, so this is not an all-or-none view. When the molecular Description A says that here is a bit of concrete, that refers to some understanding of what concrete is that involves matters beyond the borders of the thin slice.

Once one allows that a description is referential, at least to some degree, then one opens oneself up to a variety of referential descriptions. Those referential descriptions are open to judgment about the quality of the references. For example:

Equally good referential Description C: The laser hits Interstate 95, the highway that connects Washington DC and Richmond VA and points in between and beyond....

There may well be no reason to prefer Description B over Description C or vice versa — one might view the same event from several or many different perspectives. However, not all perspectives are equal:

Bad referential Description D: The laser hits Interstate 95, the highway that connects Washington DC and Hilton Head Island, South Carolina. Washington DC is the home of the United States Government, wherein Pennsylvania Avenue runs from the White House, home of the President, to the Capitol Building. The President and Congress have been arguing about the ridiculous socialist agenda of the Democrats which is sure to backfire in the next set of elections. I used to have a house on Hilton Head.

Referential Description D is problematic not because the description is referential but because the references to Washington and Hilton Head obviously reflect the writer's interests or presuppositions rather than trying dispassionately to reflect the randomly selected bit of the earth's surface.

A DES exposed description is much more like referential Description B (or C) than molecular Description A, but some commentators, perhaps including **Sutton**, **Horgan and Timmons**, and **Petitmengin** seem to think of DES results as being more like molecular Description A. That seems to be what lies behind, for example, **Horgan and Timmons**'s objection that 'Because the DES method focuses on a *very* brief time slice (what was going on experientially at the moment of the beep), the method may cut the subject off from the diachronic flow of experience over time' (p. 198).

Let's apply this metaphor to a DES example, Melanie's sample 6.4 (H&S, pp. 206–217), a sample that **Horgan and Timmons** call 'phenomenologically thin' (p. 203). Here is the summary from H&S p. 309:

Beep 6.4 (pp. 206–217): Melanie was picking flower petals out of the sink. Her experience was divided pretty evenly between the activity of picking up the petals and [innerly] hearing overlapping 'echoes' of the phrase 'nice long time' from a recently completed (but no longer ongoing) episode of inner speech [in which she had innerly said, 'Those flowers lasted for a nice long time']. (H&S, p. 207)

That is a referential description. For comparison, here is a more molecular description of this experience:

Molecular Description 6.4: Melanie was picking flower petals out of the sink. Her experience was divided pretty evenly between the activity of picking up the petals and innerly hearing three simultaneous instances of her own voice, one saying 'time', another saying 'long', and the third saying 'nice'.

From the molecular point of view, the original inner speaking occurred well before the beep and therefore does not count at all. Nor do the words 'nice long' of the first innerly heard repetition of 'nice long time' — only the word 'time' is immediately heard in the thin slice. Similarly for '[nice] long [time]' and 'nice [long time].' Such a thin-slice description tears the heart out of Melanie's experience at the moment of the beep, because *from an experiential point of view,* Melanie is *not* hearing her voice saying 'time', she is hearing her voice *echoing 'nice long* time', which itself is a fragment of an earlier spoken 'they lasted a nice long time.' Thus a description of Melanie's *experience must* refer to events outside the thin slice of the moment of the beep.

The descriptions we provided in H&S, like the Beep 6.4 description above, were written from a referential, not a molecular, point of view. We did capture some diachronic aspects of Melanie's experience. Sometimes the context reached fairly wide — referring to a debate about the World Series, referring to a remembered tool shed. It is true that we did not prompt Melanie to report the flow of her experience extending back more than a second or two before the beep because Eric and I both doubt people's ability to report such facts accurately.

I have harped incessantly on getting to the moment of the beep, and I will continue such harping because I believe that experience inheres only in moments, so to apprehend experience requires attending to moments (Hurlburt, in press). As it seems to me, most people do not ever establish the moment of their consideration and therefore are never constrained to discuss any particular experience. But *once you have adequately established what was the experience that was ongoing at the moment of the beep,* then I think it is okay to ask about and then to describe, *in a highly constrained and limited way,* the whences and whithers of that at-the-moment experience.

Targeting specific questions

Mark Engelbert and Peter Carruthers suggest that DES could profitably abandon the random-beep-driven ecological validity and the open-beginninged stance that DES typically employs. I agree, as long as the abandonment of ecological validity and open beginningedness does not also abandon the bracketing of presuppositions.

Besides ecological validity, and perhaps more importantly, the random-beep-occurring-in-natural-environments provides a head start toward bracketing presuppositions. Along with open-beginningedness, randomness selects what a DES investigation will discuss, and thus aims attention at what actually occurs regardless of whether that occurrence is thought a priori to be theoretically important. That is, randomness and open-beginningedness encourage both interviewer and subject to adopt a level playing field with respect to theoretical presuppositions, and that is hugely important, in my view (see **Presuppositions and Background Assumptions**).

Once that level playing field is securely adopted by both investigator and subject, then I think it may make sense to relax the randomness and open-beginningedness requirement. Here's an example. Golf is said to be a 'mental' game; theories abound on what golfers do and should think about on the course, based almost entirely on 19th hole retrospection. Yani Dickens and I (Dickens, 2007) sought to explore the actual experience of golfers, so we set up a tournament where we would provide golfers with beepers. But we did *not* take these subjects immediately into the tournament and sample with them there. Had we done so, it is likely that their *presuppositions* about their golf experience would have overwhelmed their *actual* experience while golfing. Instead, we randomly sampled with each golfer individually in his natural everyday *non-golf* environments for three days each. The randomness of the beeps, the open-beginningedness of the interviews, and the variety of non-golf situations helped subjects recognize the variety of their own experiences, helped the subjects build a healthy respect for trying to bracket presuppositions, helped the subjects build the skills of bracketing their own presuppositions in environments where they might not have very strong presuppositions — that is, about the nature of experience during golf.

Once the variety-of-everyday-situation sampling had helped the subjects acquire a genuine interest in what their experience was *really* like rather than in what they presuppositionally thought it should be like, *and only then*, subjects wore the beeper in the golf tournament. We found, for example, that highly skilled golfers focus more on golf than do moderately skilled golfers. In my view, that finding is believable *only because we had trained subjects to bracket presuppositions*, created in subjects a substantial interest in the actual characteristics of their experience as opposed to their golf-theoretical interest.

Although we did not do so in this study, we could have targeted specific events: we could have arranged to have specific beeps occur while in the backswing of a putt, or during the setup before the shot on the 14th tee (a wicked shot over long water to an island green); and so on.

Thus I agree with **Engelbert and Carruthers** that the typical DES method can be usefully expanded *so long as* there is some effective method of building the commitment to bracketing presuppositions and building observational skills prior to the target observations.

Siewert's Deepest Worry

> We must press sensitively worded questions to probe the content and implications of introspective judgment, to see which are worth retaining. But Hurlburt and I apparently differ regarding just what it is crucial to ask, how far to push such questioning, and the dangers of prematurely abandoning it — and it seems, the extent to which the questioners should also similarly examine themselves, while engaging in their own first-person reflection on experience. It seems — and this is my deepest worry about Hurlburt's method — that the very habits of self-reflection I would have us *cultivate*, he would evidently have us *suppress*, since he thinks they only breed error of the sort DES is called in to correct. But on my view we need just such habits of articulate alertness to our own on-going experience, and of self-examination, if we are to bring the 'personal' into the 'theoretical' as Hurlburt laudably wishes (H&S, pp. 257–60). It is just such habitual self-examination that we need to nourish the rational correction of introspectively-based conceptions of experience. (**Siewert**, pp. 87–88)

I think **Siewert** and I are not as different here as he suggests, if one has adequate appreciation for the iterative nature of DES (see above). I am *enthusiastically in favour* of 'press[ing] sensitively worded questions to probe the content and implications of introspective judgment,' *as long as one presses and pushes on an even playing field, not giving the advantage to privately created notions* (see **Presuppositions and Background Assumptions**). I strongly encourage DES investigators to be sensitive to their on-going experiences; one's own experience provides evidence of the workings of presuppositions, shows when the bracketing of presuppositions is most necessary (Hurlburt & Heavey, 2006; cf. the 'nose for presuppositions' in **Presuppositions and Background Assumptions**), and may provide a bit of insight into phenomena.

For example, I have no objection whatsoever for Eric (or me) to develop an acute and articulate awareness of his own bodily self-consciousness or lack thereof, and then to press Melanie hard on whether

her experienced self-consciousness is or is not the same as his own, as long as that pressing is on an even playing field. As long as Eric authentically has and genuinely conveys a disinterest in the direction of the result, I would encourage his saying to Melanie, 'When I examine myself, I find no bodily self-consciousness of the kind you describe, so I would like us to figure out whether you're mistaken or I am, or whether your experience is different from mine, or whether our experiences are similar but we use the language differently.' Then he should press as hard as he likes, making as careful distinctions as he likes, iteratively improving both Melanie's and his own abilities to observe and discriminate, over as many sampling days as he likes.

The practical problem is that it is high personal art authentically to have a genuine disinterest in the direction of a result. Most people (according to my observations) are presuppositionally committed to a point of view, presuppositionally primed to 'discover' what they want to discover, presuppositionally skilled at badgering the witness into corroborating the questioner's viewpoint. If those presuppositional pressures can be overcome, can be replaced with genuine, level-playing-field alertness, then I heartily agree with **Siewert:** 'we need... habits of articulate alertness to our own on-going experience.'

Difficulty/Expense

DES is often criticized as being too time-consuming, too expensive, with too much skill required, but I see that as a criticism of consciousness science, *not* of DES. Consciousness science thinks nothing of spending millions for an fMRI machine; such money could fund a lot of DES training. So the question is not about money, it is about perceived value. If the scientific community valued faithful apprehensions of pristine experience, it could have them. It would indeed require a reordering of priorities, a restructuring of the scientific community to develop and incorporate ways of recruiting, supporting, and training interviewers, as well as discriminating skilled interviewers from unskilled ones. But that could be done if the scientific community thought it important. Israeli Air Force recruitment provides an extreme model: all Israeli18-year-olds enter the military. The Israeli military gives aptitude tests and behavioural observations and determines, out of all those men and women, who *the military* wants to train to become pilots in the Air Force (it is *not* a matter of volunteering, as if self-identified-interest somehow predicts skill). Then the Air Force operates a Flight school that washes out 39 out of every 40 pilot candidates. As a result of this literally best-of-the-best selection procedure, the Israeli Air Force gets *very* good pilots. If consciousness science were so motivated, a similar scheme could be put in place: select individuals who were likely to be skilled at observing inner experience, train a bunch of them, and wash out all but the best. There is nothing impossible about this procedure.

17 Snapshots trump an accumulated life?

Sutton calls DES 'history free' and worries that I expect 17 flash snapshots to 'trump an accumulated life' of historical self-understanding (p. 125). Actually, I think DES descriptions are steeped in history (see the Diachronic section above) and I don't *expect* any trumping, even though, as an empirical fact, I frequently *observe* the subjects' sampling snapshots *do* 'trump an accumulated life'.

Historical self-understandings, like most historical accounts, are at best oversimplifications and usually substantial distortions of actual history, focusing on some events to the exclusion of others, focusing on one interpretation to the exclusion of others. Many (perhaps most) people have their favourite personal-historical accounts, usually called narratives, which they invoke often to explain or justify events and behaviour. Such told historical accounts (narratives) are part truth, part good story, part self-protection, and part self-presentation.

DES differs from other methods by relentlessly discouraging relying on (partially true) narrative explanations in favour of relying on (as unadulterated as possible) sampled experiences. Many (perhaps most) subjects recognize that suspending the narrative to get to the facts is the reverse of their usual suspending of the facts to get to the narrative. Often they find the attempt to get to the facts refreshing or relieving. The DES subject knows that she has data whose provenance she herself fully understands, data that are little or not at all driven by any agenda I have other than to get as best we can at the truth of her experience, data whose fidelity is vouched for by herself. As a result, subjects often transform their self-understandings in light of such high-quality data. I don't force this on them or expect it of them. If the subject does value her data, and does recognize that her data conflicts with her narrative (whose provenance is not well understood and whose veridicality is at some level known to be suspect), it is not surprising that she jettisons the narrative, even if — perhaps especially if — it is based on an accumulated life.

References

Akhter, S.A. (2008) *Exploring Adolescent Inner Experience*, unpublished Masters thesis, University of Nevada, Las Vegas.

Dickens, Y. (2007) *Inner Experience During Golf Performance*, unpublished Dissertation, University of Nevada, Las Vegas.

Engelbert, M. & Carruthers, P. (this symposium) Descriptive Experience Sampling: What is it good for?, *Journal of Consciousness Studies*, **18** (1).

Hill, C. (this symposium) How to study introspection, *Journal of Consciousness Studies*, **18** (1).

Horgan, T. & Timmons, M. (this symposium) Introspection and the phenomenology of free will: Problems and prospects, *Journal of Consciousness Studies*, **18** (1).

Hurlburt, R.T. (2009) Iteratively apprehending pristine experience, *Journal of Consciousness Studies*, **16** (10–12), pp. 156–188.

Hurlburt, R.T. (in press) *Investigating Pristine Inner Experience: Moments of Truth*, Cambridge: Cambridge University Press.

Hurlburt, R.T. & Akhter, S.A. (2006) The Descriptive Experience Sampling method, *Phenomenology and the Cognitive Sciences*, **5**, pp. 271–301.

Hurlburt, R.T. & Akhter, S.A. (2008) Unsymbolized thinking, *Consciousness and Cognition*, **17**, pp. 1364–1374.

Hurlburt, R.T. & Heavey, C.L. (2006) *Exploring Inner Experience: The Descriptive Experience Sampling Method*, Amsterdam and Philadelphia: John Benjamins.

Hurlburt, R.T. & Schwitzgebel, E. (2007) *Describing Inner Experience? Proponent Meets Skeptic*, Cambridge, MA: MIT Press.

Hurlburt, R.T. & Schwitzgebel, E. (this symposium) Methodological pluralism, armchair introspection, and DES as the epistemic tribunal, *Journal of Consciousness Studies*, **18** (1).

Hurlburt, R.T. & Schwitzgebel, E. (this symposium) Little or no experience outside of attention?, *Journal of Consciousness Studies*, **18** (1).

Hurlburt, R.T. & Schwitzgebel, E. (this symposium) Presuppositions and background assumptions, *Journal of Consciousness Studies*, **18** (1).

Kane, M. (this symposium) Describing, debating, and discovering inner experience, *Journal of Consciousness Studies*, **18** (1).

Klinger, E. (this symposium) Response organization of mental imagery, evaluation of Descriptive Experience Sampling, and alternatives, *Journal of Consciousness Studies*, **18** (1).

Petitmengin, C. (this symposium) Describing the experience of describing?, *Journal of Consciousness Studies*, **18** (1).

Schwitzgebel, E. (this symposium) The philosophical and psychological context of Descriptive Experience Sampling, *Journal of Consciousness Studies*, **18** (1).

Seibert, T.M. (2009) *The Inner Experience of Older Individuals*, unpublished Dissertation, University of Nevada, Las Vegas.

Siewert, C. (this symposium) Socratic introspection and the abundance of experience, *Journal of Consciousness Studies*, **18** (1).

Spener, M. (this symposium) Using first-person data about consciousness, *Journal of Consciousness Studies*, **18** (1).

Sutton, J. (this symposium) Time, experience, and Descriptive Experience Sampling, *Journal of Consciousness Studies*, **18** (1).

Eric Schwitzgebel

The Philosophical and Psychological Context of DES

In H&S[1] we contextualized our inquiry by providing three (somewhat oversimplified) historical narratives. The first narrative, emphasized especially at the beginning of Chapters 1 and 2, describes the rise of introspective science in the late 19th and early 20th centuries, its collapse in the face of methodological criticism, and the attempt of Descriptive Experience Sampling (DES) to avoid the problems that led to the collapse of the first wave of introspective psychology. The second narrative, emphasized in Chapter 3, begins with the infallibilism about current conscious experience commonly embraced by philosophers from Descartes into the 20th century, followed by the decline of philosophical infallibilism later in the 20th century but the failure of philosophers attacking infallibilism to go sufficiently far in their appreciation of the magnitude and pervasiveness of introspective error. The third narrative, scattered throughout the book (including in both the opening and the closing pages), contextualizes our inquiry in the history of science: because of the difficulty of the introspective task, consciousness studies is an immature science compared to other sciences, perhaps surprisingly so given its interest and the apparent easy availability of the data; but hopefully the data will stabilize and it will follow the path of other maturing sciences.

I interpret the commentaries of **Spener** and **Piccinini** as attempts to show how DES fits into slightly different narratives. **Engelbert and Carruthers** and **Hill**, in criticizing my pessimism about introspection, challenge Russ's and my (especially my) assertion that philosophers rejecting infallibilism didn't go far enough toward pessimism. And in presenting constructive suggestions for ways to tweak and extend DES, **Engelbert and Carruthers**, **Hill**, **Horgan and**

---

[1] See note and correspondence details on page 206 above.

Timmons, and **Kane**, present visions about how DES might fit into the future development of the historical arcs we have sketched.

On this last issue, I will just reiterate what I said in **Methodological Pluralism**: I heartily encourage a pluralism of method. The commentators' suggested methodological extensions of DES seem likely to me to be seriously problematic in various ways, but since all methods for studying consciousness are seriously problematic, the best we can do if we are not to abandon the enterprise is hope for convergent results from a variety of methods with complementary flaws. As **Kane** points out, even pretty ham-handed questions about 'mind wandering' seem to be starting to generate some useful, externally corroborated results.

Hill criticizes my introspective pessimism as founded on too monolithic a view of the nature and epistemology of introspection. Thus, I have overreached in trying to push philosophers farther into scepticism than they have already gone. **Hill** argues that although some ways of arriving at introspective judgments might be highly unreliable, others are extremely trustworthy. I partly accept this criticism. My understanding of introspection circa 2007–2008 may have been too monolithic. I am now, like **Hill**, a pluralist, in part as a result of reading **Hill**'s commentary and his 2009 book (see Schwitzgebel, in press-a). I thank him for helping me see the light! However, my polymorphism is unlike **Hill**'s in one crucial respect, relevant to the epistemology: While **Hill** characterizes introspection as driven by different processes in different cases, some of those processes very simple and reliable, I am inclined to think of introspection as normally driven by a complex confluence of processes in *each* case and thus rarely manifesting simple reliability (Schwitzgebel, in press-a).

Some of my disagreement with **Hill**, too, comes from an inclination to draw the borders of the concept of 'introspection' a bit differently. Perhaps simply saying 'it appears to me that' and then expressing a perceptual judgment is a dependable way to arrive at statements about one's own experience — but I'm inclined to think it is not an *introspective* way of doing so. There need be no sensitivity to the target experience. It could be a relatively empty cognitive act akin to thoughtlessly appending an 'I say' to a spoken utterance or a 'Yours,' before the signature line of an email. The resulting statements might be true, but if so that is a function of their structure rather than the function of any sort of appreciation of their truth. The same holds for the insertion of 'I think' into a sentence: though it transforms a sentence from one about the outside world to one, literally speaking, about one's mind, the unreflective insertion of that phrase seems to me to reflect no cognitive activity worth calling introspective, unless virtually all utterances about the world are introspective. Of course, in some cases one does really think about one's visual experience when saying 'it looks to me like...' or really reflect on the content of one's thoughts when one says 'I think....' However, in the former case, it's not clear that we don't start to seriously err (as perhaps in **Hill**'s own case of a distant object's 'looking small,' which I argue, in Schwitzgebel, 2006 and in press-b, is geometrically problematic and maybe also suspiciously culturally contingent). And the latter seems to be a special, ungeneralizable case of banal self-fulfillment, not reflecting any introspective acumen: the thought that I'm thinking that P embeds the thought that P in a way that makes it trivially, self-referentially true, like the sentence 'this sentence contains the quoted word "dog"' (Schwitzgebel, 2008, in press-b). Thus my dispute with **Hill** turns in part upon a terminological question about what deserves to be called 'introspection'.

Engelbert and Carruthers, like Hill, argue that ordinary introspection is more accurate than I acknowledge, and thus that the philosophical tradition is not as far wrong as I have said (except about the alleged introspection of attitudes, where it might be even farther wrong than I have said). **Engelbert and Carruthers** suggest that human experience is more variable than I suppose, so that some of the variation in subjective reports that I attribute to error should be attributed instead to real differences in underlying experience. They argue plausibly that people might differ immensely in the relative frequency of their visual imagery, say, versus their inner speech. However, I don't think my pessimistic arguments turn on scepticism about such matters. It's one thing to say that people differ immensely in the *proportion* of types of experience they have, and quite a different thing to say that people differ immensely in the *basic structure* of their experience. For example, I think it antecedently likely that the basic structure of people's visual imagery, when that visual imagery occurs, is the same across people. That is, I think it unlikely that some people always have sketchy imagery whereas others always have imagery replete with immense detail, or that some people have only flat, two-dimensional imagery while others have imagery with depth, or that some people experience interference between visual imagery experience and visual perceptual experience while others do not. Such differences are of course possible in principle, but I think it's legitimate to doubt that when ordinary people report such differences those reports track whatever real differences there may be in their underlying imagery experience; the empirical literature on differences in performance on imagery-related tasks finds little correlation between differences in cognitive performance and differences in subjective report (Schwitzgebel, 2002; in press-b). Possibly DES could do better, but if so, that remains to be shown. Likewise, in ordinary visual perception, it seems unlikely to me that some people normally visually experience two-degrees of clarity, rapidly moving around a hazy background, while others normally experience, in response to the same outward stimuli, a hundred degrees of stable, simultaneous clarity (Schwitzgebel, 2008; in press-b). It also seems unlikely that some people experience an elliptical apparent shape when they view a coin at an oblique angle while others do not (Schwitzgebel, 2006; in press-b). It is on matters of this sort, rather than relative frequency of different types of universally acknowledged experience, that I think we should retain a defeasible presumption that people are generally similar, pending good experimental evidence that they really do differ radically. Since the empirical evidence does not appear to defeat those presumptions of similarity, I think the most likely explanation of the differences in reporting about such matters is introspective error — though in some cases terminological differences may also play a role. (I note that Russ thinks that people *do* differ immensely in the basic structure of their experience and that the most likely explanation of the failure to discover and validate those differences is the generally inadequate methods used to apprehend inner experience.)

Spener protests, with considerable justice, that it's not entirely clear what Russ's and my goals were in our collaboration — that although we frame the book as an exploration of whether we can believe people's DES-generated reports about their inner experiences, that question lacks meat without a clear statement of what features of those reports we are interested in and what we hope to build upon them. All but the most doctrinaire sceptic or pollyannish booster would say that DES-generated reports are likely to be accurate to some degree but not perfectly. As **Spener** emphasizes, the real issue is whether the reports are accurate *enough* — and the question she poses is, enough *for what?* On this issue, as Russ and I noticed near the end of the book, Russ and I sometimes talked past each other. I wanted to do different, more theoretically ambitious, more philosophical things with the DES-generated reports than did Russ. I wanted to explore issues that turned on subtle aspects of the reports rather than on their gross outline — and I was therefore more easily dissatisfied with the reports than was Russ. This doesn't, of course, capture the whole of Russ's and my differences. After mounting this criticism, **Spener** helpfully articulates different ways in which introspective reports can cast light on philosophical issues. Of particular value, I think, is

Spener's point that even if introspective reports are often inaccurate, if we can correct for those inaccuracies or otherwise draw indirect connections between the reports and our philosophical or psychological theories, the introspective reports might still help decide among those theories. Thus, she usefully exposes and undercuts the assumption, lying behind Russ's and my narratives about the role of introspection in consciousness studies, that introspection is valuable to science only if it is accurate.

Piccinini locates H&S within the philosophical debate about whether consciousness studies uses 'private' as opposed to 'public' methods. While DES might seem to be a private method, turning on Melanie's private access to her own experiences outside the control of the laboratory, **Piccinini** argues that it is in fact a public method — which is a good thing because only public methods are, he says, scientifically legitimate.

Piccinini writes that 'a method is public [and thus scientifically legitimate] just in case different investigators can apply the method to answer the same questions, and when they do, they obtain the same data. Otherwise a method is private' (p. 105). Two difficulties with this characterization of publicity come to my mind, both of which **Piccinini** explicitly addresses: first, there seem to be scientifically legitimate, unrepeatable observations — such as of unique historical events (e.g., a brief astronomical event seen by a single astronomer). **Piccinini** responds to this difficulty by stating that in such cases the observations satisfy the 'publicity principle' — which he glosses as 'repeat*able*' and 'reprodu*cible*' (p. 107). However, it's not entirely clear what the criteria for repeatability and reproducibility are. The second difficulty, which is more fundamental, is that it's not clear why we should care about repeatability and reproducibility in principle, as opposed to corroborability, especially actual corroboration in fact. Suppose you are the only sighted person in a society of blind people. Your visual methods for detecting phenomena might be unreproducible by others (you couldn't, for example, 'teach your methods to other unbiased parties'; p. 107). But it doesn't seem that members of your scientific community should therefore dismiss your visual reports. Blind scientists might be able to corroborate those reports in many indirect ways and thus have excellent grounds for regarding your reports as legitimate evidence (perhaps under certain further conditions). Repeatability matters only because evidence acquired through repeatable methods tends to be trustworthy — especially evidence acquired through methods *in fact repeated* by different investigators with different theoretical predilections. But one can sometimes establish trustworthiness without repeatability.

Piccinini responds to this second objection by arguing that the privatism 'in the relevant sense' is committed not only to the claim that first-person data are unrepeatable but also to the claim that first-person data cannot be publicly validated. Now maybe there is a sense of privatism on which it is essential to privatism that first-person data cannot be publicly validated. I would be opposed to privatism in that sense. But so too, perhaps, would three of the four authors **Piccinini** appears to have in mind as his target privatists. Chalmers (2004) appears to contemplate third-person data showing that some first-person data are unreliable. Hatfield (2005) suggests that first-person and third-person data are on a par as evidence that should be interpreted in the light of the full array of data. Gertler (2009) explicitly says that introspective data are not 'sacrosanct' and can be undercut by, for example, neurophysiological data if the neurophysiological data have been found to correlate well with other first-person reports. Only Goldman (1997) explicitly embraces the extreme view that first-person data are incapable of public validation.

Thus, to the extent the public/private debate is about repeatability in principle, I think it misses the heart of the epistemic matter. To the extent it is really about the value of seeking external corroboration of introspective (or immediately retrospective) reports, I am wholeheartedly on the side of **Piccinini** and the publicists — and I suspect some of the so-called privatists might be too.

References

Chalmers, D.J. (2004) How can we construct a science of consciousness?, in Gazzaniga, M.S. (ed.) *The Cognitive Neurosciences III*, Cambridge, MA: MIT Press.

Engelbert, M. & Carruthers, P. (this symposium) Descriptive Experience Sampling: What is it good for?, *Journal of Consciousness Studies*, **18** (1).

Gertler, B. (2009) Introspection, in Bayne, T., Cleeremans, A. & Wilken, P. (eds.) *The Oxford Companion to Consciousness*, Oxford: Oxford University Press.

Goldman, A. (1997) Science, publicity, and consciousness, *Philosophy of Science*, **64**, pp. 525–545.

Hatfield, G. (2005) Instrospective evidence in psychology, in Achinstein, P. (ed.) *Scientific evidence*, Baltimore, MD: Johns Hopkins University Press.

Hill, C.S. (2009) *Consciousness*, Cambridge: Cambridge University Press.

Hill, C.S. (this symposium) How to study introspection, *Journal of Consciousness Studies*, **18** (1).

Horgan, T. & Timmons, M. (this symposium) Introspection and the phenomenology of free will: Problems and prospects, *Journal of Consciousness Studies*, **18** (1).

Hurlburt, R.T. & Schwitzgebel, E. (2007) *Describing Inner Experience? Proponent Meets Skeptic*, Cambridge, MA: MIT Press.

Hurlburt, R.T. & Schwitzgebel, E. (this symposium) Methodological pluralism, armchair introspection, and DES as the epistemic tribunal, *Journal of Consciousness Studies*, **18** (1).

Kane, M. (this symposium) Describing, debating, and discovering inner experience, *Journal of Consciousness Studies*, **18** (1).

Piccinini, G. (this symposium) Scientific methods ought to be public, and Descriptive Experience Sampling is one of them, *Journal of Consciousness Studies*, **18** (1).

Schwitzgebel, E. (2002) How well do we know our own conscious experience? The case of visual imagery, *Journal of Consciousness Studies*, **9** (5–6), pp. 35–53.

Schwitzgebel, E. (2006) Do things look flat?, *Philosophy & Phenomenological Research*, **72**, pp. 589–599.

Schwitzgebel, E. (2008) The unreliability of naive introspection, *Philosophical Review*, **117**, pp. 245–273.

Schwitzgebel, E. (in press a) Introspection, what?, in Smithies, D. (eds.) *Introspection and Consciousness*, Oxford: Oxford University Press.

Schwitzgebel, E. (in press b) *Perplexities of Consciousness*, Cambridge, MA: MIT Press.

Spener, M. (this symposium) Using first-person data about consciousness, *Journal of Consciousness Studies*, **18** (1).

Russell T. Hurlburt and Neda Raymond

Agency

A Case Study In Bracketing Presuppositions

This paper has two goals. First, it illustrates how presuppositions present themselves. Second, it amplifies the comment that Russ made (**Presuppositions and Background Assumptions**)[1] about **Terry Horgan and Mark Timmons**: that their own presuppositions would likely stand toxically in the way of their discovering the important features of agency.

Our interest here is the bracketing of presuppositions, which we think is of primary importance (see **Presuppositions and Background Assumptions**). We use **Horgan and Timmons** as an example because we believe that their interest in agency is important, and we hope constructively to contribute to the investigation of agency by considering an excerpt from the third-sampling-day expositional interview of 'Walt' conducted primarily by graduate student Neda Raymond under the supervision of Russ. Neda is a DES interviewer in training. She is knowledgeable about DES and recognizes the importance of the bracketing of presuppositions and is developing the bracketing skill. Focusing on a developing skill will allow us to deconstruct the bracketing process and thereby expose the process to sunlight.

Of interest here is Walt's sample 3.4, in which Walt described himself as paying attention to his body posture as he was running up the stairs. Immediately following that interview, Russ said to Neda that it had appeared that she had at least initially not believed Walt's account of sample 3.4, and Neda agreed. Russ commented that this disbelief probably reflected the operation of a presupposition that Neda had only partially bracketed: the presupposition still evidenced itself enough that Russ could sense Neda's disbelief. Neda agreed. As part

---

[1] See note and correspondence details on page 206 above.

of her endeavour to acquire the bracketing of presuppositions skill, Russ suggested that Neda write, as soon as possible, a diary entry chronicling her reactions as she had gone through the sample 3.4 interview. The object was to try to capture her whole experience, from when Walt first said he was going up the stairs to after the meeting when Russ said it seemed that Neda didn't believe him. Neda was to write this diary entry as a personal, private account, by Neda privately for Neda alone. After she had finished writing, she could elect to show it to Russ, or first bowdlerize it and then show it to Russ, or not to show it to him at all — that choice would be Neda's to make without prejudice *after* she had written the private-for-Neda account. Five hours after the sampling interview, Neda sent the diary entry to Russ with a note saying it was exactly as she had originally written it — no bowdlerization necessary. Thus the diary is retrospective, 4–5 hours after the original interview, which, while a long time by DES standards, is short by comparison to most retrospections.

We believe that Neda's diary highlights with unusual transparency the nature of the bracketing of presuppositions, so we present it below, inserted into an unedited transcript of the interview. The diary was written from Neda's memory; that is, Neda did *not* view the videotape of the interview before she wrote the diary. The 'Neda's Diary:' entries are slightly edited, leaving the sense intact but correcting irrelevancies such as misspellings, etc., and breaking the entries apart to aid the comprehension of the reader. [I wish publicly to thank and commend my co-author Neda for her willingness to expose her private process to our public inspection — Russ.]

We number by superscript each conversational turn to facilitate subsequent references to them.

Interview 3.4 (third sampling day, fourth beep)

Neda:[1] So what was going on in beep 3.4?

Walt:[2] Okay. 3.4 was in the evening of Sunday. My son was upstairs and he was in his crib and upset, and I was running upstairs to get him. And so at the beep you guys caught me about half way up the stairs. Um. My...what was in my attention was the... kind of the action of going upstairs, so the movements required to do that. So I was concentrating on, or I was aware of, um y'know, the physical act of moving. I was aware of kind of the associated tension in my y'know legs and back, and I was aware of my balance as well, basically that kind of trying not to fall over.

Neda's Diary: My immediate thought is, 'Yeah, right! There's no way you're paying attention to that level of detail as you're running toward your son's crying. You *must* have noticed the physical tension and balance stuff *after* the beep, when you're taking stock of the situation'. I'm not sure of my precise thought at that moment, but it's something pretty close to this.

Comments: (1) Presuppositions are impossible to specify in advance, both because there are so many of them and because, by definition, they exist as part of the unexamined fabric of our understanding of the world. Prior to this sampling, Neda likely *never* would have identified someone paying attention to his bodily posture as he runs upstairs as triggering a presupposition. And yet that presupposition is there, poised, ready to go when activated.

(2) Presuppositions interfere with the ability to apprehend experience faithfully. Setting aside for the moment whether Walt's experience actually was centred on his body as he went up the stairs, Neda's presupposition makes it difficult for her to apprehend *whatever* experience Walt is trying to describe. At the very least, Neda's attention is divided between her own thoughts and what Walt is saying.

(3) Presuppositions betray an already tilted playing field. Neda's disbelief comes not in the slightest because of what Walt said or didn't say or how he said or didn't say it; she was a disbeliever *pre* his saying anything.

(4) Presuppositions operate immediately — Neda doesn't *gradually* become disbelieving, she is *immediately* disbelieving. She was probably disbelieving well before Walt had even finished giving his opening paragraph — probably was disbelieving before she really understood what Walt was saying. That is the *pre* of *pre*supposition.

(5) Presuppositions have substantial personal power. Neda's reaction is not merely a cognitive 'background belief' as Eric describes them ('working assumptions about what kinds of things are relatively likely and unlikely, how the world divides up and fits together'; **Presuppositions and Background Assumptions**, p. 208). Neda's reaction is an organismic, emotionally charged way of orienting.

(6) Presuppositions are imperatives, not scepticisms. Neda *didn't believe* Walt; it was not merely that she wondered whether what he said was true.

> **N:**[3] So *right* at that moment of the beep, [snaps fingers] right before that beep kind of disturbs your awareness...
>
> **W:**[4] um hm.

N:[5] ...are you paying attention to or concentrating or aware of y'know your balance and the tension in your legs and back? Or would you say y'know after the beep goes off when you're kind of looking back at the situation, that's what...

Neda's Diary: I also begin to feel immediately 'off' somehow — uncomfortable or something along those lines. So I immediately ask him, 'so, RIGHT at the moment of the beep you say you're running up stairs, feeling tension in your legs, trying not to fall, is that right?' (or something to that effect) and he says Yes, he is.

Comments: (7) The reaction to presuppositions, like the presuppositions themselves (see 5) is organismic. Neda's bodily discomfort is a sign that her organism is resisting her own presupposition. Or perhaps the discomfort is a sign of the presupposition itself — a negative reaction to someone who would say such foolish things.

(8) Presuppositions can be bracketed. Neda *has* a presupposition, but nonetheless she asks a pretty good, pretty even-handed question, giving Walt the opportunity to clarify what he meant. That is, she is pretty successful in bracketing an existing presupposition. However:

(9) Bracketing presuppositions is a skill, and whereas Neda asks a moderately skilled presupposition-bracketed question, it is not highly skilled. Her tone, among other things, gives her away: '*Right* at that moment' has a disbelieving stress on *right*. Such aspects, while subtle, were evident enough that Russ noticed the implied criticism (and so, presumably, might Walt).

(10) There is no predetermined or fixed level of required skill for the bracketing of presuppositions. It varies based on the person, situation, etc. Apparently, Walt was not as sensitive to the implied criticism as was Russ, so Neda's bracketing was good enough in this situation. Had Walt been, for whatever reason, more sensitive, her question might not have been adequate — the implied criticism might have inhibited his attempts to describe phenomena.

W:[6] I can, I can *definitely* say that I was aware of my balance. The, y'know, maybe the tension in my legs and back was after?

Neda's Diary: And he says 'well maybe the tension was right after the beep, but the balancing was definitely at the beep,' and so now I think to myself, 'Hah! So I was right! There was no tension! He became aware of that AFTER the beep. I *knew* it!' (There WAS actually a slight, 'told you so' tinge to this thought, like I somehow had won this round of 'truth seeking').

Comments: (11) Neda's presuppositions are, at least in part, *about Neda*, not about Walt. *Neda wants to win.* This has the following corollary:

(11a) Presuppositions distract. Wanting to win necessarily distracts from the intention of wanting *to apprehend with fidelity*. (The wanting to win is further evidence that (5) presuppositions are organismic, not merely cognitive, processes.) Wanting to win, wanting to show I'm right, wanting to show that the other is wrong are frequent but not ubiquitous characteristics of presuppositions.

[pause]

N:[7] So *right* at the moment of the beep you're kind of aware of your balance?

Neda's Diary: Still not believing, I ask again, 'but RIGHT at the moment of the beep, are you actually aware of the tension in your legs and trying to balance? Or are you just running up the stairs?'

Comments: (12) Presuppositions colour experience. Note that Neda's diary reconstruction of what she said is somewhat more negative than were her actual words as transcribed from the videotape: as do most people, she recalls her *intentions* as much or more than her actual words. That is, she recalls herself as asking, disbelievingly, 'are you actually aware' when she actually said, much more neutrally, 'you're kind of aware.'

W:[8] Um hmm.

N:[9] And what... how is that awareness occurring. When you say you're aware of your balance, can you say more about [voice softens] what you mean about that?

[pause]

Neda's Diary: As I'm asking him this last part,[fn2] I start to realize that what I'm saying doesn't quite make sense, and I'm feeling a little strange about my own line of questioning. I'm feeling a little

---

[2] We make here a methodological comment about the structure of this paper. When Neda's Diary says 'As I'm asking him this last part,' it may appear that Neda's diary was written in response to viewing the transcript of the interview — that is, 'this last part' may appear to refer to what she actually said at N[9]. We emphasize that Neda wrote the diary a few hours after the interview while recalling the interview from memory, not from the transcript (which didn't yet exist) and not from watching the videotape (to which she didn't have access during the diary writing). Thus 'this last part' refers to the last part of the previous sentence in her diary, that is, to the 'Or are you just running up the stairs?' which is the last sentence in her diary entry shown after N[7]. We have 'torn apart' the diary and inserted it at what seemed relevant places in the transcript as a literary device — as a way of making the diary accessible for the reader. This is one of a few places where that tearing apart slightly

uncomfortable asking him the question. I was feeling slightly uncomfortable before this point, like I was in competition with him to PROVE that my belief was correct, and that he couldn't possibly be paying attention to balancing, because *I'd* never do that in a similar situation. But I kind of started thinking along the lines of, 'Why am I so hell bent on "proving" something about his experience that I think is true? Why am I not just accepting what he has to say about his experience? After all, it's HIS experience not mine.' (Again, I didn't think those exact words, but those words capture my thought process well.)

Comments: (13) As we said at (8), bracketing presuppositions does *not* require *eliminating* presuppositions. Neda's question at N^9 is a good, level-playing-field question, and she asks that despite the fact that her presupposition still exists. That is, Neda has found a way to set her presupposition aside, put it out of play, ask a good question anyway — that's what we mean by 'bracket'.

Bracketing presuppositions is not easy. Neda here has a real battle on her hands, not between her and Walt but between her presupposition about what people are aware of when they run up the stairs (i.e., not their balance) and the part of her genuinely trying to understand what Walt was experiencing at that moment.

> **W:**[10] [tentatively] I, I... um... It's kind of hard to describe the feeling of balance. Um, it's, y'know, whether, the best uh, the best way I could describe would be y'know is continually asking myself the question Am I about to fall? And the answer being No, or Yes, depending on whether I have my balance or not. So, um, so I guess you could say my, my spatial relation to the stairs, where I was in between the two railings, how I was angled one way or the other, forward or back, that all kind of comes to play in my awareness of balance. So my physical position. Would that, does that help?

Neda's Diary: At this point I am feeling rather uncomfortable with myself, and also kind of suddenly realizing Dr. Hurlburt is in the room; I'm feeling a little embarrassed too. I decide to 'go with' what Walt is saying regarding his physicality and paying attention to not falling over. I'm still not really convinced at this point that what he's saying was occurring was actually occurring, but I'm not feeling 'in competition' with him to prove my own correctness at this point.

---

distorts the original intention. In our judgment, that slight distortion does not materially affect the impact of the presentation. However, we do wish our process to be transparent, because the distinction between a retrospection after a few hours and a reconstruction from a transcript can sometimes be important (see Hurlburt, in press, ch. 7).]

Comments: (14) The bracketing skill is acquired over time. Neda's decision to 'go with' what Walt is saying is *not* a substantial improvement over her earlier presupposition to disbelieve him. The highly skilled interviewer would not be caught in that either/or, but would be continually evaluating the extent to which Walt's talk is consistent, subjunctified, unusual, and so on. So the fact that Neda recognized a presupposition and strove to bracket it is better than merely unthinkingly going along with the presupposition, but it does not *solve* the presupposition problem. It is a step toward that solution, which will ripen only with substantial practice.

> **N:**[11] Okay. So you're saying... right at the moment of the beep you said, you said a couple of ways that this awareness of your balance was kind of manifesting...
>
> **W:**[12] Um hm.
>
> **N:**[13] You're asking yourself over and over...
>
> **W:**[14] [interrupts] Um. Well it's not really.... That's the best way to describe it. [N: Okay] It's simply a, it's simply.... [sighs] The best way I could describe it would be um an awareness of whether or not I'm going to fall over. So I'm not, I'm not actually like mentally asking myself, Am I gonna fall, Am I gonna fall, Am I gonna fall. It's more just being conscious of whether or not... of the outcome of my physical positioning. Does that better clarify?

Neda's Diary: As he continues to speak about the details of his experience and as I'm listening more carefully, I start to believe him a little more, especially when he talks about feeling like he's thinking 'don't fall, don't fall, don't fall' but isn't actually thinking that, is just using those words to try to convey what he was experiencing — this sense of balancing as he's running up the stairs.

Comments: As part of the bracketing-skill-acquisition described in comment (14) above, this realization can help Neda become more convinced that the bracketing of presuppositions can actually be successful, which can contribute to her becoming more skillful at bracketing in the future.

Neda's Retrospection

Neda: That's the end of my diary entry. Now that I review my diary writing, I see that it does not convey how surprising was the suddenness and the strength with which this presupposition operated, and also its specificity. The presupposition arose not merely because I found Walt's experience hard to believe, but apparently because that disbelief triggered something deep in me. I had found other parts of Walt's sampling hard to believe; for example, in his sample 3.5 Walt was eating a banana and said that at the moment of the beep he was tasting yellowness — a light, fluffy slightly sweet taste. That is, he said he was tasting the *colour yellow itself*, not tasting the banana that happened to be yellow. That was mildly hard to believe, but I did *not* fight against that experience as I had fought against the running-up-stairs experience. My own experience in the interview for the two beeps was dramatically different. I strongly wanted to prove him wrong in 3.4, whereas I wanted to figure out what he meant and whether it was believable in 3.5. I have no explanation for why the running-up-stairs experience would trigger a strong reaction in me while the tasting-yellow would not.

Retrospectively I'm surprised at the strength of my resistance to the running-upstairs experience. As far as I know, I don't care one way or the other about what people feel when they run up stairs, so my resistance seems entirely out of character. And I find it striking how fast this all happened. I felt *immediately* uncomfortable in a way that is hard for me to describe. I don't know whether it is his account, my disbelief of it, or the conflict between my disbelief and the intention to bracket presuppositions that made me uncomfortable, but whatever it was, it happened *immediately*, out of the blue.

I believed, prior to my DES experience, that my presuppositions were akin to generalizations, were obvious, were easy to 'put aside,' didn't colour my apprehension of others' experience as long as I was aware that the presuppositions exist. Now I think this may be true in some cases, that certain presuppositions are knowable ahead of time and therefore can be bracketed with ease. However, this example illustrates that presuppositions are not always that straightforward or predictable.

Comments: (15) Presuppositions are themselves invisible. Neda observes her *reaction* to the presupposition, but carefully considered, Neda does not know whether her resistance arises from her feelings about agency (Walt-is-focused-on-his-*posture*-while-running), her feelings about maternality (Walt-is-focused-on-running-*while-his-baby-is-screaming*), or about some other aspect of Walt's interchange, or to some combination thereof. At most, all Neda experiences are some *results* of her presupposition: the disbelief and bodily discomfort.

Agency

Russ: In the conclusion of **Presuppositions and Background Assumptions** I raised the possibility that analysis could not resolve the bracketing of presuppositions problem — that practice, not analysis, is required. We've presented here one example of that practice, trying to illustrate, where the rubber meets the road, how presuppositions operate — without warning, powerfully, personally, irrationally. This example also illustrates how the *bracketing* of presuppositions operates — Neda asked moderately skilled, relatively level-playing-field-questions despite her presuppositions and her inner battle against it. Had Neda not recognized the importance of bracketing presuppositions, she probably never would have apprehended Walt's stair-climbing bodily focus *at all*.

This example also illustrates why I object to Eric's referring in **Presuppositions and Background Assumptions** to presuppositions as 'background beliefs' or 'assumptions'. Background beliefs and assumptions are neutral terms, comments on the base rates of phenomena. Neda is probably right about the low base rate of people's attention to their balance while running upstairs. But that base rate has little to do with Neda's presuppositional reaction, which is anything but neutral. Had Neda's reaction been tied simply to the base rate, her process would have been something like: 'Hm. Walt is saying something pretty unusual here. I should ask very careful questions to make sure that I understand what he means and try to discover if he really intends what he says.' But her actual reaction was 'I want to win!' reflecting a presupposition in action. Presuppositions are *not* merely reactions to low base rate phenomena.

Because this example is (or at least might be) about agency, it also illustrates how the failure to bracket presuppositions can be toxic to an investigation. For example, **Horgan and Timmons** seem to suggest asking *everyone* about the sense of agency. If Walt were a participant in such a study, and he reported that he was running upstairs, **Horgan and Timmons's** interviewers would ask him if he felt himself purposefully running, and he would no doubt say Yes. Thus it might appear that **Horgan and Timmons**'s interviewers would do a good job of apprehending Walt's agentive experience. However, the problem is that if they asked the same questions of *everyone* who was running upstairs, nearly everyone would say that *of course* they were purposefully running upstairs. That is unfortunate because it makes Walt's experience of attending to his running seem quite ordinary when actually it is quite unusual.

This, then, is why I think presuppositions are toxic. **Horgan and Timmons**'s presuppositional interest in the experience of agency makes it highly *unlikely* that they would discover some fundamentally important aspects of the experience of agency — that some rare individuals have powerful agentive experiences whereas most people have little or none. That is indeed an important and fascinating result about the experience of agency, which I has called the 'doing of' (Hurlburt, 1993). Most people when they run simply run; a *few* people when they run experience the *doing of* running — the premeditated placing of one foot in front of the other, the losing and maintaining of balance, and so on. But to *discover* the doing of running, investigators would have to have their presuppositions bracketed.

I applaud **Horgan and Timmon**'s interest in the experience of agency — my sense is that carefully exploring the *doing of* experience would shed important light on consciousness science and psychology. I originally wrote about the doing of experiences in my 1993 discussion of anxiety. Walt was a subject in Neda's PTSD research; PTSD is a disorder where anxiety is prominent. Hmm! There's likely a lot to be learned here, either that anxiety causes the *doing of* experience, or that the *doing of* experience causes anxiety (and so on). Sorting that through could be a substantial contribution.

But that sorting-through must be undertaken, I think, with due attention to the bracketing of presuppositions.

Learning to bracket and/or eliminate presuppositions is (or at least can be) a long-term, probably lifetime, endeavour. That learning can be a spiraling process: through this incident, Neda incrementally improved her skills of recognizing the arising of her own presuppositions and of bracketing them when they arise. At the same time she is likely to become more accepting of the existence of her own imperfections/presuppositions, and therefore may have, incrementally, less of a battle with them in the future. And as she has less of a battle, she may be able to spot newly uncovered presuppositions even faster and more skillfully. And so on. This is a lifetime process because it is presuppositions all the way down, and newly uncovered presuppositions may present new and stronger methods of defence.

The good news is that DES, with its relentless focus on concrete moments of specific experience, can present an endless stream of opportunities for presuppositions to arise, and therefore can set the occasion for an endless stream of battles, which can provide an endless stream of learning opportunities. That's what Hurlburt and Akhter (2006, p. 284) meant by 'If you let it, the randomness of the beep will break you, one presupposition at a time.'

References

Horgan, T. & Timmons, M. (this symposium) Introspection and the phenomenology of free will: Problems and prospects, *Journal of Consciousness Studies*, **18** (1).

Hurlburt, R.T. (1993) *Sampling Inner Experience in Disturbed Affect*, New York: Plenum Press.

Hurlburt, R.T. (in press) *Investigating Pristine Inner Experience: Moments of Truth*, Cambridge: Cambridge University Press.

Hurlburt, R.T. & Akhter, S.A. (2006) The Descriptive Experience Sampling method, *Phenomenology and the Cognitive Sciences*, **5**, pp. 271–301.

Hurlburt, R.T. & Schwitzgebel, E. (this symposium) Presuppositions and background assumptions, *Journal of Consciousness Studies*, **18** (1).

JCS subscriptions form (see also: imprint-academic.com/jcs)

Name ....

Address *...

....

Home phone no .... Email ....
* Credit card customers must supply cardholder registered address

ANNUAL SUBSCRIPTION RATES: Vol. 18 (2011)

12 issues. Prices inc. accelerated delivery (UK/USA), rest of world surface.
Individuals: $154/£77   **Libraries:** $560/£280   **Students:** $118/£59*
*(full-time student status evidence & course completion date required)
Individuals with UK bank accounts can also subscribe for only £19.25 per quarter by Bankers' Direct Debit (students: £14.75. Contact **sandra@imprint.co.uk** for details.

☐ Enrol my library/individual/student subscription ☐ Airmail extra: $60/£30

☐ **Free with new subscription**. Choose one of the following books:
☐ *Partial Memories*, by Ernst von Glasersfeld
☐ *Mindworlds*, by J. Andrew Ross
☐ *Ten Years of Viewing From Within*, ed. Claire Petitmengin
☐ *The Mind, The Body and the World*, ed. Brendan Wallace et al.
☐ *Trusting the Subject, Parts 1 and 2*, ed. Jack & Roepstorff
☐ *Psi Wars: Getting to grips with the paranormal* ed. J. Alcock et al.
☐ *The Varieties of Religious Experience: Centenary Essays*, ed. M. Ferrari
☐ *Emotion Experience*, ed. Evan Thompson & Giovanna Colombetti
☐ *Between Ourselves: second-person approaches* ed. Evan Thompson
☐ *The Man Who Tasted Shapes*, by Richard E. Cytowic

Back Volumes Special Offer
Full set of back volumes 1–17 (1994–2010) @ *80% discount* (online only*).
Individuals/Students: $524/£262; **Institutions:** $1904/£952.
* for online **and** print editions add £85 (UK), £175/$350 (ROW).
☐ Please enter my Individual/Institutional discount back volume order.

Payment Details
☐ Cheque (pay 'Imprint Academic') $ (US bank) or £ Sterling (UK bank)

☐ VISA ☐ MASTERCARD ☐ AMEX ☐ MAESTRO ☐ DELTA ☐ JCB

Card No .... Expiry date ...

Security code (last 3 digits on back) ..... Signed ....
Credit cards (except US Amex) charged at £ Sterling rate and converted by your card issuer

---

☐ **10% introductory discount on Volume 18 for CCDD**
We have been authorized by Barclays Bank to operate a credit card direct debit system, whereby we charge your card at subscription renewal time. We will notify you in advance to give you time to cancel the transaction and your consumer rights are fully protected by your card issuer.
I authorise Imprint Academic to recharge my card on the annual renewal date.
Signed ....

Complete and send to: Imprint Academic, PO Box 200, Exeter EX5 5HY, UK
Tel: +44 (0)1392 851550   Fax: 851178   sandra@imprint.co.uk